G. HOUTEKAMER, P. ARTIS • *MVS I/O Subsystem: Configuration Management and Performance Analysis* 0-07-002553-3

A. KAPOOR • *SNA: Architecture, Protocols, and Implementation* 0-07-033727-6

R. CROWNHART • *IBM's Workstation CICS* 0-07-014770-1

R. LAMB • *Cooperative Processing Using CICS* 0-07-036111-8

C. DANEY • *Programming in REXX* 0-07-015305-1

P. KIESEL • *REXX: Advanced Techniques for Programmers* 0-07-034600-3

J. KNEILING • *Understanding CICS Internals* 0-07-037040-0

A. FRIEND • *COBOL Application Debugging Under MVS: COBOL and COBOL II* 0-07-022453-6

H. BOOKMAN • *COBOL/370: For VS COBOL and COBOL II Programmers* 0-07-006583-7

L. BRUMBAUGH • *VSAM: Architecture, Theory, and Applications* 0-07-008606-6

B. MERROW • *VSE/ESA: Performance Management and Fine Tuning* 0-07-041793-9

J. SAVIT • *VM/CMS: Concepts and Facilities* 0-07-054977-X

T. EDDOLLS • *ASO: Automated Systems Operations for MVS* 0-07-018994-3

T. KELLER • *CICS: Capacity Planning and Performance Management* 0-07-033783-7

J. LEBERT • *CICS Essentials for Application Developers and Programmers* 0-07-035869-9

J. PORTER • *AS/400 Information Engineering* 0-07-050623-X

L. TRINDELL • *NetView: A Professional's Guide to SNA Network Management* 0-07-041984-1

To order or receive additional information on these or any other McGraw-Hill titles, in the United States please call 1-800-822-8158. In the other countries, contact your local McGraw-Hill representative.

Tony D'Amore

AS/400

AS/400

Concepts and Facilities

Tony Baritz
David Dunne

Second Edition

McGraw-Hill, Inc.

New York San Francisco Washington, D.C. Auckland Bogotá
Caracas Lisbon London Madrid Mexico City Milan
Montreal New Delhi San Juan Singapore
Sydney Tokyo Toronto

For Polina, Vicky, and Julie

Library of Congress Cataloging-in-Publication Data

Baritz, Tony.
AS/400—concepts and facilities / Tony Baritz, David Dunne. — 2nd ed.
p. cm. — (J. Ranade IBM series)
Includes index.
ISBN 0-07-018303-1 :
1. IBM AS/400 (Computer). I. Dunne, David. II. Title. III. Series.
QA76.8.I25919B37 1993
004.1'45—dc20 93-19722
CIP

1 2 3 4 5 6 7 8 9 0 DOC/DOC 9 9 8 7 6 5 4 3

ISBN 0-07-018303-1

The sponsoring editor for this book was Jerry Papke and the production supervisor was Suzanne W. Babeuf. It was set in Century Schoolbook by North Market Street Graphics.

Printed and bound by R. R. Donnelley & Sons Company.

Contents

Part 2 Development Tools

Preface

This book is intended for professional programmers and systems analysts who are interested in gaining a rapid and inclusive introduction to the AS/400—how it works and what it can do. Systems administrators and business analysts will also find it helpful in that it provides an overview of the AS/400 and what they can expect of the machine and its capabilities. Anyone familiar with the basic concepts of relational databases and modern computer systems will find this book helpful and clearly presented.

We have carefully included what is relevant and excluded that which is not actually necessary for the purpose of presenting a comprehensive, yet concise, hands-on approach to learning the important new IBM AS/400 environment.

The AS/400 is IBM's midrange component in SAA (Systems Application Architecture), facilitating both upward and downward communications and true distributed processing between micros, midranges, and mainframes. These machines can all be connected on networks which provide a means of sharing data and systems. Many companies have already implemented this strategy, creating an international network of information in which the AS/400 is the midrange component (with PCs and PS/2's on the low end, and 370 and 3090 mainframe on the high end).

IBM is committed to supporting the AS/400 architecture and environment as a standard for the next 15 years. It is the newest version of the IBM System/34, 36, and 38 family (already widely installed) and is being used to upgrade many of these. It is selling remarkably well.

Included here are the results of a careful distillation and compilation of the topics necessary for a programmer to begin working on the IBM AS/400. While this book is not intended as a complete reference work on the AS/400 environment (the actual IBM manuals take up many shelves in a library), it provides the experienced programmer with all of the tools required to begin developing and coding actual business applications in the real world. Where further research is necessary, we reference the various IBM manuals that contain technical explanations in depth.

In the interest of keeping this work practical we have included many examples of the actual code required to solve standard, everyday business projects on the AS/400. We explain the process of providing the user with a menu, getting a response, designing an input screen, creating a database, updating the database from the input screen, processing the data, and running reports and queries against this data.

These are the components of most business systems, and this book will provide the methods and real code examples which can help implement these components on the AS/400.

Part

1

Introduction and Concepts

Chapter

1

System Overview

1.1 THE MACHINE

The AS/400 is IBM's newest technology in the midrange computer market. It represents a major improvement in ease of use and system integration, and is the next step for the System 36/38 product line. Closely related to the System 38 in functionality, it incorporates the friendly user interface of the System 36. This machine is intended to complete IBM's SAA connectivity scheme between mainframe, midrange, and personal computers. Facing the growing challenge from digital connectivity and reliability features, IBM expects the AS/400 to capture the midrange market, while providing the lead in technology and functionality.

Machine organization

The machine is organized into structural, logical units. These units are known as *objects, libraries, files, members,* and *folders.*

Virtually everything in the system is regarded as an object. Libraries are objects, as are programs and databases. Libraries contain the other types of objects, like databases, source code, and compiled programs. Libraries are the primary organizational structures of the AS/400. Folders contain documents for Office/400 (see Fig. 1.1).

Object orientation

One of the revolutionary aspects of the AS/400 is its treatment of almost all data entities as objects. This includes device descriptions

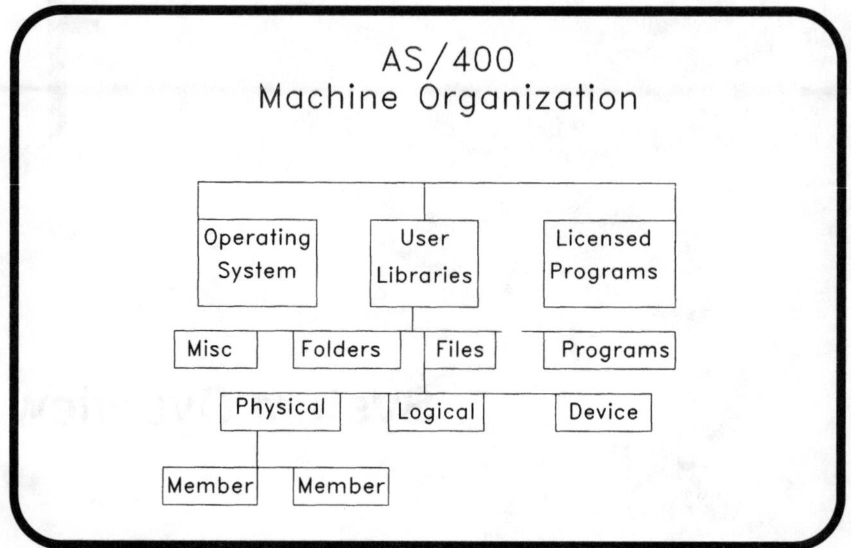

Figure 1.1 Library structure.

for terminals or printers, databases, programs, and screens. The AS/400 operating system (OS/400) stores descriptions of all objects. A user can simply name an object and the machine not only recognizes it and finds it, but knows a complete description of the object. Therefore, the system can utilize an object, once defined, with minimal user intervention.

The database

The AS/400 is set apart by its unique database handling, which is inherent in the operating system. This means that many database calls and functions are actually performed at the operating system level by coprocessors, using fast Licensed Internal Code (LIC).

Database packages and high-level languages do not have to have database manipulation engines at a high level, and the result is a much more efficient processing of data.

OS/400

The operating system OS/400 with its Command Language (CL) is powerful (over 7 million lines of code) and easy to learn. CL manages the operating system with intuitive English-like commands such as WRKOBJ (Work with Objects). These commands can be prompted at the command line to produce a menulike fill-in-the-blanks screen from which you choose the parameters you want, and fill in values for them.

Integrated application programs

Many integrated tools are available for the AS/400 which utilize the full potential of the operating system. Among these are:

Application Development Tools	**(ADT)**
System Entry Utility	(SEU)
Screen Design Aid	(SDA)
Programmer Development Manager	(PDM)
Business Graphics Utility	(BGU)
Data File Utility	(DFU)
Query	(QRY)

Office

Calendar

Display Write 4

Mail and Messages

Document and Shell Document

PC Organizer

Languages

CL

REXX

RPG/400

COBOL/400

PL1

SQL

C/400

Communications

PC Support

Performance Tuning

Performance Tools

Security

AS/400 security is among the most advanced in the industry, designed to Defense Department specifications. Security issues can become quite complex as an object may be secured by user authority, an authorization list, or a group authority. Security is based at the object level and is one of the aspects of the machine which requires an administrator to manage (QSECOFR).

Work management

Users can coordinate work flows and environments to ensure maximum machine performance and efficient business work flow. The system can be tailored to accommodate the various needs of programmers, priority users and jobs, nightly batch jobs, and other systems requirements. The system can adjust itself automatically to implement your current tasks, or you can turn this feature off and do it yourself. Work management allows manipulation of objects and their work paths through use of the Command Language.

Automatic operations

The AS/400 can perform many operations in an unattended fashion. For example, Initial Program Load (IPL), shutdown, and running of jobs or jobs streams can be set up to run automatically. Through the use of journaling, the system can track and restore database transactions and images in a forward or reverse direction. Nightly backups and housekeeping chores like cleanup of superfluous files can be automated.

Operational assistant

The AS/400 offers a menu called the Operational Assistant to help in performing many of the everyday tasks on the system. IPL, backup and restore, printing, work management, and problem handling can all be accessed through the Operational Assistant without knowing the specific CL commands. This feature brings AS/400 operations within the grasp of most users.

Automatic configuration

Advanced Peer-to-Peer Networking (APPN) has a feature which automatically configures devices when they are attached to the AS/400. APPN is what makes the AS/400 one of the most connectable platforms on the market. Just hook up a terminal or another AS/400 and the AS/400 will recognize it and configure it for communications.

User interface

English is the basis for the Control Language and the presentation screens of the AS/400. This carries into all areas of the machine from the Main Menu to online help systems. It is possible for a user to sign on the system and perform a task like copying a file without any knowledge of CL, simply by following the menus to the correct level, using the <Help> key, and the <F4> key to prompt for required parameters. The AS/400 helps you to learn its features.

1.2 LIBRARIES

Libraries are the methodology of storage on the machine. They contain everything manageable in the system. Libraries are groups of related objects, and fall into the following categories:

System libraries

System libraries contain IBM-defined system objects like the operating system, system language compilers, utilities, and descriptions of other libraries.

User libraries

These libraries hold user-defined objects like databases and application programs.

The library list

An important consideration in the use of libraries is the library list, which contains a list of libraries searched in order for a particular object. A user's library list determines where an object will be found, or if it will be found at all.

Files

A file is an object in a library which contains source code or data. For instance, all RPG source codes for one user might be stored in a file called QRPGSRC within that user's library. Remember that a file is not the actual source code or data, but an object that contains source code or data. The use of the term "file" is a bit confusing in the context of the AS/400, as it can mean a single object such as a database or program, or a group of members like program source codes.

Members

A member is where data or source code of one discrete type is stored within a file. A source file (e.g., QRPGSRC) might contain a number of members which are the actual RPG source code to be compiled. So a particular program's source code is a member of a file which may contain other members of source code of the same type.

1.3 DATABASE AND DATA DICTIONARY

As we have mentioned, the AS/400 database is one of its most innovative and useful features. Data can be described in a data dictionary, and then referenced for database structuring. The machine handles indexes and logical views automatically for you, once they are defined.

Integrated relational database

This is a machine designed expressly for managing databases. It is not necessary to manage elements of relational databases like indexing, or even to be aware of how the machine is taking care of this. Once a key is defined for a database, or a logical view or join file is set up, the machine will maintain these relations automatically. And the functions which accomplish these tasks are integrated at the operating system level, making the AS/400 an extremely powerful and effective dedicated application engine. In short, you don't have to come up with a scheme for handling or structuring data at the system level; it is already there.

The dictionary method

Databases may be created using the Interactive Data Definition Utility (IDDU), one of the machine's Advanced Development Tools (ADT). By starting IDDU, you can step through a series of screens which prompt you for entries which define the database at the field, record, and file levels. Data types may be defined with field edits, as well as database relationships. The AS/400 will construct and maintain databases for you once these values have been defined for it. It will actually write the source code for database definitions and compile it. An advantage of working with data dictionaries is consistent data definitions. Once defined, a generic field type may be referenced in a number of places, and it will always have the same properties and edits (unless overridden).

DDS

As an alternative to the data dictionary method of creating databases, you may create them by writing your own source code and compiling it into a database object. Source code for databases is known as DDS (Data Definition Specifications), and follows a format similar to program code. SEU (Source Entry Utility) is used to write the code, and then it is compiled. This method may also be used to create screens as an alternative to the Advanced Development Tool called Screen Design Aid (SDA). As with many features of the AS/400, there are multiple methods of arriving at the same end.

Migrated and native use

Code may be migrated from the System/36 or System/38 to the AS/400. However, functionality on the System/36 is limited as compared to the AS/400, and the System/38 is not as easy to use. Virtually all of the functions and options from the System 36/38 will work on the AS/400 either in native or S36/38 modes, but they represent a subset of the extended AS/400 capabilities, and there is significant machine overhead. IBM has announced that it is discontinuing the System/36 and System/38 lines and will no longer support them, so that migration appears to be inevitable at some point for these environments.

Use of the relational model

The AS/400 is based on the relational model. The AS/400 uses fixed record formats and all levels of normalization, if required. Various access paths may be built to the data in order to integrate fully the data members.

System 36 and System 38

The AS/400 is the heir to the System 36/38. Due to their popularity, the AS/400 has the ability to "emulate" those environments completely. In this way applications are ported to the new architecture. System/38 objects are compatible, but System/36 objects must be recompiled.

Enhancement or the next step

The logical progression in midrange technology for long-term MIS investment is the AS/400. Due to the advanced operating system, sophisticated office environment, integrated applications, and customer support, as well as connectivity options and the intuitive nature and quantity of help, this machine represents a leap forward in midrange computing power.

Focus on the user

The machine is very accessible to a nonprogrammer although, to take full advantage, programming knowledge is required. Nonprogrammers can quickly navigate the menu system, easily locating submenus which provide desired functions or tasks. The AS/400 is the first midrange product which can be operated entirely without command line syntax entries.

Migration

Migration is the process of moving System 36/38 applications to native AS/400 mode. IBM fully supports migration and will even migrate programs to demonstrate portability. Migration is accomplished through running your applications and database structure through IBM migration programs in order to remodel their basic structure.

1.4 THE LANGUAGES

The AS/400 is intended to support all Systems Application Architecture (SAA) standard languages, so that a program written for the mainframe 370, PS/2, or AS/400 will run on either of the other two. These languages include RPG, COBOL, C, SQL, and REXX.

RPG/400

RPG is the primary language on the System 36/38 and now on the AS/400. RPG stands for Report Program Generator, and it was originally exactly that. It has now evolved into a concise application language. Its strict column orientation can make it somewhat difficult to read and maintain, but as an alternative to COBOL it is brief and powerful.

COBOL/400

COBOL is available on the AS/400 in a version much like its PC counterpart. As many mainframe applications are written in COBOL, this language support ensures that mainframe COBOL applications can be migrated to the AS/400, with the attendant conversion. COBOL is English-like, easy to read, and widely known. However, it is wordy and more time-consuming than RPG to work in.

C/400

C is the language of choice for much software development. Many languages and applications which do not require the register speed of assembler are written in C. It is powerful, terse, easy to read, and easy to misuse. Making it available on the AS/400 indicates IBM's commitment to staying with the developing trends in software development. Drawbacks of C are the rather lengthy learning curve, and the ease with which the programmer can get into trouble.

SQL/400

SQL stands for Structured Query Language. While it is not a full-blown application language, or even a full implementation of mainframe SQL, it is a very powerful data manipulation tool which may be used interactively for queries or updates, or embedded in other code (RPG for example).

1.5 APPLICATION DEVELOPMENT TOOLS (ADT)

This tool kit is vital to every AS/400 system. It is a collection of other integrated application programs which aid the programmer in development. Source Entry Utility, Screen Design Aid, Interactive Data Definition Utility, and Program Development Manager are all part of ADT.

System Entry Utility (SEU)

SEU is the primary method of editing source code for application programs in a variety of languages. SEU includes auto syntax checking functions, and prompting for command parameters. This enables even the inexperienced programmer to use SEU easily.

Screen Design Aid (SDA)

SDA allows simple composition of screens and menus. It provides WYSIWYG (what you see is what you get) screen painting, field edits, and prompting for command procedures. SDA creates DDS and compiles automatically.

Interactive Data Definition Utility (IDDU)

IDDU allows programmers of all skill levels to define databases using a data dictionary format. IDDU creates relationships between fields and files and allows definition of key fields and formats. Changes in IDDU require more skill than simple database relationships.

DFU and Query

Data File Utility facilitates database editing and viewing, creating programs for the user for input/output. DFU allows you to create multiple formats which are analogous to logical files. Query also creates programs for the user. Query creates reports with calculations and can be used to update other database files.

1.6 HELP AND PROMPTING

Significant advances in the midrange computer, help and prompting, are useful for all skill levels. Online syntax assistance and help with parameter definition are provided through prompting, with a fill-in-the-blanks screen for possible command parameters. Help features multiple levels of definitions, a search index, and a question-and-answer feature.

The Help key

Help on the AS/400 is cursor- and context-sensitive. On almost any screen you can place the cursor in an area and receive a description and further information about the location or the function. Help is accessed through the <Help> key.

Index Search

Index Search is one of the AS/400's ways of helping you to learn the machine. If you have a question about the AS/400, you can ask it for the answer. Type STRIDXSCH at the command line and you get the Index Search screen. At the command line at the bottom of this screen you may enter a word or phrase about which you would like some information, for instance, LOGICAL FILES. The system will respond with an alphabetical list of items it has found related to the subject you typed in. You can pick one by entering a 5 next to it to display the information or definition of the topic, sometimes several screens of explanation. Enter a 6 to print the information. Try to be somewhat specific in naming the items to search for. Just saying to look for FILES would yield a list much more cumbersome to deal with than LOGICAL FILES. Index Search will define or explain virtually any subject in the AS/400 environment.

Online education (TSS)

Extensive online education and optional Discover Education give staff a common knowledge base and easily accessible tutorials for all system work.

Electronic Customer Support

ECS (Electronic Customer Support) allows IBM service direct access to the machine without an on-site visit. ECS continuously "scans" the machine, checking hardware components and other system features. ECS updates a problem log and will report problems to IBM. This reporting system is one of the most extensive ever developed by IBM.

Prompting

The <F4> key is another of the AS/400's major enhancements. Whenever a command is being issued to the operating system, using CL, you can hit the <F4> key to get a fill-in-the-blanks screen to prompt you for relevant parameters, and even to suggest viable options. With the cursor placed on any of the fields in the prompt screen, you can hit the <Help> key to get a further explanation of what might be entered into this field. This sequence is characteristic of the AS/400. Prompt for parameters to a command, and use the <Help> key to explain what is required or expected for entries. This works even when writing some types of programs—enter the command, prompt for parameters, fill in the fields, and the AS/400 will construct the line and enter it into the program for you.

Function keys

The AS/400 provides many special function keys to be used in various situations. Some provide on-screen help, while others get you out of whatever you're doing. Each facility on the machine has its own function key usages, but some of them are generic and deserve mention here:

F3 (the quit key)	stops whatever you are doing and generally sends you back one level in the direction from which you came
F4 (the invaluable prompt key)	provides fill-in-the-blanks screens for command parameter entry at the command line or in writing programs in SEU
F9	retrieves previously entered commands at the command line
F12	goes back one screen
Help	provides context-sensitive explanatory screens, depending on where the cursor is

1.7 COMMUNICATIONS

Many types of communications are supported through the AS/400. From Remote Job Entry (RJE) for System 370 applications to file transfers to and from personal systems (PCs), the machine offers a wide range of options.

Integration

Communications are part of the basic concept of the machine. The AS/400 is truly underutilized without communications to other platforms. For example, in using PC Support, cooperative processing forms a transparent APPC (Advanced Program-to-Program Communications) link with AS/400. Multiple AS/400's communicating together form a highly sophisticated, easy-to-use processing environment which can be connected to nearly all IBM platforms transparently to the user. In this way, a user in Denver can access a database in Chicago transparently.

Support

Automatic line and device recovery are examples of the refined communication ability of the AS/400. This "automatic" support can be tailored to any environment and expanded through error recovery Command Language and other programs. AS/400 supports IBM communications completely—any deviation from their products and methodologies can be problematic.

APPN, APPC, DDM

The most commonly used communication paths on the AS/400 are Advanced Peer-to-Peer Networking, Advanced Program-to-Program Communications, and Distributed Data Management. In this way, machines, programs, and databases are able to integrate in cohesive distributed systems.

Networks and connectivity

Supported networks are comprised of personal systems and LAN servers, or multiple AS/400's or System 36/38's, as well as System 370's in any combination.

1.8 SYSTEM APPLICATION ARCHITECTURE

SAA is IBM's overriding concept for the future of distributed processing. It is a unified approach to software design and interplatform communications on the AS/400, the System 370, and the PS/2. The ultimate goal of SAA is an environment which is virtually transparent to the user, so that the user is not aware that he or she is accessing a 370, even though signed on to the AS/400 or the PS/2. These three machine architectures represent the components of the SAA triangle. The AS/400 is IBM's newest concept of hardware organization. Figure 1.2 represents this new structure.

High-level machine

High-Level Language support, object orientation, and insulation from the Licensed Internal Code represent the machine interface which sets this machine apart from all others. The machine interface handles most housekeeping functions of the system, leaving operations and programmers free to deal with business applications.

Single-level storage

Unlike other machines, the AS/400 stores information in only one level. All disk storage is regarded by the operating system as virtual memory. Everything is immediately available. This single-level stor-

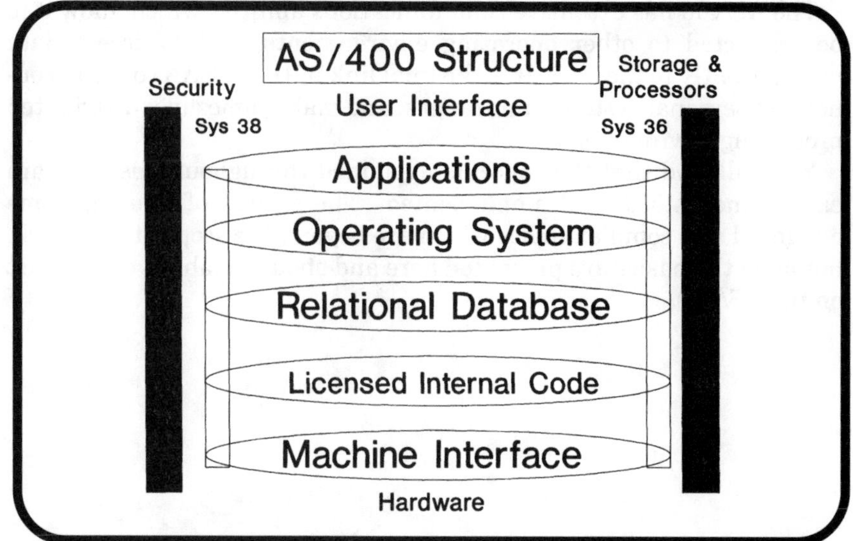

Figure 1.2 Architecture.

age allows the machine to provide the user convenient access to data segments with a minimal seek and recovery time. Whenever a segment of storage is lost, however, the entire data area is corrupted and must be reconstructed.

Contrast with data/procedure orientation

Single-level storage differs from the traditional data/procedural storage methodologies in the way empty data areas are dynamically allocated without user intervention. As opposed to JCL routines where specific storage space is allocated, the AS/400 handles this for you.

1.9 SUMMARY

The AS/400 represents a new concept in computer architecture and functionality. It is especially designed for ease of use, comprehensive help, and accessibility for the entire DP staff, not only for programmers. No longer is it necessary to wait for a programmer to get to many of your needs. Simply by following the menu structures, you can accomplish much of what you need to do.

Special functions included with the AS/400 package, such as Office, Query, and Data File Utility, allow the novice to access data for input and output very quickly, as well as to create documents, reports, and databases. For these reasons, it is important to take advantage of the machine's advanced security functions.

The AS/400 has extensive communications abilities which allow it to be connected to other operating environments, and to access data transparently to the user. It is the final link in IBM's SAA concept, connecting personal systems, midranges, and mainframes in a distributed processing environment.

You will find that the concepts explained throughout this book are easily understood and implemented. There are, of course, some advanced and complex topics which are beyond the scope of this work, but all of the basics are presented here and should enable a quick start on the AS/400.

Chapter

2

Menus and Navigation

2.1 THE MAIN MENU

The main menu on the AS/400 has eleven choices and a command line.

The AS/400 main menu allows you to select the general task you want to do. To select a menu option, type the option number on the command line and press <Enter>. To run a command, type the command on the command line and press the <Enter> key. The AS/400 provides assistance in selecting a command; press <F4> (Prompt) without typing anything and the prompting help will appear. For assistance in entering a command, type the command and press <F4> (Prompt). To get back the last commands you entered, press <F9> (Retrieve).

Signing On and the Main Menu

There are four variables which can be entered on the Sign On screen. Depending on the security setting of your system, the first two values are typically required:

USERID — This is the identification word that you are known by in the system. Typically this value is assigned by your system security officer in the user profile section of the system.

PASSWORD — This password is related directly to the USERID and, again, is initially set by the security officer. You will be prompted to change your password—

then, on a regular basis, you will be prompted to change your password to maintain security integrity of the system.

INITIAL PROGRAM — By indicating this optional value, you can immediately begin a program or job after signing on. This can be helpful particularly in programming environments where programs specify library lists and special environments before any system work can be performed. Authorization is required.

SUBSYSTEM — By specifying this optional value, you can designate the subsystem in which to operate until you change your job. Again, in a programming environment this can allow you to utilize system resources in the most effective manner (refer to Fig. 2.1).

Immediately after signing on, the AS/400 main menu will appear on your screen, unless another screen has been assigned for you. From here, depending on your sign-on authority, a menu item can be chosen, or commands can be entered. Following the menu options to other submenus, you can reach any system function (Fig. 2.2).

Entering commands on the command line

As an alternative to using the menus, menus paths, and command group menus, you can enter commands directly on the command line through the use of the command language syntax. Like most other

```
                        Sign On
                                        System . . . . . :   S9999999
                                        Subsystem . . . . :  QINTER
                                        Display . . . . . :  DUNNE

        User . . . . . . . . . . . . . .   __________
        Password . . . . . . . . . . . .
        Program/procedure . . . . . . . .  __________
        Menu . . . . . . . . . . . . . .   __________
        Current library . . . . . . . . .  __________




                                  (C) COPYRIGHT IBM CORP. 1980, 1989.
 06-53                                         S2 S9999999 KB
```

Figure 2.1 Sign-on screen.

```
MAIN                         AS/400 Main Menu
                                                     System:   S9999999
Select one of the following:

     1. User tasks
     2. Office tasks
     3. General system tasks
     4. Files, libraries, and folders
     5. Programming
     6. Communications
     7. Define or change the system
     8. Problem handling
     9. Display a menu
    10. User support and education
    11. PC Support tasks

    90. Sign off

Selection or command
===> ____________________________________________________________

F3=Exit   F4=Prompt   F9=Retrieve   F12=Cancel   F13=User support
F23=Set initial menu
(C) COPYRIGHT IBM CORP. 1980, 1991.
```

Figure 2.2 Main Menu.

commands or tasks to initiate anything on the AS/400, commands entered on the command line can be prompted through the use of <F4>.

Command group menus can be accessed by typing GO and the menu name, for example, GO CMDDLT. This command will show all of the system options concerning delete. Similarly, GO CMDxxx can be used with many of the functions on the system. Also, command groups can be accessed through types such as GO VERB, or GO MAJOR. These commands allow all verb commands to be accessed, and all major command groups to be accessed. Verb commands can be summarized as anything that acts on objects. For example:

Add commands

Clear commands

Cancel commands

Major command groups include:

File commands

Data Management commands

System Control commands

If you are lost in the system, use the major command groups (GO MAJOR) on the command line and you will quickly be able to find your way to the commands which will make the system respond to your needs (see Fig. 2.3).

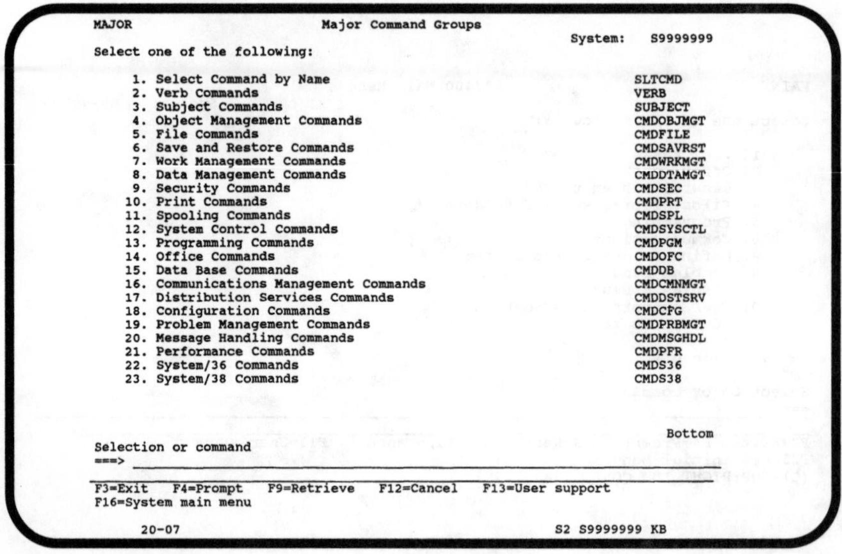

```
MAJOR                        Major Command Groups
                                                        System:   S9999999
Select one of the following:

     1. Select Command by Name                              SLTCMD
     2. Verb Commands                                       VERB
     3. Subject Commands                                    SUBJECT
     4. Object Management Commands                          CMDOBJMGT
     5. File Commands                                       CMDFILE
     6. Save and Restore Commands                           CMDSAVRST
     7. Work Management Commands                            CMDWRKMGT
     8. Data Management Commands                            CMDDTAMGT
     9. Security Commands                                   CMDSEC
    10. Print Commands                                      CMDPRT
    11. Spooling Commands                                   CMDSPL
    12. System Control Commands                             CMDSYSCTL
    13. Programming Commands                                CMDPGM
    14. Office Commands                                     CMDOFC
    15. Data Base Commands                                  CMDDB
    16. Communications Management Commands                  CMDCMNMGT
    17. Distribution Services Commands                      CMDDSTSRV
    18. Configuration Commands                              CMDCFG
    19. Problem Management Commands                         CMDPRBMGT
    20. Message Handling Commands                           CMDMSGHDL
    21. Performance Commands                                CMDPFR
    22. System/36 Commands                                  CMDS36
    23. System/38 Commands                                  CMDS38

                                                                    Bottom
Selection or command
===>

F3=Exit   F4=Prompt   F9=Retrieve   F12=Cancel   F13=User support
F16=System main menu

     20-07                                         S2 S9999999 KB
```

Figure 2.3 Major commands.

The Major menu command groups include all commands, commands by subject and commands by action (VERB). The command groups can be selected by entering the option number on the command line or typing the abbreviation for the group you want to see (refer to Fig. 2.4).

Going to other menus

The word GO followed by a menu name on the command line will take you to that menu. Type GO followed by the name of the menu and <Enter>. For example, to go to the user's tasks (USER) menu, type GO USER on the command line and press <Enter>. The menu name or menu ID is shown in the upper-left corner of the menu. For assistance in entering the GO command, type GO and press the <F4> prompt key. If at any time you cannot remember the entire menu name you can use a generic name such as GO US*; this will yield a list of all menus with US* as the first two letters of the menu name.

2.2 SUBMENUS

The Main Menu of the AS/400 takes you to various other Submenus, depending on which choice you make. Each of these other menus has menus which underlie it; in this way you can reach all of the functions of the AS/400.

At the bottom of each set of menus, a consistent set of function keys appears as follows:

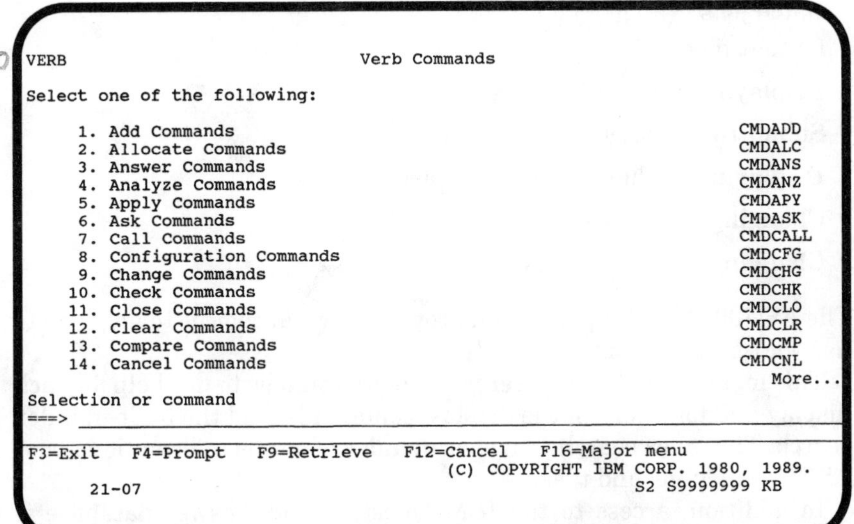

```
VERB                          Verb Commands

Select one of the following:

      1. Add Commands                                            CMDADD
      2. Allocate Commands                                       CMDALC
      3. Answer Commands                                         CMDANS
      4. Analyze Commands                                        CMDANZ
      5. Apply Commands                                          CMDAPY
      6. Ask Commands                                            CMDASK
      7. Call Commands                                           CMDCALL
      8. Configuration Commands                                  CMDCFG
      9. Change Commands                                         CMDCHG
     10. Check Commands                                          CMDCHK
     11. Close Commands                                          CMDCLO
     12. Clear Commands                                          CMDCLR
     13. Compare Commands                                        CMDCMP
     14. Cancel Commands                                         CMDCNL
                                                                   More...
Selection or command
===> ____________________________________________________________________

F3=Exit   F4=Prompt   F9=Retrieve   F12=Cancel   F16=Major menu
                                   (C) COPYRIGHT IBM CORP. 1980, 1989.
     21-07                                             S2 S9999999 KB
```

Figure 2.4 Verb commands.

F3 (the quit key)	stops whatever you are doing and generally sends you back one level
F4 (the invaluable Prompt key)	provides fill-in-the-blanks screens for command parameter entry at the command line or in writing programs in SEU
F9	causes previously keyed command to appear on the command line
F12	previous/cancel—goes back one screen
F13	user support—presents a menu of user commands
F16	major menu—takes you to the major commands menu
F23	set initial menu—sets the current menu to be the default menu at sign-on
F1	Help provides context-sensitive explanatory screens, depending where the cursor is

User tasks

This option allows you to do tasks related to your own jobs on the system, rather than everybody else's. These tasks include:

- Displaying and changing jobs

  Interactive user jobs

Batch jobs
Output files

- Displaying and sending messages
- Submitting a batch job
- Displaying or changing your library list
- Changing of passwords
- Changing of user profiles

The AS/400 User Support Menu provides several choices to help you to use your system more effectively.

This menu provides the user with choices on how to use help for each display and for fields on the display, commands, and the built-in index search. The index search provides an index of online information about AS/400 functions and tasks.

In addition, access to the IBM Question and Answer database is available from the User Tasks Menu. Product information using IBM-Link for publications and product information, capacity planning, and performance tool information is available through this menu (as seen in Fig. 2.5).

Office tasks

This option allows processing for text, handling of documents and folders, and management of other office activities:

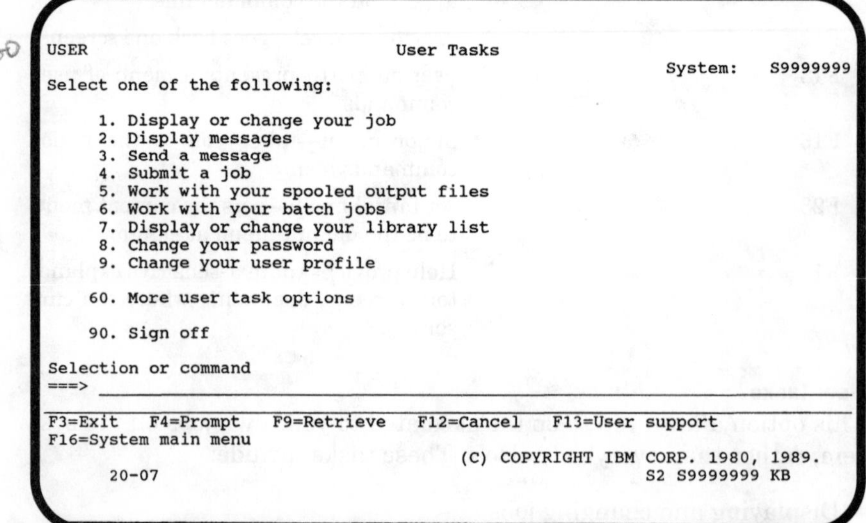

```
USER                              User Tasks
                                                   System:   S9999999
Select one of the following:

     1. Display or change your job
     2. Display messages
     3. Send a message
     4. Submit a job
     5. Work with your spooled output files
     6. Work with your batch jobs
     7. Display or change your library list
     8. Change your password
     9. Change your user profile

    60. More user task options

    90. Sign off

Selection or command
===> ____________________________________________________________

F3=Exit   F4=Prompt   F9=Retrieve   F12=Cancel   F13=User support
F16=System main menu
                                (C) COPYRIGHT IBM CORP. 1980, 1989.
     20-07                                          S2 S9999999 KB
```

Figure 2.5 User menu.

- OfficeVision/400 performs tasks related to word processing, document handling and office activities, such as use of calendars, the electronic mail system, handling of messages and notes, and library distribution functions.
- Decision support allows tasks related to database files or graphics to be performed. For example, use of Interactive Data Definition Utilities, AS/400 Query, and Business Graphic Utilities and SQL can be accessed as decision support.
- User tasks related to security for Office, working with documents and folder security, owners and authorization lists.
- Tasks related to the System Directory can be controlled from this point. This option will display the system directory, which is used for configuring Systems Network and Distribution Services (SNADS), Document Interchange Architecture (DIA), and other distribution. A system directory is a list of entries containing names, addresses, telephone numbers, and other identifying information, used with a two-part user ID to send distribution lists and other objects to the user ID.
- Tasks related to folders can be controlled from this point. A folder can contain other folders, members, and documents. For example, folders can be saved, updated, and restored from this point.

Figure 2.6 shows office tasks.

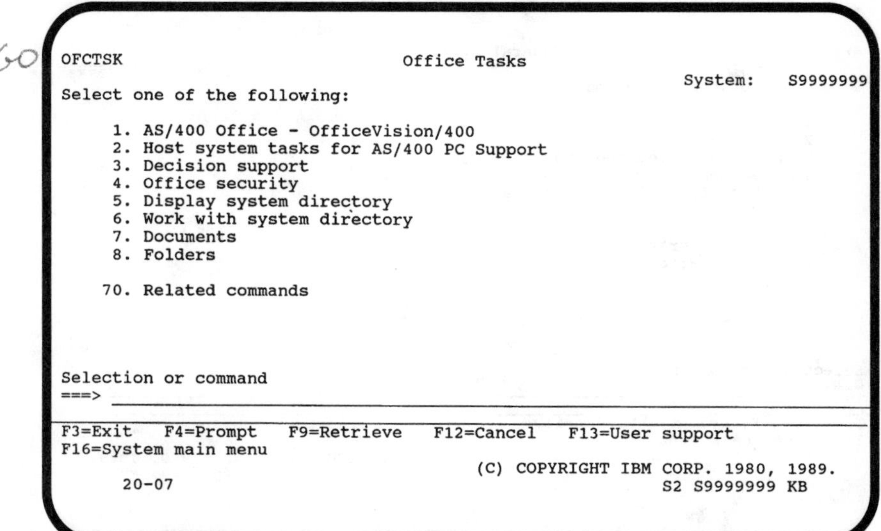

Figure 2.6 Office Tasks.

General system tasks

This option allows tasks related to all jobs on the system. For example, you can:

- Use communications or security.
- Monitor and control system jobs and messages.
- Display system or device status or system operator messages.
- Work with user data.
- Save a backup copy of an object to tape or diskette or to a save file on the system.
- Restore a copy of an object from tape or diskette or from a save file on the system.

See Fig. 2.7 on general systems tasks.

Files, libraries, and folders

This option allows users to work with user data such as:

- Data files, Distributed Data Management (DDM) files, or source files
- Libraries that contain files, programs, and other objects
- Folders that contain folder members and documents
- Host system tasks for AS/400 PC support

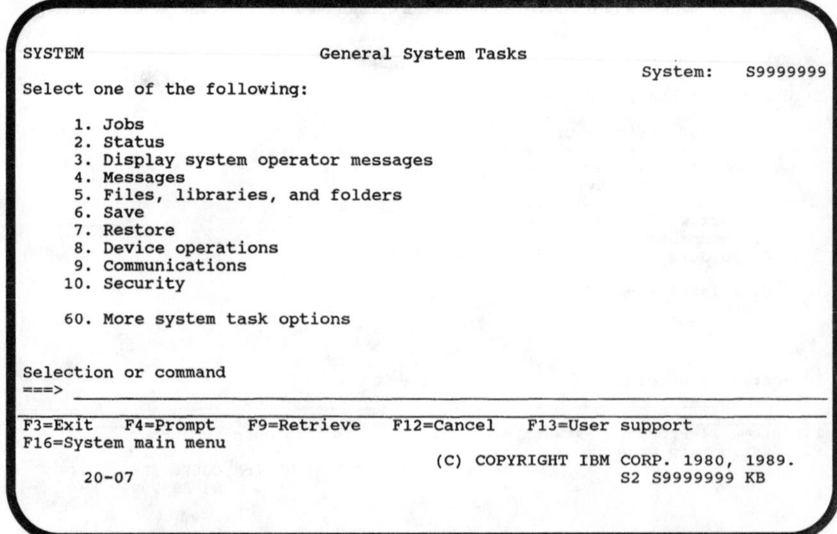

Figure 2.7 General System Tasks.

This facility is critical for the applications programmer in that it provides a convenient way to access all the objects, members, and source code which constitute a complete system (see Fig. 2.8).

Programming

This option allows users to work with programming tasks on the system by using:

- The programmer's menu to do general programming tasks
- PDM (Programming Development Manager)
- Utilities
- Programming language debug
- The SQL precompiler
- Question and Answer database(s)
- The Market Support Product to receive technical information from IBM about the AS/400 system
- Copy Screen image
- System/36 programming

Debug facilities allow commands associated with solving programming language errors. For example, you can add, change, and remove programs, pointers, and program variables.

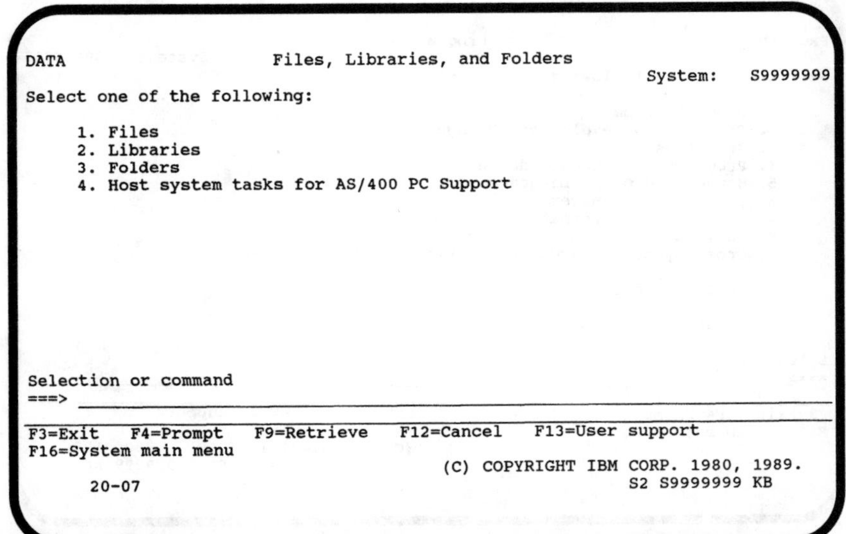

```
DATA                     Files, Libraries, and Folders
                                                          System:    S9999999
Select one of the following:

     1. Files
     2. Libraries
     3. Folders
     4. Host system tasks for AS/400 PC Support

Selection or command
===> ____________________________________________________________________

F3=Exit   F4=Prompt   F9=Retrieve   F12=Cancel   F13=User support
F16=System main menu
                                   (C) COPYRIGHT IBM CORP. 1980, 1989.
     20-07                                          S2 S9999999 KB
```

Figure 2.8 Files, Libraries, and Folders.

Options to create programs that have embedded SQL statements can also be accessed through this menu. SQL is used to put information into a database and to get and organize selected information from a database.

Question and Answer facilities allow the following:

- Search for answers to your questions by using a Question and Answer database.
- Ask questions online of your technical coordinator by using the Question and Answer database.
- Receive answers to your questions by using a Question and Answer database.

Examples of options for viewing technical information from IBM using 3270 communications in IBMLink are as follows:

- AS/400 publication and product information
- Capacity planning or Performance Tool information
- Configuration and communication information

Figure 2.9 is the Programming Menu.

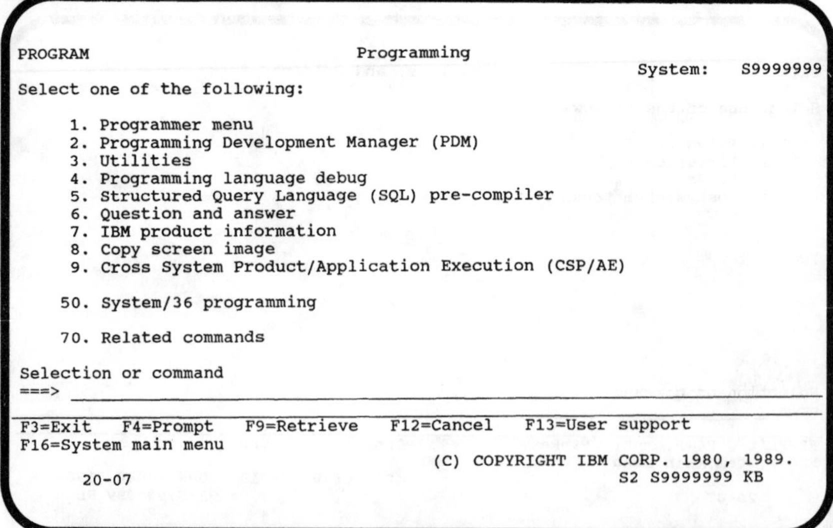

```
PROGRAM                         Programming
                                                         System:    S9999999
Select one of the following:

     1. Programmer menu
     2. Programming Development Manager (PDM)
     3. Utilities
     4. Programming language debug
     5. Structured Query Language (SQL) pre-compiler
     6. Question and answer
     7. IBM product information
     8. Copy screen image
     9. Cross System Product/Application Execution (CSP/AE)

    50. System/36 programming

    70. Related commands

Selection or command
===> ________________________________________________________________________

F3=Exit   F4=Prompt   F9=Retrieve   F12=Cancel   F13=User support
F16=System main menu
                                          (C) COPYRIGHT IBM CORP. 1980, 1989.
     20-07                                                 S2 S9999999 KB
```

Figure 2.9 Programming menu.

Communications

This option allows you to configure and control your communications network. For example, you can:

- Display communications configuration status.
- Start a job on another system.
- Configure communications.
- Manage and configure a network.
- Verify Data Links.
- Send and receive data files.

Communications are the key to the SAA (Systems Application Architecture) across multiple platforms through networks and other data linking facilities. Communications, although complex, can be accessed through menus on the system. Through the use of prompting and help information, communications can be configured and controlled easily (refer to Fig. 2.10).

Define or change the system

This option allows configuration, installation, or request of information about hardware devices (such as display stations, printers, tape

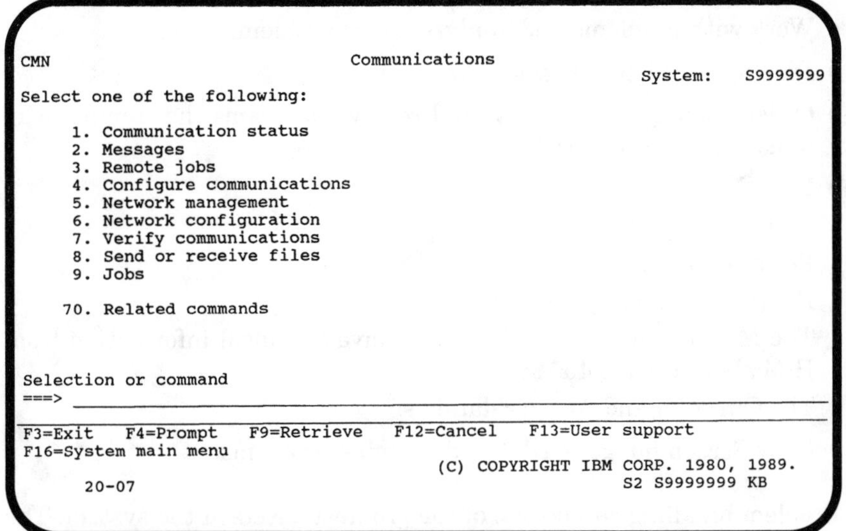

```
CMN                                 Communications
                                                          System:   S9999999
Select one of the following:

     1. Communication status
     2. Messages
     3. Remote jobs
     4. Configure communications
     5. Network management
     6. Network configuration
     7. Verify communications
     8. Send or receive files
     9. Jobs

    70. Related commands


Selection or command
===> ____________________________________________________________

F3=Exit   F4=Prompt   F9=Retrieve   F12=Cancel   F13=User support
F16=System main menu
                                          (C) COPYRIGHT IBM CORP. 1980, 1989.
     20-07                                                  S2 S9999999 KB
```

Figure 2.10 Communications menu.

devices, and controllers), and communications or security. For example, you can:

- Work with security tasks.
- Configure hardware and communications.
- Install licensed programs.
- Display and change IBM market support contact information.
- Get technical information from IBM.
- Work with a program (PTF) that replaces the affected objects in your licensed programs.
- Display or change system values which control system operations.

System values, which primarily control the main options of the system, are numerous. They provide everything from terminal inactivity time-out to controlling subsystem and library information. System values can be displayed and changed. Changes to system values generally do not take effect until the next Initial Program Load, or IPL. IPL in effect realigns the system and "cleans up," while reloading the system. (See Fig. 2.11.)

Problem handling

This option allows you to start solving general system problems. For example, you can:

- Work with problems and analyze a new problem.
- Display the history log.
- Order, display, load, apply, and remove programs that temporarily update your system (PTFs).
- Use

  Alerts

  Performance Tools

  Programming language debug

  The Market Support Product to receive technical information from IBM about the AS/400 system

  The Question and Answer database
- Copy Screen image to IBM to determine problems.

Problem handling can be one of the greatest assets of the system. The AS/400 provides problem tracking at multiple levels and interaction with IBM (Fig. 2.12).

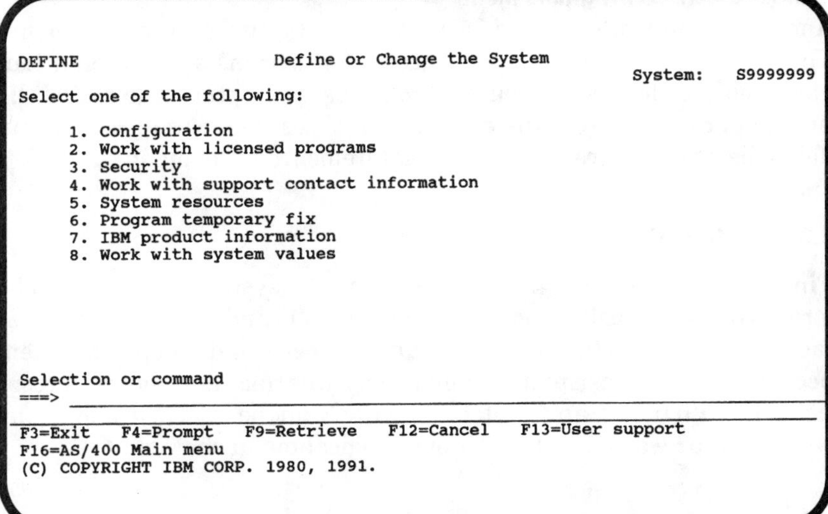

```
DEFINE                    Define or Change the System
                                                            System:   S9999999
Select one of the following:

     1. Configuration
     2. Work with licensed programs
     3. Security
     4. Work with support contact information
     5. System resources
     6. Program temporary fix
     7. IBM product information
     8. Work with system values




Selection or command
===> ______________________________________________________________________________

F3=Exit   F4=Prompt   F9=Retrieve   F12=Cancel   F13=User support
F16=AS/400 Main menu
(C) COPYRIGHT IBM CORP. 1980, 1991.
```

Figure 2.11 Define or Change the System menu.

```
PROBLEM                         Problem Handling
                                                            System:   S9999999
Select one of the following:

     1. Question and answer
     2. Work with problems
     3. Network problem handling
     4. Display system operator messages
     5. Display the history log
     6. System service tools

    60. More problem handling options

    70. Related commands



Selection or command
===> ______________________________________________________________________________

F3=Exit   F4=Prompt   F9=Retrieve   F12=Cancel   F13=User support
F16=System main menu
                                      (C) COPYRIGHT IBM CORP. 1980, 1989.
      20-07                                          S2 S9999999 KB
```

Figure 2.12 Problem Handling menu.

Manage Licensed Programs menu

Another menu you will need is the Manage Licensed Programs menu. This menu allows you to install licensed programs and national language objects for most licensed programs and optional items of the licensed programs from the distribution tapes. You can also save and delete licensed programs and optional items from the menu.

2.3 SUMMARY

Finding your way through the system and the system functions can be a relatively easy task using the systems menus and built-in navigation facilities. The AS/400 menus are an advanced and complete system because of their consistent Common User Interface and their interconnectivity. Virtually any system function can be reached simply by working your way down to it through logical menu choices.

Chapter

3

Help and Special Function Keys

Information in this chapter is perhaps the most important in the entire book—how to help yourself on the AS/400. We have stressed that the help that is included as part of the base in the AS/400 system is the most comprehensive ever developed by IBM. As IBM says, "If you want to know how this system works, just ask it." This concept is a reality on the AS/400. Help literally will guide you through concepts and design information to programming definitions and prompting for parameters.

Help is also available on the AS/400 through Electronic Customer Support (ECS), IBMLink. ECS includes national database search information, question and answer support, access to education information, order support, and service link. When accessing these services, your display station is placed in 3270 emulation mode through communications available on the AS/400.

3.1 THE HELP KEY

There are two keys for help in the AS/400 operating system (OS/400). <F1> and a specially designated <Help> key invoke help from any point in the system. Help is context-sensitive, meaning help is activated wherever the cursor is, relevant to that particular screen position. General help is also available; you can get help for the specific cursor location on screen, or for the whole screen or procedure you are performing.

When help is invoked, two screens may be activated:

1. *Cursor-sensitive help.* This type of help will explain in detail the objects and ideas presented at the current screen's cursor location.
2. *Menu level or more general level of help.* This type of help will explain the concept of the screen or command group on which you are placed.

The most common function keys are explained on the help screens.

Cursor-sensitive help. Cursor-sensitive help is invoked relative to a specific menu option item, a detailed menu, or for a specific key usage. Cursor-sensitive help defaults to the general level whenever the cursor is placed in an area that has no specific fields or other AS/400 display symbols.

3.2 INDEX SEARCH

Index Search can help you to find answers to qustions you may have about the AS/400. You can ask English-like questions and get back help screens explaining relevant topics.

Type STRIDXSCH at the command line, or hit <Help> and <F1> to the Index Search screen. At the command line at the bottom of this screen you may enter a word or phrase about which you would like some information—for instance, LOGICAL FILES. The system will respond with an alphabetical list of items it has found related to the subject you typed in.

You can pick one by entering a 5 next to it to display the information or definition of the topic, sometimes several screens of explanation. Enter a 6 next to the definition returned by Index Search to send it to the printer.

Try to be somewhat specific in naming the items to search for. Just saying to look for FILES would yield a list much more cumbersome to deal with than LOGICAL FILES. Index Search will define or explain virtually any subject in the AS/400 environment.

Depth

The AS/400 help facilities go into extensive detail. However, you will find occasionally that the help facility is not enough. For this reason, IBM provides with each system an extensive library of information. Over 300 AS/400 manuals contain over 45,000 pages. These manuals are maintained and updated with your system through the use of the IBM System Library Subscription Service (SLSS). SLSS is generally handled administratively by a user representative and your marketing representative; however, it is sometimes handled by your VAR or other system source. AS/400 documentation and manuals are also available on CD ROM. This is an excellent way to access a vast store of AS/400 information at the touch of a key on the PC.

Automatic update

Each time a new release of the operating system is installed, your online help is updated with meaningful help information, increased search topics, and tutorial system support changes in order to keep your help current.

IBM will also ship the most recent version of your manuals or pages which have changed to be inserted in your manuals.

This service ensures that you will always have the most recent information available to you and your staff online or in your system library.

Question and Answer

The Q&A database is designed to enhance end-user satisfaction with the system by allowing repetitive questions to be placed in a database easily accessible to all users. It allows selective growth and flexibility in assisting users with their day-to-day problems.

The AS/400 uses a built-in local database for questions and answers on applications, systems topics, and general information. This is accomplished through a Q&A coordinator and interaction from end users. The Question and Answer facility can also be linked to remote Q&A databases. The remote databases are available in two ways: either through IBM business partners or the national IBM Q&A database. In this way, questions can be answered remotely by an applications or systems expert and placed in your database for future use. This is an important feature in terms of end users. Especially in your initial use of the AS/400, Q&A can reduce your involvement with repetitive questions and their answers. This can be helpful when new users enter the system.

Coordinators have the ability to create, edit, distribute, and manage questions on the AS/400. Question databases can be segmented by major topic or application for your use. The coordinator is usually your institution's contact with the IBM National Database, which allows questions and answers to be linked with the latest answers for problems.

3.3 ONLINE EDUCATION

This IBM system will teach you how to use it. The AS/400 will teach concepts, tasks, ideas, and other information in a format that emulates a personal classroom, complete with quizzes.

Discover Education is an extended online education program which may be purchased separately.

Tutorial System Support

Tutorial System Support (TSS) is a base online education provided with each IBM AS/400. TSS provides a thorough introduction and overview of the AS/400. This makes education not only possible, but it can be provided for each systems staff person working with the AS/400.

Tutorial System Support covers the basics of database management, communications, files, storage on the machine, and different models of the AS/400. Online education is a concept which can provide DP staff with a consistent source of information.

In order to track your staff's progress, you may work with student information in the system. Completion dates can be monitored, as well as audience learning paths and quiz results.

Discover Education

Online education modules called Discover Education are effective staff training.

Implemented in the same way as Tutorial System Support, Discover Education is far more interactive and graphic with students. Discover Education requires students to run through a series of exercises and to interact with the system.

Discover Education modules include Implementation Topics which detail use of database in the system. Other modules, such as RPG, provide excellent basic training in RPG which can be enhanced through further instruction or practical experience.

Discover Education course modules may be completed in as little as 45 minutes—making education far more flexible for students.

Learning paths

Each of the online educational modules is accessible through a variety of learning paths. These paths are related to job descriptions which gear the education presentations to specific levels of learning.

Learning paths are divided into sections such as Programmer, and then further subdivided into experience levels. Likewise, with analyst and administrative positions, modules help you to target education to the correct staff level.

3.4 PROMPTING

One of the most important parts of the AS/400, extensive prompting is a valuable aid no matter what your skill level.

Use of the prompt

Prompting can be invoked two ways. After entering the CL command on the command line, the prompt key <F4> will produce a screen containing possible parameters of the command entered. In addition, a question mark entered before the CL command will also invoke the same parameters screen.

The advantage of the question mark's usage is specifically apparent in CL programming: when the executed program reaches a line with a question mark, the user is automatically presented with a CL parameter screen. In a program, this would allow the user to decide such things as which printer to use or other variable information. It is an integration of the interactive help environment with the compiled program.

Finding the default

Prompt parameters shown are the system default. Many of these defaults were shown as *SAME. Fortunately, this is being improved for later releases, showing you the correct parameters for the prompted information. Most parameter information is defaulted on the AS/400. You will find this to be the case consistently throughout the system.

With some CL commands, it is possible to view the defaults in more detail by using a Display command rather than a Work or Change command. Display commands will show all of the information related to the parameters. Work and/or Change commands many times present blanks where parameters may be filled in (see Chap. 4).

3.5 SYSTEM-PROVIDED REPORTS

When working in the system with WRK commands, screens will be presented that are system displays. A prime example is the Work with System Status display (Fig. 3.1). In this screen, the <F5> key can be used to refresh data (as it can in most places throughout the system) and a report can be printed. Queries can also be run against system information. System reports are a common way for you to maintain all devices on the system, such as printers.

Figure 3.2 illustrates Work with Writers.

3.6 FUNCTION KEYS

The AS/400 provides many special function keys to be used in various situations. Some provide on-screen help, while others get you out of whatever you're doing. Each facility on the machine has its own function key usages, but many of them are generic, conforming to SAA (System Application Architecture) standards, and deserve some mention here:

F3 (the quit key)	stops whatever you are doing and generally sends you back one level
F4 (the Prompt key)	provides fill-in-the-blanks screens for command parameter entry at the command line or in writing programs in SEU

```
                              Work with System Status                  S9999999
                                                              02/17/90 18:24:21
% CPU used . . . . . . . :        5.2    Auxiliary storage:
Elapsed time . . . . . . :   00:00:23      System . . . . . . . . . :    6847 M
Jobs in system . . . . . :        196      % used . . . . . . . . . :   26.4013
% addresses used:                          Total  . . . . . . . . . :    6847 M
  Permanent  . . . . . . :      4.244      Current unprotect used   :     458 M
  Temporary  . . . . . . :       .095      Max unprotect  . . . . . :     461 M

System    Pool    Reserved    Max      DB      DB    Non-DB   Non-DB
 Pool   Size (K)  Size (K)  Active   Faults   Pages  Faults    Pages
   1      7000      4409     +++       .0      .0      .1       .1
   2       852         0       6       .0      .0      .0       .0
   3      1000         0      10       .0      .0      .0       .0
   4       100         0       3       .0      .0      .0       .0
   5     20000         0      75       .0      .0     2.5      3.5
   6      6000         0       8       .0      .0      .0       .0
                                                                        More...
Command
===>
F3=Exit   F10=Restart   F11=Transition data   F12=Previous   F24=More keys

      21-07                                                  S1 S9999999 KB
```

Figure 3.1 Work system status.

```
                               Work with All Printers

Type options, press Enter.
  1=Start   2=Change   3=Hold   4=End   5=Work with   6=Release   7=Messages
  8=Queue

Opt  Device      Sts   Sep     Form Type   File        User        User Data
     PRT01       END
 _   PRT02       STR   *FILE   *ALL
 _   PRT03       STR   *FILE   *ALL
 _   PRT04       STR   *FILE   *ALL
 _   PRT05       MSGW  *FILE   *ALL        ACCT        HENRY
 _

                                                                         Bottom
Parameters for options 1, 2, 3, 4, 6 or command
===>
F3=Exit   F4=Prompt   F5=Refresh   F9=Retrieve   F11=View 2   F12=Previous

      08-03                                                  S1 S9999999 KB
```

Figure 3.2 Work writers.

F6 (the Print key)	sends the current screen or topic to the printer
F9	retrieves previously entered commands on the command line
F12	previous/cancel—goes back one screen
F13	user support—presents a menu of user commands
F16	major menu—takes you to the major commands menu
F23	set initial menu—automatically sets the user profile to use the menu currently on screen as the sign-on menu
F1	and Help provides context-sensitive explanatory screens, depending on where the cursor is

Keys for your use

Each keyboard used with the AS/400 can be mapped according to your needs. One commonly mapped key is a duplicate key which invokes a program to duplicate the last record in input mode and allows modifications to the displayed record.

3.7 ELECTRONIC CUSTOMER SUPPORT

IBMLink—the resource

IBMLink is IBM's common electronic support interface enhancing customer communications by providing access to various databases and tools. To reach IBMLink, type GO SUPPORT to get the support menu and choose "IBM Product Information," which places you in 3270 emulation mode, connected to an IBM support mainframe, online. Use this sparingly, as the connect and the 3270 emulation have significant overhead and can slow down the entire system. IBMLink provides the following:

Infolink	Information on products, education, prices, publications, dealers, and access to configurators
Orderlink	Account order information
Supportlink	Technical information about IBM products, flashes—Questions and Answers, and technical bulletins
Servicelink	Service information (e.g., problem resolution and preventive service planning)

User Functions Information and tools for IBMLink users:

How to use IBMLink, content, fastpath, PF keys

View, create, and send electronic information

File utilities, including transfer to host or PC
Comments and suggestions
Set individual user profiles

Response from IBM

IBM will provide feedback to your questions and answers or will have someone call you with the answers to your questions. Feedback is generally available with next-day response time and is very detailed. Additionally, questions can be sent to IBM for further follow-up.

The ability to ask questions is generally taken away after one year. Use this valuable facility while you have the opportunity.

Supportlink

Supportlink provides three products:

TechQA	Search a library of technical questions and answers
Flashes	U.S. system center flashes
Techbulletin	U.S. system center technical bulletins

Infolink

Infolink provides nine products:

Sales manuals	Hardware and software descriptions, prices, and software ordering information
Announcements	Announcement letters, highlights, press releases
Configurators	Tools for configuring hardware and software
Education	Source content and scheduling information
Pubs catalog	Descriptions of contents, prices, ordering information for IBM publications
SW catalog	Abstract of U.S. IBM software products with purpose benefits, and ordering information
SYS prod guide	Systems and products guide, hardware and software overviews
VPA schedules	Volume Procurement Amendment discount schedules for hardware and software products
Dealers	Dealers' names, locations, phone numbers, etc.

3.8 SUMMARY

"Imagine a computer system that can diagnose and resolve problems 24 hours a day . . ." This is just the beginning of the most comprehensive help system ever developed. Prompting, help, index searches, and Electronic Customer Support take a few minutes to learn, but will be invaluable as you use the AS/400. This is literally a computer which can teach you how to use it, and answer questions you have about it.

Chapter

4

Command Language (CL)

CL is the operating system language for the AS/400. With it, you can control the functions of the operating system (OS/400). Although there are over 700 CL commands, CL follows an English-like structure that is easy to learn and use. In fact, CL quickly becomes intuitive, so that with some experience you can guess accurately at syntax and commands.

CL has many uses on the AS/400. It can invoke a system function directly from the command line. It can be invoked from user menus so that end users do not need to know CL (avoiding potential misuse). And it can be coded and compiled into programs which have the power to call other programs, pass and receive parameters, call screens, get input from users, branch conditionally, and perform database I/O. As a command language, it is extremely powerful as well as easy to learn and use (especially compared to its predecessor, JCL).

Most AS/400 screens, including menus, contain an area at the bottom of the screen called the command line (where it says "Selection or Command ===>"). Here, you may enter CL commands and request help as to their syntax, as in Fig. 4.1.

CL uses the command prompting <F4> key to produce the prompt screen from the command line. This allows the easy inclusion of all syntactical variations on a command, simply by filling in the blanks for parameters or accepting default values. If a question mark is typed before the CL command on the command line, the system immediately

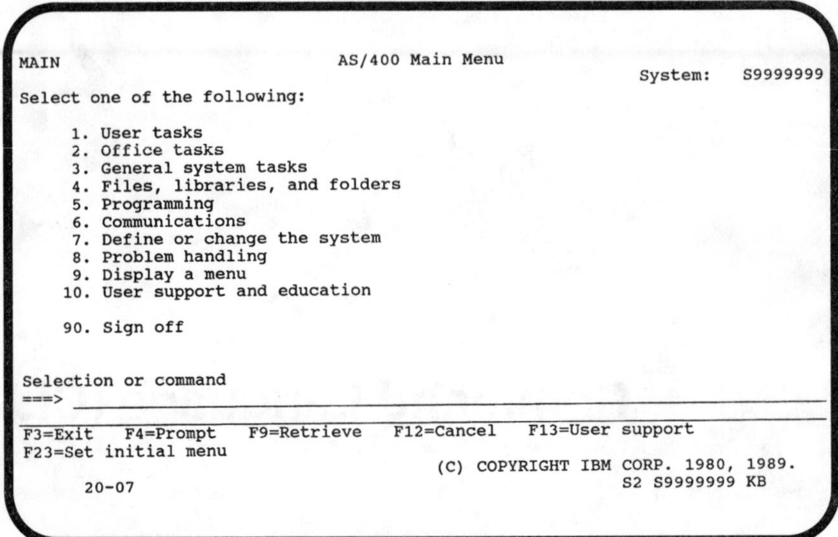

```
MAIN                              AS/400 Main Menu
                                                          System:   S9999999
Select one of the following:

     1. User tasks
     2. Office tasks
     3. General system tasks
     4. Files, libraries, and folders
     5. Programming
     6. Communications
     7. Define or change the system
     8. Problem handling
     9. Display a menu
    10. User support and education

    90. Sign off

Selection or command
===> ____________________________________________________________________

F3=Exit   F4=Prompt   F9=Retrieve   F12=Cancel   F13=User support
F23=Set initial menu
                                        (C) COPYRIGHT IBM CORP. 1980, 1989.
     20-07                                           S2 S9999999 KB
```

Figure 4.1 Menu screen with command line.

proceeds to the prompt screen. See Sec. 4.1 for more on command prompting.

CL can be used throughout the system to execute a variety of functions, some of which previously required operator attention. These functions can be written in CLPs (Command Language Programs) and called at the command line from calendars in Office (see Chap. 6) or from menus (see Chap. 16).

4.1 GENERAL SYNTAX

Three-part structure

CL is based on an English-like verb/modifier/object syntax. In addition, a number of parameters and statements may be required to qualify the basic command.

The following example shows a command which allows a user to edit a program with the System Entry Utility, an editor:

```
STRSEU
```

Notice the format: STRSEU (short for Source Entry Utility). This format is comprised of a three-letter verb abbreviation, followed by a three-letter object abbreviation. As you can see, CL is generally built from three-letter abbreviations of the function you are trying to perform.

The command statements often (but not always) include three sections, each containing a three-letter abbreviation. In the first position, there is always a three-letter verb abbreviation; the second and third positions may be shorter. Another example would be CPYF or Copy File—which has only a single letter in the second part, and no modifier. But the prototype of the CL command consists of the three-part command, each part consisting of three letters, as in CHGUSRPRF (Change User Profile).

Prompting

Most commands require more parameters than just the simple three-part CL command format. The AS/400 provides a very useful utility, called *command prompting,* to help in the completion of CL commands. To complete the aforementioned STRSEU command, type STRSEU at the command line and hit <F4> for the prompting screen. Then fill in the blanks next to the parameter prompts to complete the command. The <F10> key often provides additional optional parameters.

In Fig. 4.2, STRSEU is the command, MYLIB is the library, QRPGSRC is the source physical file (where source programs are stored), ACCOUNTS is the name of the program to edit, and RPG is the type of program (see Chap. 5 for more on libraries and objects). This complete command may be entered on the command line, if all the parameters are known, without using the prompt key:

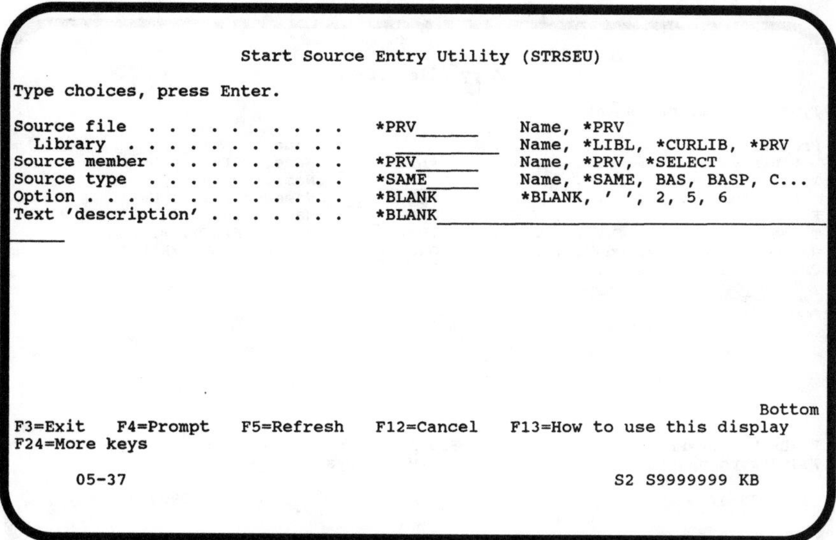

```
                    Start Source Entry Utility (STRSEU)

Type choices, press Enter.

Source file . . . . . . . . . . .   *PRV______      Name, *PRV
  Library . . . . . . . . . . . .   __________      Name, *LIBL, *CURLIB, *PRV
Source member . . . . . . . . . .   *PRV______      Name, *PRV, *SELECT
Source type . . . . . . . . . . .   *SAME_____      Name, *SAME, BAS, BASP, C...
Option . . . . . . . . . . . . .    *BLANK          *BLANK, ' ', 2, 5, 6
Text 'description' . . . . . . .    *BLANK_____________________________________
______

                                                                          Bottom
F3=Exit   F4=Prompt   F5=Refresh   F12=Cancel   F13=How to use this display
F24=More keys

     05-37                                                   S2 S9999999 KB
```

Figure 4.2 STRSEU prompt screen.

```
STRSEU MYLIB/QRPGSRC ACCOUNTS RPG
```

Another example, the command to copy a file from one library to another is Copy File:

```
CPYF
```

To prompt for the correct CPYF syntax, type CPYF at the command line and hit <F4>, producing this screen. The prompt screen may be seen in Fig. 4.3.

A complete statement might be:

```
CPYF FROMFILE(LIBNAME/FILENAME) TOFILE(LIBNAME/FILENAME)
CRTFILE(*YES)
```

This syntax tells the operating system the name of the source file for the copy operation, the target file name, and to create the target file if it does not already exist.

If you are certain of the syntax, the command could be entered directly at the command line, complete with all parameters, without using the prompting screen. Note that the <F9> key can be used to retrieve previously entered commands from memory, whether they were entered at the command line or at the prompt screen.

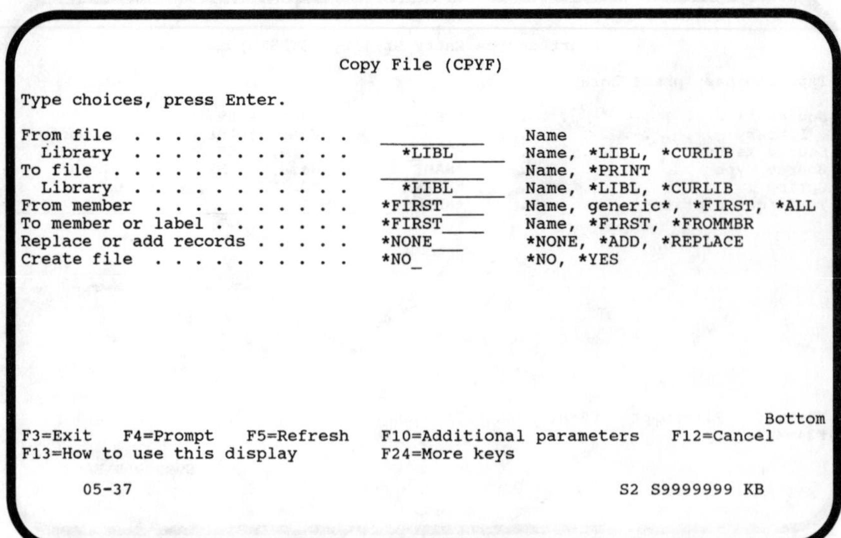

```
                              Copy File (CPYF)

Type choices, press Enter.

From file . . . . . . . . . .   __________    Name
  Library . . . . . . . . . .     *LIBL_____  Name, *LIBL, *CURLIB
To file . . . . . . . . . . .   __________    Name, *PRINT
  Library . . . . . . . . . .     *LIBL_____  Name, *LIBL, *CURLIB
From member . . . . . . . . .   *FIRST____    Name, generic*, *FIRST, *ALL
To member or label . . . . . .  *FIRST____    Name, *FIRST, *FROMMBR
Replace or add records . . . .  *NONE___      *NONE, *ADD, *REPLACE
Create file . . . . . . . . .   *NO_          *NO, *YES

                                                                     Bottom
F3=Exit   F4=Prompt   F5=Refresh   F10=Additional parameters   F12=Cancel
F13=How to use this display        F24=More keys

     05-37                                              S2 S9999999 KB
```

Figure 4.3 Prompt screen for CPYF.

Command help

Knowing all of the CL commands, optional parameters, and their values is unnecessary. Prompting for a command (typing the command at the command line and hitting <F4>) together with context- (field-) sensitive help are invaluable as aids to CL syntax construction. Field-sensitive help explains the required and optional parameters for any field on screen. Combined with command prompting, command help can provide the correct syntax for any CL command. When a CL prompt screen is active, the <Help> key will produce another screen which describes the current parameter field (where the cursor is) on the prompt screen. So, if there is a question as to what value should be entered to a field on the prompt screen, the help key will answer it. In this way, the <F4> key (prompt) and the help key facilitate CL commands. First, the command is entered at the command line, then the <F4> key produces the prompt screen, with blanks to fill in for parameters, and the help key will produce another screen which further explains any required parameter at the current cursor location in the prompt screen. See the command help screen in Fig. 4.4.

In addition to the help screen, there is often an extended help screen available which can be reached by hitting the <F2> key from a command help screen (Fig. 4.5).

The "More . . ." message at the bottom of the screen indicates that there are more pages which can be reached by the <Page Down> key.

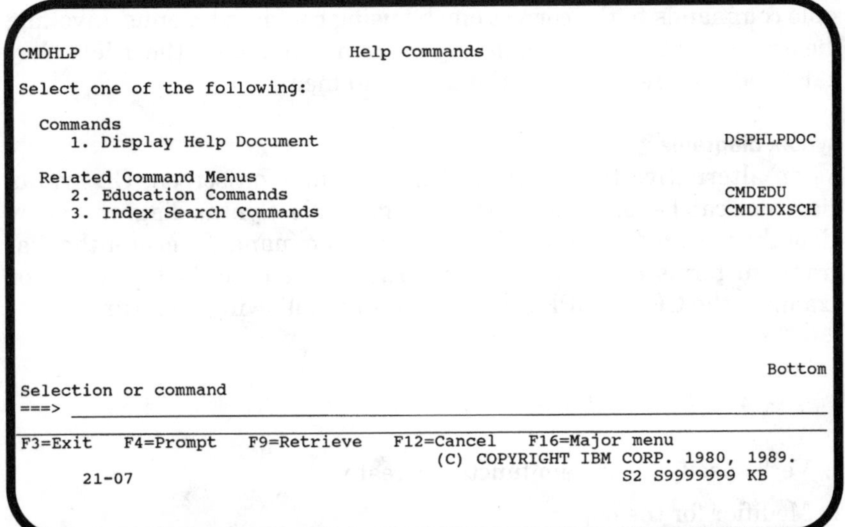

```
CMDHLP                          Help Commands

Select one of the following:

  Commands
     1. Display Help Document                                       DSPHLPDOC

  Related Command Menus
     2. Education Commands                                          CMDEDU
     3. Index Search Commands                                       CMDIDXSCH

                                                                       Bottom
Selection or command
===> ________________________________________________________________________

F3=Exit   F4=Prompt   F9=Retrieve   F12=Cancel   F16=Major menu
                                        (C) COPYRIGHT IBM CORP. 1980, 1989.
     21-07                                                  S2 S9999999 KB
```

Figure 4.4 Screen for command help.

```
HELP                               How to Use Help
How to Use Help

     Help is provided for all AS/400 displays.  The type of help provided
     depends on the location of the cursor.

        o  For all displays, the following information is provided:

           -  What the display is used for
           -  How to use the display
           -  How to use the command line if there is one
           -  How to use the entry fields and parameter line if any
           -  What function keys are active and what they do

        o  The following information is also provided for specific areas,
           depending on the type of information being displayed:

           -  Menus:  Meaning of each option
           -  Entry (prompting) displays:  Meanings and use of all values
              for each entry field
                                                                   More...
F3=Exit help   F10=Move to top   F12=Cancel   F14=Print

     01-01                                               S2 S9999999 KB
```

Figure 4.5 Screen for extended help.

Command menus

By typing GO plus the abbreviation for a group of CL commands (e.g., GO CMDSPL), a list of all related commands will appear. This list will show the actual commands, allowing you to pick one. Choosing a command, by entering a 1 next to it and hitting <Enter>, will invoke the prompting screen. In this way, you may narrow down the range of possible commands to the correct one by using command menus, invoking the prompt screen, and completing the command, using the <Help> key if desired. Figure 4.6 shows the command menu.

Syntax diagrams

As an alternative to prompting CL commands on screen, CL syntax diagrams can be found in the IBM CL manuals. Syntax diagrams show all of the parameters applicable to the CL command. Interpret the diagrams in terms of the three-part structure as described earlier. For example, the CRTSRCPF command has the following structure:

```
CRT SRC PF
 1   2   3
```

1. Verb specifying system function Create
2. Modifier for the object
3. Object (physical file)

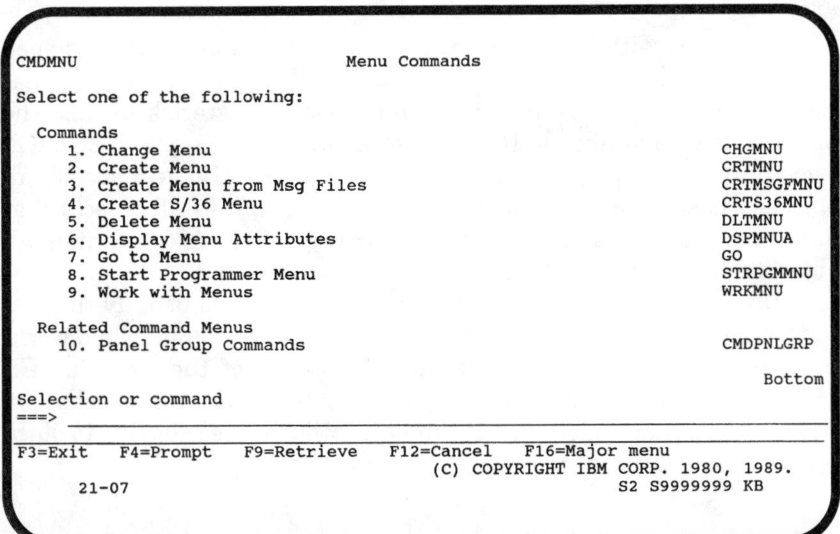

```
CMDMNU                          Menu Commands

Select one of the following:

  Commands
     1. Change Menu                                              CHGMNU
     2. Create Menu                                              CRTMNU
     3. Create Menu from Msg Files                               CRTMSGFMNU
     4. Create S/36 Menu                                         CRTS36MNU
     5. Delete Menu                                              DLTMNU
     6. Display Menu Attributes                                  DSPMNUA
     7. Go to Menu                                               GO
     8. Start Programmer Menu                                    STRPGMMNU
     9. Work with Menus                                          WRKMNU

  Related Command Menus
    10. Panel Group Commands                                     CMDPNLGRP

                                                                    Bottom
Selection or command
===> ____________________________________________________________________

F3=Exit   F4=Prompt   F9=Retrieve   F12=Cancel   F16=Major menu
                                        (C) COPYRIGHT IBM CORP. 1980, 1989.
      21-07                                           S2 S9999999 KB
```

Figure 4.6 Screen for command menu.

Syntax rules and parameters

The complete rules for syntax take up close to thirty pages in the IBM manuals. Within the scope of this book, there are a few basic rules to follow.

First, the most important of the rules—the order in which the parameters occur. Even though the parameters specified may be correct, if presented in the wrong order the AS/400 will give an error message. This is easily fixed, due to command prompting, as mentioned in Sec. 4.1. The prompt screen arranges all parameters in their correct sequence. All required parameters must occur before any optional parameters.

Second, CL usually requires use of a keyword in front of a parameter (e.g., FROMFILE(LIBNAME/FILENAME) in the CPYF example shown earlier). FROMFILE is the keyword. For each parameter, the keyword is always first, followed by the parameter values in parentheses.

Third, some CL parameters are system parameters, which require the use of an asterisk (*) before the parameter (e.g., *YES in the CPYF example).

Predefined values

As with most functions in the AS/400, Command Language has predefined values to which it will default if a CL is invoked without the complete required parameters. Be careful when entering a CL; if you press <Enter> too early, the system might provide default values which are inappropriate to your purpose.

Wildcards

When working with lists of objects, a short list is more easily managed than a complete list. When you need to specify a group of objects that contain common letters in their names, use the asterisk to take the place of the remaining letters of the name. For example, ABC* will select all objects whose names begin with ABC. *ABC will specify all objects whose names end with ABC. *ABC* specifies all objects that have the characters ABC anywhere in the name. A*C specifies all objects that begin with the character A and end with C.

*ALL provides a complete list of the objects, and is usually the system default. Subsets, or qualified object names, are helpful when working with lists of objects by limiting the scope of the list. The CL command will then operate only on the selected subset. This technique can speed searches. However, it can narrow down the selection to nothing. When this occurs a message appears:

```
No Members Match The Subsetting Criteria.
```

4.2 NAVIGATION OF CL

CL manages system objects, and the system regards everything from a database to a workstation as an object. When you prompt for parameters to a CL command, by typing the command at the command line and hitting the <F4> key, a screen presents a variety of possible parameters or functions related to the objects. You can use these screens to select an object to work with, monitor its status, and control it. Sometimes, instead of simply filling in the blanks in a prompt screen, you must step through a sequence of screens to attain the desired result.

For example, if you wanted to stop a job from running, you could step through the following screens:

1. Enter WRKACTJOB (Work with Active Jobs) at the command line to get a screen with these options, as shown in Fig. 4.7.
2. Enter option 5 (Work with) next to the subsystem or job you would like to work with, which leads to a screen with the options seen in Fig. 4.8.
3. Enter option 12 (Work with locks, if active) on the command line, which leads to a screen with more options (Fig. 4.9).
4. Enter option 1 (Work with object locks) next to the object you would like to work with, which leads to a screen with additional options, shown in Fig. 4.10.
5. Choose option 4 (End job), which will produce the result you were looking for.

The preceding was accessed through options on a series of job screens.

```
                           Work with Active Jobs                     S9999999
                                                        02/17/90  18:27:34
CPU %:      .0     Elapsed time:    00:00:00     Active jobs:   20

Type options, press Enter.
  2=Change     3=Hold   4=End      5=Work with    6=Release    8=Spooled files
  9=Exclude    10=Program stack    11=Locks

Opt  Subsystem/Job  User         Type  CPU %  Function         Status
 __  QBATCH         QSYS         SBS      .0                    DEQW
 __  QCMN           QSYS         SBS      .0                    DEQW
 __  QCTL           QSYS         SBS      .0                    DEQW
 __  QINTER         QSYS         SBS      .0                    DEQW
 __    DUNNE        USER904      INT      .0  CMD-WRKACTJOB     RUN

Parameters or command
===> ____________________________________________________________________
F3=Exit       F5=Refresh    F10=Restart statistics    F11=Display elapsed data
F12=Cancel    F24=More keys

      10-02                                              S2 S9999999 KB
```

Figure 4.7 WRKACTJOB screen.

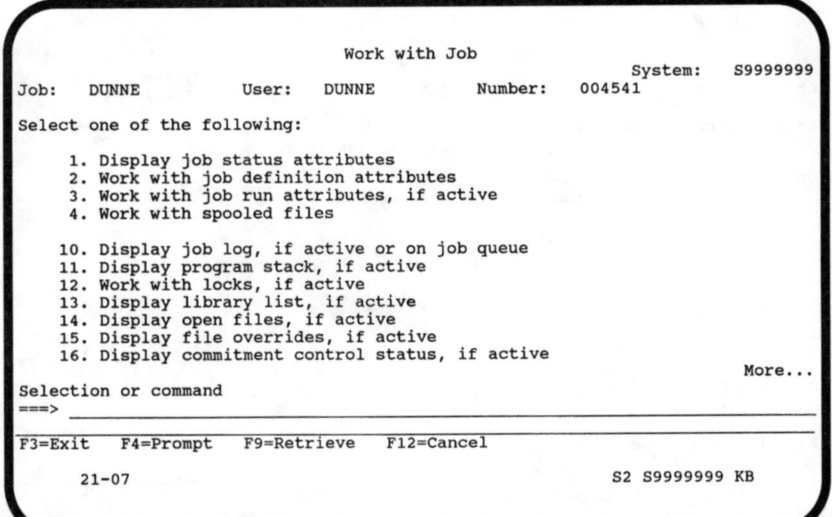

```
                               Work with Job
                                                        System:     S9999999
Job:    DUNNE          User:    DUNNE          Number:    004541

Select one of the following:

     1. Display job status attributes
     2. Work with job definition attributes
     3. Work with job run attributes, if active
     4. Work with spooled files

    10. Display job log, if active or on job queue
    11. Display program stack, if active
    12. Work with locks, if active
    13. Display library list, if active
    14. Display open files, if active
    15. Display file overrides, if active
    16. Display commitment control status, if active
                                                                     More...
Selection or command
===> ____________________________________________________________________

F3=Exit    F4=Prompt    F9=Retrieve    F12=Cancel

      21-07                                              S2 S9999999 KB
```

Figure 4.8 WRKJOB screen.

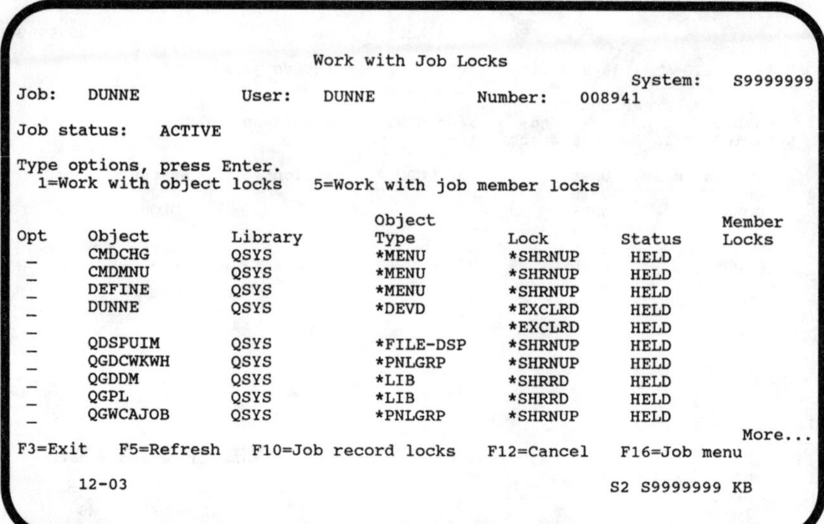

```
                         Work with Job Locks
                                                      System:   S9999999
Job:   DUNNE          User:   DUNNE          Number:   008941

Job status:   ACTIVE

Type options, press Enter.
  1=Work with object locks    5=Work with job member locks

                                       Object                                  Member
Opt   Object        Library        Type           Lock          Status     Locks
 _    CMDCHG        QSYS           *MENU          *SHRNUP        HELD
 _    CMDMNU        QSYS           *MENU          *SHRNUP        HELD
 _    DEFINE        QSYS           *MENU          *SHRNUP        HELD
 _    DUNNE         QSYS           *DEVD          *EXCLRD        HELD
 _                                                *EXCLRD        HELD
 _    QDSPUIM       QSYS           *FILE-DSP      *SHRNUP        HELD
 _    QGDCWKWH      QSYS           *PNLGRP        *SHRNUP        HELD
 _    QGDDM         QSYS           *LIB           *SHRRD         HELD
 _    QGPL          QSYS           *LIB           *SHRRD         HELD
 _    QGWCAJOB      QSYS           *PNLGRP        *SHRNUP        HELD
                                                                          More...
F3=Exit   F5=Refresh   F10=Job record locks   F12=Cancel   F16=Job menu

      12-03                                                S2 S9999999 KB
```

Figure 4.9 WRKJOBLCK screen.

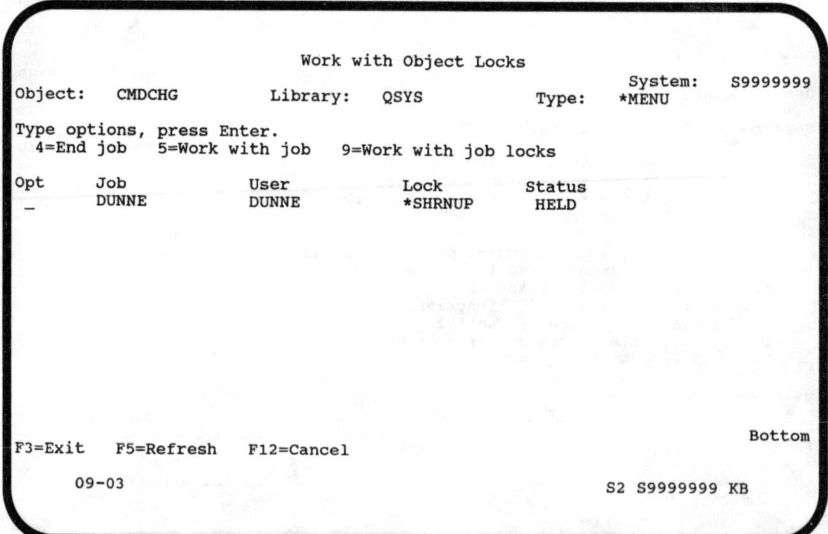

```
                        Work with Object Locks
                                                     System:   S9999999
Object:   CMDCHG          Library:   QSYS          Type:   *MENU

Type options, press Enter.
  4=End job    5=Work with job    9=Work with job locks

Opt     Job            User           Lock          Status
 _      DUNNE          DUNNE          *SHRNUP        HELD

                                                                    Bottom
F3=Exit   F5=Refresh   F12=Cancel

      09-03                                               S2 S9999999 KB
```

Figure 4.10 WRKOBJLCK screen.

Alternatively, you can work without going through all of the preceding screens. For example, the final screen could be reached directly by entering at the command line:

```
WRKOBJLCK OBJ(PGMNAME) OBJTYPE(*PGM)
```

The result of this command would be the final screen as presented in Fig. 4.10.

Or, you can use the ENDJOB command to achieve the final result of ending your job without stepping through screens at all. Although faster and more direct, you must know the appropriate command to invoke. In this case, the command is:

```
ENDJOB JOB(USERNAME/PGMNAME)
```

This command tells the operating system to end a particular job for a particular user. Since no optional parameters have been entered, the job will end using system defaults such as not deleting spool files related to the job.

4.3 COMMON AND USEFUL CL COMMANDS

There are thousands of variations of hundreds of CL commands. We include here descriptions of those command groups which we feel are most useful. See App. B for a list of selected CL commands corresponding to these command groups.

4.3.1 Major command group menus

These commands lead to screens which contain lists of the commands of the type selected. For instance, GO CMDSPL will present a screen showing all of the spool commands, allowing further selection, until you get to the actual command desired. The following is a list of the major command menus which can be reached by typing 'GO' and the command menu name listed on the right:

Selected Major Command Menus

Command Description	Command
Select command by name	SLTCMD
Verb commands	VERB
Subject commands	SUBJECT
Object management commands	CMDOBJMGT
File commands	CMDFILE

Work management commands	CMDWRKMGT
Print commands	CMDPRT
Spooling commands	CMDSPL
Programming commands	CMDPGM
Office commands	CMDOFC
Database commands	CMDDB
Message handling commands	CMDMSGHDL

Type GO MAJOR to get the complete listing of major command groups, some of which are found in the preceding list. From there you can reach any command.

See App. B for a list of selected CL commands.

Work commands

Work is done on objects. The types of objects range from definitions of devices and subsystems to system status and databases (see Chap. 5).

Generally, when a work command is issued, you are displaying, printing, creating, deleting, or performing other management of system objects. The work commands manage objects in the sense that you can change their parameters, characteristics, contents, etc. For instance, to change the print destination of a file waiting in the spool queue, you could issue the command WRKSPLF (Work Spool File).

See App. B for a list of selected work commands.

File commands

Files can be managed through a group of CL commands. These commands can create, copy, delete, and perform other functions on files. File management is an essential component of systems development and implementation.

In addition to the file management commands, there are utilities on the AS/400 to handle I/O to files. These utilities (such as Data File Utility and Query) are activated by the Start commands rather than the file commands (see Start commands following). Basic file tasks such as copy or delete are handled by the file commands, while I/O is handled through utilities.

See Appendix B for a list of selected file commands.

Display commands

Display commands allow you to display information and objects. These commands allow users only to view objects, not to change them. They are very useful for getting information on various aspects of the system, such as database structure, database contents, libraries, and documents.

See App. B for a list of selected display commands.

Print commands

Print commands manage files that are scheduled for output. With very few exceptions, these commands will not begin a print job. Use the print and spooling commands to control jobs once they have reached the queues and are waiting for an available printer. You can change printer destination or priority level, for example. Usually, the actual print job is initiated by a program, Query, Office Document, etc.

See App. B for a list of selected print commands.

Create commands

Creation of objects in the system is a vital part of working with the AS/400. With these commands, you can create libraries, objects, files, reports, user profiles, etc.

See App. B for a list of selected create commands.

Delete commands

The delete commands are used to remove objects from the system. Standard housekeeping chores often include deleting unnecessary files, queries, test routines, and jobs so that libraries do not become cluttered and unmanageable.

See App. B for a list of selected delete commands.

Start commands

Start commands initiate various AS/400 utilities or functions such as SEU (Source Entry Utility: STRSEU), SDA (Screen Design Aid: STRSDA), PDM (Program Development Manager: STRPDM), etc. All of these utilities can be reached by going through the various menus, starting with the Main Menu of the system, or they can be invoked directly from the command line with the Start commands.

See App. B for a list of selected start commands.

Other commands

Some CL commands which perform special functions do not follow the usual CL command syntax. These commands enable the user to go to a specific menu, call a program, run a Query, etc. Some of the most useful commands are:

Selected Other Commands

Go to Menu	GO menuname
Call a Program	CALL programname
Run a Query	RUNQRY queryname

See IBM Master Command Matrix Chart in the CL manual which contains all CL commands requiring parameters. In the Command Matrix Chart, verbs are cross-referenced with objects, expediting location of the desired command.

4.4 COMMAND LANGUAGE PROGRAMS (CLP)

One of the most powerful features of CL is its ability to be coded into files which manage whole job streams. These batch files are called CLPs (Control Language Programs). Use SEU (System Entry Utility, Chap. 8) to enter CL commands into a text file for compiling into an executable object (PGM). CL batch files should reside in a Source Physical File in your library. This Source Physical File can be created with the CRTSRCPF command (Create Source Physical File). An IBM naming convention suggests that you name this Source Physical File 'QCLSRC,' although that is not necessary (see Chap. 5, "Libraries, Files, and Members").

All CLP programs should begin with the PGM statement and end with the ENDPGM statement.

In between PGM and ENDPGM, any valid CL statements can occur, including some special CL statements valid only in CLP programs, such as variable declarations or IFs.

When coding the CLP in SEU (System Entry Utility), you can prompt for the correct syntax, as at the command line. Simply enter the CL command in the program and hit <F4>. This produces the prompt screen. Fill in the required parameters and hit <enter>. CL will actually enter the complete line into the source program at the current line from the prompt screen. If the syntax is incorrect, the line in the program is highlighted. Go back to the prompt screen, fix the syntax, using command help (the field-sensitive help key) if needed, and reenter the line.

Here is a sample CLP program which, when compiled, will run a program and print a form letter. The CLP declares a variable (called ABEND); clears any data from a database (called DATAFILE); calls an RPG program (called UPDTFIL), passing it the previously declared ABEND parameter; receives the ABEND parameter back when the RPG program has terminated; and, depending on the value of ABEND, branches to the end of the program or prints a form letter from AS/400 Office Documents.

```
PGM                                         /* begin pgm */
  DCL VAR(&ABEND) TYPE(*CHAR) LEN(1)        /* delare var */
  CLRPFM FILE(DATAFILE)                     /* clear file */
  CALL UPDTFIL &ABEND                       /* call pgm */
```

```
IF COND(&ABEND = 'Y') THEN(GOTO END) /* if-goto */
PRTDOC DOC(FORMLTR)                  /* print doc */
END:                                 /* label end */
ENDPGM                               /* end pgm */
```

Note carefully the use of the ampersand (&) when referring to a variable in a CLP program.

The line numbers shown in the preceding example are not actually coded into the CLP, but are provided by the SEU screen when editing the source code. We do not recommend coding actual CLP programs and compiling them until you have read Chap. 5, "Objects, Libraries, Files, and Members," and Chap. 10, "Source Entry Utility (SEU)."

Some of the special CL commands which are valid only in CLP programs are:

Selected CLP Commands

Begin program	PGM
End program	ENDPGM
Declare variable	DCL
Declare screen	DCLF
Call screen	SNDRCVF
If (conditional branch)	IF

These special CLP commands may be prompted for parameters, like any other CL command, but only from within SEU, as they cannot be entered at the command line.

Once a CLP has been created and compiled, it can be called at the command line with the CALL command, or invoked from a menu, like any other CL command. In this way, entire job streams may be run from menus, insulating the user completely from the operating system.

4.5 OPEN QUERY FILE

The Open Query File (OPNQRYF) command is a powerful SQL-based tool for database access. With it, you can open a database as a specific logical view for access by high-level languages like RPG or COBOL. You do not have to write DDS or create a logical file because OPNQRYF creates a temporary open data path for your job to run against. OPNQRYF does not affect the way Query or DFU will see the records in a database. Only high-level language programs can use it. OPNQRYF can open a database with sort keys, mapped (user-defined) fields, and record selection, so that your program is only looking at the records which concern it, in appropriate order.

OPNQRYF has the following syntax:

```
OPNQRYF FILE(Customer) QRYSLT('State *EQ "NY" ') KEYFLD(Lnam)
```

The FILE parameter specifies CUSTOMER as the name of the file being opened. The QRYSLT parameter chooses records from the database only if State is "NY" (note double quotes around a character constant). The KEYFLD parameter sorts the resulting records by the Lnam field.

OPNQRYF should be used in CL programs with OVRDBF to share open data paths, call the program, and close the open data path and delete the override, as follows:

```
OVRDBF   FILE(Customer) SHARE(*YES)
OPNQRYF  FILE(Customer) QRYSLT('State *EQ "NY" ') KEYFLD(Lnam)
CALL     PGM(Pgmname)
CLOF     FILE(Customer)
DLTOVR   FILE(Customer)
```

If you want to use a variable in the QRYSLT parameter in your CL program, you need to undergo some contortions to get it into the format that OPNQRYF demands. Notice that the QRYSLT parameter is in single quotes. It is a character string, so you must concatenate your variable into the QRYSLT parameter string. Let's say that you have gotten the State you want in the QRYSLT parameter from the user as a CL variable called &USRST. You can then incorporate this into the QRYSLT parameter like this:

```
QRYSLT('State *EQ "' *CAT &USRST *CAT '" ')
```

The QRYSLT starts with a single quote, reads through 'State *EQ " ' to the double quote required for the character parameter, tacks on a single quote to end the string, concatenates in the character variable &USRST, the single quote which resumes the QRYSLT parameter string, the variable-ending double quote, and the parameter-ending single quote. In this way, you can concatenate CL variables into OPNQRYF commands to create user-defined logical views of databases.

OPNQRYF can be prompted like any CL command with the <F4> key to get a fill-in-the-blanks window for entering the OPNQRYF parameters.

4.6 GUESSING THE PROBABLE COMMAND

Once CL commands and their syntax conventions are familiar, it is possible to guess accurately at the probable command. For instance, to work with spool files, WRKSPLF might come to mind. Type this at the command line, and hit <F4> to prompt it. If the command is valid, the prompt screen appears; if not, a message appears saying that no such command was found. If, after a few attempts, no valid command is entered, type GO MAJOR (for a list of the major command groups) or the name of another command menu to get a list from which to work your way down to the correct command.

4.7 SUMMARY

CL is the operating system language of the AS/400. It is a major advance in IBM command languages in terms of power and ease of use. The prompt key <F4>, the context-sensitive <Help> key, the extended help key <F2>, and the command menus make CL extremely accessible.

With CL, you can manage system objects, call programs, perform file operations, and generally navigate the AS/400. Many functions which previously required operator assistance or complicated JCL are immediately available at the command line and in menus.

As we have mentioned, CL is full of required and optional parameters. By making full use of prompt screens, you can supply all required and optional parameters without knowing the syntax in advance. Remember to prompt for any command or parameter which is unfamiliar and to use the help key to explain any parameter field which is unclear.

Complete CL commands, syntax diagrams, and rules are contained in the *IBM CL Reference,* volumes 1–5.

Chapter

5

Objects, Libraries, Files, and Members

5.1 OBJECTS

The AS/400 is an object-oriented machine. All entities on the AS/400 are regarded by the operating system as objects. Workstations, printers, databases, programs, source files, screens, and everything else in the system are objects. The system maintains descriptions of all its objects, which makes working with them quite simple. All you need to do is refer to a valid, existing object in the system and the AS/400 automatically knows the full description of that object. This is true in CL commands and in programs. It is therefore not necessary to define a database in detail in a program; you simply identify it properly and the AS/400 will locate it for you and make all of its predefined fields available to the program. Once defined, objects can be managed easily. And the operating system provides several useful utilities to aid in the definition, creation, and management of objects (see Part 2, "Development Tools").

5.2 LIBRARIES

All objects are contained in libraries. System libraries hold the operating system programs and functions. User libraries, created for users' profiles, contain user programs, documents, source files, and databases.

System libraries

A system library contains objects necessary for the basic operations of the AS/400. The primary system library is QSYS, which contains all other libraries. In addition, it contains profiles, device descriptions, system programs, and other system-related objects.

IBM provides approximately 40 system libraries. These libraries help to define and separate the functionality of the system. For example, all documents and folders are stored in a system library called QDOC, and the RPG compiler is stored in a library called QRPG.

A complete listing of system libraries is provided in the *IBM CL Reference,* volume 1.

User libraries

Each user has at least one library to work in. This library contains or will contain the programs, screens, and databases necessary for the user to perform work. Or, the objects may be contained in separate libraries. For example, it is common practice to have programs in one library and the databases to which they refer in another. It is therefore necessary for the system to know, when the user signs on, which libraries are to be searched for any objects referenced in CL commands or programs.

Library list

When a user sign-on (profile) is first assigned or created, a library list must be created for the user. If one is not created, the library list will default to QSYS, QGDDM, and QTEMP. The library list contains a list of library names which will be searched in order of entry for any objects required or specified by the system, by CL commands, or by programs.

It is possible to have two different objects with the same name in different libraries. In this case, the object in the library which is highest on the user's library list will be chosen for use. It is therefore critical to manage the library list efficiently and accurately to ensure that the correct objects are found by the system.

The library list can be edited or changed by the CL commands EDTLIBL and CHGLIBL. EDTLIBL with the prompt key <F4> will produce a screen showing the library list currently in use, and allow the addition, deletion, or resequencing of library names. Figure 5.1 shows the EDTLIBL screen.

Remember that any library in the the list takes precedence over any libraries named below it. This list will be searched in order for any object specified in the system, so it is important to know what is in the libraries, and which should go above others in the library list, before changing the library list.

CHGLIBL will change the library list entirely, keeping none of the libraries previously included. With the CHGLIBL command, you can reset the library list to an entirely new search path for objects.

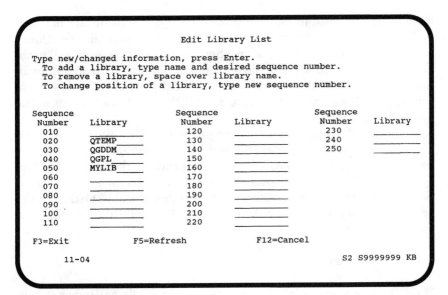

```
                          Edit Library List

Type new/changed information, press Enter.
  To add a library, type name and desired sequence number.
  To remove a library, space over library name.
  To change position of a library, type new sequence number.

Sequence                     Sequence                    Sequence
 Number    Library            Number    Library           Number    Library
  010      _________           120      _________          230      _________
  020      QTEMP____           130      _________          240      _________
  030      QGDDM____           140      _________          250      _________
  040      QGPL_____           150      _________
  050      MYLIB____           160      _________
  060      _________           170      _________
  070      _________           180      _________
  080      _________           190      _________
  090      _________           200      _________
  100      _________           210      _________
  110      _________           220      _________

F3=Exit              F5=Refresh              F12=Cancel

      11-04                                           S2 S9999999 KB
```

Figure 5.1 EDTLIBL.

Obviously, maintenance of the library list is an important feature of systems development on the AS/400. It would not be safe or feasible to expect users to enter library list commands manually before running programs which require specific search paths. Fortunately, CL implements the CL Program (see Chap. 4), which can be used to set up the library list before a program is called and to reset it if needed after program termination:

```
PGM
  CHGLIBL (LIBNAME1 LIBNAME2 LIBNAME3)
  CALL PROGRAM1
  CHGLIBL (LIBNAME2 LIBNAME4 LIBNAME5)
ENDPGM
```

The AS/400 maintains a group of special values which are used as default values for many commands (see Chap. 4). Two of these values are *CURLIB (current library) and *LIBL (library list). They are used to specify which library is the active library for any command. You can specify which library is to be used, in any CL command, or you can accept the system default: *CURLIB or *LIBL (note the use of the asterisk (*) to denote a system value).

If a library is specified by name, the system will use that particular library for its object search. This is a safe and definite method for ensuring where an object will be found. But it is inflexible. For example, if a programmer is developing a Query for a user, he or she may have some test data in his or her own library. If that library is specified by name in the Query, the programmer can be sure that the Query will find the data. But the Query, when tested and approved, will probably be copied into another user's library, for use with live data in another library. Since the Query specifically names the test data library, it will look there for input, even if the test library is not in the user's library list.

The use of *CURLIB or *LIBL can provide the flexibility needed in a situation like this. As long as the user's library list and current library (where objects are created) are set appropriately, the Query will find the correct data. Data or other objects will be found in the current library, or in the library list. This assumes that the object exists in the specified library list or current library. If it does not, the following message appears:

```
Object not found in *LIBL
```

If this happens, remedial action is required, usually editing or changing the library list. Remember that CL Programs can be used to set the library list before a program is called, then call the program. All this can be initiated from user menus. (See Chap. 19 on Application Integration.)

5.3 FILES

A file is a type of object. It may be a database, a document, a screen definition, an object which contains source code, or a number of other file types on the AS/400. All compiled objects and their underlying source codes are files.

Object creation

Objects are created in libraries. After they are created, they can be copied to other libraries for use, or they can be located where they are through the library list. Objects are created in a number of ways, depending on their types and the method of creation you prefer. System utilities can be used to create screens or databases, for example, or you can write your own source code. In the first method, the system utility actually writes the source code for you, based on an interactive definition screen, and then compiles it. In the second method, you write your own source and compile it.

Whether you use system utilities, or write your own source code and compile it, a variety of objects can be created on the AS/400 by the user or programmer. Among these are databases, screens, programs, menus, documents, and Queries (the last three can only be created through system utilities). These represent the main tools of system development on the AS/400. They are specific object types, and have special values for type as follows:

Object	Type
Database	*FILE
Display	*FILE
Program	*PGM
Menu	*MNU
Document	*DOC
Query	*QRYDFN
Message	*MSGF

Often, when specifying an object to the system for a given operation, values must be entered for object type. Remember that the asterisk (*) is part of the system name.

Source physical files

Some objects on the AS/400 may be created by writing and compiling source code. Databases, programs, and screens may be created in this way. Since these are the major components of systems development, all AS/400 programmers must be familiar with the techniques of writing source code and compiling it. It is a programming convention on the AS/400 that each type of source code resides in its own object in the programmer's library.

When a sign-on ID is first provided for the programmer, a library can be created for the programmer to work in. To create one, use the CRTLIB command (Fig. 5.2).

Now that a library exists for the programmer, objects must be created to contain the source code. These objects are called *source physical files.* They are not the actual source code, but will contain the source code. A source physical file is an object which contains source code. Within each source physical file are a group of source members of the same type, for instance, RPG programs. It is a good idea to keep all source code of the same type in the same source physical file.

Each actual program source code within the source physical file is called a *member.* In this way, libraries contain source physical files which contain members (the actual source code). All of these above the level of members are objects. To create the source physical files, use the CRTSRCPF command (see Fig. 5.3).

Standard naming conventions for the usual source physical files include:

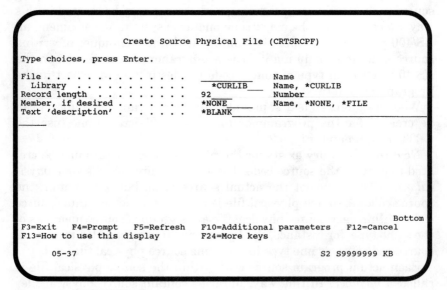

```
                       Create Library (CRTLIB)
Type choices, press Enter.

Library . . . . . . . . . . . .     __________    Name
Library type . . . . . . . . . .    *PROD         *PROD, *TEST
Text 'description' . . . . . . .    *BLANK______________________________________
______

                                                                          Bottom
F3=Exit   F4=Prompt   F5=Refresh    F10=Additional parameters   F12=Cancel
F13=How to use this display         F24=More keys

     05-37                                                  S2 S9999999 KB
```

Figure 5.2 CRTLIB screen.

```
                  Create Source Physical File (CRTSRCPF)

Type choices, press Enter.

File . . . . . . . . . . . . . .    __________    Name
  Library . . . . . . . . . . .       *CURLIB___  Name, *CURLIB
Record length . . . . . . . . .     92_____       Number
Member, if desired . . . . . . .    *NONE______   Name, *NONE, *FILE
Text 'description' . . . . . . .    *BLANK______________________________________
______

                                                                          Bottom
F3=Exit   F4=Prompt   F5=Refresh    F10=Additional parameters   F12=Cancel
F13=How to use this display         F24=More keys

     05-37                                                  S2 S9999999 KB
```

Figure 5.3 CRTSRCPF screen.

CL programs	QCLSRC
COBOL programs	QLBLSRC
RPG programs	QRPGSRC
C programs	QCSRC
Data Definition Specifications	QDDSSRC
Text files	QTXTSRC
Menus	QMENUSRC

Display definitions for screens are usually kept in QDDSSRC along with the database file source members. IBM names system libraries and source physical files with the prefix Q, as you can see.

Once the library has been created, and contains source physical files, source code can be written within the source physical files. This source code is compiled into objects which can be used or executed by the system. Source code cannot be used directly, but must be compiled first. Source code is entered into the source physical files using SEU (Source Entry Utility, Chap. 10).

Objects which are compiled from source members are created in a library specified at compile time. The system default is *CURLIB, but source members are normally compiled into objects in the same library as the member (*SRCLIB).

Database files

An AS/400 database is an object which contains data. It is usually compiled from source code Data Description Specifications (DDS), although it may be created with the CRTPF (Create Physical File) command. The DDS contains field definitions, key fields, field descriptions, etc., for the database (see Chap. 11 on creating databases).

DDS may contain key field specifications which will determine how data is organized in a given database. If specified, the key field(s) will index the records. The AS/400 handles this automatically for you.

There are two types of database definitions available to the programmer:

1. Physical files
2. Logical files

Do not confuse physical files with source physical files. Physical files are actual databases which contain records of data, whereas source physical files are objects which contain source code to be compiled. A physical file is type *FILE with attribute PF.

Logical files do not actually contain data, but are a redefinition of a physical file. In this way, a view can be created from a database (physical file) which is different from its original definition.

For instance, you may wish to specify a key other than the one specified in the DDS for a physical file, and/or limit the number of fields referenced, or even redefine the fields. This technique provides flexibility in dealing with physical files. As long as the actual data is there, you can redefine it virtually any way you want through the use of a logical file. The type of a compiled logical file is *FILE with attribute LF.

Join files are created to join multiple databases together, creating one composite record from the records in the various databases referenced. Naturally, a key field is needed to tell the system which records to join between the databases. The file type for compiled join files is *FILE with attribute LF.

Display files

Display files provide screens for the user. Like database files, they can be created by entering source code into members which are then compiled, or by using a system utility (SDA, Chap. 12).

In fact, the system makes no inherent distinction between display files and database files. Display file source code is regarded as DDS, just like database definitions. The workstation is thought of as a type of device file, usually with each line on the screen representing a record. The file type for the compiled display object is *FILE, attribute DSPF.

Program files

Programs are created by entering source code into a member of a source physical file like QRPGSRC using SEU (Chap. 10), and then compiling the source code into an executable object.

The AS/400 will check any program references to external files (such as databases or screens) during the compile to see if there are any references to undefined files or fields. If the external file referenced is not in the library list, you will get an undefined field or variable error from the compile. Once again, it is very important to maintain your library list for the task at hand, making sure that any required search paths to objects are provided.

5.4 MEMBERS

As you may have noticed, most of the work done by the programmer is within members of source physical files. Here, programs, databases, screens, etc., are defined or coded. These coded members are then compiled into the objects required for the system. These compiled objects are created by default in the same library as the source code, but this can be changed at compile time or they can be copied to other libraries.

Member List

The AS/400 provides a method for managing members, called the Member List. It is what it sounds like, a list of the members in a particular source physical file. Actually, the member list is a subfunction of a larger utility called PDM (Program Development Manager), which can also manage objects and libraries (more on this later).

Let's say you want to write an RPG program using the Member List. You reach the Member List by typing the CL command STRPDM which requires no parameters and produces the screen seen in Fig. 5.4.

Simply enter a 3 at the command line, and you are taken to the screen in Fig. 5.5, where you can specify which members to work with, in which source physical files.

Enter the library, source physical file (QRPGSRC), and members you want to work on. *ALL will get you all of the members in the specified source physical file and is the system default. Since you may have a large number of RPG programs, you would probably want to narrow down the choices for the member list. By using the asterisk (ABC*), you will get only those programs whose names begin with ABC on the member list (see Chap. 4 on qualified object names). Or, specify the member you want to work on. The screen seen in Fig. 5.6 appears.

If you are creating a new member, it obviously won't appear on the Member List. Hit <F6> to create a new member and you get the Create New Member screen (Fig. 5.7).

You may enter the member name and type, as well as a description of the member, which will appear on the member list for documentation.

To edit an existing member enter a 2 next to the desired member on the list and hit <enter>. This will start SEU where you are able to edit the source member. Most of your work occurs inside SEU (see Chap. 10

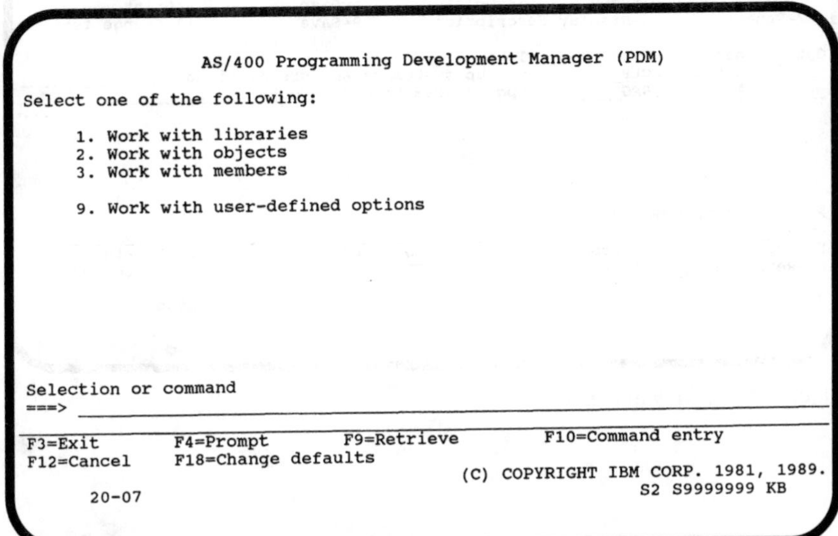

Figure 5.4 PDM screen.

```
                    Specify Members to Work With

 Type choices, press Enter.
   File . . . . . . . . . . .   QTXTSRC___    Name
     Library . . . . . . . .    QGPL______    *LIBL, *CURLIB, name
   Member:
     Name . . . . . . . . . .   MYFILE____    *ALL, name, *generic*
     Type . . . . . . . . . .   *ALL______    *ALL, type, *generic*, *BLANK











 F3=Exit    F5=Refresh    F12=Cancel
      05-32                                          S2 S9999999 KB
```

Figure 5.5 PDM select members screen.

```
                     Work with Members Using PDM
File . . . . . .  TEXTFILE__              Position to . . . . .   __________
  Library . . . .  MYLIB_____

Type options, press Enter.
  2=Edit          3=Copy       4=Delete          5=Display        6=Print
  7=Rename        8=Display description          9=Save           13=Change text

Opt  Member      Type       Text
__   SIGNON      CLP_______ Set_up_system_parameters_at_signon________________
__   UPDATE      RPG_______ rpg_program_to_update_data_________________________
                                                                       More...




Parameters or command
===> ___________________________________________________________________________
F3=Exit          F4=Prompt               F5=Refresh             F6=Create
F9=Retrieve      F12=Previous            F23=More options       F24=More keys
     11-02                                                S1 S9999999 KB
```

Figure 5.6 PDM Member List.

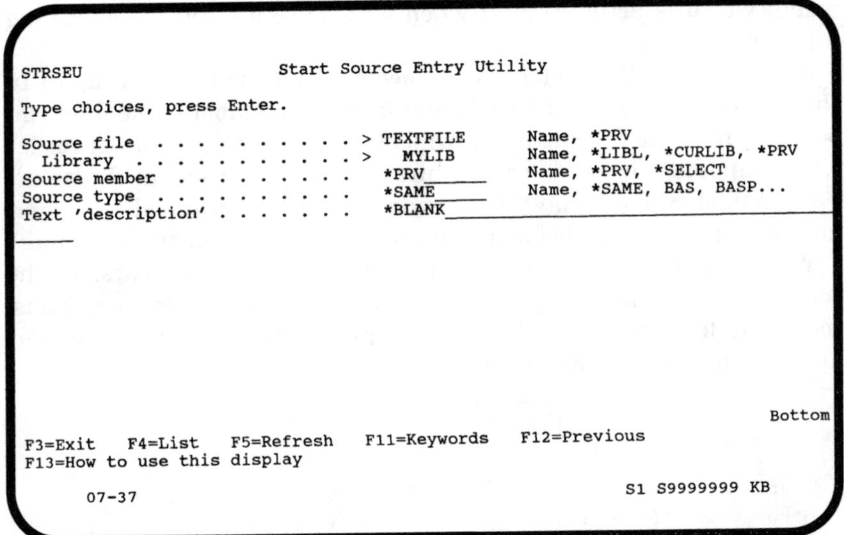

```
STRSEU                     Start Source Entry Utility

Type choices, press Enter.

Source file . . . . . . . . . . . > TEXTFILE       Name, *PRV
  Library . . . . . . . . . . . . >   MYLIB        Name, *LIBL, *CURLIB, *PRV
Source member . . . . . . . . . .   *PRV______     Name, *PRV, *SELECT
Source type . . . . . . . . . . .   *SAME_____     Name, *SAME, BAS, BASP...
Text 'description' . . . . . . .   *BLANK_____________________________________
_____

                                                                        Bottom
F3=Exit   F4=List   F5=Refresh   F11=Keywords   F12=Previous
F13=How to use this display

     07-37                                           S1 S9999999 KB
```

Figure 5.7 Create New Member screen.

on SEU). To view a source member without being able to change it enter a 5 next to the member name.

When you have edited a member, it can be compiled into an object. Simply enter a 14 next to the member you want compiled. Make sure that the member type is correct (e.g., RPG for an RPG program). This member type invokes not only the correct compiler (e.g., RPG), but also the correct type of syntax checking in SEU. The system will compile it for you. If the compile is successful, the object is now available to the system. If not, see Chap. 20, "Debugging."

Note that the 14 is not visible as an option on the member list but becomes visible as an additional option by hitting <F23> for more options.

The <F12> key will get you back to the screen previous to the member list so that you could specify another source physical file or another member to work with (see Fig. 5.7).

Multiple members

We have seen that source physical files can contain multiple members, each one being a distinct source code for compiling into an object. In addition, each physical file or display file member may contain multiple members.

Members, formats, and records

A format is a name given to a member or part of a member. Members can contain multiple formats. It is the format name (not the member name) which is actually used when writing to a database or calling a screen.

Formats, as with other AS/400 objects, can be named with up to 10 characters, which should be different from the member name. Remember that it is the format name which is referenced in a program for writes, updates, or screen calls, while a record read uses the file name.

Once the DSPF (display) object is defined in a program, all of the format names are available for screen calls (see Sec. 5.3 on programming).

Within a member, and possibly within multiple formats, is the record. A record is simply a single line of source code or data. Thus, records in formats in members in files in libraries constitute the hierarchy of the AS/400 library structure:

```
                    LIBRARY

OBJECT       OBJECT                      OBJECT
(*PGM)      (*QRYDFN)                    (*FILE)

                                  fmt1      fmt2

                           mbr1   rec       rec
                                  rec       rec
                           mbr2   rec       rec
                                  rec       rec
```

5.5 PROGRAM DEVELOPMENT MANAGER (PDM)

In addition to the invaluable member list mentioned previously, there are two other functions available from PDM: working with libraries and working with objects.

If, for instance, you wanted to copy an object (maybe a program) to another library for another user, you could type STRPDM at the command line, or hit the <F12> key to back out of the member list to the PDM screen.

Enter 2 at the command line for the Specify Objects screen (Fig. 5.8).

Enter library and object name, type, and attribute, as shown in Fig. 5.9.

Enter 3 next to the object of your choice to copy the object, and you will see the screen shown in Fig. 5.10.

Fill in the parameters for the FROM library, object and type, and the TO library. A message will appear at the bottom of the screen as to whether or not the copy operation was successful. When copying databases to other libraries, you must specify whether you want to cre-

```
                     Specify Objects to Work With

Type choices, press Enter.

  Library . . . . . . . . . .   *CURLIB___     *CURLIB, name

  Object:
    Name . . . . . . . . . . .   *ALL______     *ALL, generic*, name
    Type . . . . . . . . . . .   *ALL______     *ALL, *type
    Attribute  . . . . . . . .   *ALL______     *ALL, *BLANK, attribute







F3=Exit      F5=Refresh      F12=Previous

     05-35                                             S1 S9999999 KB
```

Figure 5.8 PDM Specify Objects screen.

```
                      Work with Objects Using PDM

Library . . . . .   QGPL______         Position to . . . . . . . .   ________
                                       Position to type  . . . . .   ________

Type options, press Enter.
  2=Change         3=Copy                         4=Delete         5=Display
  7=Rename         8=Display description          9=Save           10=Restore

Opt  Object       Type         Attribute    Text
__   UPDATE       *PGM         RPG          update data
__   ENTER        *PGM         RPG          call entry screen and edits




Parameters or command
===> ____________________________________________________________________
F3=Exit           F4=Prompt             F5=Refresh              F6=Create
F9=Retrieve       F12=Previous          F23=More options        F24=More keys
     11-02                                                S1 S9999999 KB
```

Figure 5.9 PDM Work with Objects screen.

```
CRTDUPOBJ                  Create Duplicate Object

Type choices, press Enter.

Object . . . . . . . . . . . . . > PROG04        Name, generic*, *ALL
Library  . . . . . . . . . . . . > QGPL          Name, *CURLIB
Object type  . . . . . . . . . . > *PGM          *ALL, *AUTL, *CHTFMT, *CLS...
To library . . . . . . . . . . . > QGPL______    Name, *SAME, *CURLIB
New object . . . . . . . . . . . > PROG04____    Name, *SAME




                                                                        Bottom
F3=Exit   F4=List   F5=Refresh   F11=Keywords   F12=Previous
F13=How to use this display

      08-37                                             S1 S9999999 KB
```

Figure 5.10 PDM Copy Objects screen.

ate the object in the target library (*YES) and, if the object is a database, whether you want to append to the database in the target (*ADD) or replace the records in the target (*REPLACE). The <F10> key will provide additional parameters, if needed. Remember that the <Help> key will provide a screen explaining any parameter field at the current cursor location.

Programmers might like to have the PDM screen come up automatically at sign-on, instead of the Main Menu. This can be achieved by specifying a CLP program which will run automatically upon sign-on. In this CLP program, you can issue CL commands to customize your working environment (especially CHGLIBL to set up the library list) and STRPDM to bring up the PDM screen. The command to alter what happens at sign-on is CHGUSRPRF (change user profile), and you need security officer status to do this (QSECOFR). Get your security officer to help you to customize your working environment by specifying which programs and menus will be called automatically when you sign on.

5.6 SUMMARY

Libraries are the primary structure of organization of the AS/400. Everything is an object in a library. System libraries contain the AS/400's functions, operating system, languages, utilities, etc. Users have or create their own libraries which contain a variety of objects, including executable programs, databases, and source physical files which contain source members. Source members may contain multiple formats if they are for databases or display files, although multiple formats are recommended only for display files. All source members must be compiled into objects before the AS/400 can make use of them.

The library list for a particular user tells the system where to look for any objects specified in a program or CL command. In addition, the current library setting is the default search path.

Library list management is crucial to the accurate execution of AS/400 systems because it determines where the system will look for programs, databases, screens, etc. The library list can be managed from the command line with the CL commands EDTLIBL ADDLIBLE, RMVLIBLE, and CHGLIBL. Or, CLP programs can be used for job control to set the library list and call programs, either at sign-on or at any time during your session.

Chapter

6

Security and Authority

The key to security on the AS/400 is planning. Effective security depends on establishing standards for the installation. It is extremely difficult and inefficient to try to force security into an installation that began with little or no security planning.

Two special user types are generally set up for handling security on the AS/400:

1. QSECOFR (security officer). The security officer has the "keys to the kingdom." The security officer has the highest security rating in the system and has access to all objects and functions in the system. There should only be one security officer in any system. Many times there are backup security officers in a system—disseminating "absolute" control of the system.
2. *SECADM (security administrator). In order to break up the responsibilities of the security officer, a second level of security authority is available on the AS/400. This security level is commonly given to department heads and group leaders to offer a level of localized support in security issues. There can be multiple security administrators in any system.

Especially in production, these responsibilities will become key. In the production environment, supervisors in each area might be charged with one or many of the following responsibilities:

- Change all passwords regularly.
- Create user profiles (definitions of users on the system).
- Set up initial programs and menu security as needed.
- Secure libraries from nonusers and programmers.
- Move applications from development to production libraries.
- Authorize access to system based on requests and policy.
- Log all security actions.

The security measures provided by the AS/400 can reduce the risk of users accidentally changing or destroying resources. But risk is not eliminated. Effective security requires resource controls combined with physical security and a division of duties. If this integrated security approach is not used, the system is vulnerable to possible access by unauthorized people. Overall security controls are the main responsibility of the security officer (QSECOFR).

6.1 SYSTEM SECURITY LEVELS

Different levels or configurations of security are available for the AS/400 installation. Use CHGSYSVAL SYSVAL(QSECURITY) to change the level.

Level 10. This level of security requires a user ID only. If a user ID is not present when a sign-on is created, then one is automatically created by the system.

Level 20. This level of security requires a user ID and a password. Unlike level 10, a user ID must be present on the system before a sign-on is attempted. Once signed onto the system, all users have authority to everything on the system.

Level 30. This level requires a user ID and a password, like level 20. But further security is available to secure all objects on the system and, by default, many things are secured based on a user's class (such as changes to user profiles). Level 30 is the most widely used and probably the best level of security to use on the AS/400.

Level 40. This is the most secure level of authority. Very similar to level 30, it provides the extra protection of checking that only certain types of programs can access certain objects. It is used to protect against hackers, but also adversely affects some third-party software.

Physical security

The AS/400 has a keylock switch on the system unit which can lock the system in four different modes of operation:

SECURE	The only function available in this mode is power down from a display station.
AUTO	Allows the additional function of IPL (Initial Program Load) from a remote location.
NORMAL	Allows the capability of turning the system on or off with the power switch.
MANUAL	Allows manual load of the system, manual control of functions, manual power off, different system load, DST (Dedicated Service Tools) functions.

Unlike mainframes, the AS/400 does not require an operator console associated with the system. Operatorlike functions can be done from any terminal; with appropriate authorities, the system can run "unattended."

Object and resource security

Practically everything stored in the AS/400 is an object. All objects are stored in libraries (which are also objects). Some libraries are created by users and some are provided as a standard part of the system. All files, programs, user profiles, device descriptions, etc., are objects. The security system controls access to all objects. All objects in the system have owners who play a major role in defining the security of those objects.

The security system is primarily concerned with protecting objects. All objects have common structures in their control blocks. This allows a very unified approach to security, since all objects interface the same way to the security routines. (Note that this approach is totally different from MVS, VM/CSE, or VSE security schemes, and is the basis of the AS/400's superior architecture.)

6.2 USER PROFILES

A user profile is created by a security officer or administrator to give a user specific access rights to the system. Care should be taken when creating user profiles because the user profile defines what a user can do in the system. Create user profiles for only those users who really need access to the system and grant them only the authority they need.

Useful CL commands to work with user profiles include:

DSPUSRPRF	Display user profile.
WRKUSRPRF	Work with user profile.
CHGUSRPRF	Change user profile (QSECOFR required).
CRTUSRPRF	Create user profile (QSECOFR required).
CHGPWD	Change user password (user can change own password).

A system value (QMAXSIGN) controls the number of sign-on attempts by local and remote users. This is the number of times a user is allowed to try to sign on incorrectly. Incorrect sign-on attempts can be caused by incorrect user ID, incorrect password, and a user trying to sign on a device for which he or she has no authority. Exceeding the allotted number of sign-ons results in the device or terminal being varied off. The user profile might be disabled, too, depending on system value QMAXSGNACN. Operator attention is required to reactivate the terminal and user profile.

User classes

There are five user classes which are hierarchical in authority. The classes represent different roles in the DP environment. These are convenient ways to assign special authorities to different types of users. A higher class can perform all the functions of a lower class. User classes are shown here with special authorities in parentheses keyed to the following authority types.

*SECOFR	Security officer	(123456)
*SECADM	Security administrator	(234)
*PGMR	Programmer	(34)
*SYSOPR	System operator	(34)
*USER	End user	(ad hoc)

Special authorities

In the AS/400 there are special user privileges for certain security and system administration functions. Special authorities allow certain users to administer AS/400 security and system tasks. The special authorities are not hierarchical. There are six of them:

1. *ALLOBJ allows unlimited access to everything.
2. *SECADM allows administration of user profiles.
3. *SAVSYS is for saving and restoring system tasks.
4. *JOBCTL allows manipulation of job queues and subsystems.
5. *SPLCTL allows control of spool functions.
6. *SERVICE is a special case that allows service functions.

The user class also affects what options are shown on the system menus.

Limited capability

Use may be assigned limited capability. This is an option when defining a user profile. Limited capability, when used with an appropriate initial program or initial menu, can restrict a user to almost any desired subset of system's functions.

Operations personnel should have few special authorities except *JOBCTL and *SAVSYS menus and CLP in QSYSOPR. Operators should have a separate profile for nonoperations tasks. The library is Public *EXCLUDE.

Passwords

A password is assigned at the time of creation of the user profile. The user has authority to change his or her own password, and should exercise this right regularly to ensure privacy in his or her work area. Use the CL command CHGUSRPWD.

Password management involves enforcement of several rules:

- Use easily remembered words of a reasonable length.
- Password change is required at specified intervals.
- Prevent password recycling (and short list).

Currently, the AS/400 does not support any of these actions automatically. A program or third-party software could provide these functions.

Menu access

User access to the various menus in the system can be controlled by the security officer. Users can therefore be presented with any desired menu when they sign on, and choices on system menus may be included or excluded as desired. In this way, each user's access to menus may be tailored to specific needs and security considerations.

Command access

As with menus, user access to CL commands may be restricted to a given subset or a group of user-defined commands. This is an effective means of ensuring that users who do not need potentially risky CL commands cannot find them.

Library list

Library security can authorize a group of users to an application in a library. Selected users in the group authority have access to certain functions and files in the library. This same concept can be applied to test and production libraries. The development programmer can code and test applications and, when testing is complete, can give the tested version to the user.

Users only have access to objects which are found in their library list unless they use explicitly qualified names. They can be directed to the objects necessary for their work simply by managing the entries and sequence of their library list. Likewise, they can be excluded from certain objects by excluding their libraries from the list.

Access to documents

The office system component of the AS/400 has additional security facilities for the folders and documents that comprise the unique data objects for the office system.

Access to physical files

Physical files are the databases of the system, and require proper authority to work with them. Different levels of authority are required for different operations. The owner of a physical file or database is usually the programmer who created the application. The owner of a physical file and the system security officer can grant different levels of authority to a physical file.

Physical file authorities are granted with the CL command GRTOBJAUT, and may give the following rights:

*USE	may read but not write, clear, or delete
*CHANGE	may read and write but not clear or delete
*ALL	may read, write, clear, and delete

6.3 OBJECT AUTHORITY

Objects are owned by users, and authority must be granted explicitly to those others who require access to them.

Owners

The owner of an object is the user who created it, and it is the owner who has all rights to an object and may grant rights to the object. In addition, the security officer may grant rights.

Users

Users of objects are those who must access them either directly or through programs which reference them. When an application is installed in a user area, object authorization must be carefully managed. Library lists, explicit object authority, and authorization lists must be maintained to ensure appropriate user access to required objects.

Granting authority

In AS/400 terminology, authority is the permission to access an object. The object owner and the security officer can grant or revoke authority to an object. There are a variety of detailed terms and concepts that use the word authorities. It is important to understand the difference between authority to an object and the authority to the data in an object. Operations such as allocation, moving, and renaming apply to the object. It is possible to have authority for these operations without having access to the data stored in the object. Similarly, access such as read, write, update, and delete to the data in an object can be granted selectively without having a full authority to the whole object.

There are two classes of object authority:

1. Object Control

OBJOPR	Operational, controls the use of an object and the ability to look at the description of the object. Access to a logical file can be given without granting access to the physical file. This prevents the user from corrupting a physical file. A programmer without data authority can compile using this authority, but would not be allowed to run the program.
OBJMGT	The object management authority controls the move, rename, and change attribute functions for the object.
OBJEXIST	The object existence authority controls the delete, save, restore, or transfer of ownership.
AUTLMGT	This authority is needed to manage the contents of an authorization list.

2. Data Control

READ	Controls the ability to read, write files.
ADD	Controls the ability to insert new entries.
UPDATE	Controls the ability to modify existing entries.
DELETE	Controls the ability to remove existing entries in the object.

There are four common authorities given which have special names:

*ALL	Allows unlimited access to the object and its data.
*CHANGE	Allows unlimited access to the data in the object.
*USE	Allows data to be read.
*EXCLUDE	No access to object or its data.

6.4 AUTHORIZATION LISTS

Another important security concern is authorization lists. An object may have only one authorization list associated with it. An authorization list may cover more than one object. A user can appear on many different authorization lists. Authorization lists are not affected when related objects are deleted. If an object is deleted and then restored, it is automatically linked to an existing authorization list for that object.

6.5 GROUP PROFILES

A user profile may be linked to a group profile, a concept inherited from the System/38. This allows all of the members of the group to share common attributes, common access to selected files, and common ownership to objects. A user is not required to be part of a group, and may belong to only one group.

Group profiles are used to organize users by job function, and to simplify the assignment and administration of object authorities.

6.6 OUTPUT DISTRIBUTION AND SECURITY

As in any other computing environment, printed listings or output disks cannot be protected by the system after they are written. It is very common to see confidential reports sitting in the printer output hopper waiting for the originator to pick them up. Manual distribution controls are usually required in this area.

6.7 ADDITIONAL SECURITY ISSUES

To guide security issues, there are a few practices which should be adhered to:

- CLP should be used to control the changing of objects.
- Restrict QSECOFR workstations to those who are authorized.
- Review QHST log for breach attempts.
- QSECOFR should not own objects.

In general, the environment needs to adhere to:

- Group User Profiles for programmers.
- Assign specific authorities as needed.
- Restrict access to the production environment.
- Production source should be read only for developers.

Within the production and live environment, these standards can maximize the management of users and objects:

- Group User Profiles for owning everything.
- Group Users to a single profile.
- Authorization list containing the group profile for libraries.

- Menu security limits users to menu options.
- Do not allow command entry (Qcmd).

Operations is a specialized area which requires special considerations and a great deal of attention.

6.8 SUMMARY

Security is one of the main advantages of using the AS/400. Its security scheme is modeled after one developed for the Department of Defense, and is quite rigorous if correctly managed. Level 30 security is the norm, and can be used to control everything from who can sign on, what rights they have, and which menus they can access, to user groups and authorization lists for security maintenance.

The security officer (QSECOFR) is the main implementor of system security, and it is his or her job to control the dissemination of authorizations downward to QSECADM and then to the users and programmers. All objects on the system have authorization levels associated with them, so it is possible to control exactly the working environment of all users.

An essential component of systems development, the planning of authorization and security, is key to the successful implementation of your applications.

Chapter

7

Operations

The AS/400 was designed for ease of use. It handles many system functions automatically or with a minimum of user intervention. Some functions which do require regular operator attention system include:

- Initial Program Load (IPL)
- Backup and restore
- Printing
- Work management
- Answering messages
- Installing Program Temporary Fixes (PTFs)
- Problem handling
- Housekeeping
- Upgrades

The performance of these tasks is facilitated by various menus, notably the Operational Assistant. In addition, they can be performed by entering commands at the command line, or by automating them through the use of CL programs. For instance, a CLP could be written which would wait until a specified time, perform an automatic backup of user data, then power the system off and back on again (IPL).

7.1 INITIAL PROGRAM LOAD (IPL)

The Initial Program Load reads system files from disk into main storage, preparing the operating system and verifying devices. IPL also cleans up some temporary storage used by the system in the normal course of operations. It recognizes new devices attached to the AS/400 using auto-config, and implements changed system values. Make sure that devices you want recognized by the system are powered on and correctly connected at IPL time. When IPL is finished, the Sign-On display appears on the console and display stations.

There are two forms of IPL: attended and unattended. The unattended IPL is an automatic function which, once initiated, restarts the system without user intervention. It is the normal form of IPL used in everyday operations. The keylock should be set to the Normal position for unattended IPL. The best way to perform an unattended IPL is by issuing the command: PWRDWNSYS OPTION(*IMMED) RESTART(*YES).

Attended IPL walks the user through several screens on the console, allowing changes to system values and attributes. It takes quite a while longer than the unattended IPL and is only necessary to redefine the system or the IPL procedure itself, or to install an operating system. Sometimes service personnel use an attended IPL. The keylock must be in the Manual position for an attended IPL. Use the Select switch on the control panel to show function 03. Press the Enter button. The system begins the attended IPL and presents various screens at thesystem console for the user to answer questions defining the system.

You can set up the the system to power on and off automatically by using the Power On and Off Tasks Menu (type GO POWER: see Fig. 7.1). Select option 2 to Change Power On/Off schedule and hit <F10> to change Power On/Off defaults. Here, you can set the times for the system to power on and off for each day of the week. Also, you can set how many minutes ahead of this time the system will send a message to the users.

7.2 BACKUP AND RESTORE

It is necessary to develop a backup schedule to protect your data from system failures such as disk crash or power outage. A typical plan might involve backing up user libraries daily, and performing a more complete system backup on a weekly or monthly basis to send off-site. It is not necessary to save more than once objects or libraries which do not change. This includes IBM programs, the operating system, and the licensed internal code. You can back up the unchanging data once, after an installation of the operating system or revision. After that, you might just back up user data on a daily basis. In this way, you can

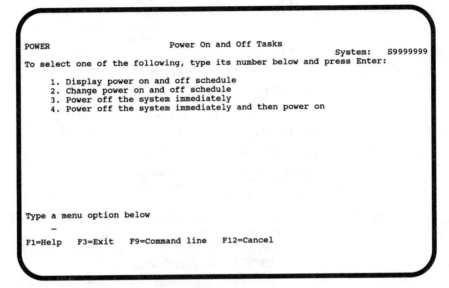

```
POWER                          Power On and Off Tasks
                                                         System:    S9999999
To select one of the following, type its number below and press Enter:

     1. Display power on and off schedule
     2. Change power on and off schedule
     3. Power off the system immediately
     4. Power off the system immediately and then power on









Type a menu option below
     _
F1=Help   F3=Exit   F9=Command line   F12=Cancel
```

Figure 7.1 Power On and Off Tasks.

always restore the operating system from the original backup, and user files from the daily backup. Entire libraries or single objects can be saved to reel tape, cartridge tape, diskette, or save file.

In order to copy data to tape and avoid conflicts with open files and performance degradation, the system should be brought to a restricted state. All subsystems can be ended with the command: ENDSBS SBS(*ALL). Backup can then be run at the system console. Backup is accomplished by issuing CL commands which instruct the operating system to copy data from disk storage to tape device. These are some of the most useful:

INZTAP	Initialize a tape for use. This command destroys any data already on the tape, and formats the tape for use by the operating system.
Example	INZTAP DEV(*TAP01)
SAVSYS	Saves all system libraries, but not user libraries. Objects saved include LIC, security objects, OS/400, distribution objects, and device configurations. This backup must be performed after a major system change, such as a new version of the operating system, but is generally unnecessary and impractical on a daily basis.
Example	SAVSYS DEV(TAP01) CLEAR(*ALL) (*Note:* CLEAR(*ALL) clears any previous data from the tape as the save proceeds.)
SAVLIB	Saves all the objects in specified libraries to tape.

Example	SAVLIB LIB(*NONSYS)	IBM licensed programs, QGPL, QUSRSYS, user libraries
	SAVLIB LIB(*IBM)	IBM licensed programs
	SAVLIB LIB(*ALLUSR)	QGPL, QUSRSYS, user libraries
	SAVLIB LIB(usrnam)	save one user library
SAVDLO	Save document library objects (OfficeVision).	
Example	SAVDLO DLO(*ALL) FLR(*ANY) DEV(TAP01)	
SAVOBJ	Save a particular object or group of objects.	
Example	SAVOBJ OBJ(objnam) LIB(libnam) DEV(TAP01) OBJTYPE(*FILE) VOL(savol) STG(*KEEP) ENDOPT(*UNLOAD)	
SAVCHGOBJ	Save only those objects which have been changed since a specified date.	
Example	SAVGHGOBJ OBJ(objnam) LIB(libnam) DEV(TAP01) OBJTYPE(*FILE) REFDATE(ddmmyy)	
SAVSECDTA	Save security data such as user profiles and object authority information.	
Example	SAVSECDTA DEV(TAP01) MAIL(*NO)	

Restoring objects from tape is performed with the following CL commands:

RSTOBJ	Restore an object or group of objects from backup into the library it was saved from.
Example	RSTOBJ OBJ(objnam) DEV(TAP01) OBJTYPE(*FILE) VOL(volnam) OPTION(*OLD)
RSTLIB	Restore an entire library from backup.
Example	RSTLIB SAVLIB(libnam) DEV(TAP01)
RSTDLO	Restore a document library object from backup.
Example	RSTDLO DLO(docnam) SAVFLR(flrnam) DEV(TAP01)
RSTUSRPRF	Restore user profiles and authorization lists.
Example	RSTUSRPRF DEV(TAP01) SEQNBR(*SEARCH) ENDOPT(*REWIND) MAIL(*YES)
RSTAUT	Restore authority to user profiles for objects.
Example	RSTAUT USRPRF(*ALL)
RSTCFG	Restore device configurations.
Example	RSTCFG DEV(TAP01) OBJ(*ALL) OBJTYE(*ALL)

Displaying the contents of a tape is performed with the following CL commands:

DSPTAP Display the contents of a backup tape on the system console.

Example DSPTAP DEV(TAP01)

As an alternative to using these CL commands at the command line, you can use the Save Menu and the Restore Menu to accomplish the same tasks. This approach has the advantages of presenting all the options to those unfamiliar with these commands and their parameters. (See Figs. 7.2 and 7.3.)

The *IBM Basic Backup and Recovery Guide* contains more information on these subjects.

7.3 OPERATIONAL ASSISTANT

OS/400 now includes the Operational Assistant to aid in performance of common daily operations tasks. This leads the user to a resolution of such problems as reports that won't print, jobs that won't run, messages that require answers, and the like. Work management can be implemented through the Operational Assistant.

AS/400 Operational Assistant is reached by typing GO ASSIST at the command line (see Fig. 7.4). From this menu you can work with printer output, jobs, and messages. You can send a message to a user or group of users and you can change your password. Device status for display stations, printers, and tape are available. Backup and tape ini-

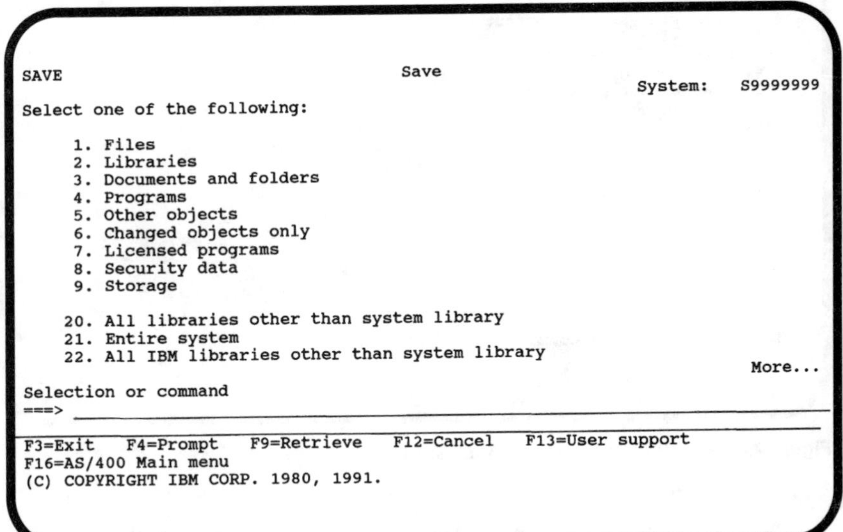

Figure 7.2 Save menu.

```
RESTORE                          Restore
                                                      System:   S9999999
Select one of the following:

     1. Files
     2. Libraries
     3. Documents and folders
     4. Programs
     5. Other objects
     6. Licensed programs

    20. All libraries other than system library
    21. The system
    22. All IBM libraries other than system library
    23. All user libraries

    50. Restore from System/36 format
                                                            More...
Selection or command
===> ________________________________________________________________

F3=Exit   F4=Prompt   F9=Retrieve   F12=Cancel   F13=User support
F16=AS/400 Main menu
(C) COPYRIGHT IBM CORP. 1980, 1991.
```

Figure 7.3 Restore menu.

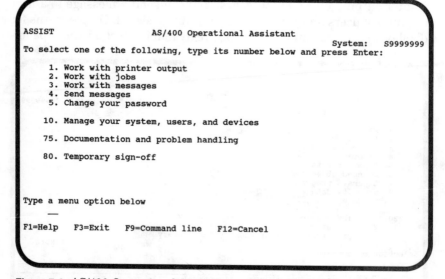

```
ASSIST                  AS/400 Operational Assistant
                                                      System:   S9999999
To select one of the following, type its number below and press Enter:

     1. Work with printer output
     2. Work with jobs
     3. Work with messages
     4. Send messages
     5. Change your password

    10. Manage your system, users, and devices

    75. Documentation and problem handling

    80. Temporary sign-off


Type a menu option below
   __

F1=Help   F3=Exit   F9=Command line   F12=Cancel
```

Figure 7.4 AS/400 Operational Assistant.

tialization can be performed. You can set up automatic power on and off of the system as well as schedule automatic cleanup tasks. Finally, you can get to documentation and problem handling. To select one of these, type its number into the menu option field and press <Enter>.

7.3.1 Print

Option 1. Work with printer output takes you to the Work with All Spooled Files screen for your user profile (see Fig. 7.5). Here you can choose the following options:

1=Send	Send file to another user.
2=Change	Change print destination, etc.
3=Hold	Hold file for later printing.
4=Delete	Delete the file.
5=Display	Look at the file.
6=Release	Release a held file.
7=Messages	Answer a message on the printer.
8=Attributes	See attributes.
9=Work with printing status	See status.
F22=Printers	See and work with all jobs on the system printers (WRKWTR).

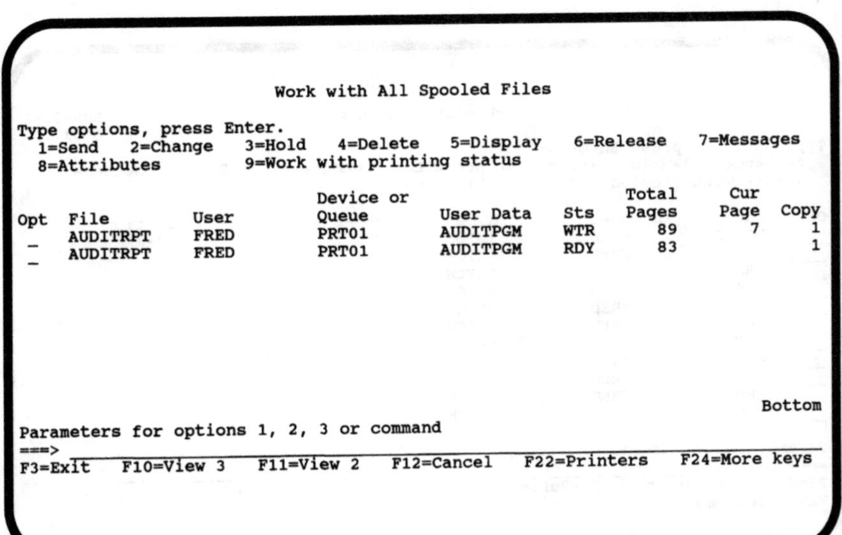

Figure 7.5 Work with All Spooled Files.

This is the first place to look when a job is not printing. See if it is spooled, if it is directed to a printer, if there is a message waiting to be answered, if it is held, etc.

7.3.2 Jobs

Option 2. Work with jobs take you to the Work with User Jobs display. Type options and press <Enter> to:

2=Change	Change a job (e.g., which queue?).
3=Hold	Hold a job to run later.
4=End	End the job.
5=Work with	Work with and investigate the job.
6=Release	Release a held job.
7=Display message	Display messages concerning jobs.
8=Work with spooled files	See spooled files for jobs.
13=Disconnect	Disconnect all jobs for device.

Look here when a job does not run. There may be a message, or it may be held. Choose "5=Work with" jobs to see job attributes, job log, and lower-level messages and open files, among other options. (See Fig. 7.6.)

7.3.3 Messages

Option 3. Work with messages produces the Display Messages screen. You can type a reply (if required) to answer the message.

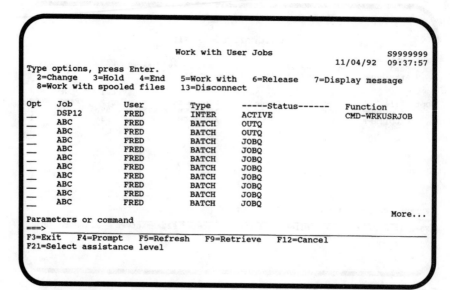

```
                              Work with User Jobs                     S9999999
                                                           11/04/92   09:37:57
Type options, press Enter.
  2=Change   3=Hold   4=End   5=Work with   6=Release   7=Display message
  8=Work with spooled files   13=Disconnect

Opt  Job        User       Type      -----Status------    Function
__   DSP12      FRED       INTER     ACTIVE               CMD-WRKUSRJOB
__   ABC        FRED       BATCH     OUTQ
__   ABC        FRED       BATCH     OUTQ
__   ABC        FRED       BATCH     JOBQ
__   ABC        FRED       BATCH     JOBQ
__   ABC        FRED       BATCH     JOBQ
__   ABC        FRED       BATCH     JOBQ
__   ABC        FRED       BATCH     JOBQ
__   ABC        FRED       BATCH     JOBQ
__   ABC        FRED       BATCH     JOBQ
__   ABC        FRED       BATCH     JOBQ
                                                                      More...
Parameters or command
===>
F3=Exit   F4=Prompt   F5=Refresh   F9=Retrieve   F12=Cancel
F21=Select assistance level
```

Figure 7.6 Work with User Jobs.

Option 4. Send messages gets you to the Send a Message screen. A message can be sent to a user or a group of users.

Option 5. Change your password. Enter current password and new password twice.

7.3.4 Work management

Option 10. Manage your system, users, and devices. This is one of the most powerful and comprehensive options on the Operational Assistant (see Fig. 7.7).

Choose 1 to check out device status (see Fig. 7.8). You can work with display devices, printer devices, tape devices, diskette devices, or print local device addresses. Options available for these types of devices include: vary on, vary off, work with job, work with description, and display mode status.

Choose number 2 from the Manage Your System menu to get to backup tasks (see Fig. 7.9). You can back up user libraries, lists of libraries, IBM libraries, or the entire system. Also, you can change library backup list and initialize a tape.

Number 11 leads to power on and off tasks. Included are display power on/off schedule, change power on/off schedule, power off the system immediately and power off the system immediately and then power on.

Selection 12 is for cleanup tasks. You can change cleanup options, start cleanup at scheduled time, start cleanup immediately and end cleanup.

```
MANAGESYS              Manage Your System, Users, and Devices
                                                          System:   S9999999
To select one of the following, type its number below and press Enter:

     1. Device status
     2. Backup tasks

    11. Power on and off tasks
    12. Cleanup tasks








Type a menu option below
    _
F1=Help   F3=Exit   F9=Command line   F12=Cancel
```

Figure 7.7 Manage Your System, Users, and Devices.

```
DEVICESTS                      Device Status
                                                        System:   S9999999
To select one of the following, type its number below and press Enter:

     1. Work with display devices
     2. Work with printer devices
     3. Work with tape devices
     4. Work with diskette devices

    10. Print local device addresses





Type a menu option below
    ___
F1=Help   F3=Exit   F9=Command line   F12=Cancel
```

Figure 7.8 Device Status.

```
BACKUP                          Backup Tasks
                                                        System:   S9999999
To select one of the following, type its number below and press Enter:

     1. Back up all user libraries
     2. Back up user libraries from the backup list

    10. Back up IBM-supplied libraries
    11. Back up the entire system

    20. Change library backup list

    30. Initialize a tape




Type a menu option below
    ___
F1=Help   F3=Exit   F9=Command line   F12=Cancel
```

Figure 7.9 Backup Tasks.

7.3.5 Documentation

Option 75. Documentation and problem handling leads to displays about how to use help, AS/400 publications, display workstation user-saving information to help resolve a problem and technical support tasks. Also there is a temporary sign-off.

7.4 UPGRADE

The AS/400 is not a static environment. Constant upgrades to software and hardware are offered by IBM. It is necessary to keep up with them to the extent that you wish to stay current with developing functionalities and technologies. The complex and evolving AS/400 operating system has occasional glitches or inefficiencies which may be solved by program temporary fixes (PTFs). In addition, IBM offers new versions and releases of the operating system at periodic intervals. Sometimes a new hardware model requires a new operating system release, or a software vendor may require a certain level of OS/400.

7.4.1 Program Temporary Fixes (PTFs)

Program temporary fixes correct problems in IBM software. New releases of OS/400 contain cumulative PTFs up to that point. Future PTFs must be installed after that. At any time, you can get a PTF or the comprehensive package of cumulative PTFs for your release level. Contact your IBM representative to see which PTFs are available, especially if you are experiencing a performance problem. PTFs can be sent on tape, or ordered online through Electronic Customer Support (ECS).

To see which PTFs you already have on your system, use the CL command: DSPPTF and prompt it with the <F4> key.

In order to implement a PTF, you must order it, install it, and apply it. PTFs may be applied either temporarily or permanently. Permanently applied PTFs cannot be removed. It is a good idea to install cumulative PTF packages every few months.

If your system is correctly configured for the modem, you can contact an IBM mainframe to download individual PTFs to you or to order a cumulative PTF on tape. Type the command SNDPTFORD SFnnnnn at the command line where nnnnn is the number of the PTF you want. To order the cumulative PTF for your current release and version, type: SNDPTFORD SF99vrm, where v is version, r is release, and m is modification.

You can order just the cover letters for the PTFs to be sent so you can review them and see what is available for the current release. PTFs are placed in a save file in QGPL when downloaded from the mainframe.

The save file is called P + PTFnumber (i.e., PSF12345 in the case of the an order for PTF # SF12345). Cover letters for the PTFs are placed as members in a file called QAPZCOVER in QGPL. Read these cover letters carefully because they often contain special instructions about installing specific PTFs.

To install PTFs it is important to follow the instructions sent with them in cover letters, whether downloaded or mailed with a tape. In general, a PTF is loaded, then applied. First, get the users off the system. Sign on as QSECOFR. Go to the PTF display with GO PTF and select option 8 to install PTFs. Device is *SERVICE for PTFs downloaded to save file or *TAP01 (or other device name) for PTFs on tape. Follow directions on screen to perform an automatic IPL, and the PTFs are applied and ready to go. PTFs can be applied immediately without doing an IPL if the program to which they apply is not in use (command: APYPTF).

Some PTFs are prerequisite to others so that a PTF installation may not work if its prerequisites are not present. The system will check for PTF prerequisites at installation time and notify you if they are not present.

Apply PTFs temporarily when you receive them, because once they are permanently applied they become part of the operating system and cannot be removed. The AS/400 maintains two storage areas for the LIC. One is called storage area A and contains the permanent version of the operating system. PTFs which are temporarily applied are in storage area B, so that IPL must be done from area B if they are to be found. The PWRDWNSYS command has an IPLSRC option which directs the IPL to the appropriate storage area.

Type GO LICPGM and select option 50 to see if the PTF installation was completed successfully.

PTF operations can be accessed through option 75 on the Operational Assistant Menu (see Fig. 7.10).

7.4.2 Versions

Every so often it becomes necessary to install a new version or release of the operating system on the AS/400. This is a time-consuming task and somewhat complicated, as it requires a correct sequence of backups and installations. Every new version or release comes with its own instructions which must be followed, so no generic instructions can be provided here.

7.5 PROBLEM HANDLING

Although the AS/400 is designed to run with a minimum of user intervention, it is impossible to avoid occasional problems. Common prob-

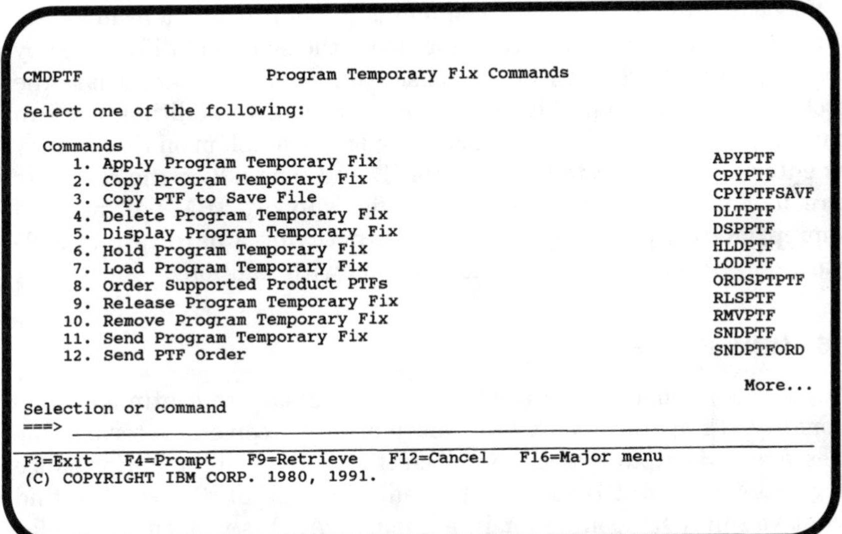

```
CMDPTF                       Program Temporary Fix Commands

Select one of the following:

  Commands
     1. Apply Program Temporary Fix                               APYPTF
     2. Copy Program Temporary Fix                                CPYPTF
     3. Copy PTF to Save File                                     CPYPTFSAVF
     4. Delete Program Temporary Fix                              DLTPTF
     5. Display Program Temporary Fix                             DSPPTF
     6. Hold Program Temporary Fix                                HLDPTF
     7. Load Program Temporary Fix                                LODPTF
     8. Order Supported Product PTFs                              ORDSPTPTF
     9. Release Program Temporary Fix                             RLSPTF
    10. Remove Program Temporary Fix                              RMVPTF
    11. Send Program Temporary Fix                                SNDPTF
    12. Send PTF Order                                            SNDPTFORD
                                                                     More...
Selection or command
===> ____________________________________________________________________

F3=Exit   F4=Prompt   F9=Retrieve   F12=Cancel   F16=Major menu
(C) COPYRIGHT IBM CORP. 1980, 1991.
```

Figure 7.10 Program Temporary Fix Commands.

lems include reports not printing, jobs which terminate abnormally, terminals that don't work, etc. Problem handling consists of isolating the cause of the problem, usually by tracking down the associated error message, and resolving it. Sometimes the resolution is as simple as answering a message and sometimes you have to call in outside help from technical support.

Several tools are provided on the AS/400 to aid in problem solving. The Q&A database as well as ECS can be helpful in solving problems. CL commands ANZPRB and WRKPRB help to provide information. Most helpful in many cases are the job logs and message queues.

The first thing to do in case of a problem is to look for any system message associated with it. A message may appear at the bottom of the screen. In this case, move the cursor onto the message and press the <Help> key for further information. Several message queues contain messages generated by the system. You can display messages for your interactive job with the DSPMSG command. Often, messages associated with a problem will turn up in QSYSOPR's message queue. These can be seen with DSPMSG QSYSOPR. Messages for a submitted job which is still active can be seen by going to the Work with Active Jobs screen (WRKACTJOB). Place the cursor next to the job you want to investigate and enter a 5. Then, on the next screen, enter a 10 to see the job log. The <F10> key will show a list of the low-level messages which are often quite detailed and tell you which commands have been issued to the system and any messages produced.

You can run the ANZPRB command to help in problem analysis. WRKPRB can also help in tracking down the source of difficulties by providing the Work with Problems screen, where you can isolate the problem ID and display further details about it. In addition, you can have the AS/400 call for help with a particular problem on this display by entering an 8 next to the problem ID and then a 2 on the resulting screen. The AS/400 will dial IBM service support. IBM will respond appropriately, by sending a PTF, or by notifying a hardware or software service representative to contact you with solutions.

7.6 HOUSEKEEPING

Any system generates data which is unnecessary to continued functionality. Temporary work files, old journals receivers, interminable message and output queues can all clutter up the system. Performance may degrade and it is difficult to wade through all that stuff to find what you may be looking for in a queue. DASD is wasted. A regular schedule of system cleanup is the answer to all of this and should be made part of the users' and operator's responsibilities.

The Cleanup Tasks Menu provides a way to automate cleanup. Operational Assistant option 10 or GO CLEANUP at the command line produce the Cleanup Tasks Menu (see Fig. 7.11). Here, you can change cleanup options for various messages, logs, journals, and OfficeVision. Set the time automatic cleanup starts each day, and

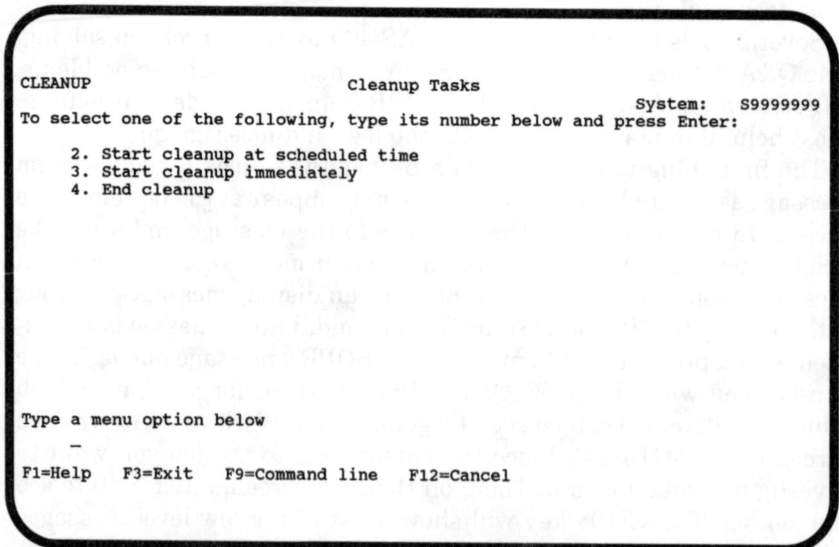

```
CLEANUP                          Cleanup Tasks
                                                       System:   S9999999
To select one of the following, type its number below and press Enter:

     2. Start cleanup at scheduled time
     3. Start cleanup immediately
     4. End cleanup









Type a menu option below
     _

F1=Help   F3=Exit   F9=Command line   F12=Cancel
```

Figure 7.11 Cleanup Tasks.

number of days to keep in each category. For instance, you might choose to get rid of all user messages after seven days. The AS/400 can be set up to perform automatic cleanup daily, at system power down or at user initiation.

In addition to automatic system cleanup, regular cleanup should be performed by users who generate personal files. Items in this category are temporary work databases, spool files, Queries, OfficeVision documents, unused access paths, etc. Some of these can get quite large and should be reviewed and managed by the user.

7.7 INSTALLATION AND HARDWARE UPGRADES

Initial installation of the system and hardware upgrades must be left to the IBM SE's and CE's engineers who come to the user site and install the AS/400. New hardware sometimes requires new software and feature cards. It is important to investigate carefully to determine the full impact of a hardware change on your system.

7.8 SUMMARY

Operations on the AS/400 are made relatively simple and painless. The Operational Assistant aids in the performance of most everyday tasks. CL commands are also available to perform work management, backup, housekeeping, and the like. These commands can, of course, be prompted for parameter values and coded into CLP programs for batch submission. Many of the routine functions of operations can be entirely automated in these ways. The operator can opt to follow the menu structure to the desired operations function as an alternative. See the *IBM Manual System Operator's Guide* for more information.

Part

2

Development Tools

Chapter

8

OfficeVision/400

8.1 OFFICE—INTEGRATED SOLUTION

Office is the word processor and task manager of the AS/400. Office is designed to help you do many everyday office tasks. It can be used to send and receive documents, look up telephone numbers, set up appointments, automatically schedule jobs to run, print form letters, and do many other things from a display station. The Office Menu can be seen in Fig. 8.1.

One major consideration of Office use is the memory it requires. If ample memory is dedicated to office functions, it will perform well.

PC support and word processing

AS/400 offers three options for word processing:

1. AS/400 Office. This word processor can be reached from any NPT (Nonprogrammable terminal) or PC attached with TDLC, SDLC, or Token-Ring. There are no special requirements or considerations for use with this set up.
2. WordPerfect. Through the use of PC Support, a shared folder contains WordPerfect (WP) version 4.2 or 5.0, in which all documents created or modified on the PC are stored. NPTs, however, do not have access to documents created through the WordPerfect interface. Since documents created in this way must be handled, printed,

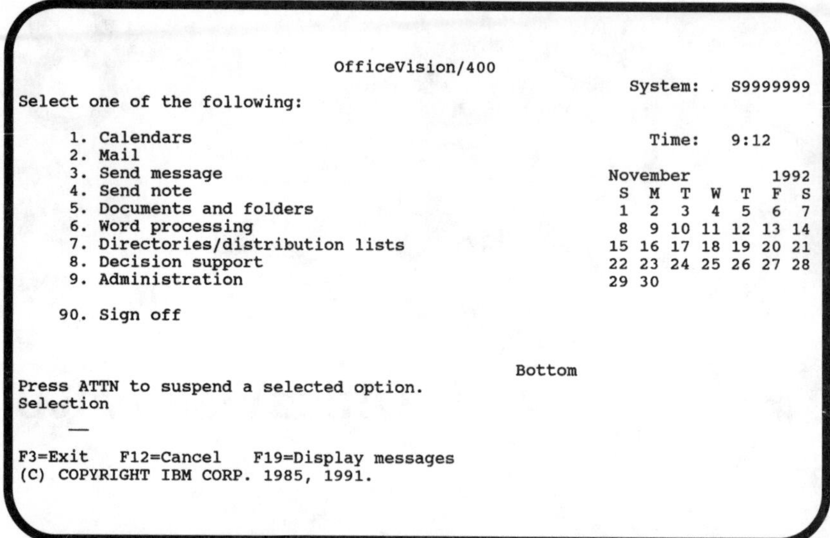

Figure 8.1 Office main menu.

or viewed through the PC interface, this is not a very convenient method of document handling on the AS/400. But it does provide the power and flexibility of PC WordPerfect.

3. Display Write 4 (DW4). Through the use of PC Support, a shared folder again contains the documents. The major difference between DW4 and WordPerfect is that DW4 does store a document in revisable form text for the AS/400 (RFTAS400). This way, any terminal can access and revise documents created through DW4.

Text assist in PCO (PC Organizer) enables PC access to AS/400 RFTAS400 documents through cooperative processing. Some of the code actually required to run the function is located on the PC and some on the AS/400. The code on the PC makes it possible to create RFTAS400 (revisable form text) on the PC. This means that PCO must be running for documents to be accessed from the PC. See the Chap. 24, "PC Support."

Office functionality

Office has an easy-to-use menu. Also, office functions can be accessed from any point in the AS/400 by use of CL commands. Office offers a range of functionality which extends from mail merge capabilities, interactive Query from within a document, electronic mail, fax interface, and more.

As with all other functions on the AS/400, help is available at the touch of the <F4> prompt key and by index search. Office allows easy switching between tasks with a few simple keystrokes. The main menu for office can be tailored to the specific user's needs.

Office begins with an understanding of messages, word processing, and calendars. These basics will allow you to handle easily everyday tasks. Full usage of integrated functions like distributions and access to shared folders is somewhat more complicated, but will make office life much easier.

All of Office is menu-driven, and merely requires choosing options from the menu screens. At the higher levels (at the menus), Office is quite simple to operate, although when you actually get into a document for editing, the combinations of keystrokes become more complex. Office has numerous configuration possibilities. Choosing an appropriate configuration is the key to effective Office use.

8.2 CALENDAR

Calendar functions include appointments, schedules, and reminders, as well as calling jobs and programs at a specific time. When Calendar is invoked, the menu in Fig. 8.2 appears.

Calendars make use of function codes which separate tasks on your calendar with a minimal amount of space.

Function codes for Calendars are referenced in Fig. 8.3.

```
                                Weekly Calendar
Function . . . . . ________    Calendar . . . .  DAVE     DUNNE____________
MON             TUE             WED             THU             FRI
02/12/90        02/13/90        02/14/90        02/15/90        02/16/90
8a__________    8a__________    8a__________    8a__________    8a__________
____________    ____________    ____________    ____________    ____________
9a__________    9a__________    9a__________    9a__________    9a__________
____________    ____________    ____________    ____________    ____________
10a_________    10a_________    10a_________    10a_________    10a_________
____________    ____________    ____________    ____________    ____________
11a_________    11a_________    11a_________    11a_________    11a_________
____________    ____________    ____________    ____________    ____________
12n_________    12n_________    12n_________    12n_________    12n_________
____________    ____________    ____________    ____________    ____________
1p__________    1p__________    1p__________    1p__________    1p__________
____________    ____________    ____________    ____________    ____________
2p__________    2p__________    2p__________    2p__________    2p__________
____________    ____________    ____________    ____________    ____________
3p__________    3p__________    3p__________    3p__________    3p__________
____________    ____________    ____________    ____________    ____________
4p__________    4p__________    4p__________    4p__________        More...
F3=Exit              F4=Prompt        F6=Add item          F9=Display item
F10=Change item      F12=Cancel       F16=Remove item      F24=More keys

    02-21                                                  S2 S9999999 KB
```

Figure 8.2 Office Calendar.

```
                         Function Keys for Calendar
F3=Exit
F4=List
F5=Refresh
F6=Six-month calendar on/off
F9=Calendar items on/off
F10=Later times
F11=Earlier times
F12=Previous
F13=More calendar tasks
F14=Extended entry
F15=Print calendar
F24=Display messages
Page keys=Later/Earlier days



Press Enter to continue.

F3=Exit   F12=Previous    F24=Display messages   Home=Calendar

     01-01                                             S1 S9999999 KB
```

Figure 8.3 Function Codes and Office.

Creation of a calendar

To create a calendar, use the calendar option from the main Office menu. On the calendar display, use <F13> (More Calendar Tasks). (See Fig. 8.4.)

Type the name of the calendar that you are creating—up to 10 characters long (no asterisk or blank in the first position). The Fig. 8.5 display will then appear.

This screen allows you to copy an existing calendar and assign an owner and manager (similar to object ownership covered in Chap. 6). There is also an option on this screen that allows someone other than yourself to manage the calendar.

Calendar appointments

Appointments are one of the most useful features of Calendar. On the AS/400 Office Menu, choose Calendars. Type an A for the appointment functions code and fill in the blanks for the options listed. Personal items can be secured on your calendar from viewing by any other user. For clarity, notes can be added to each of the appointments scheduled. You may also enter a message to be sent to remind you of the appointment, with an alarm that will sound at your display station. To send a message to yourself or others at a predetermined time, use the reminder function code (see Fig. 8.6).

To reschedule appointments, go into Calendars and you will note that each scheduled item has a number associated with it. Enter a C

```
                         More Calendar Tasks

Select one of the following:

     1. Change calendar session
     2. Work with calendars
     3. Work with groups
     4. Copy calendar items
     5. Delete calendar items
     6. Work with distribution lists
     7. Work with meetings
     8. Search remote calendars






Selection
     _
 F3=Exit    F9=Six month calendar    F12=Cancel    F19=Display messages

     21-07                                               S2 S9999999 KB
```

Figure 8.4 More Calendar Tasks.

```
                         More Calendar Tasks

Select one of the following:

     1. Change calendar session
     2. Create, change or delete calendar
     3. Change user authority to calendar
     4. Create, change or delete calendar group
     5. Change calendar group membership

Selection
     _
Type choice, press Enter.

  Calendar or calendar group . . . . . .   __________     Name
                                                          F4 for list



F3=Exit     F4=List      F5=Refresh      F12=Previous
F15=Print   F24=Display messages         Home=Calendar

     12-07                                               S1 S9999999 KB
```

Figure 8.5 Create, change, or delete Calendar.

```
                         Weekly Calendar
Function . . . .  __________  Calendar . . . .  USER___  USER______________
MON              TUE              WED              THU              FRI
02/12/90         02/13/90         02/14/90         02/15/90         02/16/90
8a_____________  8a_____________  8a_____________  8a_____________  8a_____________
________________ ________________ ________________ ________________ ________________
9a_____________  9a_____________  9a_____________  9a_____________  9a_____________
________________ ________________ ________________ ________________ ________________
10a____________  10a____________  10a____________  10a____________  10a____________
________________ ________________ ________________ ________________ ________________
11a____________  11a____________  11a____________  11a____________          More...
                              Add Item

Type choices, press Enter.
  Type of item . . . . . . . .    1       1=Event (single calendar)
                                          2=Meeting (multiple calendars)
                                          3=Reminder
                                          4=Job

  Multiple items . . . . . . .    N       Y=Yes, N=No

F3=Exit     F9=Six month calendar     F12=Cancel     F19=Display messages

     16-36                                              S2 S9999999 KB
```

Figure 8.6 Add an appointment.

function code in combination with the item number to recall an appointment and revise its contents. Thus, a function code might be C01 (change appointment 01). Appointments can be copied, removed, and listed.

Calendar reminders

An extremely useful Office function is the use of reminders. This is a message sent at a predetermined time. Reminders may be created by using the function code R in the Calendar display. The reminders themselves do not appear on the Calendar display. Instead, an R next to the day on the calendar indicates that day has a reminder. Reminders do not appear on the calendar display. You may list the calendar reminders by using the RMD functions code on the calendar display.

Calendar groups

A calendar group is a list of calendars used to schedule appointments for a set of users. Authority is necessary for the calendars you want to use.

From the More Calendar Tasks (Fig. 8.4) display (<F13> from the Calendar Display), set up a calendar group. You will be prompted to enter the list of calendars that will have membership in the calendar group. Many of the prompts that appear on this display are the same as those you used when scheduling an appointment on personal calendar. A message can be set up to remind attendees of a meeting at a predetermined time. Like the other functions of Office, meetings can be listed, rescheduled, deleted, etc.

Other functions—jobs, etc.

Jobs can be scheduled to start from the Calendar. In this way, jobs can easily be scheduled to run in the middle of the night, or whenever they are most convenient. The job must be named, and this function can be used to call CLP, which further controls the processing (see Chap. 4). Like the ADDAJE CL command, the add job function code in Calendar requires a job name and other parameters which contain all of the information necessary to run the job.

Printing calendar

There are several ways to print your calendar—the most common is to print the appointments screen. From the calendar display, use <F15>—Print Calendar and follow the prompting to print your calendar. Options for printing include format, beginning and ending dates and times, etc. Calendars can also be printed in a list format.

8.3 MAIL AND MESSAGES

Mail in Office consists of handling and sending messages, notes, documents to and from other users. Mail can be received and sent either as a printed copy or by using the electronic mail of the system.

Messages

Messages are the basic means of communicating on the AS/400, not only from one user to another, but from the system to a user and from system to system. A message is usually a few lines of text sent immediately from one place to another. The maximum length of a message is 256 characters. Messages are placed in the receiver's mail log whether or not the user is signed on. A mail log is a record of all the electronic and printed mail that a user has sent or received. When the user signs on, all the messages can be displayed.

Messages are sent to a queue, to the mail log, or both. In general, mail and messages sent through Office go to the mail log. All other messages, such as messages from the system, are directed to the user's message queue.

To send a message in Office, choose the message option from the Office Menu and follow the prompts. Use a distribution list to send a message to a group of user names, locations, and addresses. As in authorization lists in security functions, users can be added and deleted easily from a distribution list (Fig. 8.7).

Notes

The primary difference between a note and a message is that messages cannot be filed, printed, or manipulated, whereas a note can. Very

```
                              Send a Message
Type message.
 ______________________________________________________________________
_________________________________________________________________________
______________________________________________

Type distribution list and/or addressees, press F10 to send.
  Distribution list . . . . . . . . .  _______ _______  F4 for list

----Addressees-----
User ID     Address     Description                         F4 for list
________    ________
________    ________
________    ________
________    ________
________    ________
________    ________
________    ________
                                                                      Bottom
F3=Exit     F4=Prompt   F5=Refresh              F9=Attach memo slip
F10=Send    F12=Cancel  F13=Change defaults     F24=More keys

      04-04                                              S2 S9999999 KB
```

Figure 8.7 Sending a message in Office.

closely related to the message function, notes are prompted for ease of use, and also make use of the distribution list.

Notes, unlike messages, can have other attributes:

Personal	Only the recipient can view them.
High priority	Note is highlighted in the users' mail log.
Standardization	Shell document provides the correct format.

The note allows recording of the authors, a project reference, the date an action is due, etc. Notes also allow tracking so that status information is always available about notes sent to other users. A memo slip can be attached to notes and documents when sent through Office. This memo slip is similar to an action slip or routing note attached to a document circulated manually.

When a note (or any mail except a message) is received, the item may be deleted, filed, printed, or answered.

To send a note, simply choose the options, type the note, and then detail the note delivery information as in Figs. 8.8 and 8.9.

Sending documents

Like messages and notes, documents can easily be sent from one user to another. This function reduces paper, photocopying, distribution, etc. When a document is received it can be filed, acknowledged, etc. As with notes, a memo slip can be attached to a document to clarify any

```
                          Send a Note

Type mailing information, press F6 to type note.
  Subject
    ___________________________________________________
  Reference
    ___________________________________________________

Type distribution list and/or addressees, press F10 to send.
  Distribution list . . . . . . . .   _______ _______   F4 for list

----Addressees-----
User ID     Address     Description                     F4 for list
_______     _______
_______     _______
_______     _______
_______     _______
_______     _______
_______     _______
_______     _______
                                                                  Bottom
F3=Exit               F6=Type note    F9=Attach memo slip   F10=Send
F11=Change details    F12=Cancel      F13=Change defaults   F24=More keys

     05-06                                                S2 S9999999 KB
```

Figure 8.8 Note screen 1.

```
Insert Text                                                      Pg 1
DAVE999999,*INTDOC                        Typestyle 86 (12p)     Ln 11
<.:..T.2..T.:..T.3..T.:..T.4..T.:..Tv5..T.:..T.6..T.:..T.7..T.:..T.8..T.>....9
F
TO:

FROM:     DAVE  DAVE

DATE:     date
SUBJECT:
REFERENCE:
R
 START TYPING YOUR NOTE ON THE NEXT LINE.





 F1=Copy          F4=Delete         F13=Edit options      F19=Print/View
 F2=Move          F10=Send          F14=Get options       F21=Spell options
 F3=Exit/Save     F11=Insert lines  F16=Adjust/Paginate   F23=Spell aid

     15-02                                                S2 S9999999 KB
```

Figure 8.9 Note screen 2.

```
                            Send a Document

Document description . . . . :   Ascii Controller Order Letter
Document . . . . . . . . . . :   ASCII
  Folder . . . . . . . . . . :
    DAVE

Type distribution list and/or addressees, press F10 to send.
  Distribution list . . . . . . . .  ________ ________ F4 for list

----Addressees-----                                    F4 for list
User ID    Address    Description
________   ________
________   ________
________   ________
________   ________
________   ________
________   ________
________   ________
                                                                Bottom
F3=Exit    F4=List       F5=Refresh     F9=Attach memo slip
F10=Send   F11=Details   F12=Previous   F13=Change defaults

      09-40                             DM                S1 S9999999 KB
```

Figure 8.10 Send a document.

points regarding the document without creating an additional document (see Fig. 8.10).

The process of sending notes, mail, and documents is accommodated through the Systems Network Architecture Distribution Services (SNADS).

Revising mail

Notes and documents can be revised, once received by the user. In this way, responses and corrections are handled in the system, reducing paperwork. Notes and mail can be forwarded to another user. Replies can be requested and given through the mail system. Secretaries can manage mail for their bosses. Mail reports can be produced and productivity regarding in-basket mail increased.

Personal directories

A personal directory contains information you need to complete your daily work. When you create a personal directory, you determine its structure. You are really defining a personal database that is easy to manage. Personal directories can be used for everything from phone numbers to inventory control information.

Personal directories have some limitations. Unlike a standard database, reports cannot be defined for an individual case—default reports are utilized. Also, information is not sorted, indexed, or arranged in any special format. For these reasons, personal directories

```
                    View Personal Directory Entries

Directory  . . . . . :   EXAMPLEDIR   IBM-Supplied Example Telephone Directory

LAST NAME       FIRST NAME STREET ADDRESS      POSTAL CD AREA CD    PHONE
Baxter          Adam       63 Inglewood Dr     M3S 4T5   416        234-5678
Baxter          Phyllis    13-875 Codder Cr    M6B 1F2   416        987-6543
Baxter          Sonja      1786 St Laurent Blvd M8J 8R8  416        922-3444
Greenspoon      Larry      16 Anglesley        M2P 8A2   416        291-5195
Jordison        Joseph     1-A Montgomery      M5S 2L3   416        762-2166
Patterson       Katherine  709 Parkview Mall   M2L 5E3   416        456-9927
West            Charles    24 Leader Lane      M5R 4K5   416        231-6161





                                                                      Bottom
Press Enter to continue.

F3=Exit   F12=Cancel   F15=Print report   F19=Display messages

    01-01                                                   S2 S9999999 KB
```

Figure 8.11 Sample personal directory.

should have limited use. Figure 8.11 shows the Sample Personal Directory screen.

8.4 DOCUMENTS

A sophisticated word processing system has been integrated with Office. With it, you can create documents which contain special print fonts, conditional paragraphs or text, and fields from databases or queries. In addition, you can create shell documents which will print form letters from a database or Query. AS/400 documents, when used in conjunction with Queries and/or other processing (in RPG or another programming language), provide an integrated tool for processing the information on the system.

Folders

All word processing documents in the system are stored in folders. Documents and folders are stored in the AS/400 in document library QDOC. This concept is based on the office filing cabinet. A drawer (library) contains folders; within each folder are documents. Things like letters, reports, contracts, and statistical information can be organized and stored in the folders on the system. Please refer to Fig. 8.12 for a diagram of libraries, folders, and documents.

Each document contains a description which can be quite specific, allowing quick searches. Each document has:

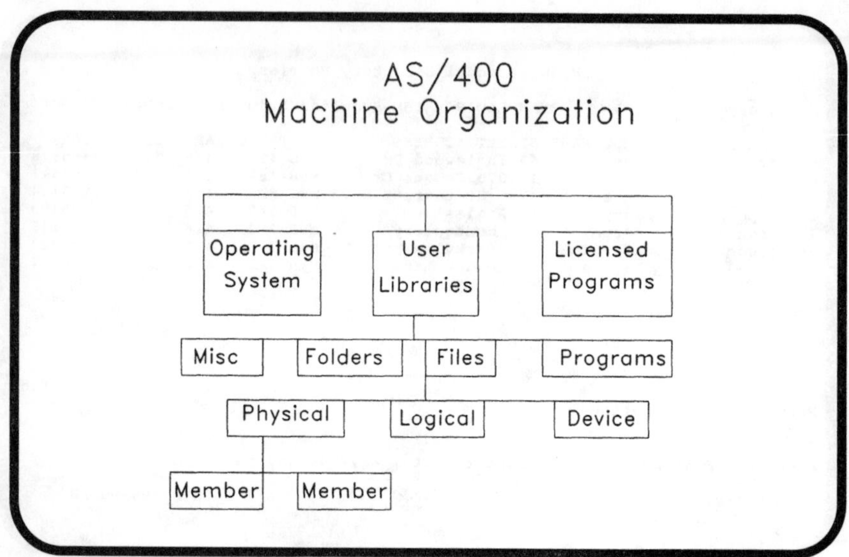

Figure 8.12 Library structure.

Name

Owner

Originator

Format

Access level (security)

Retention period

Date of creation

Date of revision

Comment

As an option, you can fill in the complete document information details screens seen in Figs. 8.13 and 8.14.

Functions

Like other document processing systems, the AS/400 Office word processing allows many standard functions. For example, a system format for documents can be set up to standardize documents, or to standardize letters, briefs, statistical formats, and drafts. All of the standard features are accessible for change, such as margins, tabs, line spacing, fonts and typestyle, first and last lines, etc.

```
                    Create Document Details                 Page 1 of 2
Profile being used . . . . :   SYSTEM        (User)

Type choices, press Enter.
  Document . . . . . . . . .   AAAA________            Name

  Document description . . .   ______________________________
  Subject  . . . . . . . . .   ______________________________
  Document to copy . . . . .   ____________
    From folder  . . . . . .   ______________________________
  Change formats/
    options  . . . . . . . .   N                       Y=Yes, N=No
  Authors  . . . . . . . . .   ____________  ____________
  Keywords . . . . . . . . .   ______________________________
______________________________________________________________
______________________________________________________________
                                                       F4 for list
  Document class . . . . . .   ____________            F4 for list
  Print as labels  . . . . .   N                       Y=Yes, N=No
                                                              More...
F3=Exit    F4=Prompt    F10=Bypass text entry      F12=Cancel

    08-33                                          S2 S9999999 KB
```

Figure 8.13 Document details screen 1.

```
                    Create Document Details                 Page 2 of 2

Type choices, press Enter.

  Project  . . . . . . . . .   ________
  Reference  . . . . . . . .   ______________________________
______________
  Status . . . . . . . . . .   ________________
  Document date  . . . . . .   ______
  Expiration date  . . . . .   ______
  Sent to  . . . . . . . . .   ______________________________
______________
  Date action due  . . . . .   ______
  Date action
    completed  . . . . . . .   ______
  Mark for
    offline storage  . . . .   1        1=Do not mark
                                        2=Mark and keep
                                        3=Mark and delete document content
                                        4=Mark and delete document

                                                               Bottom
F3=Exit          F10=Bypass text entry             F12=Cancel

    05-33                                          S2 S9999999 KB
```

Figure 8.14 Document information screen 2.

Creating a document

As you can see, working with documents in folders is very straightforward. To create a document, follow these seven steps:

1. On the AS/400 main menu, select option 6 (Word Processing).
2. Select option 1 on the Word Processing Menu.
3. On the Work with Document Display, select 1 (Create) and insert the name of the document that you wish to create.
4. Enter the Document Details as prompted for easy retrieval later.
5. Press Enter and the editing screen is shown.

Figure 8.15 shows the Editing Screen.

6. Begin typing your document just as you would on a typewriter.
7. Press <F3> (Exit/Save) and answer the prompted questions.

See Fig. 8.16, the Exit/Save Menu.

At this point, you have created, described, edited, and saved a document. The steps are easy to follow and can be taught very quickly.

Revising a document

After a document has been created, it can be revised easily in just four steps:

```
Insert Text                                                         Pg 1
AAAA,QER34X                                   Typestyle 86 (12p)    Ln 7
<2...T:...T3...T:...T4...T:...T5...Tv...T6...T:...T7...T:...T8...T:...T9>...:.










 F1=Copy          F7=Window           F15=Columns               F21=Spell options
 F2=Move          F8=Reset            F16=Adjust/Paginate       F22=Add to
 F3=Exit/Save     F9=Instructions     F17=Functions                 dictionary
 F4=Delete        F11=Insert lines    F18=Search/Replace        F23=Spell aid
 F5=Goto          F13=Edit options    F19=Print/View
 F6=Find          F14=Get options     F20=Change formats

      04-02                                                 S2 S9999999 KB
```

Figure 8.15 Editing screen.

```
                          End A Document

Type choices, press Enter.

  Save document . . . . . . . . . . .     Y                Y=Yes, N=No
    Document  . . . . . . . . . . . .     DOCNAME_____     Name, F4 for list
      Folder  . . . . . . . . . . . .                      Name, F4 for list
        QEK24X____________________________________________________________

    Display save options  . . . . .       N                Y=Yes, N=No

  Print document  . . . . . . . . . .     N                Y=Yes, N=No

    Display print options . . . . .       Y                Y=Yes, N=No




F4=Prompt   F6=Print queue      F12=Cancel

      13-40                                                S2 S9999999 KB
```

Figure 8.16 Exit and Save menu.

1. On the AS/400 main menu, choose option 6 (Word Processing).
2. On the Word Processing menu, select option 1.
3. On the Work with Documents in a folder, choose option 2 for the revise option prompt and type the name of document in the document prompt. Or, move the cursor to the document you want to revise and enter a 2 immediately to the left of the document name.
4. Make the necessary revisions and changes, and press <F3> to Exit and Save your document.

Deleting a document

1. On the AS/400 Main Menu choose option 6, Word Processing.
2. On the Word Processing menu, select option 1, Work with Documents in Folder.
3. On the Work with Document in Folder display, move the cursor to the document you want to delete and enter a 4 (delete).
4. Press the <Enter> key, and the Confirm Delete screen is shown. This screen is used throughout Office to confirm that you want to perform a delete.
5. Press the <Enter> key to confirm the delete of the document. If you decide not to delete, press <F9> to cancel the delete request.
6. Press <F3> to exit.

Printing a document

From the Work with Documents display, documents can be printed locally or on an AS/400 printer:

1. A 9 next to the document you wish to print will present you with a screen in which you may change the print options for that document, such as which printer it will go to. Enter a 6 next to the document to print it.
2. Press <Enter>, if you selected option 9, print options will appear and ask you to make changes on the default printer information. You can press enter to bypass this information. Any changes you make at this point are for this print only and are not saved.
3. Press <F3> (Exit).

Basic editing operations in a document

Having called up a document for editing in the Edit display, you should be in insert mode. Above the typing area is the scale line and the status line. On the status line is the audit window. The audit window shows any hidden control characters that are in the current cursor position.

Adjust lines. To adjust line and Page Ending, Choose the Adjust/Paginate option <F16> while on the edit display. A submenu is shown—choose selection 2 and press <Enter> to adjust and paginate.

Show options. To toggle on/off the options panel at the bottom of the Edit screen while editing a document, hit <F13> and choose "Show Fkeys option?" Enter Y to see the panel at the bottom of the screen, N to invoke full-screen editing. If you do not have the F keys memorized or written, we recommend keeping the panel at the bottom of the screen.

Center text. To center text, position the cursor anywhere on the line of the text to be centered. Press the <Alt> key plus the C key, and all text on the line is centered between the current margins. (*Note:* This function is implemented differently in Text Assist mode using PC Support.)

Center text with Text Assist/PC Support. Tab or space to the position where you want the text centered, press the <Alt> key plus the C key, and now type the text to be centered. Repeat the steps if you want to center text several times on one line. You must press the <Tab> key once to end the first centering before positioning your cursor for the next center on the same line. (*Note:* The text will not appear as centered on the display due to the code handling by PC Support and Text Assist. Text will be centered when printed.)

Copy text. Move the cursor under the first character of the text you want to copy. Press the <F1> (Copy) key and the message COPY WHAT? will be shown on the bottom of your display. Move the cursor under the last character of the text you want to copy. Press the <Enter> key and the message TO WHERE? will be shown at the bottom of the screen. Move the cursor to the location in your document where you want the text copied. Use <F5> (GoTo) to go to a specific page or line number. Finally, press the <Enter> key and the text is copied to the specified location and the cursor will be under the first character of the copied text.

Delete text. Move the cursor under the first character of the text you want to delete. Press <Del> (Delete) and the message DELETE WHAT? MOVE CURSOR PRESS ENTER is shown on the bottom of your display. Now, move the cursor under the last character of the text you want to delete. Press the <Enter> key and the text will be deleted.

In the Text Assist mode, through PC Support, the text is automatically highlighted as you move the cursor.

Insert blank lines. Move the cursor to where you want to insert blank lines and press the <Field Exit> key until you have the number of blank lines you want. (Any characters to the right of the cursor, including the character under the cursor, are moved down.)

Indent a block paragraph. Move the cursor to the beginning of the first line you want to indent. Press the <Alt> key plus the <Tab> key. A required tab is inserted in your text. This takes you to the first tab stop. Repeat this step until you arrive at the tab stop you want.

If you are creating a new paragraph at this point, simply type your text. All lines will be indented until you press the <Field Exit> key to insert a required carrier return.

If you are indenting an existing paragraph, press the enter key. All lines up to the next required carrier return will be indented.

Underline a word. As you are typing, type the word (do not space), press the <Alt> key and 'W' key.

To add an underline to an existing word, move the cursor to the first character FOLLOWING the word to be underlined, press the <Alt> key plus the 'W' key. The word is not underlined on the display unless you are using Text Assist function of PC Support, but it will be underlined when you print.

Spell check. If you have installed the language dictionaries and activated them from within Administration, use the <F21> and <F24> keys interchangeably to process.

Other functions. Other functions available from the command menu at the bottom of the editing screen include:

- Margins and tabs
- Header and footer
- Line spacing
- Typestyle
- System document formats/text profiles
- Search and replace
- Find a word
- Windowing and document movement
- End of page
- Highlight
- Boldface
- Other keys
- Goto abbreviations
- Line commands

Folder security

Folder authorization and document authorization work virtually the same for Office as they do for all other objects in the system. The primary difference is an added layer of security for Office, which is not present in the rest of the system. Each document has authority, which specifies if this is a personal document and specifies a list of authorized users to include, exclude, or provide with various levels of security. These objects can also be secured by authorization lists. (See Chap. 6.)

Office Administration requires that users be enrolled in Office before they are allowed to use any Office functions. IBM emphasizes the use of a security administrator to implement the ongoing task of security, especially in relation to Office. Office defaults to be determined include:

- How messages are handled—by you and others
- Message notifications
- Mailing address
- Phone numbers
- Calendar default information
- Word processing default information

Folder searches (finding something in Office)

It is possible to search through a folder for a theme, project, due date, etc.—basically any of the parameters defined when the document was created. You must have the proper authority to access the folders you wish to search.

8.5 SPECIAL FUNCTIONS

Function keys 1 through 24 in the Edit screen provide the following functions:

Function keys (press F1–24, CMD B–Y, or ALT B–Y)

```
1=Copy        7=Window         15=Table         21=Spell Options
2=Move        8=Cancel         16=Adjust/Pag    22=Add to Dct
3=Exit/Save   9=Instructions   17=Query File    24=Spell Aid
4=Find Char   11=Hyphenate     18=Search/Rep
5=Goto        13=Edit Options  19=Print/View
6=Find        14=Get Options   20=Chg Formats
```

Most of the special functions involving data fields, shell documents, form letters, etc., are available through the <F9> key, which brings up the Text Instructions screen:

Text instructions

Select instruction to be inserted at the cursor position:

1. Start new page CR	10. Conditional text	18. Zero index
2. Keep	11. Include	19. Summary math
3. Date	12. Data field	20. Variable
4. Time	13. Table of contents/ outline headings	21. Index
5. Document ID		22. Index entry
6. Skip lines	14. Overstrike	23. Color
7. Change font	15. Required backspace	24. Graphic
8. Numbered list	16. Help text label	25. Footnote
9. Running headings	17. Comment	26. Run

Variables

Variables may be inserted within a document from a database or Query. From the edit screen, hit <F9> (instructions). This is the key which provides most of the special processing or inclusions in a document. You see the Text Instructions Screen. Enter 12 for data fields, as in Fig. 8.17.

Next you have the Data Fields Instructions screen. Enter a '1' to print data from a data field. (See Fig. 8.18.)

Next is the Data Fields screen itself. Enter the name of the data field to include in the screen, as well as whether the data field comes from a query, document, or datafile, as shown in Fig. 8.19.

```
Insert Text                                                              Pg 1
AAAA,QASDFX                                        Typestyle 86 (12p)    Ln 7
<2...T:...T3...T:...T4...T:...T5...Tv...T6...T:...T7...T:...T8...T:...T9>...:.


                           Select Text Instruction                 Page 1 of 2

Select one of the following:
  Instruction to be Inserted at Cursor Position
     1. Start new page                          8. Numbered list
     2. Keep                                    9. Running headings
     3. Date                                   10. Conditional text
     4. Time                                   11. Include
     5. Document ID                            12. Data field
     6. Skip                                   13. Table of contents/
     7. Change font                                Outline headings

    14. Overstrike                               21. Index
    15. Required backspace                       22. Index entry
    16. Help text label                          23. Color
    17. Comment                                  24. Graphic
    18. Zero index CR                            25. Footnote
    19. Summary math                             26. Run instruction
    20. Variable
                                                                        Bottom
Selection

F3=Exit      F5=Select code      F12=Cancel

      22-07                                               S2 S9999999 KB
```

Figure 8.17 Text instructions screen.

```
Insert Text                                                       Pg 1
AAAA,QEK24X                                  Typestyle 86 (12p)   Ln 7
<2...T:...T3...T:...T4...T:...T5...Tv...T6...T:...T7...T:...T8...T:...T9>...:.


                       Select Data Field Instruction

Note: A data field may be located in either a file, Query, or document.

Select one of the following:

     1. Print the data from a data field (multiple letters or column list)

     2. Print the headings from a data field


Selection
     _
F3=Exit     F12=Cancel

  21-07                                                     S2 S9999999 KB
```

Figure 8.18 Data fields instructions screen.

```
Insert Text                                                          Pg 1
AAAA,QASFDX                                     Typestyle 86 (12p)   Ln 7
<2...T:...T3...T:...T4...T:...T5...Tv...T6...T:...T7...T:...T8...T:...T9>...:.


.&                          Data Field Instruction

This instruction prints the value of a data field from a described data
file, Query, or document.

Type choices, press Enter.
  Data field . . . . . . . .   __________     Name
    Data field source  . . .   2              1=From Merge Data Options
                                              2=*PRINT, 3=*NOTE
  Letters or list  . . . . .   1              1=Multiple letters, 2=Column list
  File ID for Query  . . . .   __
  Instruction length . . . .   12             1-255, Blank=Entire instruction

F3=Exit                    F5=Numeric editing        F6=Character editing
F9=Date/time editing       F12=Cancel                F24=More keys

     15-33                                              S2 S9999999 KB
```

Figure 8.19 Data field screen.

The next thing you see is the code for the data field which has been placed at the current cursor position in the text (Fig. 8.20).

Includes

Text may be included from other documents, by inserting a special code, and specifying where the text is to be found. Again, begin with the <F9> Text Insructions key to get the Text Instructions screen (see previous). Then enter an '11' to include text in your document from another source. You get the Include screen seen in Fig. 8.21.

Enter the name of the document you want to include, the folder it is stored in and, optionally, the page numbers you want to get from it. If you don't specify page numbers to get, you will include the entire named document into yours.

Conditional text

You may wish to include text in your document, depending on the value of a certain field in a database or query. This is simply accomplished. Start with the <F9> key for Text Instructions. Then enter a '10' for conditional text. This takes you to the Begin and End Conditional Text Instructions (.bct .ect) screen. Enter a '1' for the beginning of the conditional text. Next is the Conditional Test. Enter the condition you wish to test for (e.g., the NAME field is not blank). Figure 8.22 shows the Conditional Text Instructions screen.

```
View Document          Required Carrier Return Ins                    Pg  1
ASDFDF,ASDFDOC                                 Typestyle 172 (PSM)    Ln  48
 ....:....2....:....3....:....4....:....5....:....6...:....7....:....8....:.

______________________________________________     ________________________
                                            Applicant




F5129(1/90) #&FIELD1(F,DOC,*LIBL,*FIRST,M,)



Function Keys (Press F1-24, CMD B-Y, or ALT B-Y)
 3=Exit          5=Goto            7=Window            13=Edit Options
 4=Find Char     6=Find            8=Cancel            19=Print

                                         DM              S1 S9999999 KB
```

Figure 8.20 Data field code in text.

```
Create Document        Page End                                   Pg 1
AAAA,QSADFX                                   Typestyle 86 (12p)  Ln 7
<2...T:...T3...T:...T4...T:...T5...Tv...T6...T:...T7...T:...T8...T:...T9>...:.


.inc                              Include Instruction

This instruction marks the point in the document where another document,
or pages from that document, should be printed.

Type choices, press Enter.
  Document . . . . . . .    __________   Name, F4 for list
                                         Data field, variable name
    Folder . . . . . . .                 Name, F4 for list
                                         Data field, variable name
  Pages to include . . .
  Instruction length  . .   4            1-255, Blank=Entire instruction

F3=Exit        F4=Prompt       F12=Cancel          F16=Delete instruction

     15-30                                             S2 S9999999 KB
```

Figure 8.21 Include screen.

```
Create Document       Page End                  Ins                      Pg  1
AAAA,APLSDOC                                    Typestyle 86 (12p)       Ln  7
...1....:....2....:....3....:....4....:... 5....:....6....:....7....:....8....



          Begin and End Conditional Text Instructions (.bct .ect)
 These instructions mark the beginning and end of the text to be printed
 when the specified condition is true.

 Type choices, press Enter.
   Instruction type . . . .  1            1=Begin, 2=End
   For 1=Begin:
     Field . . . . . . . .  NAME______    Data field or variable name
       Field source . . . .  1            1=From Merge Data Options
                                          2=*PRINT, 3=Variable
     Selection criteria . .  NE           EQ, NE, GT, GE, LT, LE
     Test value . . . . . .  ' '_________________________________________
     File ID for Query  . .  __           For duplicate fields
   Instruction length . . .   4           1-255, Blank=Entire instruction
F3=Exit    F12=Previous     F15=Merge data options    F16=Delete instruction
An entry is required.
     16-30                                  DM                 S1 S9999999 KB
```

Figure 8.22 Conditional Text Instructions screen.

This series of entries will insert a code for the beginning of the conditional text instruction into your document. Next, enter the keystrokes required to insert the data field or included text from another source which will appear if the condition you entered is true (see previously mentioned Variables and/or Includes).

Finally, you must insert a code into the document to indicate where the conditional text ends. <F9> gets the Text Instructions screen.

Enter a '10' for Conditional Text, and this time enter a '2' for End Conditional Text. You now have three codes inserted into your document:

1. Begin Conditional Text (.bct)—the condition to be evaluated
2. the Data Field or Include to be inserted if the condition evaluates to true
3. End Conditional Text (.ect)

8.6 SHELL DOCUMENT

A shell document is one which is created with a number of special codes in it to gather text from various sources and run form letters from a database or query. Depending on the results of conditional text instructions (see previous), various fields, paragraphs, or documents may or may not print automatically for every record in a given data file or query. In other words, the shell document can run off form letters from a database and print the correct text for each record based on the data in that record.

Running a document from a query or database

A shell document is defined using the same techniques we have described above, inserting codes for:

- Data fields
- Includes
- Conditional text

In addition, the document has to be defined as a Multicopy Merge in order for it to generate form letters for each record in a database or Query. On the Data Field screen enter a '1' to indicate a multiple form letter.

Merging a database into a document

Instead of entering a '1' to indicate a multiple form letter, as previously, enter a '2' to indicate column list merge, in the Data Field screen. The document will then import the entire database as a column merge.

8.7 SUMMARY

Office/400 is a highly integrated product which offers calendar functions, mail, notes and messages, and word processing.

With Calendar, appointments can be managed, reminders can be routed to a terminal with a tone and/or a message, and jobs can be scheduled to start and run automatically.

Mail, notes, and messages can be handled easily through the functions of Office. It can be sent to an individual or a group, reviewed, changed, and filed (except messages, which can only be sent).

Distribution lists facilitate the routing of mail, messages, and documents to a group of users in a way which is easily implemented and maintained.

The word processing function of Office/400 is quite powerful, and easily integrated with other processing options on the AS/400, such as menus and programs (see Chap. 19). Simple documents can be created quite easily, or more complicated shell documents can be designed to run form letters from a database or Query. AS/400 Office, WordPerfect, or Display Write 4 can be used as the word processor in Office.

Issues to consider when implementing Office/400 are:

- Enrollment of users
- Authority and access to documents and folders
- Distribution lists
- Memory requirements (Office/400 requires significant overhead)
- Customized menus and environments for different users

Taken as a whole, Office/400 is an effective overall manager of everyday office tasks which can greatly streamline office operations when correctly implemented and managed.

Chapter

9

Data File Utility (DFU) and Query: Quick Input and Output

IBM provides two optional software packages which enable easy input and ouput for AS/400 databases. Data File Utility (DFU) creates a window into your database for inquiry or changes. Query is a menu-driven report writer for fast and easy reports.

9.1 DATA FILE UTILITY

DFU is a quick and convenient way to manage databases. You can input, search, change, or delete in a database without writing a program. In fact, DFU writes the program for you, once you name an AS/400 database.

Starting DFU

At the command line, type STRDFU and you get the DFU screen. (See Fig. 9.1.)

From this menu you can choose to create a permanent or temporary program to be used for access to a database. A permanent program could be created, and called from a CLP program using the DSPDTA command, for instance, to provide easy input or display. A temporary program is usually sufficient for quick manipulation of data files.

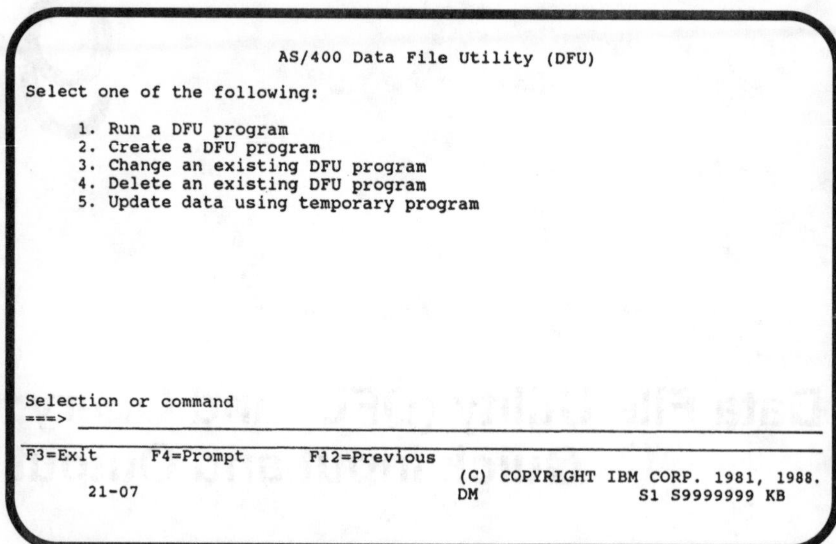

```
                    AS/400 Data File Utility (DFU)
Select one of the following:

     1. Run a DFU program
     2. Create a DFU program
     3. Change an existing DFU program
     4. Delete an existing DFU program
     5. Update data using temporary program

Selection or command
===> ____________________________________________________________

F3=Exit      F4=Prompt      F12=Previous
                                     (C) COPYRIGHT IBM CORP. 1981, 1988.
     21-07                           DM                 S1 S9999999 KB
```

Figure 9.1 DFU screen.

To create a temporary program for data I/O, choose number 5 from the DFU menu. On the next screen, enter datafile, library, and member (probably *FIRST).

The AS/400 will create a temporary program which will next present you with an I/O screen for the database you specified. Figure 9.2 shows the Temporary DFU Screen.

Finding, adding, changing records in a database

If the file is keyed, you first see a field where you can input the key value. If the input is found as a key value in the file, you are put in change mode. Otherwise, hit the <F9> key to insert a record.

Note that the function keys are:

F9	Insert
F10	Enter
F11	Change
F23	Delete

Audit log

The AS/400 will automatically maintain and print a log of records which were added, changed, or deleted in a given DFU session, unless you specify otherwise.

```
WORK WITH DATA IN A FILE                          Mode . . . . :    ENTRY
Format . . . . :    REC______                     File . . . . :    ACCOUNT

CUST NUM:           ________               STORE:              __________
ITEM CODE:          ____                   DEPT:               ___
PURCH DATE:         ________               SALES:              __________
ENTRY DATE:         ________               MANAGER:            __________
AMOUNT:             _________              AGE:                __
SEX:                _                      STATE:              __
CUST NAME:          ____________________________________

F3=Exit                  F5=Refresh                 F6=Select format
F9=Insert                F10=Entry                  F11=Change

     04-20                          DM                   S1 S9999999 KB
```

Figure 9.2 Temporary DFU screen.

9.2 QUERY

Where DFU provides easy input operations, Query enables easy output. Reports may be designed in minutes, complete with groups, subtotals, selected fields, calculated fields, etc. These Queries may then be called from a CL program with the RUNQRY command, or used interactively to have a look at database contents, or submitted to batch. Submitting to batch is the best because interactive Query uses a great deal of CPU resources.

Starting Query

At the command line, type STRQRY and you get the Query screen (Fig. 9.3).

Enter a '1' to work with Queries. You then get the Work with Queries screen. (See Fig. 9.4.)

Enter a '1' to define a new Query, or a '2' to work with an existing Query. Name the Query and specify the library in which it is located. You then get the main Query definition screen. Figure 9.5 is the Query Definition Screen.

Enter a '1' next to any function you wish to define for this particular Query in the following categories:

Defining a database for Query. Figure 9.6 illustrates the Specify File Selections screen.

```
QUERY                              Query Utilities
                                                             System:   S9999999
Select one of the following:

  Query/400
     1. Work with queries
     2. Run an existing query
     3. Delete a query

  SQL/400
    10. Start SQL/400 Query Manager

  Query management
    20. Work with query management forms
    21. Work with query management queries
    22. Start a query
    23. Analyze a Query/400 definition
                                                                       More...
Selection or command
===> ____________________________________________________________________________

F3=Exit   F4=Prompt   F9=Retrieve   F12=Cancel   F13=User support
F16=AS/400 Main menu
(C) COPYRIGHT IBM CORP. 1980, 1991.
```

Figure 9.3 Query screen.

```
                                 Work with Queries
Type choices, press Enter.

  Option  . . . . . .      _         1=Create, 2=Change, 3=Copy, 4=Delete
                                     5=Display, 6=Print definition
                                     9=Run
  Query . . . . . . .    __________  Name, F4 for list
    Library . . . . .      QGPL_____ Name, *LIBL, F4 for list











F3=Exit       F4=Prompt       F5=Refresh       F12=Cancel
                                                  (C) COPYRIGHT IBM CORP. 1988
      05-26                                            S2 S9999999 KB
```

Figure 9.4 Work with Queries screen.

```
                          Define the Query

Query . . . . . . . :   DD                  Option  . . . . . :   CREATE
  Library . . . . . :     QGPL

Type options, press Enter.  Press F21 to select all.
  1=Select

Opt    Query Definition Option
 1     Specify file selections
 _     Define result fields
 _     Select and sequence fields
 _     Select records
 _     Select sort fields
 _     Select collating sequence
 _     Specify report column formatting
 _     Select report summary functions
 _     Define report breaks
 _     Select output type and output form
 _     Specify processing options

F3=Exit                F5=Report           F12=Cancel
F13=Layout             F18=Files           F21=Select all

      11-03                                             S2 S9999999 KB
```

Figure 9.5 Query definition screen.

```
                       Specify File Selections

Type choices, press Enter.  Press F9 to specify an additional
  file selection.

  File . . . . . . . . . .   FILENAME__     Name, F4 for list
    Library  . . . . . .       QGPL______   Name, *LIBL, F4 for list
  Member . . . . . . . . .   *FIRST____     Name, *FIRST, F4 for list
  Format . . . . . . . . .   *FIRST____     Name, *FIRST, F4 for list




F3=Exit             F4=Prompt           F5=Report            F9=Add file
F12=Cancel          F13=Layout          F24=More keys

      06-29                                             S2 S9999999 KB
```

Figure 9.6 Specify File Selections.

Enter the database name, the library where it is found, the member and format name (usually *FIRST for member and format). All you really need to enter here are database name and library name. For a fast look at the data, this is all that is necessary. You can now save and run the Query <F3>. All fields will print in order, and all records will print, on the terminal. The <F9> key allows you to specify more databases, which can be joined to the primary (first) database. To refine or further format the Query, see following.

Defining result fields for Query. To define fields which are not actually contained in the database, but are derived from them at run time, enter a '1' next to 'Define Results Fields,' producing the screen shown in Fig. 9.7.

Enter a field name for the new field you are defining, a valid expression for the field definition, including values, fieldnames, and the operators:

Operator	Meaning
+	add
–	subtract
*	multiply
/	divide
SUBSTR	substring, as: SUBSTR(field1,4,2) two characters of field1 starting at the fourth position and going for two positions
||	concatenate or join characters

```
                              Define Result Fields

Type definitions using field names or constants and operators, press Enter.
  Operators:  +, -, *, /, SUBSTR, °°

Field        Expression                                Column Heading          Len   Dec
__________   _______________________________________   _____________________   __    __
             _______________________________________   _____________________
             _______________________________________   _____________________

__________   _______________________________________   _____________________   __    __
             _______________________________________   _____________________
             _______________________________________   _____________________
                                                                                  Bottom

Field                 Field
DATE                  CHG TIME
USERID                DATE 2
CHGUSRID              OBJITEM
CHGXYZ                REASON12
                                                                                  Bottom
F3=Exit               F5=Report              F9=Insert              F11=Display text
F12=Cancel            F13=Layout             F20=Reorganize         F24=More keys
```

Figure 9.7 Define Result Fields.

Select and sequence fields for Query. To narrow down the field selection and set the sequence of their display, enter a sequence number next to the field name. If you don't choose any fields, the Query will default to all fields. Figure 9.8 shows how to select and sequence fields.

Select records for Query. To narrow down the number of records selected by the Query, enter a '1' next to the 'Select Records,' yielding the Fig. 9.9 Select Records display.

Enter a field name for the test, an operator, a value, and optional additional tests with AND or OR. Valid operators include:

EQ	equals
NE	not equal
GT	greater than
GE	greater than or equal to
LT	less than
LE	less than or equal to
RANGE	in the range, i.e., RANGE 1 10
LIST	in the list, i.e., LIST 'A' 'B' 'C'
LIKE	looks like, i.e., LIKE '%ABC' (any string ending with 'ABC'; 'A_C' (any four character string starting with A, ending with C, and with any characters in the middle two positions)

Remember that all AND's are processed by Query before any OR's.

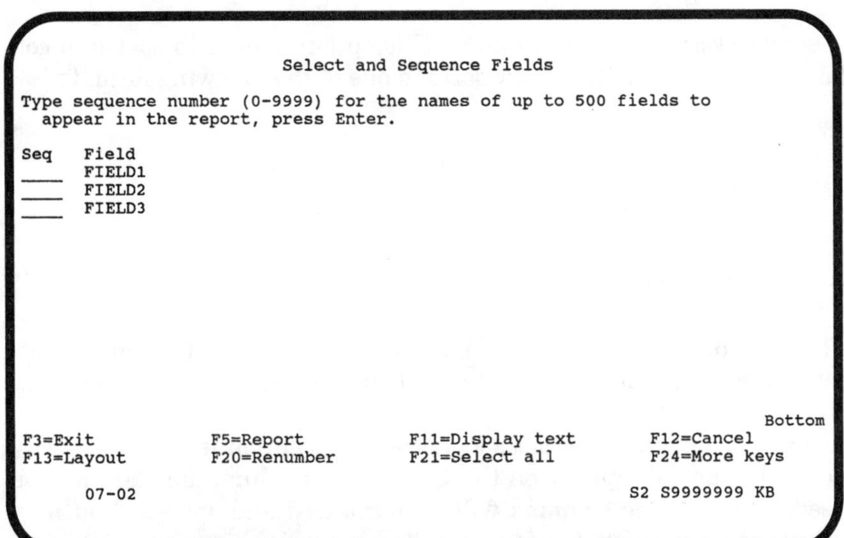

Figure 9.8 Select and Sequence Fields.

```
                              Select Records

Type comparisons, press Enter.  Specify OR to start each new group.
  Tests:  EQ, NE, LE, GE, LT, GT, RANGE, LIST, LIKE

AND/OR  Field               Test   Value (Field, Number, or 'Characters')
        FIELD1________      EQ___  'A'______________________________
______  ______________      _____  _________________________________
______  ______________      _____  _________________________________
______  ______________      _____  _________________________________
______  ______________      _____  _________________________________
______  ______________      _____  _________________________________
                                                                  Bottom
Field
FIELD1
FIELD2
FIELD3

                                                                  Bottom
F3=Exit           F5=Report           F9=Insert              F11=Display text
F12=Cancel        F13=Layout          F20=Reorganize         F24=More keys

      07-10                                                  S2 S9999999 KB
```

Figure 9.9 Select Records.

Select sort fields for Query. This is used to specify which fields will determine the indexed order for the Query. Fields may be selected here in any order and may index the file in ascending or descending order. Sort fields specified here will override key fields defined in the DDS for the file. (See Fig. 9.10.)

Select collating sequence for Query. This option is used to specify a collating sequence for the Query sorts in one of the following formats:

EBCDIC

English

User-specified

Use translation table

This option defaults to '1' (EBCDIC) and is the usual choice for collating sequence. Figure 9.11 illustrates how to select collating sequence.

Specify report column formatting for Query. This option is used to specify how columns will appear on the Query, what column headers will be used, and how the columns will be formatted and spaced. You may specify column width, header, type, and numeric edits (Fig. 9.12).

```
                         Select Sort Fields

Type sort priority (0-999) and A (Ascending) or D (Descending) for
  the names of up to 32 fields, press Enter.

Sort
Prty A/D  Field
 1__  _   FIELD1
 2__  _   FIELD2
 3__  _   FIELD3









                                                                Bottom
F3=Exit         F5=Report       F11=Display text     F12=Cancel
F13=Layout      F18=Files       F20=Renumber         F24=More keys

      08-03                                               S2 S9999999 KB
```

Figure 9.10 Select Sort Fields.

```
                         Select Collating Sequence

 The selected collating sequence will be used for character fields when
 sorting, selecting records, joining files, finding minimum and maximum
 values, and determining when a control break has occurred.

 Type choices, press Enter.

   Collating sequence
     option . . . . . . .   1            1=Use EBCDIC collating sequence
                                         2=Use English sequence
                                         3=Define a collating sequence
                                         4=Use translation table

   For choice 4=Use translation table:
     Table . . . . . . .   __________    Name, F4 for list
       Library . . . . .     __________  Name, *LIBL, F4 for list


 F3=Exit          F4=Prompt         F5=Report         F10=Process/previous
 F12=Cancel       F13=Layout        F18=Files         F23=Save as default

       11-29                                                S2 S9999999 KB
```

Figure 9.11 Select Collating Sequence.

```
                      Specify Report Column Formatting

Type information, press Enter.
  Column headings:  *NONE, aligned text lines

                   Column
Field              Spacing       Column Heading            Len  Dec   Edit
FIELD1                0          FIELD1____________          6    2
                                 __________________
                                 __________________

FIELD2                2          FIELD2____________          6    0
                                 __________________
                                 __________________

FIELD3                2          FIELD3____________         80    _
                                 __________________
                                 __________________

                                                                    Bottom
F3=Exit          F5=Report       F10=Process/previous   F12=Cancel
F13=Layout       F16=Edit        F18=Files              F23=Long comment

      08-22                                             S2 S9999999 KB
```

Figure 9.12 Specify Report Column Formatting.

Specify report summary functions for Query. Functions such as Sum, Average, Maximum, Minimum, and Count may be specified for columns. Enter the appropriate number next to the field you want, as shown in Fig. 9.13.

Define report breaks for Query. Subgroups may be specified according to sort fields. The Query will provide a report break and subtotals, if desired, at the appropriate point. Figure 9.14 is the Define Report Breaks display.

Select output type and output form for Query. This option is used to direct the output of the Query to various destinations, such as the screen, the printer, a spool file, or into a database. You may specify page headers, print width, line wrapping, title page, etc. (Fig. 9.15).

Specify processing options for Query. You may choose to use rounding and whether or not to ignore decimal data errors. Refer to Fig. 9.16, Specify Processing Options.

9.3 SUMMARY

DFU and Query provide fast, easy ways to perform input and output with AS/400 databases. Although they are more limited in control and

```
                         Select Report Summary Functions

Type options, press Enter.
  1=Total   2=Average   3=Minimum   4=Maximum   5=Count

---Options---     Field
1 _ _ _ _         FIELD1
_ _ _ _ _         FIELD2
_ _ _ _ _         FIELD3

                                                                        Bottom
F3=Exit          F5=Report        F10=Process/previous       F11=Display text
F12=Cancel       F13=Layout       F18=Files                  F23=Long comment

      07-02                                                  S2 S9999999 KB
```

Figure 9.13 Select Report Summary Functions.

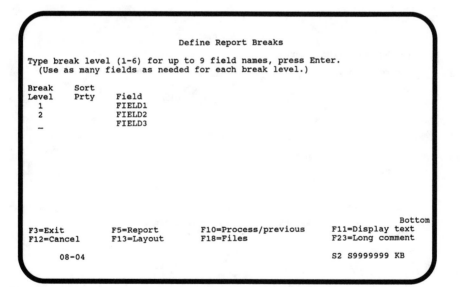

```
                              Define Report Breaks

Type break level (1-6) for up to 9 field names, press Enter.
  (Use as many fields as needed for each break level.)

Break    Sort
Level    Prty     Field
  1               FIELD1
  2               FIELD2
  _               FIELD3

                                                                        Bottom
F3=Exit          F5=Report         F10=Process/previous      F11=Display text
F12=Cancel       F13=Layout        F18=Files                 F23=Long comment

      08-04                                                  S2 S9999999 KB
```

Figure 9.14 Define Report Breaks.

```
                    Select Output Type and Output Form

Type choices, press Enter.

  Output type . . . . . . . . . . .    1       1=Display
                                               2=Printer
                                               3=Database file

  Form of output . . . . . . . . . .   1       1=Detail
                                               2=Summary only

  Line wrapping . . . . . . . . . .    N       Y=Yes, N=No
    Wrapping width . . . . . . . . .   ___     Blank, 1-198
    Record on one page . . . . . . .   N       Y=Yes, N=No




F3=Exit            F5=Report            F10=Process/previous
F12=Cancel         F13=Layout           F18=Files

      05-41                                         S2 S9999999 KB
```

Figure 9.15 Select Output Type and Output Form.

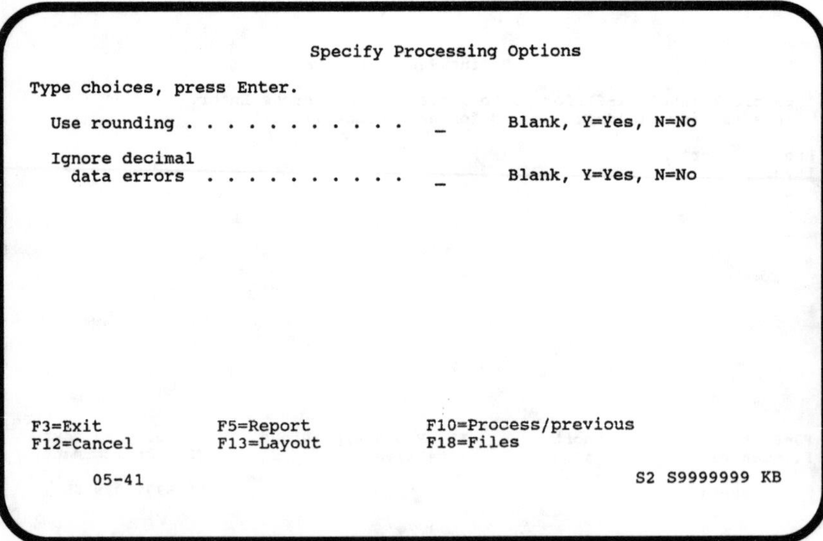

```
                    Specify Processing Options

Type choices, press Enter.

  Use rounding . . . . . . . . . . .   _       Blank, Y=Yes, N=No

  Ignore decimal
    data errors . . . . . . . . . .    _       Blank, Y=Yes, N=No




F3=Exit            F5=Report            F10=Process/previous
F12=Cancel         F13=Layout           F18=Files

      05-41                                         S2 S9999999 KB
```

Figure 9.16 Specify Processing Options.

scope than custom-written routines, what is gained in speed and convenience often makes them valuable.

DFU can allow a user to access a database within seconds, without writing a special program for I/O, but cannot provide error checking or data protection.

Query can produce straightforward reports and send the output to the screen, the printer, to another file, or into an Office document. If a high degree of user control is needed, however, as with complicated data edits or report features, it will still be necessary to write programs.

Chapter

10

Source Entry Utility (SEU)

SEU is the AS/400's Source Entry Utility. It is the editor used to enter source code into the system. It does not have the advanced text-processing capabilities of Office and DW/4 because it is intended for entering and editing source code which will then be compiled into objects. But it does have several very advanced and useful features which aid in the development of program source code, database definitions, screen generation, and debugging. These features include instant syntax checking, prompting for fill-in-the-blanks source code entry, and online field-sensitive help.

SEU can be started a number of ways: from the main menu, by typing the CL command STRSEU (start SEU), and from the PDM (Program Development Management) screen. We recommend working from the PDM screen. Type: STRPDM <Enter>. You then see the PDM screen, as shown in Fig. 10.1.

10.1 STARTING SEU FROM THE MEMBER LIST

The member list

Choose number 3 to work with members. Remember that members are the actual source code to be compiled into objects, whether they be databases, screens, or programs (see Chap. 5). This brings up the initial screen of the member list, where you can choose which members

```
                AS/400 Programming Development Manager (PDM)
Select one of the following:

     1. Work with libraries
     2. Work with objects
     3. Work with members

     9. Work with user-defined options








Selection or command
===> ____________________________________________________________________
F3=Exit        F4=Prompt       F9=Retrieve       F10=Command entry
F12=Cancel     F18=Change defaults
                                      (C) COPYRIGHT IBM CORP. 1981, 1989.
      20-07                                            S2 S9999999 KB
```

Figure 10.1 PDM screen.

you want to work on in which source physical files. This is the initial Member List screen (Fig. 10.2).

In this screen, you enter the source physical file which contains or will contain the cource code you want to work on, the library which contains this source physical file, and a parameter which will show you a list of all of the members in that source physical file (*ALL) or a selection of them. The choices may be narrowed down as follows:

*ALL	all the members in the specified source physical file
ABC*	all members starting with the letters ABC
*ABC	all members ending with the letters ABC

It is desirable to narrow down the choices if there are many members in this particular source physical file so that it will be easier to get around the Member List screen.

Also, enter the type of members you are working on so that SEU will know what type of syntax checking, prompting, and help to offer you as you work (see Sec. 10.3). Types are as follows:

RPG	RPG programs
SQL	SQL programs
CBL	COBOL programs
C	C programs
CLP	CL programs

```
                        Work with Members Using PDM

File . . . . . .    QCLPSRC___             Position to . . . . .    __________
  Library . . . .   MYLIB_____

Type options, press Enter.
  2=Edit            3=Copy      4=Delete        5=Display        6=Print
  7=Rename          8=Display description       9=Save           13=Change text

Opt  Member         Type        Text
 _   STARTUP        CLP_______  Startup_program_for_user_________________________
 _   OVRRID         CLP_______  Database_override_program________________________
 _   RPTMNU         CLP_______  Call_screen_for_reports_menu_____________________

                                                                            More...
Parameters or command
===> ______________________________________________________________________________
F3=Exit             F4=Prompt                F5=Refresh               F6=Create
F9=Retrieve         F12=Previous             F23=More options         F24=More keys

      11-02                                  DM                  S1 S9999999 KB
```

Figure 10.2 Member List screen 1.

PF	Physical File (data definition specs)
DSPF	Screen specifications
*SAME	Same type as the last one worked on

Once the parameters in this screen have been filled in, hit enter and you will come to the actual Member List shown in Fig. 10.3.

From this screen, it is easy to work on members, create members, enter source code, copy members, rename members, and compile members into objects. In addition, if you direct the output of your compilations to your spool file (highly recommended) you can work with the compile listings in the spool file from the Member List (WRKSPLF), look at the errors generated (using SEU), and return to the member list to use SEU to fix any problems and resubmit the compile (see Chap. 15 for how to do this).

Enter the following option number next to the desired member to perform the function (Fig. 10.2):

2	Edit
3	Copy
4	Delete
5	View (no changes allowed)
7	Rename
14	Compile
F6	Create new member

```
                         Specify Members to Work With

 Type choices, press Enter.

   File . . . . . . . . . .   QCLPSRC___   Name

     Library . . . . . . . .  MYLIB_____   *LIBL, *CURLIB, name

   Member:
     Name . . . . . . . . .   *ALL______   *ALL, generic*, name
     Type . . . . . . . . .   *ALL______   *ALL, *BLANK, type









 F3=Exit     F5=Refresh     F12=Previous

     05-32                            DM                  S1 S9999999 KB
```

Figure 10.3 Member List screen 2.

If you are working on a new member, hit the F6 key to create a new member, and fill in the blanks as to program name and type. Otherwise, if the member you are working on already exists, simply enter 2 next to the member in the member list and you will find yourself in SEU, looking at the member in edit mode. You can now enter source code, make changes, and use all of the functions of SEU. (See Fig. 10.4, a sample SEU screen.)

Changing edit parameters of SEU

When in SEU, you may change parameters of SEU, such as whether source code will accept lowercase input as well as uppercase by hitting <F13> (Shift-F1), and whether Page Up and Page Down move by a full page or half page. Figure 10.5 shows a Sample SEU Edit Parameter screen.

10.2 NAVIGATING SOURCE CODE IN SEU

Paging, scrolling and Go To

The SEU navigation keys operate as follows:

Page Up	Go up one screen.
Page Down	Go down one screen.
Up Arrow	Scroll upward a line at a time.
Down Arrow	Scroll downward a line at a time.

```
Columns . . . . :    1  71                    Edit                        QGPL/QCLSRC
Find  . . .  ____________________________________________                          DD
FMT **   ...+... 1 ...+... 2 ...+... 3 ...+... 4 ...+... 5 ...+... 6 ...+... 7
       *************** Beginning of data ************************************
'''''''
'''''''
'''''''
'''''''
'''''''
'''''''
'''''''
'''''''
'''''''
'''''''
'''''''
'''''''
'''''''
'''''''
'''''''
        ****************** End of data ***************************************

 F3=Exit                    F4=Prompt                    F5=Refresh
 F10=Top                    F11=Bottom                   F24=More keys
Member DD added to file QGPL/QCLSRC.
      05-09                                    DM                S1 S9999999 KB
```

Figure 10.4 Sample SEU screen.

```
                                   Edit Services

 Type choices, press Enter.

   Amount to roll . . . . . . . . . . . .   1           1=Half page
                                                        2=Full page
   Uppercase input only . . . . . . . . .   Y           Y=Yes, N=No
   Tabs on  . . . . . . . . . . . . . . .   N           Y=Yes, N=No
   Increment of insert record . . . . . .   0.01__      0.01 - 999.99

   Source type  . . . . . . . . . . . . .   CLP_______
   Syntax checking:
     When added/modified  . . . . . . . .   Y           Y=Yes, N=No
     From sequence number . . . . . . . .   _______     0000.00 - 9999.99
     To sequence number . . . . . . . . .   _______     0000.00 - 9999.99


   Set records to date  . . . . . . . . .   __/__/__    YY/MM/DD or YYMMDD

 F3=Exit                    F5=Refresh           F12=Previous
 F14=Find/Change Services                        F15=Browse/Copy Services

      05-43                                    DM              S1 S9999999 KB
```

Figure 10.5 Sample SEU edit parameter screen.

Left Arrow	One character left.
Right Arrow	One character right.
Shift-F7	One screen to left.
Shift-F8	One screen to right.

Go To. Type over a line number followed by a space in the line numbers at the left of the SEU screen and hit <Enter> to go to the line number that you input.

Finding text. Enter the text to be found (not case-sensitive) on the line after the prompt "Find" at the upper left of the SEU screen. Hit <F16> to find the text in the source.

Search and replace

Hit <F14> to bring up the Search and Replace screen. Fill in the string to search for, the string to replace it with, and optional parameters concerning whether to stop for confirmation before each replacement or not. Hit <Enter> to return to the edit screen. If you have specified confirmation for each replacement, use the <Shift>-<F4> keys to find the next occurrence of the search string, and <Shift>-<F5> to perform the replacement.

Copy and delete

Line copy. Type C over one of the line numbers at the left of the SEU screen to mark the line, cursor to the desired destination for the copy, and type B to insert the line before this line, or A to insert the block after this line. Hit <Enter> to copy the line.

Line delete. Type over D in the line numbers at the left of the SEU screen to mark the line. Hit <Enter> to delete the line.

Block copy. Type over CC in the line numbers at the left of the SEU screen to mark the beginning of the block, cursor to the end of the block, type over another CC to mark the end of the block, cursor to the desired destination for the copy, and type B to insert the block before this line, or A to insert the block after this line. Hit <Enter> to copy the block. Figure 10.6 is a sample CC block copy.

Block delete. Type over DD in the line numbers at the left of the SEU screen to mark the beginning of the block, cursor to the end of the block, type over another DD to mark the end of the block. Hit <Enter> to delete the block.

Repeat the line

Type over RP*n* in the line numbers at the left of the SEU screen to repeat the line, where *n* is the number of times to repeat the line after the current line. Hit <Enter> to repeat the line.

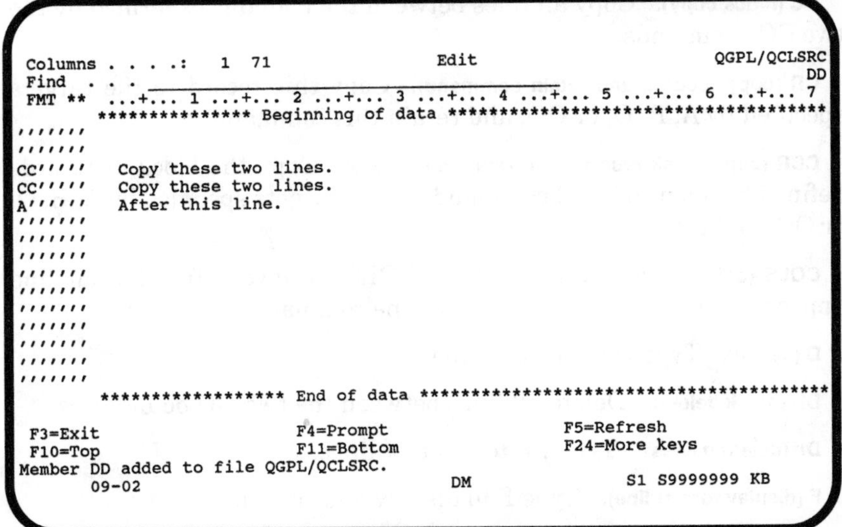

Figure 10.6 Sample CC block copy screen.

Importing text from other files

Hit <F15> to specify a file to insert in the file currently being edited in SEU. It comes in at the bottom of a split screen. To insert a section or all of it, simply follow the preceding Copy Block instructions. The <F6> key will split the screen at the current cursor location, so you may adjust how much of each window you want to see.

Summary of SEU commands

Sequence Number field displays the sequence number of the record. You may type in line commands here. Following is a list of valid line commands:

A (after). Type A in the sequence number field to move, copy, or include specified records after this record.

A*n* (after with repeat). Type An in the sequence number field to move, copy, or include specified records after this record and repeat these records n times.

B (before). Type B in the sequence number field to move, copy, or include specified records before this record.

B*n* (before with repeat). Type Bn in the sequence number field to move, copy, or include specified records before this record and repeat these records n times.

C (copy line). Copy this line to a given target.

C*n* (copy *n* lines). Copy this line plus the next n–1 lines to the target.

CC (block copy). Copy all lines between the boundaries formed by the two CC commands.

CR (copy records and retain command). Copy this record to the targets specified by A, B, O, or OO, and retain this command.

CCR (copy block records and retain command). Copy the block of records defined by a pair of CCR commands to the targets specified by A, B, O, or OO, and retain this command.

COLS (column line command). Type COLS to have a free format line appear just before the line on which the command was entered.

D (delete). Type D to delete a line.

DD (block delete). Delete all lines between the two DD boundaries.

D*n* (delete *n* lines). Type D*n* to delete *n* lines.

F (display format line). Type F to display a format line.

Fxx (display the xx format line). Type Fxx to display the xx format line.

F? (show the format selection display). Type F? to show the format selection display. From this screen choose the format you wish to display.

I (insert a line). Type I to get an insert line after this record.

IF (insert line and display format). Type IF to insert a line and display the current format before this new line.

IF*n* (insert *n* lines and display format). Type IF*n* to insert *n* lines and display the current format before the first new line.

IFxx (insert a line and display xx format). Type IFxx to insert a line and display the xx format before this new line.

IF? (show the format selection display). Type IF? to show the format selection display and insert a line with a format selected from that screen before this new line.

I*n* (insert *n* lines). Type I*n* to insert *n* lines after this record.

IP? (show High-Level Language Prompt Selection Display). Type IP? to show the High-Level Language Prompt Selection Display. An insert line will be shown in the prompt selected from this display.

IP (insert line and prompt). Type IP to insert a line and prompt for it.

IPxx (insert line with an xx prompt). Type IPxx to insert a line and display the line in the xx prompt.

IS (insert skeleton line). Type IS to display an insert line and initialize it to the data saved as the skeleton line.

IS*n* (insert *n* skeleton lines). Type IS*n* to display *n* insert lines and initialize them to the data saved as the skeleton lines.

L (shift data 1 char left). Type L to shift data in this record one character position to the left without losing data.

L*n* (shift data *n* chars left). Type L*n* to shift data in this record *n* character positions to the left without losing data.

LL (shift block 1 char to the left). Shift data defined by the boundary between and including the two LL line commands one character position to the left without losing data.

LL*n* (shift block *n* chars to the left). Shift data defined by the boundary between and including the LL*n* and LL line commands *n* character positions to the left.

LT (shift data 1 char left with truncate). Type LT to shift data in this record one character position to the left. You can lose data off the beginning of your records.

LT*n* (shift data *n* chars left with truncate). Type LT*n* to shift data in this record *n* character positions to the left. You can lose data off the beginning of your records.

LLT (shift block left with truncate). Shift data defined by the boundary between and including the two LLT line commands one position to the left. You can lose data off the beginning of your record.

LLT*n* (shift block *n* chars left with truncate). Shift data defined by the boundary between and including the LLT*n* and LLT line commands *n* positions to the left. You can lose data off the beginning of your record.

M (move a line). Type M to move a line to a given destination.

M*n* (move *n* lines). Type M*n* to move this line and the following *n*–1 lines to a chosen destination.

MM (block move). Move all records between and including the boundaries defined by the MM line commands to the target location.

O (overlay). Type O to overlay this line with the first line defined by the move, copy, or copy-repeated line command.

O*n* (overlay plus). Type O*n* to overlay this line and the following *n*–1 lines with the first *n* lines defined by the move, copy, or copy-repeated line command.

OO (block overlay). Overlay all the records between and including the boundaries defined by two OO line commands with the lines defined by the chosen destination.

MM (block move). Move all records between and including the boundaries defined by the MM line commands to the target location.

O (overlay). Type O to overlay this line with the first line defined by the move, copy, or copy-repeated line command.

O*n* (overlay plus). Type O*n* to overlay this line and the following *n*–1 lines with the first *n* lines defined by the move, copy, or copy-repeated line command.

OO (block overlay). Overlay all the records between and including the boundaries defined by two OO line commands with the lines defined by the right without losing data.

RR (block shift 1 char to the right). Shift data defined by the boundary between and including the two RR line commands one character position to the right without losing data.

RR*n* (block shift *n* chars to the right). Shift data defined by the boundary between and including the RR*n* and RR line commands *n* character positions to the right, without losing data.

RRT (shift block right with truncate). Shift data defined by the boundary between and including the two RRT line commands one position to the right. You can lose data off the end of your records.

RRT*n* (shift block *n* chars right with truncate). Shift data defined by the boundary between and including the RRT*n* and RRT line commands *n* positions to the right. You can lose data off the end of your records.

RT (shift data 1 char right with truncate). Type RT to shift data in this record one character position to the right. You can lose data off the end of your records.

RT*n* (shift data *n* chars right with truncate). Type RT*n* to shift data in this record *n* character positions to the right. You can lose data off the end of your records.

RP (repeat line). Type RP to repeat this line before the next line.

RP*n* (repeat line *n* times). Type RP*n* to repeat this line *n* times.

RPP (block repeat). Repeat all lines defined by the boundary between the two RPP line commands.

RPP*n* (block repeat). Repeat all lines defined by the boundary between the two RPP line commands *n* times.

S (skeleton line). Type S to define this data line as the skeleton line.

SF, (show first record). Type SF to show the first record of the exclude group.

SF*n* (show first *n* records). Type SF*n* to show the first *n* records of the exclude group.

SL (show last record). Type SL to show the last record of the exclude group.

SL*n* (show last *n* records). Type SL*n* to show the last *n* records of the exclude group.

TABS (display tabs record). Type TABS to set and show the tabs for the display. To use the tabs you set, specify Y (Yes) for the "Tabs on" field on the Edit Services display.

W (display member from column 1). Type W to display the member beginning in column 1.

Wn (display member from column n). Type Wn to display the member beginning in column n.

X (exclude). Type an X next to the record you would like excluded.

X*n* (exclude plus). Type X*n* to exclude this record and the next *n*–1 records.

XX (block exclude). Exclude all lines between the boundaries formed by the two XX line commands.

Plus (roll member forward). Type +*n* to roll the member forward *n* lines.

Minus (roll member backward). Type –*n* to roll the member backward *n* lines.

10.3 A SMART EDITOR

SEU provides a number of very helpful aids for writing source code. Among these are syntax checking, prompting, and field-sensitive help.

Prompting for syntax

Remember, when you entered SEU from the PDM screen, you entered a File Type for the member you are working on. This is how SEU knows what type of syntax checking to do for you as you enter source lines. If you do not have the correct prompt type, you can set it right by typing over IP? in the line numbers at the left of the SEU screen. SEU will then show you a list of possible prompt values with definitions of each. Choose the appropriate one, entering it in the space provided on the prompt type screen, and hit <Enter> to return to SEU. Figure 10.7 illustrates a prompt-type request (in the line numbers) for a help screen.

```
 Columns . . . :    1  71           Edit                        QGPL/QCLSRC
 Find  . . .                                                            DD
 FMT **   ...+... 1 ...+... 2 ...+... 3 ...+... 4 ...+... 5 ...+... 6 ...+... 7
          *************** Beginning of data ***************************************
0001.00 PGM
0002.00
IP?3.00   WRKACTJOB
0004.00
0005.00   1234
0006.00
0007.00 ENDPGM
          ***************** End of data *****************************************






 F3=Exit                    F4=Prompt                 F5=Refresh
 F10=Top                    F11=Bottom                F24=More keys
String beginning '1234        ' not valid command name.
       09-03                               DM                S1 S9999999 KB
```

Figure 10.7 Prompt types from help screen.

Syntax checking

When SEU is set to the correct prompt type for whatever you are working on, the <F4> key will produce a fill-in-the-blanks form at the bottom of the SEU screen for you to enter commands, values, parameters, variables, etc. Figure 10.9 shows a sample SEU prompt screen for a line of RPG code. If anything is entered incorrectly for the type of program you are working on, SEU will highlight the offending field, place the cursor in it, and wait for a correction. For instance, in writing an RPG program, if a command is entered in a column where it doesn't belong, SEU will respond with a screen like that seen in Fig. 10.8. (Note message at bottom of screen.)

SEU will not catch all types of errors. For instance, it would not know if you are referencing an undefined variable. These and other kinds of compilation errors must wait for actual compilation to show up. But SEU can be very helpful in pinpointing immediately upon input syntax errors like misspelling a command, column misplacement, and missing parameters. When all components of a command line are correct, you may hit <Enter> and SEU will insert the line into the program at the current location.

Syntax help

When the cursor is positioned in one of the fields in the prompt window, you may hit the <Help> key to get online help for that particular

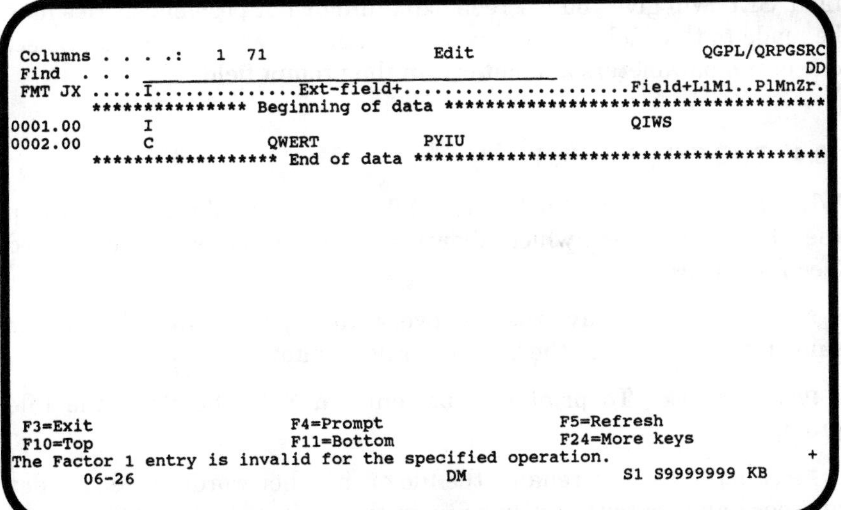
```
Columns . . . .:   1  71                Edit                  QGPL/QRPGSRC
Find  . . .                                                             DD
FMT JX .....I..............Ext-field+....................Field+L1M1..PlMnZr.
        **************** Beginning of data **************************************
0001.00      I                                             QIWS
0002.00      C              QWERT          PYIU
        ****************** End of data ******************************************

F3=Exit                     F4=Prompt                 F5=Refresh
F10=Top                     F11=Bottom                F24=More keys
The Factor 1 entry is invalid for the specified operation.              +
      06-26                             DM                S1 S9999999 KB
```

Figure 10.8 Sample RPG error in prompt screen.

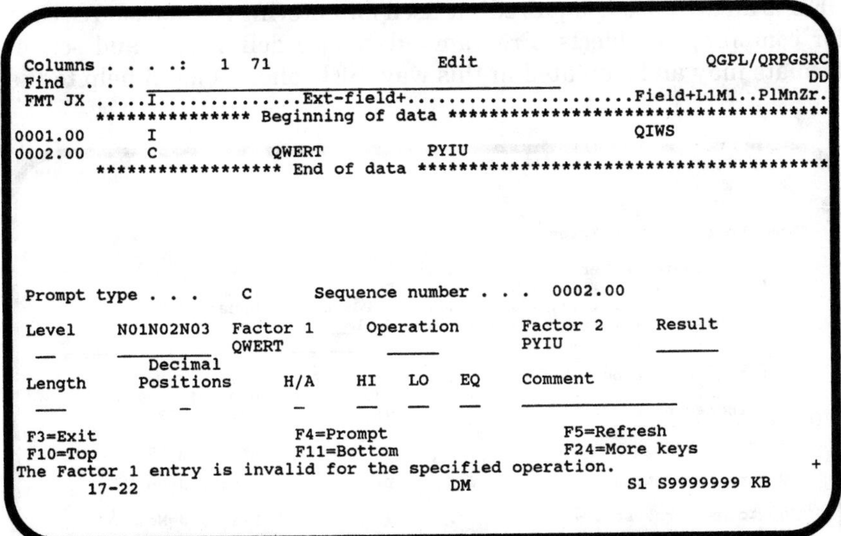
```
Columns . . . .:   1  71                Edit                  QGPL/QRPGSRC
Find  . . .                                                             DD
FMT JX .....I..............Ext-field+....................Field+L1M1..PlMnZr.
        **************** Beginning of data **************************************
0001.00      I                                             QIWS
0002.00      C              QWERT          PYIU
        ****************** End of data ******************************************

Prompt type . . .     C      Sequence number . . .  0002.00

Level    N01N02N03  Factor 1      Operation      Factor 2      Result
                    QWERT                        PYIU
            Decimal
Length     Positions     H/A    HI    LO    EQ     Comment

F3=Exit                     F4=Prompt                 F5=Refresh
F10=Top                     F11=Bottom                F24=More keys
The Factor 1 entry is invalid for the specified operation.              +
      17-22                             DM                S1 S9999999 KB
```

Figure 10.9 Sample SEU help in prompt screen.

field. SEU will give you a screen explaining what possible entries may be made to that field in whatever language you are working in. Select one of the parameters and enter it in the prompt field.

10.4 THE EXIT SCREEN

When finished editing the file, hit <F3> to save the file. This brings up the SEU Exit screen, which allows several parameters to be entered (see Fig. 10.10).

Saving the file. To save the file, overwrite a previous version by the same name, enter Y to the Save the File prompt.

Printing the file. To print the file, enter a Y to the Print the File prompt.

Renaming the file. To rename the file or, in other words, save it under another name, enter the new name in the member-name prompt.

10.5 SUMMARY

SEU is an advanced, smart editor used for entering AS/400 source code for compiling to objects. Programs, database definitions, and screen formats may all be created in this way. SEU offers a lot of help to the

```
                                    Exit

 Type choices, press Enter.

   Change/create member . . . . . . . .   Y             Y=Yes, N=No
     Member . . . . . . . . . . . . . .   DD________    Name
     File . . . . . . . . . . . . . . .   QRPGSRC___    Name
       Library . . . . . . . . . . . . .  QGPL______    Name
     Text . . . . . . . . . . . . . . .   ___________________________________

     Resequence member . . . . . . . . .  Y             Y=Yes, N=No
       Start . . . . . . . . . . . . . .  0001.00       0000.01 - 9999.99
       Increment . . . . . . . . . . . .  01.00         00.01 - 99.99

   Print member . . . . . . . . . . . .   N             Y=Yes, N=No

   Return to editing . . . . . . . . . .  Y             Y=Yes, N=No

   Go to member list . . . . . . . . . .  N             Y=Yes, N=No

 F3=Exit        F5=Refresh        F12=Previous

 Member contains syntax errors.
      05-42                                DM              S1 S9999999 KB
```

Figure 10.10 SEU Exit screen.

programmer in that it is aware of the type of source code being entered and can detect syntax errors upon entry, before compiling. It also offers field-sensitive help at the touch of the <Help> key, which explains which parameters or commands are expected in certain positions in an AS/400 source member. Learning to use its features can cut down remarkably on development time as well as on frustration. We are not aware of another editor which is as smart or helpful as SEU in entering source code and catching syntax errors.

Chapter

11

Database: Data Definition Specifications (DDS) and Interactive Data Definition Utility (IDDU)

Databases can be defined two ways on the AS/400. You can code and compile your own Data Definition Specifications (DDS) for databases, or you can use the Interactive Data Definition Utility (IDDU) to create a data dictionary and dependent databases. Writing your own DDS is somewhat more flexible, but requires a knowledge of data definition coding techniques. The IDDU approach offers consistent data files based on a common data dictionary, and ease of use with a menu-driven user interface for designing databases, but is more cumbersome to change. We will explore both methods.

There are two ways to describe and define data—internal and external. Internal or program description allows:

Specific field selection and use

Multiple data definitions

Naming inconsistency

External or system described allows:

Data always known by the same name and attributes

Field selection done through "logical views"

Since the AS/400 is a database-oriented machine, the normal way to handle databases is to use externally described files which are accessed by the application programs. This method takes advantage of automatic database functions on the AS/400 and saves coding time when writing programs.

11.1 DATA DEFINITION SPECIFICATIONS

Data Definition Specifications are source code. You write them in much the same manner as you would write a program, and then you compile them. DDS compiles into an object of type *FILE and contains data. Actually, physical files contain data, while logical and join files are altered views of the physical files. The DDS itself does not contain data but is the source code for compiling into objects (physical files) which contain the data. Here is a simple DDS which defines a database with two fields: NAME and AMOUNT.

```
A          R ACCT
A            NAME         20          COLHDG('Name')
A            AMOUNT        8S 2       COLHDG('Amount')
A          K NAME
```

ACCT is the record format name, as opposed to the DDS member name. The member name will be the default name of the compiled database object used in programs for reads, while the format name is the name used in programs for writes and updates.

```
NAME      20        COLHDG('Name')
```

Name field, 20 char (DDS knows it is char because there is no decimal position, as there is in the Amount field). The default column heading for the field is 'Name' as defined in the keyword COLHDG, and it will automatically be used by AS/400 functions such as Query and SDA.

```
AMOUNT     8S 2   COLHDG('Amount')
```

Amount field, 8 byte zoned with 2 decimals. Column heading is 'Amount.'

```
K NAME
```

'Name' is the key field, which will be used automatically by the AS/400 to keep the index for this file current. Key fields may be overridden by Logical files or Query sort groups.

Source files

The first step in creating a database according to the DDS method is to write source code defining the database. This source code must reside somewhere, and it is an AS/400 convention to keep all source code of a similar type in a source physical file. A source physical file is simply a bucket to hold source code of one type (see Chap. 5). It is a convention to name the source physical file for DDS as QDDSSRC, although you can call it by any valid name. So, if you want to write DDS, you should create a QDDSSRC in your library if one does not exist.

Members

Source code resides in a member of a source physical file. Source physical files contain members, each of which contains code defining a particular object to be compiled. Use SEU to write the code in each of these DDS members in QDDSSRC. SEU is a smart editor, so when you tell it that you are writing DDS code for a physical file (type PF), for example, it will know what kind of syntax checking, help, and prompting to offer.

Record formats

DDS defines a database record. The source code has a name, which will be the name of the database, once compiled. You might name your DDS as ACCOUNTS. This is the database name, but the database also needs a record name (format) which is used for writing to the database. Use the database name for reads, and the record or format name for writes. If the database is called ACCOUNTS you might make the format name ACCT. So you would read ACCOUNTS but write to ACCT when you refer to the database later, in your programs.

A format name is specified in DDS, is usually the first specification, and is coded as follows:

```
A          R ACCT
```

Fields

Fields are defined in DDS simply by entering a field name, type, and length. Various keywords may be added (see following), but name and length are the minimum definitions for a field and often suffice. Keep in mind that RPG is the most prevalent language on the AS/400 and only allows six characters in field names. So, if you don't want to end up redefining field names for RPG, keep them to six characters or less. The two primary data types are alpha and zoned decimal. They are defined as follows:

DDS for Alpha field:

```
A       NAME           20A          COLHDG('Name')
```

DDS for Zoned Decimal field (8 byte with 2 decimals):

```
A        AMOUNT          8S 2      COLHDG('Amount')
```

Packed decimal fields require a name, length, a P instead of an S, and a decimal length. Alpha fields require only a name and length. They do not strictly require the A because the absence of decimal length implies alpha type.

Key fields

A key field is a field by which the database will be ordered. You do not have to handle this indexing of the database beyond defining the key field(s) in the DDS. The AS/400 takes care of keeping indexes current for specified key fields. Multiple key fields (keys composed of more than one field) are achieved by listing the key fields in order of significance, at the end of the DDS:

```
A          K NAME
```

The 'UNIQUE' keyword at the beginning of a DDS indicates that only one record can exist for a given key value.

Key fields must, of course, be fields already defined in the DDS. See "Logical Files" (following) for redefining key fields.

Field edits

DDS may specify keywords for data edits as ranges or possible field values for the database. The AS/400 can then reference these values in applications and displays to determine whether the input is valid according to the DDS, issuing messages if it is not. Keywords which further define DDS fields include:

COLHDG	Provide a column heading which will be used by Query, DFU, SDA, or any other AS/400 database functions.
COMP	Compare the field to a value for entry validity.
DESCEND	A keyed field has descending sequence.
EDTCDE	Specify a special code for numeric edits.
EDTWRD	Specify a picture clause for a field.
RANGE	Specify a range for field input.
REF	Specify, at the file level, which file is to be referenced for external field definitions.
REFFLD	Specify, at the field level, which field definition from the REF file will be referenced.
TEXT	Include a text description of the field for documentation.

UNIQUE	Specify, at the record format level, that the key is unique and duplicate key entries will not be allowed.
VALUES	Specify allowable values for input.

The database—physical files

Physical files are the primary units of data capture on the AS/400. They contain the actual data. The are defined in DDS, with the type of PF. Once defined and compiled, they may be accessed for input, reads, writes, etc. Remember that any further definition and compiling of the physical file will drop any data which may have been contained in the file and that DDS changes necessitate recompiling of any programs or objects which reference the physical file, to avoid level checks at run time. These occur when a program tries to access a file which has been changed and recompiled since the program was last compiled.

Logical files

Logical files provide alternate views of previously defined physical files. Key fields may be altered, fields may be included or omitted, and filter conditions may be placed on the database. Logical files do not actually contain any data, but redesign the way the data in a physical file is accessed. Their file type is LF.

A logical file must have a line which defines the physical file to which it refers, and a line for every field redefinition which it contains. If no fields are explicitly specified, the logical file will default to all fields. If any fields are specified, it will contain only those fields.

```
A       R ACCT                          PFILE('ACCOUNTS')
A         NAME         20               COLHDG('Name')
A         AMOUNT        8S 2            COLHDG('Amount')
A       K AMOUNT
```

The preceding DDS defines a logical file which redefines the key for physical file ACCOUNTS. The new key is the AMOUNT field. Note the record format name (ACCT) which matches the physical file record format name. The PFILE keyword is required and indicates which physical file is being redefined here in the logical file. The resulting logical file will contain only two fields, NAME and AMOUNT, and will be ordered by AMOUNT.

We could even redefine the NAME field from the physical file as the first five characters, like this:

```
A         NAME5         5               SUBSTR(NAME,1,5)
```

Join files

Join files create a view of two or more physical or logical files as if they were one. You might want to answer a user's question with a screen which shows a join file, combining fields from various databases. Remember that join files may be read but not written to or updated. You cannot use a join file for output, only individual files.

11.2 INTERACTIVE DATA DEFINITION UTILITY

IDDU is the IBM system utility that allows database definition. Through IDDU, definition of DDS is made simple and can be prompted. IDDU is a preferable method of database definition for many users due to the database dictionary feature of IDDU. The data dictionary provides good documentation for future reference, but also requires maintenance. In most cases, maintenance of the data dictionary and the database files is more cumbersome through IDDU than directly through creation of your own DDS.

The traditional method of database management stores all data in a fixed format record, and the programmer controls the data description. The relational method of database management on which the AS/400 is based is especially easy to access through IDDU:

1. Data is known to the operating system.
2. Each element of data is unique.
3. All programs deal with logical records.
4. It is easy to use by importing external data descriptions.

Starting IDDU

The CL command STRIDD begins the utility. The IDDU menu is then presented to the user as shown in Fig. 11.1.

By selecting a menu option, the user is guided through all of the steps of defining a database from start to finish. All work done in each of the sections of IDDU must be done through the dictionary.

Files

Files are initially created without fields in IDDU. They can be defined, however, using predefined record formats, thus requiring predefinition of the fields.

At the file level, as in DDS, you can define several parameters:

ALTSEQ	the alternate collating sequence table for ordering key entries
LIFO	duplicates key retrieval order

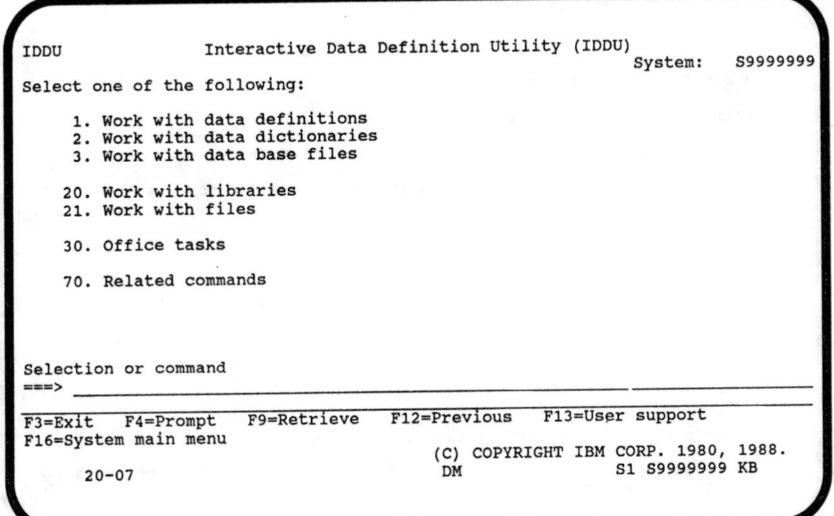
```
IDDU              Interactive Data Definition Utility (IDDU)
                                                    System:    S9999999
Select one of the following:

     1. Work with data definitions
     2. Work with data dictionaries
     3. Work with data base files

    20. Work with libraries
    21. Work with files

    30. Office tasks

    70. Related commands



Selection or command
===> ____________________________________________________________

F3=Exit   F4=Prompt   F9=Retrieve   F12=Previous   F13=User support
F16=System main menu
                                   (C) COPYRIGHT IBM CORP. 1980, 1988.
     20-07                         DM              S1 S9999999 KB
```

Figure 11.1 IDDU menu options.

REF	specifies the file, library, and (if necessary) the format to be used by all reference field definitions in the file
Unique	specifies that no duplicates may occur in key field

Record format

Record formats must be created through the data dictionary. The record format allows the file to have a primary logical view. This format will show specified fields in a defined sequence. From this point, fields can also be defined. The best way to define the record format is to have fields already defined in the dictionary. Please refer to Fig. 11.2.

At the record level, the format specifies the name of the file containing the record format that you are referencing for this file. There are no field specifications allowed, but key field names are required.

You are allowed a 50-character description of the record. It is passed to the HLL (High-Level Language) on compile. More than 50 characters are allowed but not carried to other parts of the system.

Fields

Fields must be created through a similar process for dictionaries and formats. There are two basic types of fields that can be defined in the system: (1) character (2) and numeric (with four types).

Character fields can be defined in length from 1 to 32,766.

On the AS/400 there are four types of numeric fields:

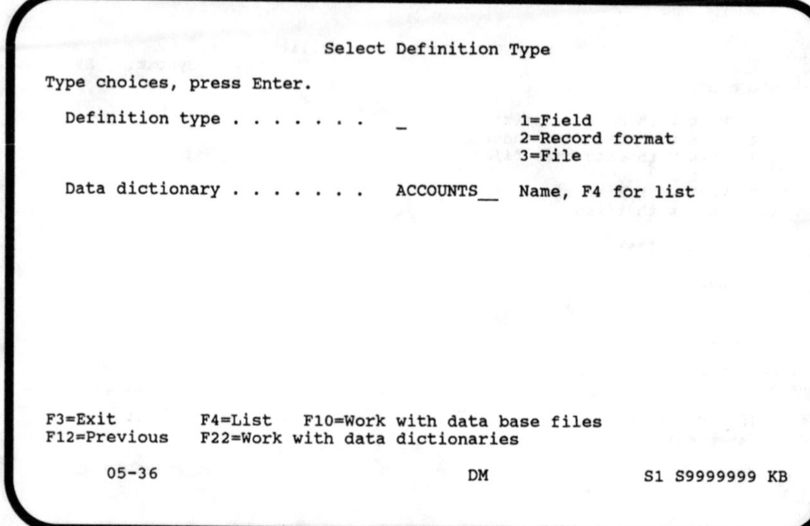

```
                    Select Definition Type
Type choices, press Enter.

  Definition type . . . . . . .   _            1=Field
                                               2=Record format
                                               3=File

  Data dictionary . . . . . . .   ACCOUNTS__   Name, F4 for list







F3=Exit        F4=List   F10=Work with data base files
F12=Previous   F22=Work with data dictionaries

      05-36                        DM                  S1 S9999999 KB
```

Figure 11.2 Create and select field definitions.

1. Zoned
2. Packed
3. Binary
4. Floating point

For all field types, IDDU lets you predefine the column headings for field use, numeric editing qualities, comments, and keyboard shift information. These include signs, leading zero information, decimal point definitions, and field lengths.

Up to seven key fields can be specified.

Database

The database created through IDDU will be fully documented and will outline all of the relationships present. IDDU database must have files, record formats, and fields.

11.3 DATA DICTIONARY

The first step in using IDDU (although it is not the first menu option) is the data dictionary. Creation of the dictionary requires a name located in a specific library and definition of the default authority for the dictionary.

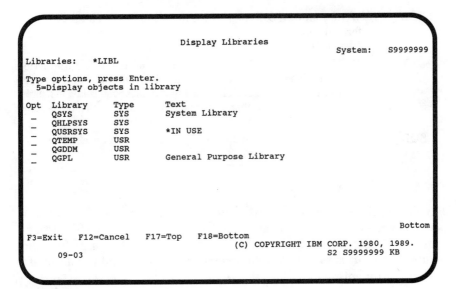

```
                        Display Libraries
                                                   System:   S9999999
Libraries:    *LIBL

Type options, press Enter.
  5=Display objects in library

Opt  Library      Type      Text
 _   QSYS         SYS       System Library
 _   QHLPSYS      SYS
 _   QUSRSYS      SYS       *IN USE
 _   QTEMP        USR
 _   QGDDM        USR
 _   QGPL         USR       General Purpose Library

                                                               Bottom
F3=Exit   F12=Cancel   F17=Top   F18=Bottom
                                  (C) COPYRIGHT IBM CORP. 1980, 1989.
     09-03                                     S2 S9999999 KB
```

Figure 11.3 DSPLIB display.

Using the display library function (CL Command DSPLIB), choose which library to use (see Fig. 11.3).

Maintenance

This is the most difficult part of use of IDDU. Each time the database is altered, the data present in the current database must be copied into another file, the dictionary altered, and the data mapped back into the new database. As you can guess, this can be a very time-consuming process.

For the novice, there is a very clear path—IDDU. IDDU allows full access to all of the functionality of the built-in AS/400 system through prompting. For the experienced user, IDDU will be cumbersome and less flexible than definition of your own DDS.

In addition to DDS and IDDU, files can be created through:

CRTPF	create physical file
SQL	tables
Query	as output from another file

File definition methodologies

CRTPF — Use the CL command with RCDLEN parameter to create a file. This method is OK for a quick definition of a file, but does not offer much flexibility in terms of field definitions and edits.

DDS — Write your own DDS using SEU and compile the database object for full control over fields, edit codes, etc. This requires knowledge of DDS coding techniques as well as SEU.

IDDU — Use IDDU to step through the menus and create a data dictionary and dependent databases. Data is normalized and screens aid in the definition of fields, edits, and database relations. This method makes it cumbersome to change field definitions as compared to the DDS method.

SQL — Use SQL CREATE TABE command to create a database.

11.4 SUMMARY

Typically, the AS/400 offers several ways to get to the same result: the creation of a database. You can use IDDU to walk through the system-provided screens and create a data dictionary, databases, fields, and edits. Data refers to the data dictionary for formats, and the database is self-documenting.

Alternately, you can write your own DDS and compile it into a database. With practice, this method will prove to be more efficient, faster, and more flexible than the IDDU method. However, you do not benefit from the self-documenting features of the IDDU method, and data is not automatically formatted by reference. Nevertheless, the DDS method is preferred by most programmers.

Chapter

12

Creating Screens and Menus with Screen Design Aid (SDA)

Screen Design Aid (SDA), which is part of the Application Development Tools package, provides an easy-to-use interface to design, create, and maintain displays, menus, and online help screens to use with programs you develop. One of the first things to know about SDA is that there are currently three versions available to you:

AS/400 environment. This environment is used to develop and process displays to be used in the AS/400 environment.

System/38 environment. This version also allows development of displays to be used on the System/38 or in the System/38 environment of the AS/400 system. You can also use this version to process displays migrated from the System/38 System.

System/36 environment. This version is used to develop displays for a System/36 or the System/36 environment of the AS/400 System.

You can use Screen Design Aid for menus and displays which collectively are refered to as *screens,* and to create online help in all but the System/38 environment. As with all other environments on the AS/400, the system is accessed through a series of menu options. The displays define the screens a user works with when using an application program.

12.1 STARTING SDA

Type STRSDA at the command line to start SDA.

When you work with SDA, you need to understand the relationship between display files, records, and fields. A display file contains one or more records. Each record specifies all the characteristics of one display. Each display is composed of fields, which are designated as input, output, or both (input and output). SDA defines some of the common terms in a slightly different way.

SDA uses the term *field* in two ways:

1. In relation to DDS, *field* refers to the item you specify for defining your display.
2. In relation to database files, the term field refers to items that you define for storing your data.

SDA uses the term *record* in two different ways:

1. Within DDS, all the fields on a display are grouped together and called a record. To DDS, a record represents a display. When you create a display, SDA asks you for a record name to be used for the display. After you compile your DDS to create a display file, you reference each display in the display file by its record name. When you test a display file, SDA asks you for the record name within the display file you want to test.
2. Within a database file, a record consists of group of fields and their definitions. It is used to store data. The record itself resides inside a database file. When you retrieve field definitions from a database file, SDA will prompt for the name of the database record format in addition to the database file name.

SDA uses the term *file* in two different ways:

1. In reference to a display file, once SDA has generated the DDS statements from the displays you defined, you must compile the DDS so that you can use the display. The compile output is a compiled object, called a *display file.*
2. In reference to a database file, a file is used to store your data. The file used by SDA to store a DDS screen source member is known as a *source file.* The file you retrieve data definitions from is known as a *database file.*

A note about DDS: On the AS/400 system, displays are described by a language called Data Description Specifications. DDS defines databases as well as screens. The language consists of a special set of words to define the displays. These special words are called *keywords.*

DDS groups all the fields on the display into one record and all the records within a member into a file. Keywords that define a field are known as *field-level keywords;* keywords that define a display record are known as *record-level keywords;* and keywords that define the whole file (all the records) are known a *file-level keywords*.

There are a number of ways to start SDA, depending on the version you want to use. This chapter will address only the AS/400 SDA.

Type STRSDA on an AS/400 command line and press <Enter>. The Screen Design Aid menu appears (Fig. 12.1).

You can also start SDA by typing '17' (Change using SDA) next to a member of type MNUDDS, MNUCMD, or DSPF on the Work with Members on the PDM screen. Press <Enter>. You will go to either the Design Screens display or the Design Menus display, depending on the type of the member you selected.

12.2 MENUS

A menu is composed of the following two parts:

1. A display file
2. A set of commands associated with the menu options

In the AS/400 environment, the display file contains the menu image, a message file contains the commands, and a menu object contains the name of the display file and the message file.

```
                         AS/400 Screen Design Aid (SDA)
Select one of the following:

     1. Design screens
     2. Design menus
     3. Test display files










Selection or command
===> ____________________________________________________________________

F3=Exit   F4=Prompt   F9=Retrieve   F12=Cancel
                                       (C) COPYRIGHT IBM CORP. 1981, 1989.
     21-07                                             S2 S9999999 KB
```

Figure 12.1 SDA menu.

Designing the menu

A menu is a list of numbered options from which the user makes a selection. Each option is a brief description of the job that is run if the operator selects that number. The system runs the job associated with the option number on the menu.

The user needs only to know when and how to make a selection. In selecting an option number for a menu description, the user does not need to know any commands. Using menus can reduce the amount of typing and the chance of error.

If you are using AS/400 SDA, remember that the menus must be maintained through SDA, and the results cannot be predicted if the code is maintained in any other way than through SDA.

Creating the menu and its parts

An AS/400 menu definition consists of two different DDS source file members: the menu source member and the command source member. These members are automatically created by the SDA source file you specify. The menu source member paints the screen for the user, telling what the selector option number does and describing what appears on the display when the menu appears. This definition includes any descriptive text associated with an option number, the placement of the option numbers, and the name and title of the menu. The menu source also holds the online help source for the menu. The command source member tells the system which commands or statements to use to run a job when the operator selects an option number.

You cannot change the size of AS/400 menus, and menu names cannot be more than eight characters long. As an aid, rows 1 through 20 are a default menu outline that is consistent with IBM menu standards. You can change this default to anything that you want. All editing attributes and color characters are recognized in this area. The first position (row 1, column 1) of this area is reserved by SDA as an attribute byte. Any attempt to put something in this position results in a keyboard error.

Row 21 is the command line prompt. The text of the command line prompt can be changed to anything you want, up to a maximum of 38 characters. If you create a menu image that you want to use as a default, use the following example:

Type STRPDM and press <Enter>. The AS/400 Programming Development Manager (PDM) menu appears.

Select option 3 (Work with Members) and press <Enter>. The Specify Members to Work With display appears.

Type the file and library name that your menu is stored in and press <Enter>. The Work with Members Using PDM display appears.

Type a new name for the member and press <Enter>. The Work with Members Using PDM display appears.

Type 17, Change Using SDA, in the option column beside the new member, and press <Enter>. The Specified Menu Function display will appear.

Saving and compiling the menu

The following steps explain how you save and compile the menu image:

Press either <F3> or <F12> on the Specify Menu functions display to get the exit menus display as shown in Fig. 12.2.

The DDS member name is the name of your menu. The command member is the name of your menu with Q appended. You cannot change either of these names at this point because the naming convention is required by the menu function of SDA.

Using the primary predefined defaults for this display, the menu source will be presented.

Calling the menu

In order to use the menu created, look at the following example to help you with your menus. Unlike testing displays, you are actually running the commands when you test your menu.

Type GO menuname on the command line of the Screen Design Aid menu.

```
                              Exit Menus

File . . . . . . . :    QCLPSRC          DDS member . . . . . :    DAVE
  Library . . . . :       QGPL           Commands member . . . :   DAVEQQ

Type choices, press Enter.

  Save new or updated menu source . . .   Y             Y=Yes, N=No
    Source file . . . . . . . . . . . .   QCLPSRC___    Name
      Library . . . . . . . . . . . . .   QGPL______    Name, *LIBL, *CURLIB
    Text . . . . . . . . . . . . . . . .  ______________________________________
_____________
    Replace menu members . . . . . . . .  Y             Y=Yes, N=No


  Create menu objects  . . . . . . . . .  Y             Y=Yes, N=No
                                                        F4 for Prompt
    Object library . . . . . . . . . . .  QGPL______    Name, *CURLIB
    Replace menu objects . . . . . . . .  Y             Y=Yes, N=No


F3=Exit      F4=Prompt      F12=Cancel

      08-45                                             S2 S9999999 KB
```

Figure 12.2 Exit Menus display.

```
BACKUP                          AS/400 BACKUP MAIN MENU

Select one of the following:

     1. Sales files
     2. Inventory files
     3. Customer files
     4. System files
     5. Full Backup

     6. Signoff





Selection or command
===> ____________________________________________________________

F3=Exit   F4=Prompt   F9=Retrieve   F12=Previous
F13=User support      F16=Main menu

     20-07                               DM                  S1 S9999999 KB
```

Figure 12.3 Menu sample.

Press <Enter>. The menu is displayed as shown in Fig. 12.3.

When the menu appears, you can choose any of the options or command prompts. By using the <F3> prompt listed on the bottom, you can exit the menus.

12.3 SCREENS

Screens or simple displays are easily created. Be sure that you have the proper authority to call source files, for example, QDDSSRC, which is the IBM-supplied DDS source file.

A series of SDA displays are used to design and create displays as follows:

Screen Design Aid

Design Screens

Work with Screens

Select Field Keywords

Select Database Files

Select Database Records

Select Database Fields

Save DDS, Create Display File

Some of the SDA displays have special extensions to define special field indicators or long parameters. In such cases, the following apply:

- When indicators are allowed on a display, you can get to an indicators display by typing + in the indicators prompt anywhere in SDA.
- When duplicate keywords (such as INDTXT) are allowed, you can page through those keywords by typing + or – in the 'More . . .' prompt for the keyword.
- When long parameters are allowed (with the EDTWRD keyword), you can get extension space by typing + in the 'More . . .' prompt for the keyword. The 'More . . .' prompt is not displayed if the field length is shorter than the standard input field for the keyword.
- When you press <F3> on the display, you lose all the input from the display. SDA does no processing.
- Keywords that are not valid for the record or file type being processed do not appear on the displays.

Designing the screen layout

You can use the work screen to design your file maintenance and inquiry displays. The work screen appears with the field names you selected along the bottom. The file names you selected on the Select Database Fields display appear in multiple-field mode at the bottom of the work screen. The plus sign at the end of the field name list indicates there are more field names. Page down to display more field names.

Labels can easily be placed on the screen, next to database fields. Highlights, deletes, and other things can be placed on the screen and can be prompted using AS/400 help.

In addition, overlapping fields can be placed on the screen. Conditional indicators are easily manipulated and invoked through a menu-based work screen. Fields are moved and changed by typing a series of arrows in front of fields to be moved.

By specifying a cursor position, you place the cursor in a particular field each time the display appears.

The range limit allows checking types of numbers which users can type into fields.

A subfile is a group of records with the same record name. Subfile records and subfile control records can be used to examine and possibly change records and fields from a database file on a scrolling display. The subfile is defined in DDS (manual or SDA) and must be loaded, updated, and managed by the application program. The group or records in the subfile is read from and written to a display in a single operation. Subfiles are a rather complicated technique, and are beyond the scope of this book.

Display files, like every other part of application programming, require testing and modification.

Text and data fields

You can select fields from a database file to place at the bottom of the work screen. You then can use work-screen symbols to correctly position the fields on the work screen.

You can also use a ruler to line up fields on the work screen. <F14> acts like a switch: press it once to display the ruler, and press it again to remove the ruler.

Data types, input-output, field edits, and display attributes

You can assign display attributes to fields on the work screen to change a field's appearance (color, highlighting, and so on). You can also define your own fields instead of selecting them from the database file.

In addition, fields can be formatted, adding zeros and commas for example, for edit codes as well as plus and minus signs.

Use <F3> to exit, and the work screen is finished. Sample screens can then be viewed and reedited for the final touches.

Designing the online help

You can create online help information to supply explanations of displays or menus a user sees when running application programs. You can specify online help information for the AS/400 displays and menu you create.

You can define areas within the display, called *help areas.* Each help area is defined by a specification in the application format, called an H specification. Help areas provide information for users that can be kept on the system separate from the application program. You can add online help information to an existing application program by making changes to existing displays and creating help displays.

When the user presses <Help> on a display, the online help information you created for that display appears. The operator can page through the various help displays by using the <PageUp> and <PageDown> keys. The operator leaves the help function by pressing <Enter> and returning to the display. The display is left unchanged. This functionality is only available in the advanced program called SDA on the AS/400.

You can write help information at both the file and the field level. File-level help information is more general and defines the default help for the file. This information is specified directly on the Select Help Keywords display and appears when the user presses <Help> and the cursor is outside all of the defined help areas. You can define only one file-level help display.

Record-level help information is more specific. This information is specified on displays, and is associated with a field or a set of fields on the display. Online help information appears when the user presses <Help> and the cursor is in a defined help area. You can define more than one set of help displays per record.

Similarly, help information can easily be created for menu sources.

Use of symbols and attributes in SDA

Use the work screen symbols to move a field name or prompt from the bottom row of the work screen to where you want it to appear on the display. The following table lists symbols which can be used to import fields and headers to the display:

Single mode	Multiple-field mode	Meaning
&	&n	Place the database field and its associated attributes in this position.
&L	&nL	Place the database field in this position with the column heading to the left. Put a colon after the column heading. The column heading and the field heading are separated by two blanks.
&R	&nR	Place the database field in this position, with a column heading to the right. The column heading and field are separated by two blanks.
&C or :	&nC	Place the database field in this position with the column heading above the field. The column heading is left-aligned with alphabetic field and right-aligned with numeric fields.
&P	&nP	Place only the prompt for the database field in this position. Use the column heading for the prompt.

12.4 WRITING YOUR OWN SCREEN CODE

You may generate your own screens using the techniques of DDS coding (see Chap. 11).

Using SEU to generate DDS for screens

SDA automatically generates Data Description Specifications (DDS) code. However, you may prefer to work through SEU, writing your own source code for screen DDS and then compiling it. At first, it is advisable to use SDA to generate your screens. Then you can browse the source code that SDA writes to see how it is done. Use SEU to browse the code (using '5' to browse from the PDM menu, so you don't inadvertently change it).

Once you are familiar with the source techniques of screen DDS, you can copy one of these screens and change the source to generate your own screens, often more quickly than by using SDA. Remember to use a file type of DSPF for screen DDS, so that the compiler will know what to do with it. Otherwise, writing your own screen DDS is much like writing any other program. You edit the source from the PDM screen, using SEU, and then compile it into an object. Remember that when any screen is recompiled or changed, any programs which call it must also be recompiled to avoid level checks. The following is an example of DDS which defines a screen.

Define screen size, highlight, <Print> key active, <F3> key active with message at bottom of screen. <F3> will return indicator 99 set on if the user presses it.

```
A                                      DSPSIZ(24 80 *DS3)
A                                      CHGINPDFT(HI CS)
A                                      PRINT
A                                      CF03(99 'F3 = exit')
```

Record format name ORDSCR which is the name actually used to call the screen from a program in RPG or another AS/400 language.

```
A          R ORDSCR
```

Labels to go on screen at given row and column coordinates. Note the keyword COLOR(BLU) which makes 'F3 = Quit' appear in blue at the bottom of the screen (23 10).

```
A                                  1 22'ORDER ENTRY SCREEN'
A                                  4  3'Code:'
A                                  6  3'Qty:'
A                                  8  3'Price:'
A                                 10  3'Name:'
A                                 12  3'Address:'
A                                 14  3'City/State:'
A                                 23 10'F3=Quit'
A                                 COLOR(BLU)
```

Fields to go on screen at given row and column coordinates. Fields are named and defined as to type:

```
A          CODE           2    B  4 16COLOR(TRQ)
```

2 char, both input and ouput, at row 4 column 16, color is turquoise.

```
A          QTY            3Y 0B  6 16COLOR(TRQ)
```

3-byte zoned number (Y), no decimals, both input and output at row 6, column 16.

```
A       PRICE         6Y 2B  8 16EDTCDE(4)
```

6-byte zoned number, two decimals, both input and output, EDTCDE (edit code) is 4 (no leading zeros, trailing minus sign).

```
A       CSTNAM        25    B 10 16COLOR(TRQ)
A       ADD1          25    B 12 16COLOR(TRQ)
A       ADD2          25    B 14 16COLOR(TRQ)
```

Menus are most easily created through SDA.

Passing data to and from programs

Parameter passing to and from programs is handled in much the same way as is database handling. Any variable or field known to the screen is also known to the calling program by name and need not be defined in the program.

Calling the screen

Once a screen is coded and compiled, it may be called from a variety of other programs. CLP, RPG, and COBOL can all call screens designed with SDA or DDS.

RPG screen call. The screen's file name must have been defined in the F specs as a Combined, Full-procedural File (CF).

```
SCREEN   CF      E    WORKSTN    (declare the screen)
EXFMTscr                         (call the screen)
```

The EXFMT call refers to the format name of the screen, not the file name.

CLP screen call

```
DCLF    screen  /* declare the screen */
SNDRCVF scr     /* call the screen */
```

The DCLF statement refers to the file name of the screen, while the SNDRCVF statement calls the format name of the screen.

12.5 SUMMARY

According to IBM, SDA offers several advantages over traditional methods of designing displays:

- It generates Data Description Specifications (DDS). You do not need extensive knowledge of the DDS coding forms, keywords, or syntax to use SDA.

- It presents displays in functional groups to make DDS keyword selections easier at the file, record, or field level.
- It allows you to select fields from existing database files to design displays.
- It allows you to see the display you are designing or changing as you work on it.
- It allows you to test displays with the data and status of the condition indicators specified for each test.
- It allows you to create menus as well as the message files (for AS/400 environment SDA) or the control language (CL) programs (for the System/38 environment SDA) required to run the menus.
- It allows you to create a display file from the DDS source statements SDA creates.
- It supplies error messages with explanations. Diagnostics are supplied for conflicting source statements when selection of DDS keywords occurs.

Chapter

13

Tools

The AS/400 is a platform which uses extensive and diverse software products. Some of these are from IBM and some are from third-party vendors. The initial software configuration of an AS/400 will probably miss out on some useful and important tools which can improve on ease of use and funcionality of the system. Communications as well as Graphical User Interface and database access can be enhanced by the use of these tools. Selected tools are presented in this chapter.

13.1 QUSRTOOL

The AS/400 is shipped with a library called QUSRTOOL, which has source code for various useful utilities and commands. These are not a part of the standard set of OS/400 commands, but are provided by IBM as a toolbox of optional useful functions. They are coded in RPG, PL/1, and Pascal and must be compiled before you can use them. These routines are exemplary in that they show you how you can develop your own system programs to help with managing your AS/400 and developing applications. QPGMR can access these files in QUSRTOOL through PDM. A source file called QATTINFO in QUSRTOOL contains member AAAMAP, which is IBM's listing and documentation of the tools found in this library. Print it out to see names and descriptions of additional functions available in this library. The source files are:

QATTCL	CL source
QATTCMD	command definitions
QATTDDS	DDS source
QATTINFO	documentation of QUSRTOOL
QATTPAS	Pascal source
QATTPL1	PL/1 source
QATTRPG	RPG source

QUSRTOOL is grouped into seven functional categories:

1. PC Support Configuration Tools, to create and change PC Support objects for SDLC, Token-Ring, and twin-axial connections
2. Graphics Tools, to convert graphics into GDDM format and produce output
3. Group Jobs Made Easy, to facilitate group jobs
4. Menu Work Management Functions, to provide a menu for work management function access
5. Storage Space Management Tools, to manage DASD utilization and cleanup
6. Example Communications Configurations, to show how to configure and change communications from a menu
7. Programming Tips and Techniques, to provide examples of programs and routines to be used in application development

Since the source code in QUSRTOOL is replaced by future releases, copy them to a user library for modification and compiling. QUSRTOOL contains examples of some of the more creative solutions to AS/400 problems.

13.2 CODE/400

IBM says, "AD/Cycle CODE/400 provides cohesive edit, compile, and debug facilities, operating in a window environment on an IBM PS/2 workstation in cooperation with a System/370 or AS/400 host." Cooperative Development Environment (CODE/400) is IBM's implementation of OS/2's Presentation Manager as a development environment for AS/400 applications. This strategy takes advantage of the graphics capabilities of OS/2, and the PC in general, to enhance and facilitate application development tasks such as editing code and debugging systems. Although the AS/400 provides adequate tools in the form of SEU and Debug, CODE/400 offers some advantages over the AS/400 platform. Among these is the fact that program development can largely be relegated to the PC. The AS/400 is still required, however, to perform final compiling, one of the most CPU-intensive aspects of program development. CODE/400 has a precompiler which performs syntax and variable checking. Relatively clean code can thus be submitted to the AS/400, reducing the number of AS/400 compiles.

There are three major components to CODE/400: the Editor, DDS Design Utility (DSU), and the Debug Tool:

The Editor combines a PC word-processing feel with SEU's knowledge of source types and syntax checking. You can edit source files which reside on the AS/400 or on the PC. You only need to resort to OS/400 for compiling. Pull-down menus and such PC features as Cut and Paste are available for source editing. Color (Token Highlighting) is used to highlight different kinds of lines and components in the source code, making deciphering RPG much easier, for example. Online help is extensive in pop-up windows. You can set up an interactive error list in a window so that you can monitor errors as they occur, as the result of code verification, precompile, or actual AS/400 compile. Click on the error with the mouse and an extensive explanation appears. CODE/400 performs syntax checking like SEU, as well as program verification and precompiling. AS/400 objects such as files are checked to verify field references. The precompiler does not actually create the executable program, but it does reveal many of the problems which need to be fixed, reducing the AS/400's share of program development in most cases to the final compile.

The DDS Design Utility (DSU) makes database design easier and faster, using the GUI interface of OS/2. Especially for screen and report design, the WYSIWYG features can expedite development dramatically, while taking some of the real drudgery out of it. Using the mouse, you can now literally paint screens and reports using click and drag techniques. No longer do you need to know what column a title occupies on a screen, counting the spaces. Just put it where you want it visually. All features of DDS, including keywords and subfiles, can be implemented more easily with the mouse than by coding DDS in SEU. You can scroll through lists of available database fields and pop them onto the screen where you want them. If a field is the wrong size, just click on it and drag it to the right size. Help text windows are defined by clicking upper-left and lower-right coordinates. You can set on indicators to see what would happen to the screen or report as if a program had set them.

The Debug Tool is a major advance over the AS/400 facilities of STRDBG, ADDBKP and ADDTRC. Once the program is compiled on the AS/400, you can use the Debug Tool to provide a wealth of information about program execution. It will step through the program, showing the program variables changing in a window as the various breakpoints are reached. This is an extremely powerful tool which allows you to interact with the application through windows. The Command/Log window has a command line for issuing Debug commands. The Debug Frame window shows the parts of the program. The Source window has the source code listing. The Step/Run window allows access to the Step and Run features to start and stop the program at the various points. The Global/Local Monitor Lists show the current states of various variables at different program points. In a window, you can view or modify variables at any point in the program.

Hardware requirements for CODE/400 include an 80386 or greater PC processor, minimum of 10 Mb of RAM and 60 Mb of disk. It will run better with more, however; for example, 15 Mb RAM and 120 Mb disk. Extended edition 1.3 of OS/2 or higher is also required, as well as PC Support and a Token-Ring (TRLAN), twinax, or SDLC connection. V2R1M1 of OS/400, ADT, and current PTFs are also necessary. CODE/400 consists of a PC component at the workstation and an AS/400 component, priced according to your model.

13.3 ADVANCED FUNCTION PRINTING

Advanced Function Printing (AFP) enables the connection of the AS/400 to high-speed page printers. A variety of sophisticated capabilities and options are provided such as multiple-up printing, S/370 automated print routing, electronic forms, S/370 LINE Data PAGEDEF support, and more. A mixture of text, vector data, and imaging is generated automatically as an object-oriented data stream. Four types of printed output supported are Native AS/400 (from AS/400), Advanced Function Printing Data Stream (AFPDS from AS/400 or S/370), and LINE Data and AFPDSLINE (from S/370). A number of printers are supported, mostly laser IPDS printers, connected by Twinax, SDLC, and Token-Ring. Many fonts and styles, as well as graphics, are implemented by AFP. You can create overlays using PC GUI to merge with application data on the AS/400 to generate sophisticated documents. AFP can print simplex, duplex, tumble, overlay electronic forms, and specify paper bins, among other capabilities. Print Manager/400, a function of OS/400, allows you to create applications which are portable to other SAA platforms. Included in the AFP package are three utilities called AFP Utilities/400:

1. The Overlay Utility can generate graphics overlays interactively.
2. The Print Format Utility is an interactive report generator. Menus allow the creation of text and data merge in a Print Format Definition (PFD).
3. The Resource Manager Utility controls overlays and page segments, allowing copy, rename, delete, etc.

13.4 MULTIMEDIA HOST SUPPORT/400

This product interacts with a multimedia presentation on the PC, taking advantage of the graphics capabilities of that platform in a sophisticated connection with AS/400-driven applications. Video, images, and sound may be produced for help, documentation, or product descriptions. Touchscreen buttons can be set up for use with the application and the multimedia presentation images. A wide selection of display fonts is available. Up to four national languages may be invoked for any given application. Multimedia objects may be displayed in a window on the 5250 type terminal. While the PS/2 handles the graphics application, the AS/400 provides the database handling, using each machine for its best features in true distributed processing. In short, you can set up a multimedia front end on the PC or PS/2 for accessing the AS/400. At the touch of a button, a terminal can now call up pictures and sounds from an AS/400 application. Through PC Support, tables are downloaded to the PC to communicate with PS/2 programs, which can access multimedia objects from disk and display them. The PS/2 makes use of run-time modules installed in shared folders on the AS/400. Requirements include a MicroChannel 386 PS/2, DOS 5.0, 2 Mb of memory, a VGA monitor, an M-Motion card, PC Support, and a videodisk player.

13.5 FACSIMILE SUPPORT

Facsimile Support/400 brings fax right into the AS/400 database. Again, the PC serves as the interface or front end to the AS/400. But it is only used as a communications controller to the telephone lines. The application is resident on the AS/400. The PC contains printer microcode to emulate the IBM 3816 printer, a remote Advanced Function Printer (AFP). AFP Utilities/400 features which can be output to a 3816 printer can also be incorporated into faxes. Faxes are spooled, just like printer output, and can be controlled in the same way. QFFSNDFAX is the output queue for faxes where they can be held, released, deleted, or prioritized. The application can create a local Intellegent Printer Data Stream (IPDS) and use the SNDFAX command to spool the fax. SNDFAX allows you to send the fax immediately or later. Incoming faxes are treated as scanner data, and stored in a database file on the AS/400 as members. They can be printed to IBM printers or displayed on a PC as Revisable Form Text Document Content Architecture (RFT:DCA) in a shared folder. It is not really revisable, though, because it is not character-based, it is an image. Up to 60 telephone lines can be configured for simultaneous use with Facsimile Support/400.

This feature requires a 386 or 486 MicroChannel PC, OS/2. This may be attached to the AS/400 through Token-Ring, Ethernet, or twinax. Also, you must have a FaxConcentrator Adaptor/A internal fax modem. Software consists of a PC module and the usual tier-priced AS/400 component.

13.6 WSRIPL/400

Workstation Remote IPL is a way to control LAN stations which exist on a Token-Ring. Instead of using local disk drives on the Programmable Work Stations (PWS), a diskette image on the AS/400's disk storage is set up to appear as local disk to the PWS. In this way, the network administrator can access all of the local PC software in a central location (the AS/400). You don't have to run around the office trying to update everyone's software at lunchtime or after hours. This scheme brings the local PC disks under AS/400 security measures, a much more effective environment for preventing software incompatibilities, inconsistencies, or abuses. Connecting another PS/2 to the Token-Ring with WSRIPL is simply a matter of plugging it in. WSRIPL will automatically configure it when it is turned on, making AS/400 diskette image software available to it.

13.7 WINDOWTOOL/400

This tool allows you to create windows on the AS/400 without going through all the trouble of DDS, CL, and/or RPG. Interfaces which support Common User Access (CUA) standards can be created. Pop-up menus, action bars, database pop-up windows, and help boxes can be created. PCs can be set up with mouse or touchscreen interfaces. This feature allows you to set up PC-like, Windows-like environments as front ends for AS/400 applications. Navigate menus, call programs, and interact with the user through CUA screens instead of the AS/400 look. WindowTool/400 can be integrated with Rumba/400 (see following) to enhance the Windows effects.

13.8 IMAGEPLUS

ImagePlus satisfies the image processing needs of a business by providing the standard features of imaging. You can scan a document, import a document, and print a document. Also, you can store, index, and retrieve documents. ImagePlus is implemented through special imaging Application Program Interfaces (APIs) which may be called from RPG or COBOL programs. DOS or OS/2 can be used at the PC to provide cooperative image processing functions, using the PC for much of the CPU-intensive imaging work.

Requirements include ImagePlus Workfolder Application Facility (WAF), a MicroChannel 386 PS/2, PS/2 Token-Ring Adapter/A, PS/2 ImagePlus Workstation Programs, VGA display, and printer and scanner options.

13.9 CALLPATH/400

CallPath/400 uses Application Programming Interfaces to integrate AS/400 applications and data with voice and telephone services. The AS/400 can communicate through CallPath/400 with private branch exchange (PBX) switches. Intelligent answering is supported as well as consultation and voice and data transfer. When someone calls in, the AS/400 can look up their file automatically, based on a taped question and telephone keypad answer. When the operator answers the phone, the AS/400 can already have the relevant file up on the screen, and can even set up a transfer of the call and consultation with another phone. CallPath/400 supports Integrated Services Digital Network (ISDN) protocols to enable dialing from a database and selective answering strategies based on what happens on the other end.

13.10 APPLICATION PROGRAM DRIVER

IBM provides the Application Program Driver (APD) tool to help with customizing AS/400 application user interfaces. Menu Creation and Control aids in providing consistent, friendly menus with help for running applications. Multiple Installation Support, Security, Application Installation, Save/Restore, Batch Job Scheduling/Control, Restart Monitoring, and Conflict Management are also included. Menus can easily be set up with security to ensure that only authorized users are allowed access to desired functions. Fastpath commands allow users to go directly to a function without stepping through menus.

13.11 BUSINESS GRAPHICS UTILITY

Business Graphics Utility (BGU) is an IBM package which adds graphics to AS/400 applications for reports and presentations. Colorful charts of many types can be created with BGU for display on screen or printing with any graphics-capable IPDS printer. Line graphs, bar charts, and histograms, as well as Venn diagrams and pie charts with cross sections, all in color, can be created. You can control the size of characters and draw boxes. BGU supports up to eight plotter pens, automatic paper feeding, output rotation, and manual override of spool parameters. Color monitors supported include 5292-2 Color Display Station for the AS/400 or VGA PC monitors.

13.12 PERFORMANCE TOOLS/400

This IBM utility is a powerful set of functions which can show you exactly how efficiently your system is running. It collects and displays data on the performance of the AS/400 and helps you to analyze the data and manage the system. The Performance Advisor makes recommendations to improve the performance of the current system, and can implement them if you so wish. PT/400 lets you work through a series of menus to get to screens which show graphics representations of the current system workload over a period of time. You can monitor throughput, response times at a local or remote site, DASD usage, and communications statistics. Diagnostic reports are generated and can be viewed on the terminal or printed. The system can be viewed as a whole or in sections. The Capacity Planning Function lets you ask the question "What if . . ." in relation to new applications and hardware. This tool is quite valuable in achieving maximum performance from an existing system configuration. It is available in a less expensive starter version as Performance Tools Subset/400 for smaller systems.

13.13 SYSTEMS ADMINISTRATION TOOLS/400

IBM provides Systems Administration Tools/400 (SAT/400) to help with the management of AS/400 at multiple sites. The Central System Administration Tools run at the central site, and Distributed Systems Administration Tools run on the remote system. Change Management, Distribution Mangement, Problem Management, Configuration Management, and Asset Management are all features of SAT/400. You can also use this tool to control the distribution of files, applications, PTFs, network resources, hardware, software, and data through the network. Many other functions, such as password management and passthrough session tracking, are included. This package can help to reduce the time required to track multiple systems.

13.14 IQ

Interactive Query (IQ) is a Query/400-like SQL-based report generator which offers several advantages over Query/400. Like Query, IQ offers file joins, result fields, field and record selection, sorts and breaks, and report formatting. Output may be to a report or to another file. However, IQ also allows conditional result fields, a valuable feature. Conditional result fields allow you to create a user-defined field based on values in the database. For instance, you might want to create a field called DISCOUNT which contains 10 percent of the AMOUNT field *if* the amount field is over $1000. You can't do this with Query/400 (it's the *if* part you can't do). This feature comes in handy in any number of situations. Also, you can join files on a result field, another valuable ability. IQ provides the ability to pass parameters into the query from a CL program so that you can automate the running of queries from a menu, reflecting different months or regions, or whatever parameters are passed in from CL. These parameters can be used for sorts, breaks, and in the report headers. Break-level calculations are available, as well as date arithmetic, data-type conversions from alpha to numeric and numeric to alpha, and downloading reports to PC applications. These few additional features make IQ an effective and powerful tool for report generation on the AS/400.

13.15 DBU

Data Base Utility can be used with AS/400 databases as a superior alternative to IBM's Data File Utility (DFU). DBU allows you to browse a database in multiple- or single-record mode. You can easily go to a record number or perform a key search. Records can be added, changed, or deleted with the touch of a function key. You can select fields and order the way they appear on screen. In addition, you can look at all of the available access paths (logical files) which are built on the particular physical file being viewed. Shown here are all of the parameters which define the logical files, including keys and select/omit specifications. Just enter an 'X' next to one of these logical files on the display to begin using this file in DBU. It is easy to switch between field selections and logical views of files. DBU provides a quick access into AS/400 databases for interactive record queries or updates.

13.16 RUMBA/400

RUMBA/400 from Wall Data was developed in conjunction with IBM according to AS/400 Application Program Interfaces (APIs). Offered as an add-on to PC support, it provides cooperative processing in the form of a dialogue manager. RUMBA operates from a shared folder on the AS/400, just like PC Support. Through Windows 3.0 GUI-based architecture and PC Support, RUMBA makes calls on AS/400 applications to access midrange data. Scroll bars, icons, and push buttons are the familiar components of the RUMBA interface. File transfer between the PC and AS/400 or S/370 is available as a menu option of Version 2.2

along with auto-sign-on to the AS/400. As with other Windows products, RUMBA allows you to shrink the AS/400 session in a sizable graphics window and move it around the screen, or it can be turned into an icon for later retrieval. Now the AS/400 has become just another item on the Windows desktop ready to be accessed when needed.

You can click the mouse on the AS/400 function key descriptions or on menu options to execute them. Macros are included to allow you to script interaction with the AS/400 and to run PC programs. You can read screen positions, determine responses to various messages, and set up entire transactions with the AS/400 as if you were picking options, hitting function keys, and answering messages. A QuickStep drop-down menu can then be set up so that you can press a button on it and execute your macros. Any customization can be saved in a PC configuration file so that it can be invoked in the future when you start RUMBA. Using Dynamic Data Exchange (DDE) in conjunction with RUMBA's Hotlinks, you can cut and paste data back and forth between the AS/400 and the PC Windows Clipboard into RUMBA. RUMBA allows you to open up multiple AS/400 sessions and even 3270 sessions and size them in various windows around the PC screen. This is truly an SAA application with the PC, the AS/400, and the S/370 running in windows on a programmable workstation (PWS). When you use RUMBA to check your mail in Office, you see a mailbox with the little red flag up if you have mail. Just open it up and take out your letters.

Additional tools are available from Wall Data for RUMBA. Tools for the Administrator lets the RUMBA administrator manage RUMBA profiles. Tools for DDE let you set up advanced data links to the AS/400. Tools for EHLLAPI enable Windows and C applications to exchange data with RUMBA. Tools for Toolbook enables the use of the Asymetrix Toolbook to create graphics alterations and applications for screens (to make the AS/400 look like a PC).

Twinax, asynchronous, SDLC, Token-Ring, or Ethernet connections suffice to communicate with the host. It is recommended that you use plenty of resources to run this product through Windows, more than Wall Data suggests. An 80386 machine with 4 Mb or more of RAM and 40 Mb of disk would be the minimum for satisfactory performance of any Windows task-swapping procedure.

13.17 SHOWCASE VISTA

ShowCase VISTA provides PC to AS/400 database access, using the PC as a front end. Microsoft Windows or any Dynamic Data Exchange (DDE) applications can be integrated. Excel or Lotus 1-2-3 for Windows or Microsoft Word can interface with the AS/400 through VISTA to allow data retrieval from the midrange host. Query functions are implemented to the AS/400 databases, including SQL interface, query timers, user prompts, control breaks, and subtotal capability. It is possible to set up spreadsheets, using this product, which contain formulas that access SQL/400 queries. In this way, the PC is used as a familiar front end to AS/400 data. An executive who is familiar with spreadsheet usage can access AS/400 databases without even knowing how to sign on. This is a user-friendly approach for making the AS/400 Database Manager available from a PC application front end for those users familiar with PC practices.

13.18 EMERALD EMULATION

As a less expensive alternative to the Token-Ring/PC Support PC connection, Emerald can be used to provide a twinax workstation connection through gateways. NetLynx and PCLynx are the components of this configuaration. Netlynx runs at the gateway, while PClynx runs at the workstation. Local, remote, and even DEC connections can be set up through Netlynx. Address pooling allows users to sign on to the next available gateway (AS/400) session without allocating specific sessions to individual users. This saves on gateway resources and ports.

In this configuration, a PC is used as a gateway to set up seven sessions to the AS/400. The AS/400 sees only seven normal 5250 terminals attached, while the gateway PC translates protocol for seven other PCs on the network to perform 5250 terminal and printer emulation and file transfer. Also available from Emerald is Emerald Transfer Utility (ETU) which performs file transfers to and from the host. The connection software for each individual station can be installed on the network, so that all PCs can log on to the network and access a standard, centralized version instead of having local versions on everyone's hard drive. No Token-Ring card or PC Support is necessary. It should be noted, however, that some specialized functions designed to work with PC Support will not be available.

13.19 PATHFINDER

Pathfinder is a utility package for the AS/400 which offers a number of useful techniques and facilities. Among these are a network configuration utility and an object cross-reference. You can scan source files to find strings and can also find unreferenced objects. Mass program create is a useful feature in application development. Also contained are job explosion, flow charts, outfiles, file analysis, APIs, user-defined options, field cross-reference, object last used, and spacing charts.

13.20 SUMMARY

Many tools are available from IBM and third-party vendors to enhance the functionality of the AS/400. Graphics and PC-based Graphics User Interface (GUI) applications are rapidly bringing the AS/400 into the Windows world complete with pop-up and pull-down menus and push buttons for the mouse. Utilities are available to ease input, update, and output of reports on the AS/400 as an alternative to writing code. Performance, communications, and multiple sites can be managed much more easily with the aid of some of these tools. Take the time to become familiar with the existing and constantly emerging tools for the system in order to maximize the efficiency and ease of use of your installation.

Part

3

Languages

Chapter

14

RPG/400

14.1 OVERVIEW OF RPG/400

RPG is an acronym for Report Program Generator, and this was initially its function—to create reports. But it can be used for a variety of purposes, including I/O and screen calls, so that entire systems can be written in RPG. It is somewhat idiosyncratic. But the learning curve is not very long and, once is has become familiar, it is a quick and powerful development tool. RPG is the primary development language used on the AS/400.

Columns

RPG is, more than any other language, column-oriented. That is, everything in an RPG program must be in the correct column or it will generate a syntax error. This seems to be an arbitrary feature, at first, but the fact that SEU (Chap. 10) knows RPG syntax is extremely helpful. The prompt key <F4> in SEU will provide a fill-in-the-blanks screen for RPG commands, making it unnecessary for the programmer to know much about which column things go in.

Probably the main disadvantage of RPG's column requirements is the inability to indent loops and logic blocks, making RPG difficult to read and maintain later. All commands must begin in the same column. So, which END goes with which IF? The compile listing offers some help here, as we shall see in Chap. 20, "Debugging."

The sample program which we provide will provide an order entry screen for the user and update an order entry file.

14.2 SECTIONS AND SPECIFICATIONS

14.2.1 Sections

RPG programs are written in sections, called *specifications,* which must occur in order and are identified by a letter in column 6:

H	Header specs	program identification
F	File specs	file definitions
E	Extension specs	array declaration
I	Input specs	further data definitions, data structures, renames
C	Calc specs	the commands and main program
O	Output specs	report writing

Note, in the following sample RPG program, that each line of code begins with a letter (H, F, or C) in column 6. This is how RPG knows what type of line is being coded, and how SEU knows what type of prompting and syntax checking to do for you. A comment is indicated by an asterisk in column 7. It is not important at this stage to understand all of this code; just look it over for the different types of specs and the column-oriented format. We will go through it in detail later.

```
H* INPUT ORDERS
H*
FORDER  UF E           K            DISK            A
FORDDSP CF E                        WORKSTN
C*
C            LOOP    TAG
C*
C                    MOVE *BLANK    CODE
C                    MOVE *BLANK    CSTNAM
C                    MOVE *BLANK    ADD1
C                    MOVE *BLANK    ADD2
C                    Z-ADD0         QTY
C                    Z-ADD0         PRICE
C*
C                    EXFMTORDSCR
C*
C           *IN99    IFEQ '1'
C                    GOTO END
C                    END
C*
C            CODE    CHAINORDER             77
```

```
C          QTY    MULT PRICE     TOT
C*
C          *IN77  IFNE '1'
C                 UPDATORD
C                 ELSE
C                 WRITEORD
C                 END
C*
C                 GOTO LOOP
C*
C          END    TAG
C                 SETON                      LR
```

Advantages. RPG is terse and efficient. It does a lot of the work for you in terms of I/O and reports. Its data manipulation structures are flexible and useful. It is quick to write.

Limitations. Maintaining or rereading RPG can be difficult because of the lack of indentation in the source code. For this reason, it is important to document the code fully. Also, complex calculations or logical tests can be difficult in RPG.

14.2.2 Specifications

RPG is coded in different sections, each with its own type of specification.

Header specs

The first type of spec coded in an RPG program is the header spec. While the header is optional, it provides identifying information about the program and should be included. You may specify your name, the program name, and a description of the program's function. The '*' in the seventh position indicates a comment line.

```
H*  INPUT ORDERS
```

File specs

File specs are critical to an RPG program. They identify each externally defined file to be referenced by the program, and indicate what its function will be. Remember that screens are considered to be files, just like physical files and logical files. The following two file specs identify, to the RPG program, a data file and a screen file:

```
FORDER   UF  E        K           DISK           A
FORDDSP  CF  E                    WORKSTN
```

Many things must be defined about the files in the file specs. Here is a breakdown of the first foregoing file spec:

F	Indicates that this is a File spec.
ORDER	The filename.
U	File will be used for Update.
F	File is Full procedural, can be used for chaining, updates, adds, deletes, etc.
E	File is defined Externally to RPG (in DDS).
K	File is keyed. The AS/400 will recognize which keys were defined in the DDS for this file and will automatically maintain the index.
DISK	File resides on disk.
A	Records can be added to this file.

Note that, since RPG expects certain parameters in specific columns, you do not have to separate these parameters with blanks. RPG knows what the entry means because of the column it is in. This helps to give RPG its run-on aspect, where commands run into parameters without blanks in-between. In fact, sometimes a blank in a specific column has a particular meaning for RPG, as we shall see later.

It is extremely important to define accurately the files you need to use, as to type and program function, or the program will not work. In fact, it probably will not even compile with bad file specs. The important things to remember are:

- The file name (up to eight characters) immediately follows the F spec.
- Next is the file usage:

I	input
O	output
IP	input primary
UF	update full procedural (for chaining or finds)
CF	combined full procedural (for screens)

All of this is made much easier by SEU, which will provide you with a fill-in-the-blanks prompt screen after you type in the 'F' to column 6, so that SEU knows what type of RPG spec to prompt for. See Fig. 14.1, an SEU Prompt Screen for File Specs.

Extension specs

Extension specs have an 'E' in column 6 and are used to define run-time arrays. Since our sample program is fairly simple, we do not have a run-time array, but if we did it would be defined like this:

```
Columns . . . .:   1  71              Edit                     USRLIB/QRPGSRC
Find . . .      ________________________________________             ORDR
FMT *   ..... *. 1 ...+... 2 ...+... 3 ...+... 4 ...+... 5 ...+... 6 ...+... 7
        *************** Beginning of data ****************************************
0001.00        H*  INPUT ORDERS
0002.00        H*
0003.00        FORDER   UF  E              K          DISK                    A
0004.00        FORDDSP  CF  E                         WORKSTN
0005.00        C*

Prompt type . . .    FX      Sequence number . . .   0003.00

              File       File            End of                   File
Filename      Type     Designation        File      Sequence     Format
ORDER___       U          F                _           _           E

 Mode of              Record
Processing         Address Type        Device        Continuation
    _                   K              DISK___            _
                           File           File
 Exit      Entry         Addition       Condition
______    ______            A              __

F3=Exit                      F4=Prompt                  F5=Refresh
F10=Top                      F11=Bottom                 F24=More keys

      14-02                               DM              S1          KB
```

Figure 14.1 SEU prompt screen for file specs.

```
E            NAME     25  1
```

The preceding defines a 25-element array with 1 byte in each element to contain a variable called NAME. Array elements could be referenced in the program by array name and element number as: NAME,3.

Input specs

Input specs, like extension specs, are used for further internal definition of the data for the RPG program. Redefines or data structures may be accomplished with input specs. Again, our little program does not require input specs, but they look like this:

Redefine variables A, B, and C as elements of array X for input screen USRSCR

```
IUSRSCR
I            A            X,1
I            B            X,2
I            C            X,3
```

Set up data structure to break down variable TIME into HRS and MNS where HRS is position 1–2 of TIME and MNS is 3–4

```
I       DS
I                     1  4 TIME
I                     1  2 HRS
I                     3  4 MNS
```

Calculation specs

Calc specs are generally the heart of an RPG program. It is here that the specific file and data processing takes place, commands occur, and logic flow is implemented. Here is a calc spec which initializes a variable called CODE with blanks:

```
 C            MOVE *BLANK    CODE
```

To define CODE as a variable and initialize with blanks, we need only add the field length to the preceding.

```
 C            MOVE *BLANK    CODE  10
```

See the section on Op codes for details on the commands found in the calc specs.

Output specs

Output specs are the last type of specs found in an RPG program (tables may follow them, however). It is here that lines are output to files for storage and/or printing. Although output specs occur physically last in the RPG program, they can be executed at any time from the calc specs. Our program contains no output specs, as the syntax can get rather complex and we wish to keep the example both simple and useful. By way of example, though, here is an output spec which can be executed by the Op code EXCPT to print a line containing the label 'DATE: ' and the system date to a previously defined file called OUTFILE (you could use IBM-supplied printer file QPRINT instead):

```
 OOUTFILE H   2
 O            E          LINE1
 O                                50 'DATE: '
 O                       UDATE Y  62
```

14.3 OP CODES

RPG calls commands Op codes. The general syntax for Op codes is as follows:

```
FMT C .....CLON01N02N03Factor1+++OpcdeFactor2+++ResultLenDHHiLoEqComments++++
```

Command:

```
         C          A        ADD  1        B
         spec       Factor1  Op   Factor2  Result
         type                     code
         'C'
```

The main components of a calc spec are the 'C' which identifies the line as a calc spec, Factor1 which is related somehow to Factor2 through the action of the Op code, and the outcome is placed in Result. In the preceding example, Factor1 (A) is Opcoded (ADD) to Factor2 (1) to give Result (B). In other words B = A + 1.

Additional parameters include the N01N02N03 you see on the left of the preceding syntax line for indicator use (more later), and the HiLoEq on the right of the syntax line, also for indicators.

The SEU prompt screen helps with Op code construction, as illustrated by Fig. 14.2.

There are not that many of them, and they fall into the following categories.

Assignment operators and initialization of variables

RPG variable names can be only up to six characters long. It is important to remember this because the column positions provided for variable names will not accept anything longer. And, when referencing array elements, the entire array element must fit into six characters, including the array index, as in: ARR,12. That is all the space you get, so when defining arrays keep the array name to three characters or less. Also, when defining databases for RPG using DDS or IDDU, remember to keep the variable names to six characters or less.

If a data file is correctly identified in the F specs in an RPG program, all of its field names become automatically available to the program.

```
Prompt type . . .    C       Sequence number . . .   0146.00

Level     N01N02N03  Factor 1     Operation      Factor 2      Result
___       _________  __________     Z-ADD        UDATE_____    DATE__
               Decimal
Length      Positions       H/A    HI    LO    EQ    Comment
___            _             _     __    __    __    ______________

F3=Exit                    F4=Prompt                F5=Refresh
F10=Top                    F11=Bottom               F24=More keys

      05-03                                              S1 S         KB
```

Figure 14.2 SEU prompt screen for op codes.

RPG creates variables of the same names as the DDS field names for internal use by the RPG program. And these field names are automatically passed to and returned from any screen which is called from the RPG program.

These are some of the more useful Op codes to handle data:

Z-ADD initialize to zero and add a number to a numeric variable

```
C          Z-ADDO        QTY
```

MOVE to move a variable to another variable (left-truncated if necessary)

```
C          MOVE 'HELLO'   GREET
```

MOVEL to move a string to a character variable (right-truncated if necessary)

```
C          MOVEL'HELLO'   GREET
```

MOVEA to move a string to an array or vice versa

```
C          MOVEA'HELLO'   GREET
```

Variables can be initialized simply by adding the defining parameters—length and decimal positions—to the preceding Op codes. For example, to define and initialize the variable QTY:

```
C        Z-ADDO        QTY    20
```

This tells RPG to set up a variable called QTY with two digits and no decimals, and to initialize it to zero (Z-ADD0). It is simply the two numbers 2 and 0 in the appropriate columns which tell RPG to declare this variable. If you forget this, you will get an undefined variable error at compile time.

A variable needs to be defined only once. After this, you may refer to it without the defining numerals. To define a character variable, put in only the variable length, and leave out the decimal portion.

```
C     MOVE 'HELLO'  GREET  5
```

The missing decimal portion of this initialization is an example of how nothing in a certain column means something to RPG (that this is a character type declaration).

Mathematical operators

RPG is a bit lengthy when it comes to complex mathematical calculations, because only one operator can be used on any line of code. Therefore, algebraic expressions like

```
a = x * (b/c)
```

are not available in RPG. You would have to build this expression up one operation at a time (see following).

The basic RPG operators are ADD, SUB, MULT, and DIV. The syntax is as follows:

Algebra: A = X + Y

```
RPG:    C         X        ADD  Y        A
```

Algebra: A = X − Y

```
RPG:    C         X        SUB  Y        A
```

Algebra: A = X * Y

```
RPG:    C         X        MULT Y        A
```

Algebra: A = X / Y

```
RPG:    C         X        DIV  Y        A
```

Algebra: A = X * (B/C)

Build in stages

```
RPG:    C         B        DIV  C        A
        C         X        MULT A        A
```

Again, SEU helps with the construction of expressions by providing the prompt screen at the touch of the <F4> key. Figure 14.3 shows the Op Code Prompt Screen.

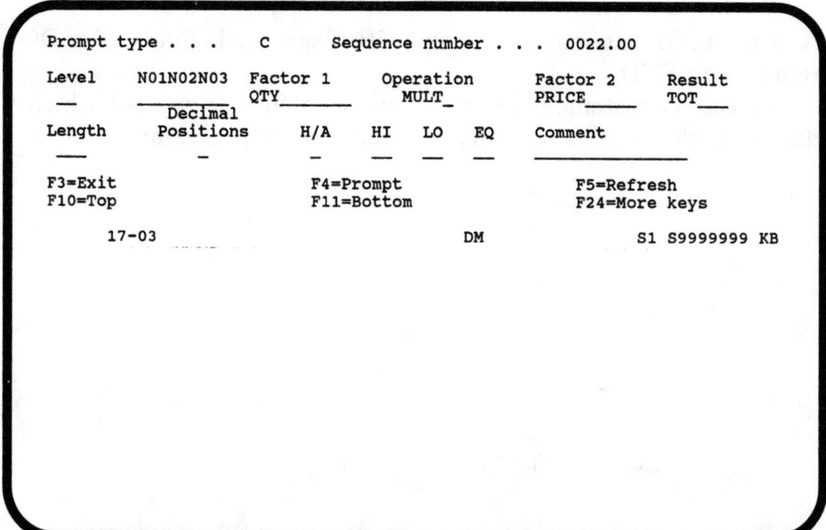

```
Prompt type . . .    C      Sequence number . . .  0022.00

Level    N01N02N03  Factor 1      Operation      Factor 2     Result
__       _________  QTY_______      MULT_        PRICE_____   TOT___
              Decimal
Length     Positions        H/A    HI   LO   EQ    Comment
____          _              _     __   __   __    ______________

F3=Exit                     F4=Prompt                 F5=Refresh
F10=Top                     F11=Bottom                F24=More keys

      17-03                                DM             S1 S9999999 KB
```

Figure 14.3 SEU prompt screen for calc specs.

Logic: If, Do While, and GoTo

RPG provides the basic logic operators IF, DO WHILE, and GOTO for directing program flow. They include:

	If	Or	And	Do While
Equal	IFEQ	OREQ	ANDEQ	DOWEQ
Not equal	IFNE	ORNE	ANDNE	DOWNE
Less than	IFLT	ORLT	ANDLT	DOWLT
Greater than	IFGT	ORGT	ANDGT	DOWGT

Logic. If A is greater than B, or C is equal to 1, go to START.

```
RPG:    C     A     IFGT B
        C     C     OREQ 1
        C           GOTO START
                    END
```

Note the END statement at the end of the logic block. Every IF or DOW requires an END.

Logic. Add 1 to X while X is less than 25.

```
RPG:    C     X     DOWLT25
        C     X     ADD  1       X
                    END
```

Note the END statement at the end of the logic block. Every IF or DOW requires an END.

The GOTO statement redirects program flow to a label which is defined with the TAG Op code, as in our sample program:

```
C         *IN99     IFEQ '1'
C                   GOTO END
C                   END
C*
.
.
.
C*
C         END       TAG
C                   SETON          LR
```

I/O: Record Find, Read, Update, and Write

RPG Op codes for database I/O include:

EXFMT Executes a screen which has been designed and compiled externally to RPG, passing RPG fields to it.

```
C                  EXFMTORDSCR
```

CHAIN Finds the named value in the index, reads record, sets on RPG special indicator (77 in this case) if not found.

```
C                  CHAINORDER          77
```

READ Reads the next record, sets on indicator 77 if end-of-file.

```
C                  READ ORDER          77
```

READE Sets pointer to next record with same index value, on special indicator 77 if not found.

```
C                  READEORDER          77
```

SETGT Sets the pointer to next record with a value greater than named value, sets on indicator 77 if not found. Does not read the record, you must issue a READ.

```
C                  SETGTORDER          77
```

UPDAT Update the current record (requires record format name, not database name).

```
C                  UPDATORD
```

WRITE Add new record to database (requires record format name, not database name).

```
C                  WRITEORD            77
```

SEU provides a prompting screen to help with the construction of RPG I/O statements in the calc specs. Refer to Fig. 14.4.

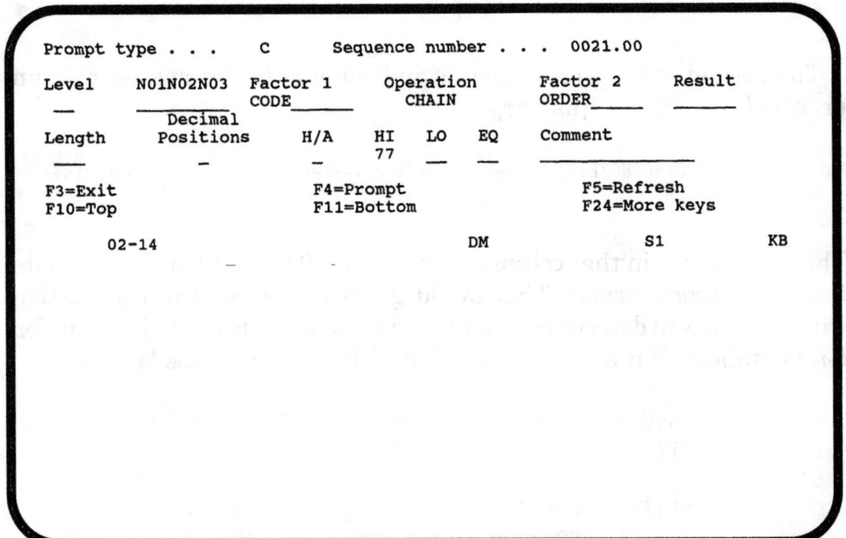

Figure 14.4 Calc specs prompt screen.

14.4 INDICATORS

RPG maintains special indicators to help with program logic flow and control. These indicators can be referenced in two ways. First with the *INnn syntax:

```
C                  EXFMTORDSCR
C*
C        *IN99     IFEQ '1'
C                  GOTO END
C                  END
```

The preceding code says:

> Do a screen (EXFMTORDSCR). If Indicator 99 is set on ('1') after user exits the screen go to the end label. Indicator 99 was defined in the screen, in SDA, to signal that the <F3> key was hit by user.

RPG allows the setting of indicators 01 through 99 to be used by the programmer as program flags. These indicators can be used to tell when a file is at end-of-file, when a certain condition is true, what key a user has hit in a screen, etc.

The programmer can set on indicator 12 with this statement:

```
C              SETON           12
```

and set it back off with:

```
C              SETOF           12
```

The second way to reference an indicator is in the special column provided by RPG for this purpose:

```
FMT C .....CL0N01N02N03Factor1+++OpcdeFactor2+++ResultLenDHHiLoEqComments++++
             N99               UPDATORD
```

The N99 means, in that column, if indicator 99 is not turned on, update the ORD record format. This would generally be used in conjunction with a CHAIN to determine whether a record already exists in the index for a database. If it does exist, use UPDAT; otherwise, use WRITE:

```
C          CODE     CHAINORDER              77
C          QTY      MULT PRICE     TOT
C*
C          *IN77    IFNE '1'
C                   UPDATORD
C                   ELSE
```

```
C                     WRITEORD
C                     END
```

Could be:

```
C  N77                UPDATORD
C   77                WRITEORD
```

What is gained in brevity is lost in clarity, however, and we recommend the IFNE construction used here.

RPG maintains a set of special indicators which it uses to determine program flow and branching. The only one we need concern ourselves with is LR. LR is an indicator which tells RPG whether the last record has been read in an input file. RPG is allowed to exit the program since LR is set on, either by the RPG cycle (see following), or by programmer intervention.

Our program was terminated with a GOTO which directed program flow to the END TAG. This is not sufficient to end the program, however. We had to add a SETON LR to tell RPG that processing is complete.

```
C           END       TAG
C                     SETON           LR
```

14.5 THE RPG CYCLE

RPG has an automatic cycle which it will follow. The programmer can define one of the data files as an input primary (IP) file in the F spec. RPG will then read one record at a time from this file, performing all of the logic in the Calc specs for each record in the input primary file, and set on LR (last record) when the input primary file is at end-of-file.

Input primary files

A file is defined as input primary with this syntax:

```
FORDER   IP  E       K     DISK
```

This file definition will read one record at a time from the file defined as IP (input primary) and perform all Calc spec logic for each record.

Circumventing the RPG cycle

Input primary only works if you can read one record at a time from this file, until it is finished, and then quit. If you need to jump around in the file, you will need to maintain your own program I/O logic with CHAINs and GOTOs and SETON LRs, as in our sample program.

14.6 SAMPLE PROGRAM

```
FORDER   UF  E           K        DISK          A
C*
C              LOOP      TAG
C                        EXFMTORDSCR
C*
C              *IN99     IFEQ '1'
C                        GOTO END
C                        END
C*
C              CODE      CHAINORDER            77
C              *IN77     IFNE '1'
C                        UPDATORD
C                        ELSE
C                        WRITEORD
C                        END
C*
C                        GOTO LOOP
C*
C              END       TAG
C                        SETON                 LR
```

Some programmers ignore the RPG cycle or don't learn it, preferring to manage the logic and flow of RPG I/O themselves, explicitly. If this method is used, and it is often preferred by programmers who come from other backgrounds and are therefore used to handling explicit I/O calls and looping, you must remember to use the GOTO along with the TAG to control program I/O flow. And use SETON LR to terminate the program when end-of-file has occurred as shown by indicator usage:

```
C      CODE     CHAINORDER                   77
C      *IN77    IFEQ '1'
C               GOTO END
C               END
C*
C      END      TAG
C               SETON                        LR
```

14.7 SUMMARY

RPG is a powerful language. It has its own I/O cycle, which makes some of the file handling automatic. And it is a concise language, so that applications can be written with a minimum of code lines.

While requiring very specific column placement for everything that goes into the program code, SEU is very helpful in providing fill-in-the-blanks prompt screens which take care of column placement for you.

RPG programs are coded in sections which have different functions, and the lines of code in these sections are called *specs*. Specs fall into the following categories.

H	Header specs	program identification
F	File specs	file definitions
E	Extension specs	array declaration
I	Input specs	further data definitions
C	Calc specs	the commands and main program
O	Output specs	report writing

RPG is relatively easy to write, once its syntax is understood, but it is more difficult to read and maintain, because of the inability to indent control and logic blocks. Nevertheless, it is the preferred language for applications development of the AS/400.

Chapter 15

COBOL/400

15.1 OVERVIEW OF COBOL/400

COBOL is the oldest and most widely used of the computer languages we are discussing here. It is becoming more prevalent on the AS/400 and it is pervasive in the business world. Increasingly, commercial applications written in COBOL on other platforms are being ported to the AS/400. This includes migration and downsizing. Most commercial applications of the 1960s and 1970s were written in COBOL, and many of them are still in use. COBOL is an acronym for Common Business Oriented Language. Its English-like syntax and vocabulary make it one of the easiest computer languages to read and understand.

Columns

COBOL requires some coding in specific columns, but is not nearly as strict in this regard as RPG. Mostly, it is necessary to code Division and Section headers, paragraph names, and a few other special program statements starting in area A (columns 8 through 11). All other statements must be in area B (columns 12 through 72). See following for more on specific placement of statements.

Divisions and Sections

COBOL programs are comprised of four basic Divisions:

1. Identification Division
2. Environment Division
3. Data Division
4. Procedure Division

Within each of these Divisions may be found various Sections, declarations, paragraphs, statements, and clauses.

Advantages

One of the primary advantages of COBOL is that it is so English-like in syntax and vocabulary. This feature makes it much more accessible to those not specifically trained in computer languages, so that business analysts can usually understand what a COBOL program is doing.

It can be indented liberally, clearly showing flow of control and sectional form. Variables can be given long names (up to 30 characters) which clearly indicate their nature, as opposed to the six-character limit in RPG. Also, COBOL is the standard language of applications development over the last couple of decades.

Limitations

COBOL, however, because of its English-like syntax, is rather wordy, and programs usually end up being considerably longer than those written in RPG or C. These other two languages are generally gaining acceptance as more efficient development environments than the older COBOL, and many applications are being converted, especially into C. Still, COBOL is widely used and maintained, and the AS/400 supports a version of it (COBOL/400).

15.2 IDENTIFICATION DIVISION

The first of the four required Divisions in any COBOL program is the Identification Division. It looks like this:

```
IDENTIFICATION DIVISION.
PROGRAM-ID.  ORDERS.
```

These are the only two lines strictly required by the compiler. The first line is the division header. The second is the PROGRAM-ID paragraph. Note the periods to end each line. Every COBOL statement must end with a period.

15.3 ENVIRONMENT DIVISION

Next is the Environment Division, where devices and files are defined. The Configuration Section identifies the computer hardware being used, and is optional.

```
ENVIRONMENT DIVISION.

CONFIGURATION SECTION.
SOURCE-COMPUTER. AS400.
OBJECT-COMPUTER. AS400.
```

The most important feature of the Environment Division is the Input-Output Section which specifies which files and devices will be used by the program, in the following format:

```
INPUT-OUTPUT SECTION.

FILE-CONTROL.

       SELECT ACCOUNTS-FILE
          ASSIGN TO DATABASE-ACCOUNTS
          ORGANIZATION IS INDEXED
          ACCESS MODE  IS DYNAMIC
          FILE STATUS  IS ACCOUNTS-FILE-STATUS
          RECORD KEY   IS EXTERNALLY-DESCRIBED-KEY.

       SELECT PRINT-FILE
          ASSIGN TO PRINTER-QPRINT.
```

The File-Control in the Input-Output Section of the Environment Division specifies that an AS/400 disk database called ACCOUNTS will be referred to by a program file called ACCOUNTS-FILE, and that a file called PRINT-FILE will go to the printer.

ACCOUNTS-FILE is defined as referring to a database called ACCOUNTS, which is indexed, dynamic access. A program-defined field called ACCOUNTS-FILE-STATUS is used to indicate the file status for I/O, and the record key is defined externally to the program, in the DDS for the file ACCOUNTS. These specifications define the external file to the program and tell the compiler where to route program requests for input or output. They are used in conjunction with later statements in the Procedure Division, which refer to files and/or devices for I/O.

15.4 DATA DIVISION

Here, data is defined, formatted, initialized, and made available to the program. The specific format for the Data Division is as follows:

```
DATA DIVISION.

FILE SECTION.

FD ACCOUNTS-FILE
```

```
       LABEL RECORDS ARE STANDARD.

    01 ACCOUNTS-RECORD.
       COPY DDS-ALL-FORMATS OF ACCOUNTS.

    FD PRINT-FILE
       LABEL RECORDS ARE OMITTED.
    01 PRINT-RECORD                    PIC X(132).
```

Note that file specs begin with the letters "FD" (File Description) in the File Section. LABEL RECORDS ARE STANDARD refers to a standard AS/400 datafile. Then comes the format name of the data file, as defined in FILE-CONTROL. This format name is preceded by a level "01" indicator, specifying that it is a record format name. The COPY DDS-ALL-FORMATS statement will import to the program the record structure and field names of the AS/400 database, which has already been defined externally to the program in DDS. The format of PRINT-FILE's PRINT-RECORD format is defined here, inside the program, consisting of 132 characters.

Working-Storage Section

Like the File Section, the Working-Storage Section defines data. It defines data not from external files, but for variables to be used internally by the program. The "01" level indicator is generally a record format name for a group of internal variables, while "05" level indicators define the actual variables themselves. The "77" level indicator defines a special flag variable to be used for program I/O control, in this case. Here is where the internal program-defined fields of RPT-REC are defined for later output to the PRINT-FILE.

```
 WORKING-STORAGE SECTION.

  77 ACCOUNTS-FILE-STATUS          PIC XX        VALUE SPACES.

  01 RPT-REC.
     05 FNAME                      PIC X(15)     VALUE SPACES.
     05 LNAME                      PIC X(20)     VALUE SPACES.
     05 AMOUNT                     PIC 9999V99   VALUE ZERO.
     05 BIG-ORDER                  PIC X         VALUE SPACES.
```

Picture clause

Finally, each field may have a Picture clause identifying its type. PIC X(20) indicates a 20-character alpha type field, while PIC S9(2) defines a 9-byte numeric field with two decimal places. Fields can be initialized when declared, as previously with the Value Clause. VALUE ZERO initializes a field to numeric zero.

15.5 PROCEDURE DIVISION

The last division in a COBOL program is the Procedure Division, and it is here that all logic and processing takes place. It begins with the following header:

```
PROCEDURE DIVISION.
```

The first statement in the Procedure Division is the A000-MAIN-ROUTINE, which is the main calling routine of a COBOL program. Here, the two files defined in the program are opened.

```
A000-MAIN-ROUTINE.
     OPEN INPUT ACCOUNTS-FILE
          OUTPUT PRINT-FILE.
```

In the Procedure Division are I/O calls, calculations, and data manipulations.

Assignment operators and initialization of variables

We have seen that the declaration and initialization of variables takes place in the Environment Division (see previous). Any variables not declared will generate compiler errors. In addition to the method described previously, where variables are initialized at declaration (with the VALUE clause), they can be initialized with the MOVE command, as follows:

```
MOVE "ANDY" TO NAME.
MOVE 10.5 TO AMOUNT.
```

Mathematical operators

COBOL has reserved words which perform the standard mathmatical operations, or you may use the COMPUTE statement with algebraic notation. The following two statements perform the same mathematical operation:

```
ADD A TO B GIVING C.

COMPUTE C = A + B.
```

The first statement uses the COBOL-reserved words, while the second uses standard algebraic notation in conjunction with the COMPUTE statement. The more complex calculations become, the more it is advisable to use the COMPUTE statement with algebraic notation. These are the COBOL math operators:

```
ADD        +
SUBTRACT   -
```

```
DIVIDE     /
MULTIPLY   *
EXPONENT   **
```

Open and close

COBOL must open files before they can be used. This is done with the OPEN statement, specifying whether the file will be used for input or output:

```
OPEN INPUT  ACCOUNTS-FILE
     OUTPUT PRINT-FILE.
```

Files may be defined as INPUT for input, OUTPUT for output, or I/O for both. Once the file has been opened correctly, it is available for program reads and writes.

At the end of a program, files are closed with this simple syntax:

```
CLOSE ACCOUNTS-FILE
      PRINT-FILE.
```

which closes the two files (ACCOUNTS-FILE and PRINT-FILE) previously defined in the Data Division and opened in the Procedure Division.

Read

To read the next sequential record of a file, use this statement:

```
READ ACCOUNTS-FILE NEXT
     AT END
      GO TO B003-EXIT.
```

This statement reads the next ACCOUNTS-FILE record. (Remember that ACCOUNTS-FILE is a program defined name for the disk file ACCOUNTS.) When the system encounters the end-of-file condition on the read operation, the program will branch to the Procedure Division paragraph named B003-EXIT, as a result of the AT END clause, terminating program execution.

Move

The MOVE statement is used to move a variable from one location to another, for instance, from a field in the database being read to a program-defined field or a field in the output file.

```
MOVE LSTNAM OF ACCT OF ACCOUNTS-RECORD
  TO LNAME OF RPT-REC.
```

This command will take the LSTNAM field from the most recent read of ACCOUNTS-FILE (ACCOUNTS) and copy it into the LNAME field of the RPT-REC program-defined format. Note the use of the externally defined record format name in the MOVE statement (ACCT). It is the format name defined in the DDS for the ACCOUNTS file when it was created.

It is necessary to know the external database name, the external format name, and the internally defined record name in order to use fields in the program.

Write

To write a record to a printer file with COBOL, use the WRITE statement:

```
WRITE PRINT-RECORD FROM RPT-REC AFTER 1.
```

This statement will write out the program-defined format called RPT-REC to the printer file called PRINT-RECORD after skipping one line.

To update a record at the current file pointer location in a disk file, use the REWRITE statement:

```
REWRITE OUTPUT-RECORD FROM ORDER-WS.
```

15.6 LOGIC: IF, DO WHILE, AND PERFORM

Program logic and testing is accomplished through the use of IF, DO WHILE, and PERFORM. The most basic and useful test is the IF, which takes the following form:

```
IF AMOUNT OF RPT-REC > 1000
  MOVE "*" TO BIG-ORDER OF RPT-REC
  PERFORM B001-DISCOUNT
ELSE
  MOVE SPACES TO BIG-ORDER OF RPT-REC.
```

In this way, we have tested the amount read from the ACCOUNTS file and set a field called BIG-ORDER in RPT-REC to "*" if AMOUNT is over 1000. Additionally, we will branch to a Procedure Division paragraph called B000-DISCOUNT. This is a subroutine, and is called with the PERFORM statement. It is simply a label or paragraph name, followed by commands, which in this case will issue a 3 percent discount to any account with an amount over $1000, before continuing with the processing.

```
B001-DISCOUNT.
COMPUTE AMOUNT = AMOUNT * .97.
```

Note the use of the ELSE in the IF. This tells the program what action to perform if the condition in the IF is not met.

The program is terminated by the use of the STOP RUN statement in the B003-EXIT paragraph, after the files are closed.

```
B003-EXIT.
    CLOSE ACCOUNTS-FILE
          PRINT-FILE.
    STOP RUN.
```

15.7 SAMPLE PROGRAM

```
IDENTIFICATION DIVISION.
PROGRAM-ID.  ORDERS.

ENVIRONMENT DIVISION.

CONFIGURATION SECTION.
SOURCE-COMPUTER.  AS400.
OBJECT-COMPUTER.  AS400.

INPUT-OUTPUT SECTION.

FILE-CONTROL.
      SELECT ACCOUNTS-FILE
         ASSIGN TO DATABASE-ACCOUNTS
         ORGANIZATION IS INDEXED
         ACCESS MODE  IS DYNAMIC
         FILE STATUS  IS ACCOUNTS-FILE-STATUS
         RECORD KEY   IS EXTERNALLY-DESCRIBED-KEY.

      SELECT PRINT-FILE
         ASSIGN TO PRINTER-QPRINT.

DATA DIVISION.

FILE SECTION.

FD ACCOUNTS-FILE
   LABEL RECORDS ARE STANDARD.

01 ACCOUNTS-RECORD.
   COPY DDS-ALL-FORMATS OF ACCOUNTS.

FD PRINT-FILE
   LABEL RECORDS ARE OMITTED.

01 PRINT-RECORD                        PIC X(132).
```

```
/
WORKING-STORAGE SECTION.

77 ACCOUNTS-FILE-STATUS            PIC XX       VALUE SPACES.
01 RPT-REC.
   05 FNAME                        PIC X(15)    VALUE SPACES.
   05 LNAME                        PIC X(20)    VALUE SPACES.
   05 AMOUNT                       PIC 9999V99  VALUE ZERO.
   05 BIG-ORDER                    PIC X        VALUE SPACES.

PROCEDURE DIVISION.

A000-MAIN-ROUTINE.
    OPEN INPUT ACCOUNTS-FILE
         OUTPUT PRINT-FILE.

B000-READ-RECORD.
    READ ACCOUNTS-FILE NEXT
         AT END
          GO TO B003-EXIT.

   MOVE LSTNAM OF ACCT OF ACCOUNTS-RECORD
     TO LNAME OF RPT-REC.

   MOVE FSTNAM OF ACCT OF ACCOUNTS-RECORD
     TO FNAME OF RPT-REC.

   MOVE AMT OF ACCT OF ACCOUNTS-RECORD
     TO AMOUNT OF RPT-REC.

   IF AMOUNT OF RPT-REC > 1000
     MOVE "*" TO BIG-ORDER OF RPT-REC
     PERFORM B001-DISCOUNT
   ELSE
     MOVE SPACES TO BIG-ORDER OF RPT-REC.

   PERFORM B002-WRITE-RECORD.
   GO TO B000-READ-RECORD.

B001-DISCOUNT.
    COMPUTE AMOUNT = AMOUNT * .97.

B002-WRITE-RECORD.
    WRITE PRINT-RECORD FROM RPT-REC AFTER 1.

B003-EXIT.
    CLOSE ACCOUNTS-FILE
          PRINT-FILE.
    STOP RUN.
```

15.7 SUMMARY

Although somewhat wordy, COBOL is relatively easy to understand and analyze, even for those not technically trained in computer languages. Especially as compared to the rigid column formatting of RPG, and the highly symbolic syntax of C, COBOL most resembles English in syntax and structure.

COBOL has been the dominant mainframe applications development language for several years, and many applications have been ported over to the AS/400 from mainframe COBOL routines. It is not the primary language on the AS/400, but there is no doubt that it remains useful and that a familiarity with it will make one more adaptable to systems development in the commercial world.

Chapter

16

C

16.1 OVERVIEW OF C/400

C is powerful, efficient, and difficult. Of the four languages we are discussing here, it the least amenable to a brief description. It is, however, the language of choice for much software development these days; many other high-level languages have C as their source code. It will possibly become the one language which is most suitable for portable code across IBM's SAA platforms, running on the micro, midrange, and mainframe environments with minimal conversion requirements.

Advantages

The main advantages of C are its efficent, compact code, its flexibility, and its portability. Compared to a COBOL program, C code is very compact. COBOL is seen by many to be a language of the past and, while many business applications are written in COBOL and are still being maintained, many corporations are making the conversion to C. If any computer language can be described as the language of the future, it is probably C.

Limitations

C has a rather lengthy learning curve. Primarily this is because C does not insulate the user from the operating system. It is necessary to understand elements of disk I/O and addressing to become fully adept at C. Issues such as structures and unions, and especially pointers, are complex and take some getting used to.

Hazards of C

C can also be a dangerous language. It protects the user less than most languages from programming errors. It will let you do some very undesirable operations, like overwriting your data areas, without any warning messages. There is no bounds checking in C, so that if you set up an array of 10 elements and make the mistake of writing more than 10 elements to it, C will write the extra elements to somewhere, without warning you. There is no telling where these extra elements will go; they might even overwrite program code or part of the operating system. In addition, the current implementation of the C compiler on the AS/400 does not provide level checks against databases (whether the C program references a database which has changed since the last compile). So you must monitor this yourself. We expect this to change in future releases. Be careful with C!

Functions and link libraries

One of the features that makes C so flexible and powerful is the fact that there is no one standard set of functions and libraries for C. You choose the functions and libraries you need for a particular application, and specify them to the compiler and linker. You can write your own functions or use some of the many functions which are provided as part of the many add-on C function libraries, of which there are more available all the time. The basic C language has only 28 keywords; all the rest is made up of these commands in the form of user or library functions.

16.2 PREPROCESSOR DIRECTIVES

It is necessary to tell C which special functions will be included in the code you are writing. These directions are called preprocessor directives, and are found at the beginning of any C program. All preprocessor directives are preceded by the # character in the code.

Includes

The Include is the most common form of preprocessor directive. It tells the C compiler to go out and look for special files to include in your code, defining certain data elements for functions or operations you intend to perform. Include files all have .h as their file extension. STDIO (standard I/O) is the most common Include, and makes available to your program standard I/O operations, such as getting input from the user terminal.

Without the Include, this input would not work. It is therefore necessary to know in advance which functions you will be using and to incorporate the appropriate Includes in your program. Consult the IBM C function manual for which function calls require which Includes.

```
#include <stdio.h>
```

Include files are largely composed of multiple defines and data declarations, providing consistent usage of special terms in C programs.

Defines

Defines are another type of preprocessor directive, a way to set up special data names for use by your program. For instance, if you want to specify that the data name SUCCESS will indicate a successful read of a record, you would need to define SUCCESS as being equivalent to the return code for a successful read.

```
#define SUCCESS 1
```

Defines take the form of macro substitution, so that any time the program encounters a Defined term, it will substitute the characters indicated in the preprocessor definition. In the preceding example, the program will substitute the character 1 for the term SUCCESS.

16.3 DATA TYPES

C has only a few data types, which need to be declared to the program before they are used.

Assignment operators and initialization of variables

Data items must be explicitly declared before they are referenced in the C program. You must provide the data type and name. There are a few data types in C:

char	1-byte character
int	integer
float	single-precision floating-point numeric
double	double-precision floating-point numeric
short	short integer
long	long integer
unsigned	unsigned integer, no negatives; therefore twice as large as int

The actual number of bytes in each of the numeric type declarations is machine-dependent and will be assigned by the compiler at compile time. This feature adds to the portability of C across platforms, since data types will change automatically to accommodate the particular machine on which the code is being compiled.

The most common forms of data type are char, int, and float. Here is a declaration for character variable name and an integer variable x which will be used in the program:

```
char name;
int  x;
```

Multiple variables can be declared in one line:

```
int  x,y,z;
```

Variables can be initialized in the declaration:

```
char name = "A";
int  x    = 1;
```

Arrays are declared like any other data type with an additional parameter in square brackets indicating array length:

```
char name[25];
```

Note the use of the semicolon (;) which is used in C to denote the end of a statement. By far the most popular bug in C is forgetting the semicolon at the end of a statement.

C is case-sensitive, so that X and x are two different variable names. Lowercase is the de facto standard for writing C code. White space or blanks in the code may be used freely in most situations to make the code more readable in terms of indentation and blank lines.

16.4 KEYWORDS

There are only 28 inherent keywords in C. Everything else is either user-defined, or imported through Includes or external-link library functions. The C keywords are:

auto	double	if	static
break	else	int	structure
case	entry	long	switch
char	extern	register	typedef
continue	float	return	union
default	for	short	unsigned
do	goto	sizeof	while

You will notice that the C keywords have to do with variable declarations of various types, and with control of logic flow. C provides logic control in the form of:

if	for	goto	case
else	while	switch	break

More will be said on this later (see Sec. 16.8).

16.5 MATHEMATICAL OPERATORS

C's mathematical operators are very straightforward, and can be used to write algebraic-like expression in the C program:

+	add
–	subtract
*	multiply
/	divide
%	modulus

Parentheses are used to group operations in an expression. An expression such as this is possible in C:

```
a = ((b*c)/r) - 1;
```

Of course, all of these variables must have been declared previous to the expression.

There is no exponential operator. You must use a function for this.

16.6 ASSIGNMENT AND COMPARISON

As we have seen, assignment of values to C variables is easily accomplished as in:

```
x = 1;
name = "Fred";
```

Comparison of data items for purposes of logic flow requires the use of these operators:

==	equals
!=	does not equal
>	is greater than
>=	is greater than or equal to
<	is less than
<=	is less than or equal to

Note that the comparison for "is equal to" requires the double equal sign, = =. It is a common mistake to use a single equal sign for comparison purposes. Correct syntax is as follows:

```
if(a == b)
```

These comparison operators are found within the parentheses associated with flow of control words like 'if,' 'while,' 'for,' or 'switch' and 'case.'

16.7 FUNCTIONS

Most of the power of C is available through functions. These functions are of two types: library functions that come with the compiler, and user functions that you write yourself. There are more libraries of functions for C available all the time to handle whatever special tasks you might have, from screen handling to file I/O. It is therefore necessary to become familiar with the function libraries available for C. In addition, most C functions require special Includes to define standard variables used by the function libraries, so you must know which Includes are needed. There are literally hundreds of special functions available for C. We will explain a few of the standard C functions.

16.7.1 C functions

Functions are called in C in the form: funcname(arg1, arg2), where funcname is the name of the C function and arg1 and arg2 are the parameters passed to it. Of course, not all functions have two arguments.

All C programs must begin (after the preprocessor directives) with the main() function. This is the first statement in the body of a C program and has the following simple form:

```
main()
```

The main() function may be adapted to receive calling parameters from the command line (see manual).

16.7.2 User-defined functions

In addition to the functions which come with your C compiler, you may create your own functions in C. In fact, much of the processing required by your program will be written as function calls. To write a function, you must identify it, declare variables which are used inside it, write the code in it, and return a value to the function call:

```
userfunc(a,b)

int a,b;
{
        int c;
        c = a + b;
        return(c);
}
```

This is a user-defined function called userfunc which will receive two variables (a and b) from the calling routine. It will add a to b, giving c, all three of which are declared in the function. It will then return the value of c (not the variable name c) to the calling routine.

Parameter passing to functions

The preceding is a user-defined function which will return the result of a + b as the value of variable c when called by the program. The return value of the function simply substitutes for the function after it is called. So the function call:

```
x = userfunc(q,r);
```

will pass the integer variables q and r to the function, receive them into variables a and b, add them together, and return them to the calling statement as variable c. Assuming that variables q and r have been previously declared as int and have the values of 1 and 2, respectively, the function call evaluates to x = 3. You must pass the function the same type of variable that it declares in its variable declarations.

The variable x, which receives back the return value from the function call, must be the same type as the function's internally declared return variable c, an integer. Variable names inside the function have nothing to do with variable names which are passed to it. They are separate variables altogether. The values of the variables in the calling routine are passed, in order, into the function's declared variables, in order. The function's return value is passed back to the calling routine.

Functions are called simply by naming them as:

```
printf("This is a C function \n");
```

This function will print the string inside the quotes on the terminal. The \n is a newline character which places the cursor on the following line on the screen. Note the semicolon to complete the function call.

Not all functions receive a return value, as with the preceding printf() function call.

16.7.3 Input and output functions

C has no commands for I/O. All I/O is handled through function calls.

Fopen()

The fopen() function opens a datafile for I/O by the program. Remember that C does not shield you from elements of the operating system, like pointers and addressing, so you must declare a special type of variable called a *file pointer* in order to handle files. Also, you need to include <stdio.h> to handle file I/O.

```
#include <stdio.h>
```

Declare a file pointer:

```
FILE *datafile;
```

This file pointer is a special variable which will contain the actual machine address of the file being handled. Note the asterisk, which is a necessary part of a pointer declaration.

Open the file:

```
datafile = fopen("data.txt","r+");
```

This statement opens an existing datafile named data.txt in the update (read-write) mode and assigns the location of the file to file pointer 'datafile.'

The preceding statement will open the data file for update, assuming that it exists and that all goes well. It is much safer to use it in the following form, however:

```
if ((datafile = fopen("data.txt","r+")) != NULL)
```

Here, we are testing to make sure that the fopen() function does not return special variable NULL (defined in the <stdio.h> Include) before we proceed with file I/O.

Seem confusing? Pointers *are* confusing and take some practice. They are one of the least accessible features of the C language. However, remembering the necessary Includes and file pointer declarations, and using the preceding syntax for fopen(), you will be able to access files. Be very careful with the file mode (the second parameter in the fopen() call). The wrong one can create unfortunate effects, such as clearing an existing file.

See the manual for additional features of the fopen() and other functions.

Fclose()

As opposed to the fopen() function, fclose() is simple. It goes like this:

```
fclose(datafile);
```

Scanf()

Scanf() reads a formatted data stream from the terminal. It requires the following Includes and declarations to get a number and a name from the user:

```
#include <stdio.h>

int   num;
char name[15];
```

Note that the variable name is declared as an array with 15 elements.

Scanf() takes the following form:

```
scanf("%4d, %15s", &num, name);
```

where the values in double quotes are format specifications for the values to be read, num and name, in order of appearance. The percent sign indicates a format spec, the d means decimal and the s means string. So the format specs tell scanf() to expect a 4-digit decimal and a 15-character string from the user. Following the format specs are the names of the variables to receive the input. Nonarray variable names require the '&' character as shown.

See the manual for further format specs and details of scanf().

Fscanf()

Fscanf() reads a formatted data stream from a data file. It requires the following includes and declarations to get a number and a name from the file:

```
#include <stdio.h>

int   num;
char name[15];
FILE *filename;
```

Note that the variable name is declared as an array with 15 elements, and that we need a file pointer declared with a '*.'

Fscanf() takes the following form:

```
fscanf(filename, "%4d, %15s", &num, name);
```

The fscanf() format specs follow the same rules as the scanf() format specs. The above fscanf() function will read a 4-digit integer and a 15-character name from the current location of the file specified by file name. The file pointer is positioned to the next character after the fscanf() is finished reading. Remember that you must account for all characters in a file when using fscanf(), including a possible carriage return and line feed at the end of a record. The next fscanf() function will not automatically get the next record, but will proceed from wherever you have left the file pointer after the last operation, so it is critical to account explicitly for every byte in a record when using C.

The file being read with fscanf() must have been opened already for reading by fopen().

Printf()

Printf() writes strings to the terminal for communicating with the user. It requires the following Include to print a message to the terminal:

```
#include <stdio.h>
```

Printf() takes this form:

```
printf("Please enter number and name: ");
```

In conjunction with scanf(), printf() can be used to put messages on the screen and get input back for interactive processing.

Fprintf()

Fprintf() writes a formatted data stream into a data file. It requires the following Includes and declarations to write a number and a name to the file:

```
#include <stdio.h>

int    num;
char name[15];
FILE *filename;
```

Fprintf() takes the following form:

```
fprintf(filename,"%4d, %15s, \n", &num, name);
```

The fprintf() format specs follow the same rules as the fscanf() format specs. The foregoing fprintf() function will write a 4-digit integer, a 15-character name, and a carriage return into the current location of the file specified by file name. The file pointer is positioned to the next character after the fprintf() is finished writing. Remember that you must account for all characters in a file when using fprintf(), including carriage return and line feed, as seen in the \n (newline) character in the format specs.

The file being written with fprintf() must have been opened already for writing by fopen().

16.8 LOGIC: IF, WHILE, FOR AND SWITCH

C provides keywords for handling flow of control logic. You can test variables and branch to other parts of the program depending on the results of the test.

If

IF is the most common form of logic testing. It has this syntax:

```
if(x == 1)
        funcname();
```

The preceding If statement says to perform the function funcname() if x is equal to 1. Note the double equal sign (= =) used for comparison testing.

C also has an else:

```
if(x == 1)
        funcnam1();
else
        funcnam2();
```

While

The While statement in C will iterate a loop until the While condition is met:

```
while(x <= 10)
{
        x = x + 1;
}
```

The preceding While loop will add 1 to x until x becomes greater than 10. Note the use of the curly brackets to enclose the body of the While loop. This practice tells the compiler where the While loop ends.

For

The For statement provides a compact method for performing an iteration. The preceding While loop could be written as a For:

```
for(x = 1; x <= 10; x++);
```

This For loop says that beginning with x = 1, and continuing while x <= 10, increment x. Note the shorthand notation for incrementing x (x++).

Switch

Switch is C's case statement. It tests a succession of possible cases, executing the correct one.

```
switch(x)
{
        case 1:
            func1();
            break;

        case 2:
            func2();
            break;

        default:
            break;
}
```

The preceding will test variable x. If it is 1, func1() will be called; if it is 2, func2() will be called. The Default statement, last of the Case statements, will execute if no previous case has been matched. The Break statement is required in the Switch syntax. It causes flow to leave the loop after its associated Case or Default has been met and executed.

Goto

C has a Goto statement for purposes of branching. It has this form:

```
if(x == 1)
        goto label;
```

where label is a name in the program followed by a colon:

```
label:
```

If the condition in the test is matched, the program will branch to label: and continue processing with the line after it.

Of course, in a structured language such as C, Goto's are frowned on, structured control being the preferred method. But sometimes they are the easiest and clearest method of directing flow of control.

16.9 SAMPLE PROGRAM

Here is a simple C program to get an order code, customer name, quantity, and price from the user. Then the total is calculated from price and quantity. Finally, the entire record is written into the ORDERS.TXT datafile. Note the use of /* comment */ for documentation in the code.

```
/*  ORDERS (to input orders)  */

/* includes */

#include <stdio.h>

/* variable declarations */

int code   = 0;
char name[15];
int qty      = 0;
float price  = 0;
float total  = 0;
FILE  *datafile;

/* main program */

main()

/* Get the customer data from user */

printf("\n Customer Name: ");
scanf("%15s", name);

printf("\n Customer Number: ");
scanf("%4d", &code);

printf("\n Quantity: ");
scanf("%4d", &qty);

printf("\n Price: ");
scanf("%8.2e", &price);

/* calculate the total from quantity and price */

total = qty * price;

/* open the file data.txt */

if ((datafile = fopen("data.txt","r+")) != NULL)

/* write to data.txt */

fprintf(filename," %15s,%4d,%4d,%8.2e,%8.2e% \n",
                   name,code,qty, price, total);

/* NOTE THE \n IN THE ABOVE FORMAT SPEC TO ISSUE CARRIAGE
   RETURN IN C. YOU MUST ACCOUNT FOR EVERYTHING */
```

```
/* close data.txt */

fclose(datafile);
```

16.8 SUMMARY

C is a powerful and flexible high-level language. While it is useful and adaptable to many situations, it is rather difficult, and the learning curve is high. Its flexibility and complexity are simultaneously advantageous and difficult to acquire.

Once its peculiarities are mastered, however, C becomes an ideal development environment in that it offers custom tailoring of the language, its functions, and features to each situation. No other language approaches it for high-level function coupled with low-level access. Those who work fluently in C swear by it.

It seems that C is positioned well to become a standard development language of the future, porting easily across IBM's SAA platforms.

Chapter

17

Structured Query Language (SQL)

17.1 OVERVIEW

In order to utilize fully Structured Query Language (SQL), as with all languages supported on the AS/400, you must possess an understanding of system administration, database structure, and application programming. If these concepts are clear, using SQL can allow you to harness the full functionality of the AS/400 very quickly. With SQL, you can create, maintain, and report on databases efficiently. For a fast view or update of AS/400 data, it is hard to beat SQL.

SQL subset

The implementation of SQL on the AS/400 is a subset of the mainframe version of SQL.

The future and portability

SQL is geared toward Systems Applications Architecture (SAA), allowing application programs to be ported from platform to platform. The SAA definition, a set of software interfaces, conventions, and protocols, provides a framework for programmers to write applications. SQL is the only language which lends itself toward use of multiple system hardware platforms, software, and data.

Advantages

The Structured Query Language is a language used to access data in a relational database. SQL is unlike many languages because you do not have to code a complicated sequence of instructions explaining how to get to the data. SQL will allow you to access data using a single SELECT statement directed toward the database manager in the AS/400's operating system. The database manager allows access and maintains the data. This tandem of simple and powerful SQL commands working together with the AS/400's database manager is a very useful and efficient feature of the machine.

Limitations

The basics of SQL can be learned quickly, but SQL requires some practice in order to harness its full power. Performance is one of the most significant issues. Structuring code in a logical sequence, with range delimiters for searches, using indexed files, and yielding a manageable set of records, will allow you to take full advantage of the power of SQL. Also, SQL is primarily a data selection utility, and does not offer the complete control over screens, processing, data edits, or calculations which are characteristic of RPG and other high-level languages.

17.2 SQL COMMAND LANGUAGE STRUCTURE

With an English-like syntax, SQL lets the user change, define, and modify data through a set of logical commands. These commands have a syntax and structure which, like CL, may be prompted interactively or programmed and compiled.

SQL Data Dictionary

Tables and views are maintained by the database manager containing information about data structures in the database. A catalog table contains information about tables, views, and indexes. Tables and views in a catalog are like any other database tables and views. You can use SQL statements to retrieve data in the catalog in the same way you retrieve data from any other table in the system. The catalog is always kept up to date with the latest information by the database manager.

Tables

Relational databases are based on a collection of tables. Tables are structures made up of columns and rows. Values (or individual data items) occur at the intersection of every column and row. A column is a set of values of the same structure, like a field. A row is a set of values forming a record.

A table is created with the CREATE TABLE statement to contain data. When a program or command is run in SQL, a result table is created which is a subset of rows that the database manager selects or generates from one or more other database tables. The following defines a table.

```
CREATE TABLE username.tablename
   (NAME      CHAR(20)          NOT NULL WITH DEFAULT,
   AMOUNT     DECIMAL(7,2)      NOT NULL WITH DEFAULT,
   DEPT       CHAR(3)           NOT NULL WITH DEFAULT)
```

The preceding statement defines a table for a user. Note the period between the user name and the table name. Three fields are defined: NAME, with 20 characters; AMOUNT, with a 7-digit number containing two decimals; and DEPT, with three characters. NOT NULL WITH DEFAULT means that the field cannot contain a null value, and that it is initialized with default values (blank for char, and 0 for decimal).

Views

There are usually several ways to look at your data. Views provide an alternate way of viewing data in one or more tables. In a view, rows and columns may be selected and ordered, as with logical files. Views can be created and used as true tables. These can work transparently to users who never need know they are working with a view and not with a table.

Views differ from tables in that a table requires disk storage, but a view does not. A view's definition is stored in the catalog. No data is stored in a view and, therefore, no index can be created for a view. However, an index created for a table on which a view is based can be utilized and will generally improve the performance of the view. Here is a view definition, based on the foregoing table definition, selecting only the NAME and AMOUNT fields, and only those records in the table whose AMOUNT field is greater than 1000:

```
CREATE VIEW username.viewname
            (NAME, AMOUNT)
            AS SELECT ALL
            NAME, AMOUNT, DEPT
            FROM username.tablename
            WHERE AMOUNT > 1000
```

Indexes

A word about indexes, a concept which, when implemented correctly, will significantly improve performance. An index is an ordered set of pointers (called keys) to rows of a database table. Every index is based on the data values in at least one or more table columns. Each index is stored as an object separate from the database. Indexes are built and maintained automatically when requested.

Using SQL, access to data is faster when using a index. Indexes ensure that each row in a database is unique, and cannot have rows with identical key values.

17.3 INTERACTIVE SQL

Interactive SQL is properly referred to as Dynamic SQL. Dynamic SQL allows ad hoc SQL statements and queries to a table. Programs can be written in other languages that request or read SQL statements from a terminal where the user is located at the time the application is implemented. Finally, Dynamic SQL allows you to create your own native SQL programs. In this way you could easily develop your own SQL-based query set. This methodology can be compared to creating your own commands in Control Language.

To start an interactive SQL session, type at the command line:

```
STRSQL
```

17.4 EMBEDDED SQL

Another use of SQL is to embed SQL statements inside RPG, or COBOL application programs. When SQL is used in this way, it is correctly referred to as Static SQL. The primary point to remember is that the SQL statements must be fully coded into the application program at the time that they are precompiled, inside SQL blocks in the RPG or other program.

Embedding SQL in RPG and COBOL

SQL programs can be written to contain static SQL statements. Before an RPG or COBOL program containing static SQL statements is compiled, the code must be submitted to the SQL precompiler. The precompiled SQL flags the SQL statements as commands and then includes the instructions to call the database manager and invoke your instructions. All SQL syntax is checked at this precompile stage. Then, when compiling your RPG or COBOL program, the compiler can understand and process the program.

With SQL, calling programs using RPG or COBOL are referred to as *host structures.* Host structures are defined by statements of the host language. In this way, SQL can access data and determine other parameter information about the data with far fewer instructions than the host language.

SQL statements can be embedded in an application program, and many can be issued interactively. Static SQL does have some statements and instructions that cannot be used interactively.

We have been using the phrase "embedded in an application program," defined as the ability to specify statements in a source program that will be submitted to an SQL precompiler for processing before compiling the host structure.

The phrase "issued interactively" means that you can invoke a statement using the interactive portion of SQL.

Some statements can only be embedded in application programs and are not executable statements. The precompiler processes these statements and reports any errors it encounters. All executable statements embedded in an application program should be tested.

The technique of embedding SQL in host programs is more complex than that of running interactive SQL statements, and we leave the technical explanations to the IBM SQL manuals.

17.5 LANGUAGE ELEMENTS

Data as it is handled in SQL is divided into several types. The smallest unit of data that can be manipulated in SQL is called a *value*. SQL interprets data types based on the source of the data, which could include constants, host language variables, functions, and expressions.

The following statements are the basis of SQL/400:

SELECT	Select records (rows) from a database or table based on criteria.
UPDATE	Update fields in records (rows).
FETCH	Retrieve the next record (row) of a table into host variables in calling program (e.g., RPG).
INSERT	Insert a record (row) into a table.
DELETE	Delete a record or records from a table.

Each statement may contain a number of clauses, and even have nested statements and clauses. The sequence of SQL clauses in statements is as follows:

FROM	which database is being operated on
WHERE	record selection
GROUP BY	record grouping
HAVING	group selection
ORDER BY	indexing the results based on field contents

Numbers and strings are not compatible for comparison. Thus, numbers and alphabetic strings cannot be compared, numbers cannot be assigned to alphabetic columns or variables, and strings cannot be assigned numeric columns or variables.

Another important element of the SQL language is a host variable. A host variable is an RPG, or COBOL data item, that is referenced in an SQL statement. Host variables should not begin with the characters SQL or RDI. Host variables are defined by statements of the host language.

Basic predicates

A predicate in SQL is an expression followed by a comparison operator and another expression.

The null is not operational in this implementation of SQL. Therefore, if your statements indicate that either value is a null, the result of a predicate operation would be unknown and basically nonfunctional. All of the results of a predicate are true or false.

Comparison operators

x = y	x is equal to y
x]= y	x is not equal to y
x<> y	x is not equal to y
x < y	x is less than y
x > y	x is greater than y
x<= y	x is less than or equal to y
x>= y	x is greater than or equal to y
x]< y	x is not less than y
x]> y	x is not greater than y

Some practical examples of comparison operators are:

```
ID = '123456789'
COST < 200
```

In addition, the BETWEEN predicate is used to compare a value with a range of values.

```
value-X BETWEEN value-Y AND value-Z
is also equivalent to the search condition:
value-X >= value-Y AND value-X <= value-Z
```

SELECT statement

The SELECT statement creates a result table which is usually a subset of the database.

FROM clause

The FROM clause specifies which database is being operated on.

```
SELECT * FROM database
```

This SQL command selects all fields (*) from the database, and does not filter out any records.

```
SELECT NAME, AMOUNT FROM database
```

This command selects only the named fields, NAME, and AMOUNT from the database.

WHERE clause

The WHERE clause narrows down the records affected or returned by the SELECT.

```
SELECT NAME, AMOUNT, DEPT FROM database
       WHERE AMOUNT > 100
```

It returns only those records whose AMOUNT is greater than 100.

GROUP BY clause

The GROUP BY clause groups the results of a SELECT by a field value:

```
SELECT NAME, AMOUNT, DEPT FROM database
       WHERE AMOUNT > 100
       GROUP BY DEPT
```

The preceding statement would select records from the database if AMOUNT is greater than 100. The resulting table is grouped by the DEPT field.

HAVING clause

The HAVING clause defines which groups will be shown. It is similar to the function of the WHERE clause in the SELECT statement:

```
SELECT NAME, AMOUNT, DEPT FROM database
       WHERE AMOUNT > 100
       GROUP BY DEPT
       HAVING MAX(AMOUNT) > 1000
```

Only departments with a maximum amount in any record greater 1000 will be shown.

ORDER BY clause

The ORDER BY clause indexes the results returned:

```
SELECT NAME, AMOUNT, DEPT FROM database
        WHERE AMOUNT > 100
        GROUP BY DEPT
        HAVING MAX(AMOUNT) > 1000
        ORDER BY NAME ASC
```

The results will be in alphabetical order for the NAME field, grouped into departments, in ASCending sequence (the default). Descending sequence is signified by DESC.

UPDATE statement

The UPDATE statement can be used to replace fields in a database with a new value, based on a test. For instance, if you wanted to replace all DISCOUNT fields in a database called ACCOUNTS with .10 for only those records where AMOUNT is greater than 1000:

```
UPDATE ACCOUNTS SET DISCOUNT = .10
        WHERE AMOUNT > 1000
```

Be careful with the UPDATE statement, as it will actually change all of the indicated fields in the relevant records. But this is a very quick and easy way to update databases, with a one-line interactive command as opposed to the entire program, which would have to be written and compiled in RPG or COBOL.

Functions

SQL provides functions which may be used in the SELECT and other statements. They include:

SUM()	Sum the field.
AVG()	Average the field.
MAX()	Find the maximum value in the field.
MIN()	Find the minimum value in the field.

These functions may be used to get quick numeric results from a database. Inside the parentheses, include the name of the field you want to SUM, or whatever. For instance, to see the sum of the AMOUNT field from database ACCOUNTS:

```
STRSQL

SELECT SUM(AMOUNT) FROM ACCOUNTS
```

This will return an on-screen summation of the AMOUNT field.

17.6 SQL AND SYSTEMS APPLICATION ARCHITECTURE (SAA)

SQL is one of the first applications from IBM which truly represents the future of Systems Application Architecture. SAA is designed to incorporate data manipulation across any IBM platform. When SQL reaches its full implementation, it will be easy for any user to query, define, or modify data or database structures. It is our opinion that SQL must first reach the level of a consistent implementation on each platform before this can easily be achieved. Currently, the AS/400 implementation of SQL is a subset of the mainframe implementation and the PS/2 version is being defined.

17.7 JOB LOCKS

All SQL programs execute as part of a job. A job generally involves one or more programs, requiring the database manager to allocate resources and locks on files (databases). Locking is used to maintain data integrity when several programs request access at the same time, preventing, for example, updates of the same column or row of data at the same time.

17.8 SUMMARY

An extensive data definition and manipulation capacity is provided through SQL/400. This language can create tables or databases, indexes, and views of the data.

SQL is a very friendly language and does not take a great deal of time to learn. SQL can easily be introduced and implemented in the same day, in a basic form, unlike some of the other AS/400 application languages. SQL is made for users of all skill levels. As you become more adept in the use of SQL, you will find subtleties in using the language, such as indexes from a base table. As its name only partly implies, Structured Query Language allows users to query, retrieve, update, and delete data in a database.

SQL is a future direction in database methodology, especially where multiple systems and platforms are involved. Eventually, IBM intends for SQL calls to run transparently across platforms, so that an SQL query on a PS/2 could access a database on an AS/400 and update a database on a mainframe, all transparently to the user. The potential power of this kind of development environment is obvious.

SQL is fully documented in your IBM manuals and they provide full reference and further expansion of the topics listed here.

Chapter

18

REXX (Restructured EXtended eXecutor)

18.1 REXX OVERVIEW

400/REXX is a structured programming language which is part of OS/400, and may be seen as an extension to CL. For command processing or simple applications, it can be very useful. What might take many lines of CL—string handling, for instance—can be handled by one REXX statement. It is adapted from the System/370 MVS environment and is SAA's official prodedural language. While most of the tasks which can be accomplished in REXX are also addressable by CL, REXX is easier to use in many cases and has many built-in functions which can save a lot of time. CL commands can be inserted right into REXX routines, although SEU can't help out with CL prompting in the REXX environment. Its logical constructs are more structured than CL, offering DO WHILE, WHILE, UNTIL, and FOR loops as well as SELECT. Recursive calls are supported for flexibility. I/O to the terminal is easier than in any other AS/400 language or utility.

REXX is interpreted, not compiled. First you enter the REXX source code, and then you run it through the REXX interpreter without compiling. There is no compiled program object because REXX runs right from the source code. This means that it is convenient as well as slower than most compiled programs. In addition, its I/O scheme is rudimentary, allowing only sequential reads of only one input file.

QREXSRC is the source physical file which should be used to contain REXX programs or members of source type REXX. SEU is used to edit REXX programs. REXX programs are composed of various clauses of the following types:

Null clauses	/* this is a comment */, or blank lines
Assignments	A = 'Hi'
Instructions	REXX keywords
Labels	markers in a program for subroutines invoked with CALL (for example, SUBRTN1: is a label)
Commands	literal clauses that are run by other programs, like CL

18.2 VARIABLES

Variables are easily declared in REXX. In fact, they do not have to be declared at all in the strict sense. All REXX variables are characters, although REXX can perform math with them if they represent valid numbers. A = 123 assigns a character 123 to variable A and this variable can then be treated interchangeably as a character or a number by the program. You can do math with it, concatenate it, or substring it.

Variable names can be 250 characters long and can contain alpha characters or numbers (the first character must be alpha). REXX is not case-sensitive, so that "A" is the same as "a" in a variable name. The symbols !, ?, and _ are also valid in REXX. A99_!? is a valid REXX variable name, even if somewhat obscure.

Variables can be assigned values in several ways.

Assignment	A = 3
ARG	receives and assigns parameters when the program is called
PULL	gets input from external data queue or user input to a variable from the keyboard if queue is empty

See the discussion of REXX instructions for more detail on ARG and PULL.

Variables can be displayed with the SAY instruction:

```
SAY var1 var2  /* shows the values of var1 and var2 on screen */
```

If a variable is not yet assigned, the SAY instruction will merely repeat the name of the variable on screen, in uppercase.

You can use the period in compound symbols or names to create arrays. The first part of the name is called the *stem,* while the second part is the *tail.* The tail may be numeric or alpha. Array elements may be of different types. Here is an array declaration to contain months of the year:

```
month.1 = "January"
month.2 = "February"
month.3 = "March"
month.4 = "April"
month.5 = "May"
```

. . . etc.

If the program knows the number of the month, it can access the array element containing its name. 'SAY month.4' results in 'April' being displayed on the screen. This is an example of a one-dimensional array. Two-dimensional arrays are possible as well, as in var.3.2, etc.

All REXX variables are global in scope. They are available throughout the program unless they are made local with the PROCEDURE instruction. PROCEDURE as the first statement in a called subroutine limits the visibility of variables to the local routine. The main program's variables are not visible to the subroutine, and the subroutine's variables are deleted on return to the main program. Variables may be passed by value into the subroutine with the ARG instruction:

```
CALL SUBRTN x

SUBRTN:
PROCEDURE
ARG var1
.
.
.
RETURN var1
```

The preceding is a subroutine identified by the label SUBRTN:. The PROCEDURE instruction hides all main program variables from the routine. The ARG instruction receives one passed parameter into the local variable called var1. The CALL instruction invokes SUBRTN and passes the value of x into the local variable var1. The RETURN instruction sends the value of var1 back to the special REXX variable RESULT, which is used just for this. It contains the value passed back from the most recently called subroutine. Main program variables can be made visible to the subroutine with the PROCEDURE EXPOSE instruction. All main program variables which follow the EXPOSE word will be visible:

```
PROCEDURE EXPOSE amount custname
```

This makes only the main program variables called 'amount' and 'custname' visible to the routine.

18.3 OPERATORS AND EXPRESSIONS

REXX offers several operators to be used in building and testing expressions. Expressions are used for variable assignment, SAYing, or testing in IF or other logical constructs.

Arithmetic operators

`+` add
`–` subtract
`*` multiply
`/` divide
`%` divide and return the integer part of result
`//` divide and return the remainder
`**` exponentiation
`||` concatenate (with characters or even with numbers)

Example

```
var1 = (2 * 3) || "b"
```

Result: 6b

Logical operators

`&` AND
`|` OR
`&&` XOR
`\` NOT
`¬` NOT (same as \)
`==` strictly equal
`=` equal
`^=` NOT equal
`>` greater than
`<` less than
`>=` greater than or equal to
`<=` less than or equal to

Example

```
IF (var1 = var2 & var1 <= 11) | var2 = 35
```

You can see that expression construction in REXX is quite sophisticated, especially since there are many more special operators available (see the IBM 400/REXX manual). The preceding are the most commonly used.

18.4 KEYWORDS

REXX has keywords which constitute the instructions of the language. These instructions, together with the built-in REXX functions, implement the functionality of REXX. Their syntax is not complex.

ARG As the first instruction in a REXX program, ARG receives the parameter string which was passed into the program and parses it into REXX variables. The parameter can be up to 3000 characters long, and is parsed by words (blank delimitation). ARG is shorthand for PARSE UPPER ARG.

```
ARG var1 var2
```

CALL Invokes an internal subroutine or external program, possibly passing it parameters.

```
CALL pgmname parm
```

DO Indicates that the following instructions are to be executed as a group until the END is encountered. Usually used with IF or select to provide a list of instructions to be performed if the condition is met. Without DO, only the first instruction following the IF is executed.

```
IF a = b THEN
  DO
    instruction
    instruction
    instruction
  END
```

DO WHILE Executes the instructions which follow, up to the END, in a recurring loop until the condition becomes false.

```
DO WHILE x = 0
  instruction
  instruction
  instruction
END
```

DO UNTIL Executes the instructions which follow, up to the END, in a recurring loop until the condition becomes true.

```
DO UNTIL x = 0
  instruction
  instruction
  instruction
END
```

DO *x* Indicates that the DO group is to be performed *x* times. The following executes the list of instructions 10 times.

```
DO 10
  instruction
  instruction
  instruction
END
```

DO FOREVER An endless loop which will execute until the EXIT instruction is encountered.

DROP Clears the external data queue.

EXCSBR Executes a subroutine.

```
EXCSBR subnam
```

EXIT Terminates program execution. EXIT can return a value to a calling program as in:

```
EXIT('1')
```

IF Indicates an instruction to be performed if a logical condition is true. The optional ELSE clause indicates what is to happen if the condition is false.

```
IF a = b
  THEN instruction
  ELSE instruction
```

INTERPRET Evaluates an expression, using its returned value as text to be processed by the program.

```
INTERPRET "call" pgmnam
```

ITERATE Skips all remaining loop instructions and goes directly to the loop test.

LEAVE Ends a loop and continues processing with the instruction following the loop's END.

NOP Indicates that No OPeration is to be performed following an IF. You must have some instruction after an IF or an ELSE, so if you intend for nothing to occur, use NOP.

```
IF a = b THEN
  NOP
ELSE
  instruction
```

PARSE WITH Divides various types of input strings into variables using templates. REXX assumes that it can break the input string into words delimited by spaces and assign each to a variable. Periods can be used as null placeholders to skip a word. The following divides up an input variable into six words, of which only the first, fourth, and sixth are assigned to variable names. Since there are fewer variables than input words, the entire end of the input string is put into the last variable name (var3).

```
inputvar = '10 is the number after eight and nine'
PARSE VAR inputvar WITH var1 . . var2 . var3

  /* var1 contains '10' */
  /* var2 contains 'number' */
  /* var3 contains 'eight and nine' */
```

PARSE LINEIN Takes input from the keyboard (STDIN) regardless of whether there is data on the data queue (see **PULL**).

PARSE PULL (or just PULL) Gets input from the REXX external data queue. If the queue is empty, PULL waits for user input at the keyboard. In any case, the data is placed into a variable, usually used after a SAY instruction which provides direction to the user. The following waits for the user to input two variables from the keyboard, hitting the <Enter> key each time. PULL is shorthand for PARSE UPPER PULL.

```
PULL var1 var2
```

Or, you can PARSE PULL by positional patterns in the input string. In this way, you can read a nondelimited input file and parse it into fields.

```
if the data queue contains '10ABC356.99'
PARSE PULL inputvar WITH var1 2 var2 3 var3

  /* var1 contains 2 positions '10' */
  /* var2 contains 3 positions 'ABC' */
  /* var3 contains the rest '356.99' */
```

(See IBM manual *Programming: Procedures Language 400/REXX* for complexities of PARSE instructions).

PROCEDURE Hides the variables of the current subroutine from the calling program and vice versa. This creates local, as opposed to public, variables. Use ARG to receive variables into the subroutine and RETURN with RESULT to return values to the caller.

PUSH Places strings on top of the data queue.

QUEUE Places strings on the bottom of the data queue.

RETURN Returns from a subroutine.

SAY Displays text between quotation marks on the terminal.

```
SAY 'Please enter your name: '
```

SELECT A case statement which selects one of a series of operations to perform, based on a logical test.

```
SELECT
  WHEN x = 1 THEN ...
  WHEN x = 2 THEN ...
  WHEN x = 3 THEN ...
  OTHERWISE ...
```

Long instructions can be continued on the next line by using the comma character. Multiple instructions can be combined on the same line with the semicolon.

18.5 FUNCTIONS AND SUBROUTINES

REXX has many functions which make it easier and faster to write than CL. Internal functions are user-defined, while external functions are provided by the REXX language. Both types are recursive, they may call themselves. A function is called simply by naming it and passing its parameters in parentheses: FNCNAM(var1, var2). The function routine returns a value which substitutes for the function call in the calling program.

A subroutine is invoked using the REXX CALL instruction: CALL SBRNAM var1. There are not parentheses around the parameters in a REXX subroutine call. A function always returns a value, while a subroutine may or may not. Otherwise, they are quite similar. They consist of code at the end of the program which is identified by a REXX label (with a semicolon). When invoked, REXX branches to the label and continues processing until it encounters the RETURN. Then it goes back to the place in the calling program where it left off. In the case of a function, the returned value is substituted for the function call in the code (e.g., SAY DATE(U) evaluates to SAY '12/31/93').

The PROCEDURE instruction, following the function or subroutine label, makes all variables created in the routine local. Main program variables cannot be seen by the routine, and the routine's variables evaporate on return to the calling program. Parameters are passed in with the ARG instruction, and are passed back with the RETURN instruction. If PROCEDURE is not used, all variables are global and can be accessed by name in the main program and the routines. When a subroutine RETURNS a value, it is passed back in the special REXX variable called RESULT. This may then be accessed by the program.

These are some of the more useful REXX external functions:

DATE Returns the system date in various formats.

```
SAY DATE('U')      /* returns mm/dd/yy */
```

FORMAT Adjusts and rounds the display of a variable.

```
FORMAT(amount,9,2)
```

LEFT Returns leftmost portion of a string.

```
LEFT(string,4)
```

LENGTH Returns the length of a string.

MAX Returns the largest of a group of numbers.

```
MAX(a,b,c)
```

MIN Returns the smallest of a group of numbers.

```
MIN(a,b,c)
```

OVERLAY Writes over a portion of a string with a given value.

```
OVERLAY(string,'ABC',4)  /* writes 'ABC' over string starting at
                            position 4 */
```

RIGHT Returns the rightmost portion of a string.

```
RIGHT(string,7)
```

STRIP Removes leading or trailing space from a string.

```
STRIP(string)
```

SUBSTR Substring by starting position and length.

```
SUBSTR('123456789',5,2)  /* returns '56' */
```

TIME Returns the system time.

```
SAY TIME()   /* returns hh:mm:ss */
```

TRANSLATE Changes characters within a string.

```
TRANSLATE(string,' ','!')   /* changes all spaces in string to ! */
```

It is possible to call external routines from REXX, and these external routines may by written in other languages. The preceding are the most common and useful of REXX's string manipulation functions. Many more are contained in the IBM REXX manuals.

18.6 COMMANDS

Commands are lines contained in quotes which are passed to CL (the default command environment) for execution. 'STRPDM' as the only contents of the REXX line will be passed to CL to start PDM. This is a very powerful feature of REXX because it means that virtually all functions of CL are available from within REXX, as well as all REXX functions. In this way, REXX is a command extension to CL.

To submit a job with a parameter to batch from REXX:

```
'SBMJOB CMD(CALL PGM(pgmname) PARM(&var1))'
```

The quotes around the CL command identify it as a command to be passed by REXX to the CL environment. Note the use of the ampersand (&) in the passing of REXX variable 'var1' to CL. Commands are executed in CL and then processing is returned to REXX along with a return code which can be accessed through REXX special variable RC. A '0' return code (RC = 0) indicates successful completion of the command.

Although CL is the default command environment, REXX can also pass commands into the Common Programming Interface Communications environment (CPICOMM). SAA CPI commands can be issued for communications functions.

18.7 I/O AND THE REXX EXTERNAL DATA QUEUE

REXX does not take advantage of the AS/400's database architecture with its attendant external file descriptions. Instead, it uses an external data queue to communicate with the world outside the REXX program. REXX can read from and write to the external data queue as well as clear it. This external data queue is created when the job is started and lasts for the duration of the job, not for the duration of the current interactive REXX invocation. Therefore, a REXX program can end and leave a data queue out there with data in it. This is useful for communicating between programs. It can also be a problem if you forget that there is already data in the queue when you start up a REXX program. REXX can read from the data queue or the keyboard for user input. You can PUSH data onto the top of the queue or PULL data off. This is like a stack of plates: the last one you put on is the first one you take off the top, or Last In First Out (LIFO).

REXX uses stream I/O and data parsing to read records and fields from a database via the data queue. The file names STDIN and STDOUT are the only two file names REXX knows. They refer by default to the keyboard (STDIN) and display (STDOUT). They can be redirected by the CL command OVRDBF to physical files. When STDIN and STDOUT are not overridden, the Extended Program Model (EPM) controls the REXX session and displays output on the terminal. The interpreter automatically opens and closes STDIN and STDOUT for the program. DDS and display files are not required for this, which is a significant convenience of REXX. Paging up and down, <F9> for retrieval and <F3> program termination are supported by EPM. In this way, interaction with the user is quite easily accomplished, using the SAY and PULL instructions. EPM handles the rest.

REXX can read from and write to data files as well. First, you have to override to the database files from STDIN and/or STDOUT, the only input file names that REXX recognizes. Only one input file is allowed, as with CL, and only sequential reads are supported. You can get around this limitation by starting another REXX invocation to read another file and return values to the original REXX program via the data queue. Obviously, this is not the language to use for complex I/O requirements such as key field random access or backing up the record pointer. But small, simple applications which require sequential I/O with a database can be developed very quickly using the features of REXX.

The instructions and functions which deal with the data queue are:

PUSH Places a line at the top of the queue. The last line PUSH'd is the first one PULL'd (LIFO).

```
PUSH var1
```

PULL Takes a line off the top of the queue, or from STDIN if the queue is empty (see instructions: PARSE PULL).

```
PULL var1
```

QUEUE Places a line at the bottom of the queue.

```
QUEUE var1
```

QUEUED A function which returns the number of lines in the queue.

```
DO QUEUED()  /* this will execute a do loop for the number of lines in
                the queue, which is a handy way to process the whole
                queue */
```

OVRDBF Actually a CL command which can be used in the REXX program to override STDIN to an AS/400 database.

STDIN The only input file REXX can use.

STDOUT The only output file REXX can use.

You can also add a REXX external data queue buffer with ADDREXBUF and remove one with RMVREXBUF.

18.8 RUNNING REXX

You run the REXX program by using the STRREXPRC command in CL or in another REXX program:

```
STRREXPRC SRCFILE(QGPL/QREXSRC) SRCMBR(PGMNAME) PARM('A 123')
```

The ARG instruction in the REXX program could receive these two parameters into two variable names, parsing them by space delimitation.

REXX allows only one parameter to be passed as a character string when the procedure is called with STRREXPRC. This parameter can be up to 3000 characters long and should be contained in quotes (which are not passed to the called REXX program). Then you have to parse it inside the REXX routine to contruct the various constituent parameters needed by the program. The EXIT statement allows the return of values to another REXX program. If you want to pass parameters to another program in another language, you have to use the QREXQ API which uses the QREXQ data queue for PUSHing and PULLing parameters used between programs. One program pushes data onto the queue, and then the next program pulls it off and uses it.

If you have a problem or bug with a REXX program, you can use the TRACE instruction to display the results of REXX operations:

TRACE INTERMEDIATES	Shows the result of each operation.
TRACE RESULTS	Shows results of expressions.
TRACE NORMAL	Shows only commands which might cause failure condition.
TRACE ERRORS	Shows commands which could cause error or failure.
TRACE ?R	The question mark makes TRACE interactive, waiting for the user to hit <Enter> before continuing; the R means RESULTS.

REXX programs can be run from the PDM Work with Members screen. Just put a '16' next to the member name of the REXX program you want to run. Also, you can use the QREXX API to call REXX programs (STRREXPRC).

18.9 SAMPLE REXX PROGRAM

Here is a sample REXX program which uses some of the most useful of the foregoing instructions and functions. It parses a parameter which is passed in to determine the user name and the report date. Then the program calls a subroutine to get the password, a special one for Fred, the supervisor. Fred can then run three reports while the other users can only run two. These reports are invoked by passing CL commands out to the CL environment. Two of these reports submit Queries to batch, while the third calls a CL program and passes it a CL parameter.

```
/* This is a REXX program to run programs based on passwords */

ARG CALLPARM    /* receives calling parameter into REXX variable */

PARSE VAR CALLPARM WITH USRDAT USRNAM     /* parses callparm into*/
                                          /* USRDAT and USRNAM   */

CALL SUPER                          /* supervisor password subroutine */

IF USRNAM = 'FRED' & PASSWORD = 'X99' THEN DO
 SAY '1. Management Report'         /* supervisor menu */
 SAY '2. User Report 1'
 SAY '3. User Report 2'
 END
ELSE DO
```

```
  SAY '1. User Report 1'          /* user menu */
  SAY '2. User Report 2'
  END
  PULL CHOICE                     /* get user choice from keyboard */

 SELECT                           /* process the choice */

   WHEN CHOICE = 1 & PASSWORD = 'X99'  /* supervisor report #1? */
     THEN 'SBMJOB CMD(RUNQRY QRY1)'    /* CL command to submit Query */
                                       /* to batch */

   WHEN (CHOICE = 2 & PASSWORD = 'X99')|(CHOICE = 1 & PASSWORD = 'ABC')
     THEN 'SBMJOB CMD(RUNQRY QRY2)'

   WHEN (CHOICE = 3 & PASSWORD = 'X99')|(CHOICE = 2 & PASSWORD = 'ABC')

     THEN 'SBMJOB CMD(CALL RPT2 (&USRDAT))' /* CL command to submit CL   */
                                            /* program to batch with    */
 END                                        /* CL parameter &USRDAT     */

 EXIT                             /* terminate REXX program */

 SUPER:                           /* label to identify subroutine */

   SAY 'What is your password? '
                                  /* message on screen */
   PULL password                  /* gets password from user */

   IF PASSWORD ¬= 'X99' & PASSWORD ¬= 'ABC' THEN
     EXIT                         /* incorrect password terminates */
   ELSE
     RETURN PASSWORD
```

18.10 SUMMARY

REXX is a very useful procedural language provided by IBM as part of OS/400. As an extension to CL, REXX can make programming job control much easier and faster. It offers many built-in functions not available in CL, especially for advanced string handling which can be quite cumbersome in CL. Modern structured constructs like DO WHILE and SELECT also make REXX more convenient than CL. In addition, CL commands can be run right from the REXX program. And REXX is able to put messages right on the screen and receive answers back from the user by automatically using the Extended Program Model (EPM). This means you can easily interact with the user right from the REXX program, without having to write DDS for DSPF (or SDA). REXX is also used as a standard SAA language on the System/370 and PS/2 or PC.

Chapter

19

Application Integration

19.1 WHAT IS API?

Application Integration is the ultimate power of the AS/400. Entirely integrated and coordinated procedures may be designed and implemented once the components of API are understood. With it, you can specify a menu to initiate a CL program which calls an RPG or a COBOL program to update a database, possibly on another computer, and then run a shell document from Office, printing form letters from that database—all of this from one menu choice or even from a Calendar setup which runs a batch automatically in the middle of the night.

Integration

The AS/400 provides an integrated and seamless interface between the various powerful functions of the machine's operating system. You can call a program written in any language supported by the AS/400 (RPG, COBOL, PL1, CL, C). These programs can, in turn, call displays designed with SDA, update databases, etc. CL has logic structures, so that parameters can be passed to the called programs, and they can return values which determine how the CL program will branch after the call. This is a very powerful feature. It means that all components of an API can be dynamically responsive to values returned from other areas.

CL can even initiate the printing of documents or shell documents in Office, which can query a database and print various paragraphs, or not, depending on the query results. The entire range of integrations on the AS/400 is flexible and powerful, and usually provides a variety of possible solutions to most problems.

Putting together the pieces

Of course, integration is one of the most advanced and complicated techniques on the machine because it involves knowledge of many different areas and skills. It is not uncommon for APIs to involve, for instance:

Menus	designed with SDA
Screens	designed with SDA or coded in DDS
Databases	designed with IDDU or coded in DDS, physical files and/or logical files
CLP	programs written in SEU and compiled
RPG	programs written in SEU and compiled
QRY	Query/400
Office	documents created with DW/4

The benefit of being able to work with all of these functions or tools is the ability create a streamlined, customized application which any user can initiate at the touch of a single key, from a menu.

19.2 MENUS

Menus are often involved in APIs because they provide a simple front end for the user. Using Screen Design Aid (SDA), menus can be created very quickly, and can call any program in the system, passing parameters to it if desired. In addition, a menu can call any other menu, so the menu is a powerful and safe front end for the user interface. And the user's profile can be set up so that the user is automatically placed at any desired menu upon sign-on, and signed off when quitting this menu.

The front end for users

One of the primary goals of API development is to insulate the user from the complexities and hazards of the operating system. Also, APIs provide a rapid and highly synchronized processing environment, ensuring the correct sequence of modules and allowing other controls to be enacted, transparently to the user.

Passing parameters based on user selection

When designing a menu in SDA (see Chap. 12), it is possible to set up a program call from the menu by entering a CL CALL command at the screen which underlies the menu design screen, and which appears when you hit the <F10> key. Just add a parameter to the CALL command to pass it to the called program as:

```
CALL REPORT 3
```

This example calls a compiled program called REPORT and passes it a number 3 as a parameter.

19.3 CL PROGRAMS

CL files as drivers called from menus

Often, a CL program is invoked from the menu because of the power of CL to manage the rest of the job stream. Job control is, after all, one of the main functions of CL interacting with the operating system. CL programs can:

clear physical files (databases)

call programs and pass parameters

print an Office document

branch conditionally

call screens and pass parameters

run Queries

call menus

override databases and printer files

They can, in fact, invoke any function on the AS/400, and are the logical control center for an API called from a menu.

Receiving parameters from menus and programs

CLP programs can pass and receive parameters by value. The first line of any CLP program is PGM, as we have seen in Chap. 4. Variables must be declared next:

```
PGM
DCL VAR(&ABEND) TYPE(*CHAR) LEN(1)
```

Note that the variable is declared using the CL DCL VAR command, and that its name is preceded with the ampersand, within parentheses. The ampersand is required, as are the additional parameters—type and length. Once declared, this variable can be passed to a called program and received back, controlling logic flow in the CLP (see following).

File handling

Often, it is necessary to clear any data from a database before processing begins. This cannot be done from an RPG or COBOL program. To initialize a database in this way, use the CLRPFM command in a CLP:

```
0003.00   CLRPFM FILE(DATAFILE)
```

Remember that any user invoking this command or a program containing this command must have *ALL authority to the database (see Chap. 6).

Display files

CLP programs can call displays which get input from the user and return a value for conditional branching. In this way, the user may be prompted for any kind of interaction needed by the application—for instance, mounting a tape or reacting to an unexpected error condition in the processing. First, the screen must be declared to the CLP:

```
DCLF SCREEN              (this is the file name)
```

Once the screen has been declared, the CL command which calls a screen is:

```
SNDRCVF SCR              (this is the format name)
```

Calling other programs

CLP may call other compiled programs. The command is CALL and it is followed by the name of the program to be called and optional parameter(s) to be passed:

```
0004.00   CALL UPDTFIL &ABEND
```

Note the ampersand '&' as a prefix to the passed parameter. Remember that this parameter must have been previously declared in the first line of the CLP after the PGM statement (see previous).

Logic: If and GoTo

When a CLP program receives return of control from a called program, any valid parameter passed will also be returned, automatically. The value of this parameter is now available for conditional testing and branching. In the example we are using, the following statement will test the value of the passed parameter &ABEND. If the program which was called has changed the value of &ABEND to a 'Y' the CLP program will branch to a label with the name of 'END.' Otherwise, program flow passes to the next line:

```
IF COND(&ABEND = 'Y') THEN(GOTO END)
.
.
.
END:
ENDPGM
```

19.4 OTHER PROGRAM CALLS

CLPs may call any other valid compiled program within the AS/400, including other CLPs. When processing is finished in the called program, control is returned to the calling CLP, along with any parameter passed. Likewise, RPG programs may call COBOL routines or CLPs, etc. One of the most powerful features of the AS/400 architecture is this transparency of compiled object. The system regards all executable objects in the same way, regardless of the source language.

Parameters are received in order, as passed. If the number of parameters received in this way is less than the number passed, the program will abort. Be careful to receive the same number of parameters as passed; receiving too many parameters results in a compiler error. Once parameters have been received correctly, they are available to the program for processing and may even be passed to another program and received back. Call is by positional value of the incoming parameters, so that you can assign any name to the parameters coming from another program. In other words, a list of values, not variable names, is received from the calling program, and you assign names to the values as they come in. When flow of control returns to the calling program, these parameter values are returned automatically to the parameter names in the calling program.

Program calls

RPG, as well as COBOL and C, can be called from CLP or another language. Consult the various IBM language manuals to see how the parameters passed from a calling program are received into the called program, and how they are returned. The extreme flexibility of interprogram calls is one of the important benefits of API development on the AS/400.

Displays

User screens are designed using SDA, or written in DDS. Once compiled, they may be called from any compiled program, whether it be CLP, RPG, or any other AS/400 language. Be aware of level checks when integrating applications. A program must be recompiled when any database or screen on which it depends has been recompiled.

File reads, writes, and updates

File maintenance (i.e., copy, delete, or clear) is handled by CLPs, using the usual CL commands for these functions. File I/O (i.e., searches, reads, writes, and updates) is handled in the compiled program usually called from a CLP. This called program will be in one of the AS/400 languages (RPG, C, etc.).

19.5 QUERIES

Once a Query has been defined to the AS/400 with the STRQRY command, it is a simple matter to call it from a CLP:

```
0005.00   RUNQRY QRY(QRYNAME)
```

The Query, as defined, will contain the library and data file to which it refers. Optionally, it may contain printer routing and format parameters.

19.6 DOCUMENTS AND SHELL DOCUMENTS

Documents which have been defined to Office may be called by the PRTDOC command:

```
0006.00   PRTDOC DOC(FORMLTR) FLR(FOLDER)
```

This command prints a document from a folder. This document may have been created with multiple form letters specified from a Query, included data fields, conditional paragraphs, or any of the other features available in Office.

19.7 SUMMARY

Application integration coordinates the power of the AS/400's various functions. Menus may call CLPs which in turn may call other programs, Queries, documents, etc. Parameters may be passed back and forth between the various components through API, enabling conditional branching in any module, depending on values returned from other modules.

Integrations provide a transparent and safe front end for the user. The user may simply choose an option from a menu to initiate the most complex series of procedures. APIs may also be run from Calendar, automatically or in batch, so that there is no user involvement at all.

An effective usage of integrations can provide an elegant and seamless solution to virtually any problem or algorithm. This requires a thorough knowledge of the features and functions of the AS/400, and represents the ultimate integrated power of the machine.

Chapter

20

Debugging

20.1 COMPILING

Once a program has been written using SEU, it is a simple matter to compile it. If you are working in PDM, as we have suggested, you simply need to enter a number '14' next to the source code entry on the PDM screen. This will submit the program to the appropriate compiler, as indicated by the source code type.

20.2 COMPILE LISTING

When the compiler finishes with the program, it will send a compile listing to the printer. We suggest that you alter this procedure so that the compile listing goes into an output queue instead of to the printer. That way, you don't have to run to the printer every time you compile, and you can use the editor on the compile listing to search more quickly for errors. You can even call up the original source code and the compile listing in windows in SEU so that you can view the errors and the source at the same time, working back and forth.

To send the compile listing to a spool file, you need first to create an output queue: CRTOUTQ outqname. Then you need to indicate that all your output is to be directed to the output queue: CHGUSRPRF username OUTQ(outqname). You will have to get your security officer to do this for you, since it requires QSECOFR or QSECADM authority. If you do this, remember that all output will go to the OUTQ and will have to be printed explicitly from there, using the WRKSPLF command.

Error severity levels

The compile listing will contain various severity levels of errors, assuming there are any. You know the compile was successful when there are no errors above severity level 10. Level 20 severity and above are fatal errors, that is, the program will not successfully be compiled into an executable object.

20.3 WORKING IN THE SPOOL FILE

If you have directed your compile listings to a spool file in your output queue (see previous), you can work quickly and easily on compiler errors.

After you have submitted the program to the compiler by placing a number 14 next to it on the PDM Work With Members screen, you can go immediately to the spool file by entering an 'SP' next to the member name on the PDM screen, or type WRKSPLF at the command line. This brings up the output queue for spool files. There may be many entries here, because every job you perform which creates output will end up here. It is important to manage your spool (output) queue, deleting unnecessary entries when you are finished with them so that the spool queue does not become cluttered.

Identifying the error

When you have the compile listed on the spool queue, wait until the status changes from OPN to RDY. For a long program, this may take a little while. Place a number 5 next to it when it is RDY and hit <Enter> to bring up the compile listing. On the line which says Control, enter a b and hit <Enter> to get you to the bottom of the compile listing. Here you will see the numbers of errors by various severity levels. If there are none, there is a message "Program Has Been Created" and you are successful. Unfortunately, this is not all that common with complex programs, so you will have to track the source of the errors and debug. Figures 20.1 and 20.2 illustrate Working in the Spool File.

Locating the cause of the error

Just above the severity level listing at the bottom of the program are the error codes for what went wrong. Page up to these error codes and jot them down, along with the brief description of the error. Then go back up to the top of the listing by entering a t in the control line at the top of the screen. Now go down one line to the Find line and enter one of the error codes. Once that is entered hit <F16> to find that error code

```
                    Work with All Spooled Files

Type options, press Enter.
  2=Change   3=Hold   4=Delete   5=Display   6=Release   8=Attributes

                              Device or                    Total    Cur
Opt  File          User       Queue       User Data  Sts   Pages   Page  Copy
 5   PROG1         BARITZ     QPRINT                 RDY       1            1
 _   QPJOBLOG      BARITZ     QPRINT      BARITZ     RDY       3            1

                                                                      Bottom
Parameters for option 2 or command
===> ____________________________________________________________________
F3=Exit   F10=View 3   F11=View 2   F12=Cancel   F22=Printers   F24=More keys

     08-03                                                 S2 S9999999 KB
```

Figure 20.1 Working in the spool file.

```
                                Display Spooled File
File . . . . . :     DB                                  Page/Line    20/44
Control . . . . .    B_____                              Columns      1 - 78
Find  . . . . . .    ______________________________
*...+....1....+....2....+....3....+....4....+....5....+....6....+....7....+...
 &YY                   300        *CHAR                2          1200    1400    1500
 Defined Labels
 Label               Defined         References
 END                   7800            1900
 START                  800            7700
                      * * * * *    E N D    O F   C R O S S   R E F E R E N C E
 5738SS1 V2R1M1   920306                       Control Language                 WIN
                                               Message Summary
               Severity
 Total         0-9   10-19   20-29   30-39   40-49   50-59   60-69   70-79   80-89   90
   217          0      1       0       0       0       0       0       0       0
 Program DB created in library XXXXRPT. Maximum error severity 10.
                              * * * * *   E N D   O F   M E S S A G E   S U M
                                * * * * *   E N D   O F   C O M P I L A T I O
                                                                          Bottom
F3=Exit   F12=Cancel   F19=Left   F20=Right   F24=More keys
```

Figure 20.2 Working in the spool file.

in the source code. The editor will find the offending line of code and you will see the code with several stars next to it.

Often you can tell from the error description that you have noted what is wrong with the line of code. If not, look up the error code in the appropriate error messages manual. Make a note of the line numbers of the errors in the source code.

An alternate method is to bring the compiler listing into a window underneath the actual source code, so that you can look back and forth between them. When you have the source code up on the screen in SEU, hit <F15> to bring up a window. Enter a number '2' to bring in the spool file and name the spool file. Hit <Enter>. A window will appear at the current cursor position. You can change the window position with the <F6> key. Now you can work back and forth between the compiler listing and the source code.

Correcting the error

Once you have determined the nature of your compiler errors, go back to the PDM edit screen (if you are not already there, in split screen). In the line numbers at the left of the screen, enter the line number of an error, which you have previously noted. At the appropriate line number, correct the code.

Resubmitting the compile

When you think you have corrected all errors, leave SEU by hitting the <F3> key, and resubmit the compile by entering a number 14 again next to the source entry in the PDM screen. Continue these steps until you get a clean compile ('Program Has Been Created' at the bottom of the compile listing), as can be seen in Fig. 20.2.

20.4 DEBUG

Sometimes a program will compile cleanly, but still does not accomplish what you intended. The results are off somehow. You need to look at the results of the processing as the program is running. You need DEBUG.

Starting DEBUG

Once the program has compiled successfully, you may run a debug on it, showing contents of variables at line numbers of your choice. To start debug, type:

```
STRDBG pgmname UPDPROD(*YES)
```

where PGMNAME is the name of the program you want to debug. UPDPROD(*YES) means that you want to run the program on existing data files specified in the program, changing data where required.

Setting breakpoints

Once debug has been started, you can set breakpoints at line numbers in the program where you want to stop, and specify variables you want to look at.

```
ADDBKP STMT(23500) PGMVAR( (X) (NAME) )
```

This breakpoint statement will cause the program to stop at line 235 and will show you, on the screen, the contents of variables X and NAME. Note the use of the zeroes after the line number. These are required. Breakpoints must be set at executable line numbers. You cannot set a breakpoint at a line number for a comment line, for instance.

Now, just call the program in the usual way:

```
CALL PGMNAME
```

It will stop at the indicated line number and reveal its variable contents.

To remove a breakpoint:

```
RMVBKP STMT(23500)
```

To end DEBUG:

```
ENDDBG
```

You must end and restart DEBUG every time you recompile.

Displaying variable contents

When you are in the variable window at a breakpoint, you may display additional variables if you wish by hitting the <F10> key and entering variable names. You will see any variables specified in the ADDBKP statement plus those additionally identified.

20.5 COMMON ERRORS

There are several common types of compiler errors, most of which are easily avoided or fixed.

Unidentified or redefined variables

Using undeclared variables or fields results in a compiler error. Coding x = x + 1 when x has not been defined, or redefining an existing field with different attributes, will cause an error.

Data type mismatches are also fairly common. Do not try to add 1.5 to the letter a.

Undeclared or incorrectly declared files

Files must be opened correctly. Opening a file in read-only mode and then trying to write to it will result in compiler errors. Referring to a file by an incorrect name will get you a multiplicity of errors from "Undefined variable" to "file does not exist."

Incorrect or missing syntax

It is easy enough to forget or mistype required syntax, possibly an IF without an END in RPG, or a missing { in C. Missing periods are common in COBOL. All required correct syntax must be present in order for a program to compile correctly. Typos are also very common in this category (Rezd instead of Read, for instance).

Objects not found in library list

Files named in the program must be accessible through the library list at compile time (see Chap. 5). This applies to display files as well as physical files and logical files.

Objects not recompiled when necessary

Level checks result when a file is recompiled without recompiling programs which depend on it. If, for instance, a database structure is changed, the programs which reference it must also be recompiled to pick up the change. This applies to physical files, display files, and programs.

20.6 SUMMARY

The AS/400 environment makes compiling and debugging quite efficient. You can compile from the PDM screen simply by entering a number 14 next to the source file. You can redirect your compile listing output to an output queue where you can edit the spool file with SEU. You can edit the source file and the error file in windows, simultaneously, in SEU, working back and forth.

DEBUG allows you to set breakpoints and reveal and modify variable contents at any executable line number in the program.

Chapter 21

SYNON

21.1 CASE AND SYNON

Computer Aided Software Engineering (CASE) tools have been making a significant contribution to the development of in-house projects and applications. Some shops have even made the transition from a team of programmers to a team of business analysts who are trained in the use of CASE. These shops claim that they have not touched a line of code in months or years, preferring to design the system with the help of CASE tools and let the tools actually generate the system and the source code.

SYNON is the major CASE tool for the AS/400. It is a program that writes programs. IBM has made SYNON their only AD/Cycle partner for the AS/400. The IBM endorsement means that SYNON will continue to be a major player in applications development on the AS/400.

The guiding principle of CASE is to have a repository of stock objects, consisting of standard subroutines and programs. Let's face it, most systems involve the same sort of processes, with variations. You have to input data to a screen, validate it with edits, store it in a relational database, possibly process it, and retrieve it in meaningful reports. That's usually about it. SYNON provides a way to begin with reliable modules for these functions, and tailors them to a specific design of your data. Then it writes the code in RPG or COBOL and compiles the entire system. The SYNON development scheme involves data modeling, functional specifications, prototyping, documentation, and code generation.

Obviously, this is not an inexpensive capability. And it requires extensive training and practice for the users to become adept at manipulating the data dictionary and navigating the action diagrams. SYNON offers training and consulting to help the initiate. The fact that more than 2000 sites are using SYNON probably attests to its productivity. They say it will cut 20 to 80 percent out of development time, a fact which accounts for the 20 percent of total users who are themselves software vendors. Ease of maintenance of existing systems is another selling point of SYNON. The user can generally locate the intended fix quickly and modify it easily by using the SYNON interface.

SYNON now offers SYNON/CSG which has client/server capability. Applications can be generated from a single design that uses the cooperative processing capabilities of the AS/400 and the PS/2. Also, SYNON can run under MVS and AIX. The intent of SYNON is not to be limited to a single platform, but to take advantage of and adhere to IBM's SAA concept, providing functionality across a range of systems.

21.2 DATA MODELING

The entire concept of SYNON begins with the data model. A data model is a structured description of your relational database. This requires a rigorous thinking through of the purposes and requirements of your business and its data processing function. Throughout, SYNON takes this sort of top-down approach. Analysis is the key and primary function, followed by system generation at the final stage.

A data model must be normalized. It must be:

- Comprehensive, containing all relevant bits of information
- Nonredundant, containing each data item only once
- Consistent, applying the same rules for data definition throughout

The data model is not the actual database but a symbolic representation of the details of the business model. The data model is developed from the business model and leads to the construction of the database in the following manner:

- Analyzes the business model
- Develops the data model
- Generates the actual database

Meetings and discussions between the analyst's users lead to an accurate business model. It is important to take special care at this point, because everything else depends on it. Once the business data is determined, you have to delimit the business functions. In other words, here is the information—what do you do with it? This involves thinking about appropriate access paths to the data.

A data model is necessarily a somewhat simplified view of the actual business. Not all of the daily operations in an office are represented in the data model, nor should they be (for instance, talking at the coffee machine and searching for lost files). The business and data models should consist of essential business functions which can effectively be computerized.

21.3 DESIGN PROCESS

The data model is a blueprint for the design of the system. The designer must decide what is critical, what is included, and what is unnecessary. Disagreements will naturally arise on these subjects, and it is important to have a strategy for dealing with them in a productive manner. The whole idea behind SYNON is to spend a majority of time on business analysis, and leave actual generation of the system programs, and even the database itself, to the CASE tool. Thus the system is data-driven and object-oriented, minimizing the effects of individual programming styles and techniques.

Since SYNON knows the data structure through the data dictionary, it can very easily provide a standard input screen for a given purpose. It simply creates a module, based on certain assumptions, to allow input to the data fields which constitute the object or entity in question (maybe an order entry or a request for payment). If SYNON's assumptions about what you need in module functionality are not accurate or complete, you can modify the supplied module through action diagrams.

SYNON depends on this modularity of function or object-oriented design. Business data is analyzed into entities (functional groups), and then a modular process can be applied to the entities. 'Send a bill to a client' is a possible operation for SYNON to perform automatically once it knows what constitutes a bill and a client. These things are known to it through data modeling.

First, design a process flow diagram of the business area being analyzed. Use these symbolic representations of the business items:

Item	Symbol	SYNON implementation
A task or process	Rectangle	Function
Piece of information	Oval	Capture entity
Document or file	Tray	Entity
Person, department	Diamond	Reference entity
Movement	Lines or arrows	Access path

You can see that once the items are understood and diagrammed correctly, it is fairly easy to translate them into SYNON components.

21.4 SYNON SCREENS

The three main screens of SYNON are:

Edit Database Relations
Edit Access Paths
Edit Functions

They show the flow of SYNON thinking. First define the data, then access it, then process it. It is a top-down approach.

21.5 SYNON FUNCTION KEYS

SYNON provides several function keys to facilitate processing options in the various screens.

Screen design keys

F1	exit
F3	left 40 columns
F4	right 40 columns
F5	edit screen format details for format at cursor position
F6	cancel current operation
F7	edit screen format relations for format at cursor position
F8	pick up or put down field at cursor position
F9	move field to beginning of next line
F10	add one space before field at cursor
F11	move field at cursor to one line before
F12	align fields in format below cursor
F13	fast exit
F14	display SYNON/2 Map
F15	to left margin
F16	to right margin
F17	display list of screen formats
F18	edit display attributes of field at cursor
F19	add new function to screen after cursor field
F20	edit function field at cursor
F21	move cursor field to next line, same column
F22	remove a space before cursor field

F23	add new constants to screen
F24	align all fields in format with field at cursor
<Enter>	edit field details of cursor field
<Help>	display help text

Action diagram keys

F1	return to previous level
F5	display user exit points for code changes; select one
F6	cancel current move
F13	fast exit
F14	display SYNON/2 Map

Action diagram line selection

Ix	insert new construct
IS	display user exit points
IA	action
IC	case condition
IX	new condition within case
IT	iteration
I*	comment
I+	action is *ADD built-in function
I–	action is *SUB built-in function
I=	action is *MOVE built-in function
F	edit action or conditions
FF	edit action parameters
C	copy this construct to mark 'A'
M	move this construct to mark 'A'
A	mark target position
D	delete construct
H	hide construct
S	show construct
Z	zoom line show only indicated construct
U	unzoom line
T	return to top level of diagram

21.6 ENTITY AND ATTRIBUTE

Defining entities is one of the primary tasks in using SYNON. A SYNON entity is something about which it is necessary to capture data. It could be a company, client, supplier, customer, product, or any other discrete unit about which you need to capture and retrieve data. The entire business can be broken down into entities. There are two basic types of SYNON entities: the reference entity (REF) and the capture entity (CPT). The reference entity is something that is used by the system for lookup and generally doesn't change from day to day. For instance, if data entry is inputting order forms, you want to make sure that the orders are for existing products. Therefore, you have a products lookup table—a reference entity. The daily transactions of the business, in this case the actual orders, are the capture entity. Generally, capture entities are verified or clarified by reference entities.

Entities have attributes which can be defined. An attribute is a property of an entity which consists of a field, file, or access path definition within the entity. For example, phone number is an attribute of the customer entity. Attributes are often derived from the documents which flow through the company daily.

21.7 FIELD ATTRIBUTES

Attributes (or field types) are defined in SYNON at the DEFINE OBJECTS display with these types:

CDE	code	A
VNM	valid file name	A
NBR	number	N
PCT	percent	N
PRC	price	N
QTY	quantity	N
VAL	money	N
DTE	date	N
TME	time	N
TXT	text	A
NAR	narrative	A
STS	status	A
REF	reference/based on other field	

Attributes have characteristics, or elements, which further define them. These include attribute type, name, description, data type, length, null permitted, special validation, allowed values, default values, and heading. You can see that this stage is very similar to traditional file and field definition (e.g., DDS), but more extensive. SYNON allows the specification of validation attributes for fields. These include the usual DDS type of validation such as uppercase, as well as special SYNON check conditions. In this way, SYNON is able to enforce default and special edits for fields when they are referenced for input in the system. These special edits are called *check conditions* in SYNON terminology. They have four types:

VAL	used for status type fields, it specifies a value ('A')
CMP	compares the field entry to a value (greater than 10)
RNG	allows a range of input values (15–23)
LST	list of acceptable entries ('MA' 'CT' 'NY')

When two fields have exactly the same attributes, they are said to share the same domain. A domain is the totality of a SYNON object's attributes. In this case, the fields having the same domain can and should be defined with the REF attribute, which refers it to the domain of another field:

```
VarA   10 alpha
VarB   REF         VarA
```

Virtual fields are those which are not present in the primary file, but are accessed through relational joins to other files. The REFERS TO relation is a mechanism to join one file to another such that a field in the primary causes a key field lookup in the referred-to file (see "Relations" following).

21.8 RELATIONS

Relations define the association between files (entities) or between files and fields and are part of file definition. They are the interconnections used to achieve a meaningful data model and relational database. SYNON uses eight types of relational verbs, of which the first four are the most useful:

SYNON relation	Meaning
REFERS TO	Nonkey field which is key in another file
OWNED BY	Key field in transactional (owned) file key which is also key in owning file
KNOWN BY	Primary unique key
HAS	A nonkey field
DEFINED AS	Defines the file descriptively
EXTENDED BY	Optional file which extends fields of a file
INCLUDES	A list of nonkey fields
QUALIFIED BY	Primary key for continuous variable

If you have an order file which references a customer file through a customer number, you could use the following relations:

ORDER	KNOWN BY	ORDER NUMBER
ORDER	HAS	QUANTITY
ORDER	HAS	PRICE
ORDER	HAS	CUSTOMER NUMBER
ORDER	REFERS TO	CUSTOMER
CUSTOMER	KNOWN BY	CUSTOMER NUMBER
CUSTOMER	HAS	NAME
CUSTOMER	HAS	ADDRESS
CUSTOMER	HAS	PHONE NUMBER

The preceding causes SYNON to sequence the CUSTOMER database by customer code, the ORDER database by order number, and to relate the two files so that ORDER's customer number is linked to CUSTOMER's customer number. This defines an access path which will automatically be used to find the right customer by number when an order is created. In this way, access paths to the data can be defined right along with the data by using English-like expressions. The designer does not have to worry about logical files and access paths; SYNON handles it automatically. Key fields are defined by these relational verbs in the Edit Database Relations screen. Key in relations by entering subject, relation, and object to this screen. Enter a D to delete a relation (designer only). Relations cannot be deleted until any dependent relations are deleted.

21.9 ACCESS PATHS

SYNON databases of types REF or CPT (reference or capture) are automatically defined with three default access paths:

PHY is a physical file which is not keyed (arrival sequence). Other types of logical access paths are based on this type of file.

UPD is a logical file whose keyed access path is used to update the file. The key is derived from the relations defined. There may be more than one update file for any physical file.

RTV is a logical or a join file used to retrieve records from the file based on defined relational keys. It can contain virtual fields. RTV files are associated with corresponding UPD files.

Two additional access path types are optional:

RSQ is a resequence file that defines a key other than the originally defined key in the relations. Each RSQ file has an RTV associated with it. These correspond to the various logical files or access paths created to handle specific situations in standard AS/400 DDS.

SPN is span file that corresponds to the AS/400 join file. The span file defines a format which contains fields from two or more databases. Each SPN has an RTV associated with it.

Define objects

The DEFINE OBJECTS display allows you to specify SYNON names and file types for objects. This creates a DEFINED AS relation for the file. Relations specified for objects not yet defined will cause them to appear on the DEFINE OBJECTS display.

21.10 FUNCTIONS

SYNON functions are procedures which are applied to the objects described previously: files, fields, and entities. These functions are the various modules which ultimately constitute the system. Functions are defined in terms of name, type, and an access path on which it will operate. At this point, you can begin to see the automated properties of SYNON. No one has written any DDS or created logical files or written RPG or COBOL programs. Yet you are able to generate input routines for a given set of records from a database. SYNON uses its extensive data modeling and entity definitions to create default assumptions about what it is that you intend to do. If SYNON is not correct about the details of what you need, you can get into the function through Action Diagrams and modify it.

Functions come in three types: standard functions, built-in functions, and field functions.

Database functions are used to process the database.

Device functions define interactive screens and reports.

Message functions produce messages for the user on the screen.

User functions can plug in user-written routines where necessary.

21.11 SYNON STANDARD FUNCTIONS

Standard functions are contained in SYNON to provide useful common procedures. For instance, it is usually necessary to allow user access and update to a database through an access path. Once the fields are known through the access path, SYNON can create a standard input screen. SYNON provides a set of standard functions which may be associated with a user-defined access path to satisfy the usual ADD, CHANGE, INQUIRE, and DELETE needs of database maintenance. Their central theory seems to be the question, "Why reinvent the wheel?" Most database routines bear a strong resemblance to one another, so that to a large extent they can be made generic. If these SYNON standard functions are not exactly what you need right out of the box, you can alter them fairly easily. A lot of time is saved by not having to code every screen or routine from scratch, over and over.

Database functions allow access to the data contained in physical files and accessed through the database relations and access paths you set up. These default functions include:

CRTOBJ (create object)	Add a record to a database. Default values will ensure the record does not exist. If it does, a message is issued to the user. Requires UPD-type access path.
CHGOBJ (change object)	Update a record in a database. Ensures that the record does exist. Requires UPD-type access path.
DLTOBJ (delete object)	Ensures that the record exists and deletes it from the database. Requires UPD-type access path.
RTVOBJ (retrieve object)	Gets data from the database for processing. Requires RTV- or RSQ-type access path.

Message functions provide the necessary interaction with the user and are implemented in the same way as typical OS/400 messages. Message functions are of several types as follows:

SNDINFMSG (send information message)

SNDERRMSG (send error message)

SNDCMPMSG (send completion message)

EXCMSG (execute message)

RTVMSG (retrieve message)

Device functions control the way data is displayed on the screen or sent to the printer. Fields are treated differently in the various kinds of screen device functions. By choosing the correct type, you get the kind of field processing you want. For example, EDTRCD allows changes to a key field while DSPFIL screens do not. Use the Edit Screen Design display to edit the automatic default SYNON screen format the user will see. If you have ever worked with subfiles, you know how much time is saved by using these device functions. The device functions consist of the following types:

Single-record displays

DSPRCD (display record)	Output only for display.
EDTRCD (edit record)	Change nonkey fields on existing records. In add mode, all fields are input.
PMTRCD (prompt record)	

Multiple-record displays (subfiles)

SELRCD (select record)	Output display to select a record. Only the selection field is input.
DSPFIL (display file)	Output-only listing.
EDTFIL (edit file)	change nonkey fields on existing records. In add mode, all fields are input.

Transaction record displays (one to many, header and subfile)

DSPTRN (display transaction)	Output only.
EDTTRN (edit transaction)	Input and output for changes to existing transaction records related to a master record.

These EDT functions allow input to nonkey fields, while key fields are protected. DSP-type functions are output only for display purposes. SYNON provides standard function key usage to implement and navigate through the devices or screens:

F1	Exit, no update
F2	Go to previous screen
F9	Change mode
F11	Delete mode
Enter	Accept the screen for update
PageDown	Previous page
PageUp	Following page
Help	Show help screen

21.12 PRINT FUNCTIONS

Print functions are provided by SYNON to facilitate the design of output and reports. They consist of device designs (PRTFIL, a print file used as design for reports), parameters, and action diagrams.

21.13 BUILT-IN FUNCTIONS

Built-in SYNON functions provide math and control of flow. Arithmetic functions perform the usual math routines of add, subtract, divide, and multiply. More complex calculations may be provided through a user function.

Control functions are used to exit or quit a function, or commit or roll back changes in commitment control.

Built-in functions include:

*ADD	*COMMIT	*EXITPGM
*SUB	*ROLLBACK	*QUIT
*MULT		
*DIV		

21.14 FIELD FUNCTIONS

Field functions are calculated fields which do not actually reside in the database, but are derived from values in the database. For example, if you have a price field and a quantity field in the database, you could use a function field to calculate the total price and display it on the screen. SYNON provides some functions which may be used in function fields, like Sum, Count, Maximum, and Minimum. Alternatively, if you need something a bit more complex, use an action diagram (see following) to define a user field function. Field functions return a single value, which is the value of the calculated field. They include:

FLDSUM	calculated field for totals on a field
FLDCNT	calculated count field
FLDMAX	maximum result field
FLDMIN	minimum result field
FLDUSR	user-defined field
FLDDRV	user-defined calculated field

Functions may be implemented as external functions or separate HLL programs; internal functions (which are like subroutines in the calling function) or message functions are calls to standard OS/400 messages.

Functions are defined in terms of parameters, device designs, and action diagrams. In other words, they are composed of incoming and outgoing values, user screens and/or reports, and procedures which act on the access path.

Parameters are those variables which are passed into the function when it is called and those which are received back from the function when it returns at run time. These parameters refer to defined SYNON fields and have four possible types or usages, similar to DDS field types:

Input only	The function receives a value at run time but does not return a value. This type is generally used for display purposes where it is not necessary for the user to enter data.
Output only	The function receives no incoming value for the field, but returns a value to the calling function. The user may input a value to a field on screen. This type is often used to prompt the user.
Both	The function receives an incoming value and returns a value as well. This can be used to show the user a field from the database and allow a change or update.
Neither	The function does no parameter passing to or from calling routines or functions. This parameter type is used for strictly internal use by the function.

21.15 ACTION DIAGRAMS

Action diagrams are the key to code generation in SYNON. They are like a programming language in that they are a structured, logical sequence of procedures and functions. Once the data has been specified and functions designed, action diagrams are the way to tie it all together into a logical, executable system. This is as close as you will get to writing actual code using SYNON. Actually, SYNON generates the code from the interaction of data specifications (access paths) and function designs which are named and used in the action diagrams. Both SYNON standard functions and user-defined functions can be specified in the action diagrams.

The Edit Action Diagrams screen invokes the interactive action diagram editor. Using this tool, you can create and change action diagrams. Objects and functions are selected and connected in logical sequence to build up the various procedures of the system. Action diagrams allow logical constructs such as IF and CASE structures to guide the flow of logic.

Automatic default action diagrams are created by SYNON for use with most of the SYNON standard functions. These reflect the SYNON thinking that the various possible types of procedures you want to perform on the database can be expressed generically. They can, of course, be modified with the interactive action diagram editor. Not all parts of the action diagrams are accessible to the editor. Some parts are protected from user editing if the function needs them for correct operation. Most editing has to do with adding on functionality to an already existing module, for example, adding edits or field validations which SYNON cannot foresee. Sections of the action diagram which are accessible to user editing are called "User Exit Points" and are indicated by arrows on the right of the diagram.

The user can insert, delete, or move unprotected constructs in the action diagrams by entering the following commands in the lines to the left of the actual action diagram constructs:

IS	insert sequence
IA	insert action
IC	insert condition
II	insert iteration
D	delete construct to right
M	move construct to right to position following 'A'

As SYNON functions may call other SYNON functions or user-defined functions and procedures, great flexibility is provided through the use of action diagrams to tailor the system to your needs. You can specify actions to be performed based on conditional field testing in the action diagram or on user interaction such as function key usage or prompting. While you are not actually writing code in the action diagram, you are specifying how the code will be written by SYNON. It is a higher view of things and tends to focus the user more on a top-down, data-driven approach.

21.16 SERVICES MENU

The Services Menu is a critical point in the SYNON scheme. From here you can submit the system for compilation. The actual code is generated (RPG or COBOL, at your request) and compiled into an executable system. Also, the Documentation Menu is accessible from here for generating various levels of technical, detailed text about the current state of the system. You can display all functions in the system, where they are used, details about their design, and action diagrams associated with them. Access path information is available at the Services Menu, too, showing format details, fields, relations, logical file parameters, and the like. This is a very useful feature of SYNON because it virtually documents the system for you, constantly reflecting the latest changes to the system and answering the developer's questions about design issues.

21.17 SUMMARY

While SYNON does require a lengthy learning curve, and a knowledge of relational database structure, it can greatly decrease the length of development projects and maintenance when used by trained analysts. Data models, standard functions, and action diagrams are the components manipulated by the skilled designer to create a system from user specifications. This is essentially an analytical tool which facilitates the definition of the database and its relations, and the functions or procedures which are to operate on the database through the access paths. Once these components have been specified to SYNON, it can generate the source code and the actual compiled system. Automatic default functions and action diagrams are provided by SYNON based on the data definitions and the functions specified. The user may alter these to suit particular purposes or needs. When mastered, SYNON becomes a powerful tool in generating fully functional systems in a fraction of the time required by traditional hand-coding techniques.

Part

4

Networks

Chapter

22

Communications: SNA and SAA

Communications is one of the most powerful as well as complicated features of the AS/400. This machine is designed specifically with connections to other platforms in mind. Together with the System/370 mainframe and the PC, the AS/400 rounds out IBM's System Application Architecture (SAA) strategy for communications between different platforms. These three completely different kinds of architectures can communicate as equals or peers by using IBM's System Network Architecture (SNA) together with SAA features such as Advanced Program-to-Program Communications (APPC) and Advanced Peer-to-Peer Networking (APPN). Before getting into the specifics of intersystems connections, it is a good idea to take a brief look at SNA and SAA.

22.1 SYSTEM NETWORK ARCHITECTURE (SNA)

IBM's SNA describes logical structures, protocols, formats, and procedures for implementing and controlling networks. Elements of SNA have been around for years in the form of the System/370-type connections to terminals such as Virtual Telecommunications Access Method (VTAM). This implements a type 5 SNA node which uses a System Services Control Point (SSCP) to act as host. This is the traditional host relationship to the network. The host has the communications functions, and the devices which communicate with it are dumb. They can activate functions on the host, but cannot do any processing on their own. This is a hierarchical relationship in which the mainframe is the intelligent master and the peripheral terminal is the dumb slave. 3270-terminal emulation allows remote systems like PCs to communicate with the System/370 host, but only as dumb terminals.

SNA is a protocol stack composed of seven layers:

1. Physical control
2. Data link control
3. Path control
4. Transmission control
5. Data flow control
6. Presentation services
7. Transaction services

The first three (or lower) layers of SNA are concerned with the physical connection on the network. These layers are called the node type. The top four layers of the SNA protocol stack are called the Logical Unit (LU). They handle the software services of communications.

Mainframes (type 5 nodes) represent the most powerful node types with their communications controllers (type 4 node). Known as the subarea node, they provide a powerful and extensive set of networking facilities. They route network traffic and support a multitude of connections. This type of node supports the traditional host/workstation network scheme. Peer-to-peer capability is not supported, however.

22.2 ADVANCED PEER-TO-PEER NETWORK (APPN)

SNA node type 2.1 was introduced to enable peer-to-peer connectivity as an advanced alternative to 3270-type-terminal emulation. These nodes are called Low Entry Networking (LEN) nodes because they do not require the mainframe. Although the mainframe is a type 4 and 5 network node, it can look like a type 2.1 node to the network when running VTAM and NCP together. In this way, the mainframe can participate in node type 2.1 peer-to-peer networking, but only as an end node. Advanced Peer-to-Peer Networking (APPN) is a recent enhancement to node type 2.1 networking which implements dynamic networking capabilities between network nodes. APPN allows 2.1 network nodes to reconfigure themselves automatically in response to changes in the APPN network. A mainframe node is not required to direct traffic between 2.1-type nodes. APPN services include connectivity services, directory services, route selection services, session services, and data transport services.

Independent or peer-to-peer-type connections involve the establishment and maintenance of a link between network nodes which function as equals and do not require the services of an SSCP or mainframe host to mediate beween them. Advanced Peer-to-Peer Networking (APPN) is the AS/400 implementation of this strategy. Mainframes do not use APPN. It is a cutting edge feature of the AS/400, making it much easier to configure than mainframes.

Three network topologies are supported at the physical or data link layer to support peer-to-peer connections:

Token-Ring

Synchronous Data Link Control (SDLC)

X.25 Packet-Switching

These topologies can be used to connect three families of IBM computers:

System/370

AS/400 (System/36 and System/38)

PC (PS/2)

In turn, these three families of computers can be connected together in varying relationships, as node types. End nodes are those which can function as host, receiving requests from the network and furnishing a response in the form of an object or data stream. Network nodes can originate a request, serve a request, or simply route a request through to the appropriate node for a response. SNA node type 2.1 is essential for SAA-style communications because it supports peer-to-peer connections where each node can initiate, respond, pass through, or terminate. 2.1-type nodes can function as peers, or with the 370 as host (end node) to a network. The AS/400 can function both as an end node (host) or as a network node. Generally, PCs are used as network nodes in conjunction with larger machines because of the superior CPU power and DASD capabilities of the 370 and AS/400. However, PCs are also being used as servers in their own right, as they become more powerful. A typical SAA network configuration is shown in Fig. 22.1.

There are three types of nodes which can be used in the APPN network:

LEN End Node	No APPN dynamic networking functions but still can connect as node type 2.1 to APPN network.
APPN End Node	APPN autoconfiguration but only as end of network. No routing or directory services.
APPN Network Node	Full APPN function including routing, directory services, dynamic reconfiguration. No System/370, only AS/400 and PC.

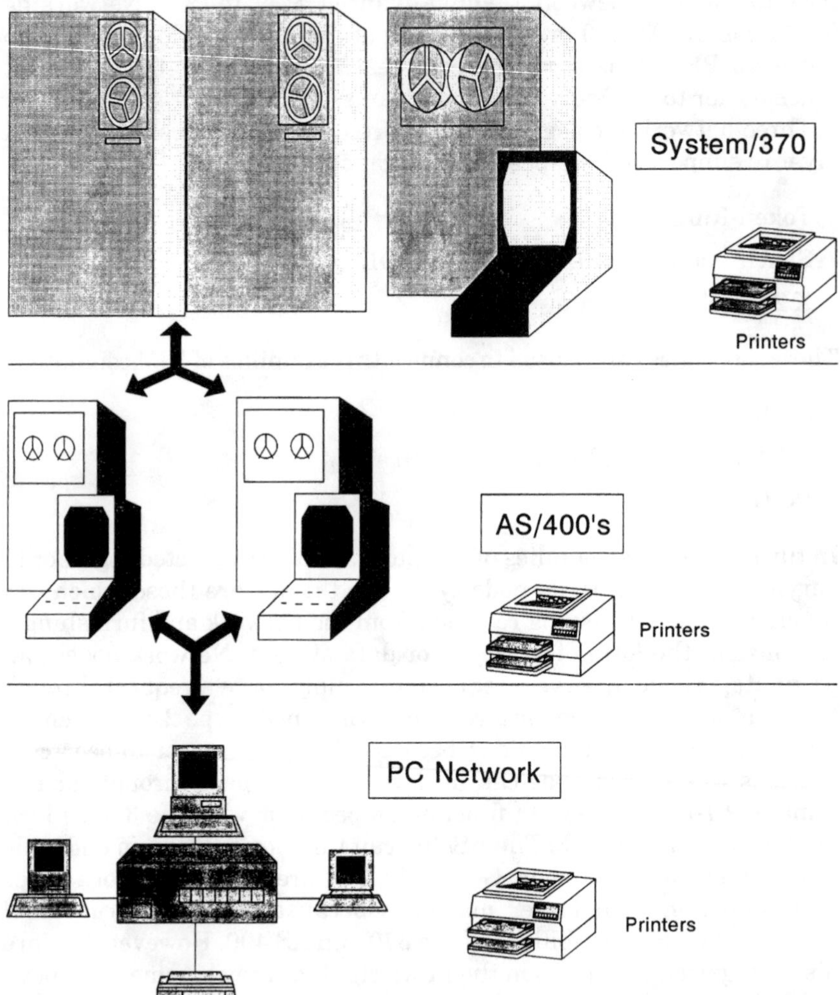

Figure 22.1 Typical SAA network configuration.

Advanced Peer-to-Peer Networking (APPN) is an important feature of SAA/SNA connectivity and node type 2.1. Dynamic networking capabilities allow network nodes to configure themselves automatically and to recognize the addition or removal of remote nodes. It is what offers the ability to connect as peers without using the services of the System/370 as interpreter or host. It runs on the AS/400, System/36, and PC, providing dynamic networking capabilities between them. APPN also allows display station pass-through in which a user can sign on one system and pass through it to another peer system on the network, accessing the remote systems data and programs. The user can be on a PC, for example, sign on to one AS/400 and access data on another AS/400 without being directly connected between the PC and the remote AS/400. This is a very important feature of APPN and SNA because it allows network connections to configure themselves dynamically in an any-to-any relationship. True distributed processing is a result of this kind of peer relationship between network nodes. Only these peer-to-peer features of SNA are included in the SAA network definition, although the hierarchical host-to-workstation relationship is still supported.

22.3 LOGICAL UNIT 6.2

Logical Unit (LU) 6.2 was designed to work with SNA node type 2.1, providing Advanced Program-to-Program Communications (APPC) facilities to interconnect the PC, AS/400 (also System/36 and System/38), and System/370. LU 6.2, or APPC as it is more often called, allows remote systems to communicate and synchronize distributed processing between themselves. LU 6.2 has features to control transaction and commitment control in the event of an error on the network. LU 6.2 controls conversations between programs and platforms involved in distributed processing, supporting multiple sessions at the same time between 2.1-type nodes. Application Services like DIA, DDM, SNADS, SNAMS, and DRDA are implemented through LU 6.2 by transaction programs. The LU handles the SNA protocols for transfer of requests, and answers between local and remote transaction programs. LU 6.2 support is provide by VTAM/NCP on the mainframe, OS/400 APPC on the AS/400, and OS/2 EE Communications Manager on the PC.

22.4 APPLICATION PROGRAMMING INTERFACE

Application Programming Interfaces (API) were designed to talk between systems and platforms and provide true distributed processing. This scheme takes advantage of the fact that all three platforms in the SAA world are intelligent, and each can offer its own advantages. Systems can be developed which run across the boundaries of platforms, using the strengths of each.

LU 6.2 contains verbs which can be used in programs to invoke networking functions. These function calls from an application program to the Logical Unit are known as Application Programming Interfaces (API). They enable high-level languages to communicate directly with the operating system and networking features of the LU. It is the use of these APIs which enables the development of software and application services such as electronic mail (DIA).

IBM has provided SAA Common Programming Interface for Communications (CPIC) to standardize programming access to LU 6.2. A standard set of LU 6.2 protocol boundary verbs can be used to communicate with remote LU 6.2 applications. A conversation is set up between partner programs running on different platforms.

22.5 SYSTEM APPLICATION ARCHITECTURE (SAA)

SAA is IBM's master plan for the future of distributed processing. It provides a unified approach to software design and interplatform communications on the AS/400, the System/370, and the PS/2. The ultimate goal of SAA is an environment which is virtually transparent to the user, who is not aware of accessing a 370, even though signed on to the AS/400 or the PS/2. These three machine architectures represent the components of the SAA triangle.

SAA provides intersystem connections and cooperative processing. It has several facets. One is to provide a standard and consistent interface for users across the various platforms. The goal of this is that a user would not need a great deal of training to move from a productive position on the AS/400, for instance, to the PC. Common User Access (CUA), as it is called, implements this standardized approach primarily in screens and in keyboard usage. Also, SAA attempts to standardize the programming environments across the platforms, offering standard languages on all three. Common Programming Interface (CPI) is IBM's attempt to provide a consistent application development environment. Last, Common Communications Support (CCS) is IBM's communications standardization scheme, and perhaps the most successful of the three standards to date. The SNA-based ability for intelligent peers (type 2.1 nodes) to communicate and share resources enables CCS. Obviously, IBM has a long way to go in providing a seamless integration of these different computer systems, but the APPC and APPN features of SNA and CCS are a good start.

22.6 COMMON COMMUNICATIONS SUPPORT

CCS is composed of a complex group of physical network connections, functions, and protocols which, taken together, provide a consistent way to communicate between the PC, AS/400, and System/370. These functions fall into the following groups.

Data link controls. The physical connections, hardware, communications lines, modems, workstations, controllers, and protocols used to connect network nodes. They include Synchronous Data Link Control (SDLC), Token-Ring, and X.25 networks.

Network node. The SNA node type 2.1 devices which are being connected. They are capable of routing and handling directory services for APPN in order to maintain the dynamic networking functions.

Objects. Formatted data and tokens of discrete types contained in data streams and suitable for transmission and interpretation between SAA platforms:

PTOCA	Presentation Text Object Content Architecture
IOCA	Image Object Content Architecture
GOCA	Graphics Object Content Architecture
FOCA	Font Object Content Architecture
FDOCA	Formatted Data Object Content Architecture

Data streams. Standardized formats for collections of objects which are used to transfer data between SAA platforms for various purposes such as print serving or distributed databases:

3270	Data Stream
CDRA	Character Data Representation Architecture
IPDS	Intellegent Printer Data Stream
RFT:DCA	Revisable Form Text: Document Content Architecture
MO:DCA	Mixed Object: Document Content Architecture

Session services. LU 6.2 functions consisting of APPC protocols to provide data communications support.

Application services. Features of APPC which provide distributed functions. These represent some of the real benefits of SAA communications and include the following:

DIA	Document Interchange Architecture
SNADS	System Network Architecture/Distribution Services
DDM	Distributed Data Management
DRDA	Distributed Relational Database Architecture
SNAMS	System Network Architecture/Management Services

22.7 APPLICATION SERVICES

Part of the Logical Unit (upper) section of the SNA protocol stack is the Applications Services. This is the group of functions which serves the needs of network users. These services may be requested by any LU 6.2 of any other node on the SAA network.

DIA. Document Interchange Architecture enables electronic mail and the exchange of information and documents between OfficeVision/400 users and applications. Users can send and receive documents and messages both locally and remotely. Document library services offer a filing system for documents which allows their storage, retrieval, and distributions across the full range of SAA platforms. This service is implemented as a client server relationship between a Source-Recipient Node (SRN) and an Office System Node (OSN). DIA is supported in OfficeVision/MVS and DISOSS on the mainframe, OfficeVision/400 on the AS/400, and in OfficeVision/2 on the PS/2.

SNADS. System Network Architecture/Distribution Services is an asynchronous distribution service capable of storing data or information for later delivery. Sometimes called *store and forward,* this ability is central to the electronic mail function. However, it is also useful in other respects, such as distributing files, programs, messages, or other types of objects to multiple remote users. For this to work, SNADS must be supported on all platforms involved in the exchange. Distribution queues, such as document library services queues and VM/MVS bridge queues, are used to route objects to other systems. A system distribution directory contains system addresses and names of authorized SNADS users. OS/400 can use SNADS to exchange objects between systems using APPC and APPN. Distribution Service Units (DSU) use routing tables which contain unique system and user names to coordinate the network distribution of objects.

VM/MVS bridge. Enables transfer of DIA documents, OfficeVision documents, notes, messages, and other objects such as print files and data files between AS/400 and VM/370. AS/400 SNA communicates with System/370 VTAM/NCP and VM/RSCS. This facility used to be called PROFS Bridge and is contained in the AS/400 Communications Utility.

DDM. Distributed Data Management allows AS/400 users and applications to access data on remote systems and vice versa. The AS/400 is the source system and the remote system is called the target system. APPC and APPN support enable DDM to access files and records remotely. You can find, update, delete, and add records to the target database just as if it were right here on the local disk drive. Also supported are file operations such as copy, delete, and rename. A file can be copied from target to source computer, for instance. The user, programmer, and application do not need to know where the file resides—DDM handles all that transparently. DDM, part of the Database Manager, performs client-server requests between the source and target systems.

Of course, both ends of the source/target connections must be running SAA-compliant DDM. DDM/CICS on the mainframe supports target functions, while AS/400 DDM can be both source and target.

DRDA. Distributed Relational Database Architecture is an SAA enhancement to remote database acess using DDM level 3. An SQL interface allows applications to access a relational database which is spread out on the SNA peer network. DRDA manages the remote portions of SQL data requests using the FDOCA and CDRA standard formats for data interchange between systems. A system of two-stage commitment control is implemented by DRDA to ensure database integrity across the network.

SNAMS. System Network Architecture/Management Services provides a way to maintain the entire network from a central point. Issues such as configuration and problem management as well as performance tuning can be monitored from one machine. Alerts originating anywhere on the SNA network are forwarded to the focal point for centralized control. Network nodes fall into three SNAMS categories:

Entry Point	a network node which has its own management support
Focal Point	central control location which monitors information and alerts from other points in the network
Service Point	a non-SNA device which uses a protocol converter to communicate and relay information to the Focal Point for network management

NetView running on the mainframe is an example of a SNAMS control point. It offers several useful facilities to monitor and control the network. NetView can monitor response time, performance, hardware faults, and distribute network management commands around the network.

22.8 AS/400 NETWORK MANAGEMENT

SMU. AS/400 Systems Management Utilities can be purchased from IBM to enable an AS/400 to provided system management services for other AS/400's in the network. The service provider can handle PTF orders, create problem logs, notify operators of alerts, analyze problems on remote systems, and forward requests to IBM.

The AS/400 uses APPC/APPN to function as a Control Point for networks. It can act as a Focal Point or an Entry Point. Or it can be a nested Focal Point in a more complicated network using Spheres of Control. In this scheme, AS/400's are configured as Focal Points, Primary Focal Points, or Default Focal Points to direct alerts to the appropriate AS/400 on the network. For instance, computers B and C might report to computer A, while E reports to D and D reports to A. A and D are therefore Focal Points, with A being the Primary Focal Point.

22.9 SUMMARY

SNA is a collection of IBM networking protocols and procedures. It consists of seven layers, called the *protocol stack,* which provide services from the Data Link Control to the Application Services. SAA is IBM's grand plan for connecting diverse platforms and architectures. It is based upon three platforms, the System/370, the AS/400, and the PC or PS/2. Distributed functions and cooperative processing depend on intelligent communications between these three platforms. Node type 2.1 was developed to enable peer-to-peer sessions between devices which no longer require the routing services of the mainframe SSCP. APPN is an extension to node type 2.1, providing dynamic network configuration and intelligent routing of network sessions. LU 6.2 works intimately with node type 2.1 to enable session services consisting of APPC protocols to provide communications support. Riding on top of LU 6.2 and using the physical connections of 2.1 nodes are the Applications Services: DIA, SNADS, DDM, DRDA, and SNAMS.

Chapter

23

Configuring Networks

Setting up networks using the Intersystem Communications Function (ICF) of the AS/400 is a complex task. However, a lot of support is provided by the machine itself, as usual, in the form of help and parameter prompting. Autoconfiguration is also a major saver in terms of time and headaches. Advanced Peer-to-Peer Networking (APPN) has several features which enable dynamic configuration of the network, without human intervention. The AS/400 can be connected to other AS/400's or System/3x's, System/370's, or PC intelligent workstation networks. Many APPC services become available by doing so, including Document Interchange Architecture (DIA), Distributed Data Management (DDM), System Network Architecture/Distribution Services (SNADS), Distributed Relational Database Architecture (DRDA), and others. The AS/400 is uniquely designed to enable peer networking with all of the attendant advantages.

23.1 AS/400 CONNECTIONS

SNA-SAA-style communications are conceived with three basic platforms in mind. These systems are designed for connectivity with each other. They form the IBM SAA communications triangle:

System/370

AS/400

PS/2 (PC)

The AS/400 9406 is shipped with a Base Communications Subsystem consisting of a Multiline Communications Controller, adapter card, and cables for two lines. One of these lines is an EIA 232/V.24 Enhanced Cable for Electronic Customer Support (ECS) at 2400 bps SDLC. There is only one additional available line in this standard configuration, which is another EIA 232/V.24 Enhanced Cable, supporting up to 19,200 bps. The Base System supports asynchronous, bisynchronous, SDLC, or X.25 communications. This configuration can be expanded through ordering Line Expansion Features at initial order time to expand to four or eight communications lines. Up to 10 additional communications subsystems can be added to the AS/400 9406, bringing the total of communications lines up to between 16 and 48, depending on the model.

The AS/400 can also support up to four LAN attachments for either Token-Ring or Ethernet networks using feature cards:

Token-Ring 6034 adapter at 4 megabytes per second

Token-Ring 6134 adapter at 16 megabytes per second

Ethernet 2635 adapter at 10 megabytes per second

The AS/400 can connect to a wide variety of devices, in various capacities. It can function as a host for remote workstations like 5250 terminals, 3270 terminals, Point of Sale (POS) devices, and Personal Computers. The AS/400 can host another AS/400 or System/36 or System/38. In addition, it can connect to the System 370 family of mainframes. Connections are even possible to non-IBM devices through TCP/IP. A diverse group of modems and communications controllers can be used to connect the AS/400 to other platforms. These remote connections can be accomplished through:

IBM System Network Architecture (SNA)

Binary Synchronous Communications Equivalence Link (BSCEL)

Asynchronous Communications

Transmission Control Protocol/Internet Protocol (TCP/IP)

These communications protocols can support several data link protocols and network interfaces, such as:

Synchronous Data Link Control (SDLC)

Binary Synchronous Communications (BSC)

Asynchronous

IBM Token-Ring Network

Ethernet

X.25

It is obvious that the range of possibilities is extensive and open-ended. We will concentrate on IBM SNA communications using the features of APPN and APPC.

23.2 CONFIGURING APPN

Advanced Peer-to-Peer Networking (APPN) as implemented by OS/400 provides distributed directory searches, session routing, and dynamic route selection. These constitute dynamic networking between node type 2.1 peer computers. These computers can even reconfigure themselves automatically to recognize a new or removed network node.

The first step in configuring for communications is to define the network by using CL to create the following AS/400 objects in order:

1. *Line descriptions* (*LIND) describe the attached physical communications line. Parameters such as line protocol, line speed, and switching are defined. You have to vary on-line descriptions before use. WRKCFGSTS *LIN will show you the current status of line descriptions.
2. *Controller descriptions* (*CTLD) describe the attached controllers, local or remote. Here you can define which lines go with which controller and the telephone number for dial-up of the remote controller. If the line is nonswitched, you have to vary it off before you do the controller description, then vary it back on. APPN automatically creates some types of controllers if QAUTOVRT is not zero. These can be customized.
3. *Device descriptions* (*DEVD) describe attached devices or logical units. Each device attached to a communications controller must have a device description. Here, you define device type, controller association, addressing, and device protocols in use. APPN automatically creates device configurations for remote sessions which request communications.
4. *Mode descriptions* (*MODD) describes APPC session limits and parameters for APPN paths. These are used for APPN and APPC. On the System/370 side are mode descriptions for DSNX, DHCF, 3270 emulation, RJE, and SNUF (see following).
5. *Class-of-service descriptions* (*COSD) describe the APPN link and node routing criteria. These entries define which network nodes can and should be used for dynamic route selection. Link speed, transmission priority, connection cost, and security are delineated.

Configuration List is a list of local and remote locations, pass-through parameters, and addresses.

Remote Location Names are used by the system to implement ICF. They refer to a logical name for a device description to be used in accessing remote functions. APPN can search the network when a remote location name is used to find the correct device description to use; or the remote location name can be specified as part of the device description. In this way, an application program can reference a device name in an Intersystem Communications Function (ICF) file which is associated with a remote location name (see Sec. 23.3). APPN will take over to search the network for the remote location name for the device. This is how DDM and 5250 display station pass-through are supported by APPN. You cannot request a specific device description when using APPN; it is selected automatically by the routing features of APPN. The system searches alphabetically for the device description as a corresponding remote location name, and will use it if it is varied on and not already in use.

Automatic Configuration is a significant aid in establishing APPN type networks. For instance, if you attach a PC network to the AS/400 via a twinax line (TDLC), the AS/400 will automatically recognize the presence of all the new workstations as they request sessions and will automatically create APPC controller and device descriptions for them. The system can also create device descriptions for virtual devices used in pass-through and for TCP/IP connections to dissimilar platforms.

You can manually configure the AS/400 communications objects by using menus (number 6 for Communications Menu from the AS/400 Main Menu) or CL commands with prompting for parameters (F4 key). Use CRT or WRK commands as follows:

WRKLIND	work with line descriptions (Fig. 23.1)
WRKCTLD	work with controller descriptions (Fig. 23.2)
WRKDEVD	work with device descriptions (Fig. 23.3)
WRKMODD	work with mode descriptions (Fig. 23.4)
WRKCOSD	work with class-of-service descriptions (Fig. 23.5)
WRKCFGL	work with configuration lists (Fig. 23.6)
WRKCFGSTS	work with configuration status (see Fig. 23.7) to determine the current status of lines, controllers, and devices
DSPCNNSTS	display connection status
WRKHWDRSC	work with hardware resources for a listing of available attached devices

The preceding Work With commands yield lists of the configuration objects of a particular type. For instance, WRKDEVD produces a list of

```
                    Work with Line Descriptions
                                                   System:    S9999999
Position to  . . . . .   __________    Starting characters

Type options, press Enter.
  2=Change    3=Copy    4=Delete    5=Display    6=Print    7=Rename
  8=Work with status    9=Retrieve source

Opt   Line           Type      Text
 _    QESLINE        *SDLC
 _    QTILINE        *SDLC
 _    SWTLIN01       *SDLC     XXXX Line

                                                                Bottom
Parameters or command
===>
F3=Exit   F4=Prompt   F5=Refresh   F6=Create   F9=Retrieve   F12=Cancel
F14=Work with status
```

Figure 23.1 Work with Line Descriptions.

```
                  Work with Controller Descriptions
                                                   System:    S9999999
Position to  . . . . .   __________    Starting characters

Type options, press Enter.
  2=Change    3=Copy    4=Delete    5=Display    6=Print    7=Rename
  8=Work with status    9=Retrieve source      12=Print device addresses

Opt   Controller    Type      Text
__    CTL01         6140      Controller description created during IPL.
__    CTL02         6140      CREATED BY AUTO-CONFIGURATION
__    QCTL          6140      Controller description created during IPL.
__    QESCTL        *HOST
__    QTICTL        *HOST
__    SWTCU01       5251      Switched Line Controller
__    SWTCU02       5394      Switched Line Controller

                                                                Bottom
Parameters or command
===>
F3=Exit   F4=Prompt   F5=Refresh   F6=Create   F9=Retrieve   F12=Cancel
F14=Work with status
```

Figure 23.2 Work with Controller Descriptions.

```
                     Work with Device Descriptions
                                                      System:   S9999999
Position to  . . . . .   ________   Starting characters

Type options, press Enter.
  2=Change   3=Copy   4=Delete   5=Display   6=Print   7=Rename
  8=Work with status   9=Retrieve source

Opt   Device       Type     Text
 _    DKT01        9331     CREATED BY AUTO-CONFIGURATION
 _    DSP01        3197     CREATED BY AUTO-CONFIGURATION
 _    DSP02        3197     CREATED BY AUTO-CONFIGURATION
 _    DSP03        3196     CREATED BY AUTO-CONFIGURATION
 _    DSP04        5251     CREATED BY AUTO-CONFIGURATION
 _    DSP05        5251     CREATED BY AUTO-CONFIGURATION
 _    DSP06        5251     CREATED BY AUTO-CONFIGURATION
 _    DSP07        5251     CREATED BY AUTO-CONFIGURATION
 _    DSP08        5251     CREATED BY AUTO-CONFIGURATION
                                                              More...
Parameters or command
===>
F3=Exit   F4=Prompt   F5=Refresh   F6=Create   F9=Retrieve   F12=Cancel
F14=Work with status
```

Figure 23.3 Work with Device Descriptions.

```
                     Work with Mode Descriptions
                                                      System:   S9999999
Position to  . . . . .   ________   Starting characters

Type options, press Enter.
  2=Change   3=Copy   4=Delete   5=Display   6=Print   9=Retrieve source

Option     Mode        Text
  _        #BATCH      This Mode is IBM Supplied
  _        #BATCHSC    This Mode is IBM Supplied
  _        #INTER      This Mode is IBM Supplied
  _        #INTERSC    This Mode is IBM Supplied
  _        BLANK       This Mode is IBM Supplied
  _        LU62
  _        QSPWTR      This mode is IBM supplied

                                                               Bottom
Parameters or command
===>
F3=Exit   F4=Prompt   F5=Refresh   F6=Create   F9=Retrieve   F12=Cancel
```

Figure 23.4 Work with Mode Descriptions.

```
                 Work with Class-of-Service Descriptions
                                                       System:    S9999999
Position to  . . . . .  ________    Starting characters

Type options, press Enter.
  2=Change   3=Copy   4=Delete   5=Display   6=Print   9=Retrieve source

Option      COS          Text
  _         #BATCH       This COSD is IBM Supplied
  _         #BATCHSC     This COSD is IBM Supplied
  _         #CONNECT     This COSD is IBM Supplied
  _         #INTER       This COSD is IBM Supplied
  _         #INTERSC     This COSD is IBM Supplied

                                                                    Bottom
Parameters or command
===> _________________________________________________________________
F3=Exit   F4=Prompt   F5=Refresh   F6=Create   F9=Retrieve   F12=Cancel
```

Figure 23.5 Work with Class-of-Service Descriptions.

```
                      Work with Configuration Lists
                                                       System:    S9999999
Position to  . . . . .  __________    Starting characters

Type options, press Enter.
  2=Change   3=Copy   4=Delete   5=Display   6=Print   7=Rename

Opt  List         Type         Text

  (No configuration lists selected)

                                                                    Bottom
Parameters or command
===> _________________________________________________________________
F3=Exit   F4=Prompt   F5=Refresh   F6=Create   F9=Retrieve   F12=Cancel
```

Figure 23.6 Work with Configuration Lists.

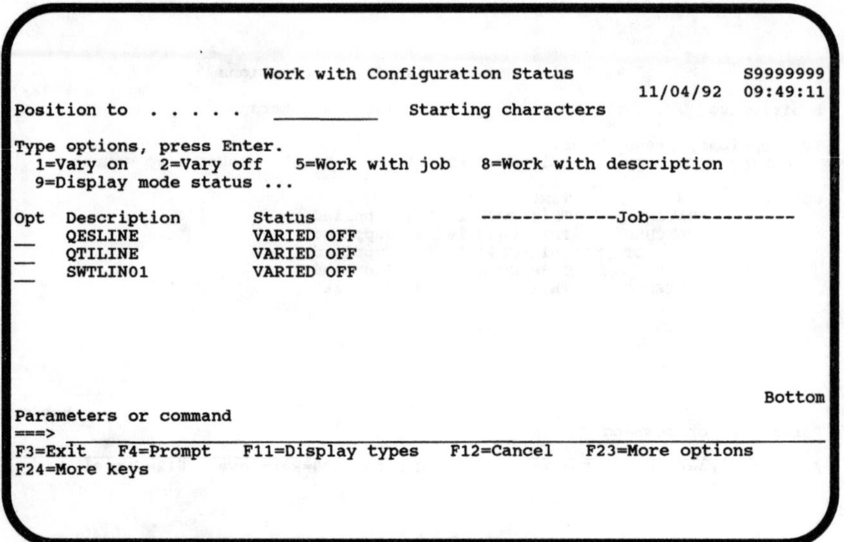

```
                        Work with Configuration Status              S9999999
                                                          11/04/92  09:49:11
Position to . . . . .  __________    Starting characters

Type options, press Enter.
  1=Vary on   2=Vary off   5=Work with job   8=Work with description
  9=Display mode status ...

Opt  Description       Status              -------------Job--------------
__   QESLINE           VARIED OFF
__   QTILINE           VARIED OFF
__   SWTLIN01          VARIED OFF

                                                                      Bottom
Parameters or command
===>
F3=Exit   F4=Prompt   F11=Display types   F12=Cancel   F23=More options
F24=More keys
```

Figure 23.7 Work with Configuration Status.

attached devices with which you can work in the following ways by entering option numbers to the left of the object listed:

2	Change	to alter parameters
3	Copy	to copy to another description for a similar device
4	Delete	to delete the description
5	Display	to show the description without allowing changes
6	Print	to send the description to printer or output queue
8	Work with Status	to work with the status of the object description (same as WRKCFGSTS)
9	Retrieve Source	to create CL source for the description
<F6>	Create new description (or use CRT instead of WRK, e.g., CRTLIND in the place of WRKLIND)	

Of course, proper authority is required to perform these tasks on communications objects, as with any tasks performed on AS/400 objects.

23.3 CONFIGURING APPC

Advanced Program-to-Program Communications (APPC) is a feature of OS/400 which enables communications protocols to other platforms and devices. LU 6.2 provides the remote system connection protocols between IBM Network node type 2.1 platforms (see Chap. 22). APPC is the AS/400 implementation of SNA LU 6.2, enabling remote programs to communicate between SNA type 2.1 nodes. APPC provides a group of verbs which can be used in high-level language programs to establish Intersystem Communications Function (ICF). Peer systems in this type of network can communicate without the mediating services of a host.

APPC can be configured through CL commands or the AS/400 communications menu. APPC configurations consist of:

- Line description for the physical line and link protocol
- APPC or host controller description for adjacent system type
- APPC device description for the remote logical device
- Mode description for session characteristics

APPC can be configured without APPN where the nodes are attached as Low Entry Networking (LEN) nodes and do not perform APPN functions such as autoconfiguration and pass-through. Specify APPN(*NO) on the controller description to configure an AS/400 as a LEN node. The absence of APPN dynamic network configuration means that a LEN node must explicitly configure all remote locations which will communicate. With APPC you can select a specific device description for communications to determine which line and controller you want to use on the host. This is not possible when using APPN which performs dynamic device and route selection.

APPC support needs to be varied on and off just like a workstation device or printer. Use VRYCFG STATUS(*ON) to establish APPC connections to remote location names.

23.4 PROGRAMMING APPC

Intersystem Communications Function (ICF) lets programmers access remote systems transparently, without being concerned with or even aware of the complexities of intersystem communications protocols. High-level language programs can use communications functions to accomplish this remote access. Communications functions are invoked in the program and return codes can be tested to determine the completion status of each operation. Device descriptions provide the necessary information for the system to establish these remote communications between programs or physical devices. The program performs I/O requests to a special type of file, actually an ICF file, as though it were accessing to an ordinary local physical file. APPC and APPN handle the rest, providing the link between the local ICF file and a remote ICF file. DDS is used to create the ICF file, using system-supplied formats.

First, create an ICF file with CRTICF. This file is the mechanism which is used by APPC and APPN to establish a link with a remote system. ADDICFDEVE or OVRICFDEVE are used to allow the program to access the ICF file. Its parameters consist of:

PGMDEV	program device name for the application to refer to
RMTLOCNAME	remote location name specified
DEV	remote device description name
LCLLOCNAME	local location name
MODE	mode name for remote location
RMTNETID	remote network ID
FMTSLT	type of record selection
CNVTYPE	conversation type

The following are some of the verb types which execute Intersystem Communications Functions (ICF) from applications:

OPEN/ACQUIRE	Establishes a session with the remote platform.
EVOKE	Starts a remote program to participate in the logical connection or transaction.
WRITE	Sends data to the remote location.
FORCE-DATA	Flushes the buffer.
CONFIRM	Acknowledges receipt of data at the other end.
FAIL	Sends message to remote system that operation has failed.
FORMAT-NAME	Sends the record format name to the remote location for mapped conversations.
READ	Get remote data.
INVITE	Get remote input data, used with READ-FROM-INVITED-PROGRAM-DEVICES function.
DETACH	End the transaction.
RELEASE	End the session.

RPG/400, C/400, and COBOL/400 support APPC functions. Refer to their IBM manuals for details of syntax and implementation of APPC verbs and functions.

Any system in APPC communication can bind or unbind sessions. APPC establishes and controls sessions to satisfy application requests. Synchronous or asynchronous conversations allow programs to communicate with each other directly and constantly (synchronous) or intermittently with sessions shared by multiple programs (asynchronous). Mapped Conversations use system processing to construct data streams, while Basic Conversations assume that the application program is formatting the data stream explicitly for transmission.

Prestart jobs allow the programmer to start a program on the remote system so that it is up and running when a local request goes out to it, saving response time. ICF file support is available in RPG/400, COBOL/400, and C/400.

Services enabled by APPC include DIA, SNADS, DDM, display station pass-through, PC Support, file transfer, and SNAMS.

23.5 SYSTEM/370 NETWORK

The AS/400 can function as a network node in a network hosted by a System/370 mainframe. APPC handles all the protocol conversions necessary for communications between these two platforms. The AS/400 is an SNA node type 2.1 (peer) and the System/370 looks like a 2.1 node by virtue of running VTAM/NCP (even though it is really a type 4 and type 5 node). The AS/400 can perform network routing and pass-through services as a network node, while the System/370 is an end node and functions as a host or server. The AS/400 must be defined to VTAM/NCP on the host. Line, controller, and device descriptions must be created on the AS/400. The following are standard configurations for AS/400 to System/370 communications:

Standard Configurations

Define AS/400 to host VTAM/NCP	
Create line description	CRTLINETH
	CRTLINSDLC
	CRTLINTRN
	CRTLINX25
Create controller description	CRTCTLAPPC
	CRTCTLHOST
Create device description	CRTDEVAPPC

In addition to the preceding standard configurations, specific types of services require additional configurations as follows.

Alerts. These notify the network operator at the network focal point when a problem occurs at a site remote to the System/370. NetView running at the mainframe focal point is able to monitor alerts coming in from the network. At the AS/400 end, you use OS/400 commands to determine which messages are forwarded to the focal point.

Additional configurations

Create controller description	CHGNETA

Distributed Systems Node Executive (DSNX). You can control the exchange of data and programs throughout the network from a central AS/400 through the use of DSNX. In a network which is controlled by a System/370 host using NetView, the AS/400 can use DSNX to distribute job streams and files to remote platforms. DSNX aids in the maintenance and distribution of AS/400 objects among other AS/400's System/36's and System/38's and PC networks under the control of NetView running on the System/370. Distribution requests can be routed upward and outward through the host System/370 NetView Data Manager or outward to AS/400's and PCs using SNADS.

Additional configurations

Create device description	CRTDEVSNUF

Distributed Host Command Facility (DHFC). The AS/400 can participate in the Host Command Facility (HFC) network through the use of DHFC. In this way, users at the host can access AS/400 data and programs from their 3270 terminals as if they were local 5250's.

SNA Upline Facility (SNUF). This allows AS/400 users to communicate with the System/370 to implement distributed processing both interactively and in batch. SNUF enables the AS/400 to initiate procedures on a remote System/370 which is running CICS/VS or IMS/VS. Conversely, these remote systems can communicate with the AS/400 to initiate programs. 3270 data stream APIs are also supported for terminal or printer sessions.

Additional configurations

Create device description	CRTDEVSNUF
Create ICF file for SNUF	CRTICFF
Add program device to ICF file	ADDICFDEVE

3270 display station pass-through. A remote 3270 display station attached to the AS/400 can pass through it on the way to a remote System/370, without the need for data stream translation. In this way, the AS/400 acts as a link between the remote 3270 terminal on one side, and the remote System/370 on the other. This feature of APPN allows the remote 3270 terminal to toggle between an AS/400 session and a System/370 session. See AS/400 configuration, Sec. 23.3, for configurations of pass-through.

Remote 3270 and 3270 emulation. The AS/400 can play host to remote 3270 terminals through SDLC, X.25, or Token-Ring line protocols. In addition, the AS/400 can emulate the 3270 type of terminal in communicating with the System/370, so that an AS/400 user can appear to the System/370 just like a local 3270 terminal. The AS/400 looks like a 3274 Control Unit to the remote System/370. Emulated terminal sessions and printer sessions work just as if they were local on the System/370. The 3270 data stream is translated into a 5250-type data stream so that the AS/400 thinks it is talking directly to one of its native, local devices.

Additional configurations

Start 3270 emulation	STREML3270

VM/MVS Bridge. This used to be called RSCS/PROFS Bridge. It provides distribution services between SNADS and System/370 RSCS or Job Entry Subsystem. Documents, files, and messages can be sent over the VM/MVS Bridge.

Additional configurations

Configure VM/MVS Bridge	CFGRPDS

Remote Job Entry (RJE). This is a feature of the AS/400's Communications Utilities which allows an AS/400 terminal user to submit a job to the System/370 host on the network.

23.6 AS/400, SYSTEM/36, AND SYSTEM/38 NETWORK

The AS/400 can participate in a peer network with other AS/400's, System/36's, and System/38's. In this type of network, peer nodes communicate as equals. The AS/400's can be network nodes, with pass-through and dynamic APPN routing, or end nodes. In general, to configure for any peer-type communications, you first need the usual configurations:

Standard Configurations:

Create line description	CRTLINETH
	CRTLINSDLC
	CRTLINTRN
	CRTLINX25
Create controller description	CRTCTLAPPC
	CRTCTLHOST
Create device description	CRTDEVAPPC
Create class-of-service descriptions	CRTCOSD
Define mode description	CRTMODD

In addition to these standard configurations, each communications feature of ICF might require additional configurations as follows.

Advanced Program-to-Program Communications (APPC). This is the interface to SNA node type 2.1 architecture and LU 6.2. It enables communication between programs running concurrently on separate platforms.

Additional configurations

Define network attributes	CHGNETA
Create ICF file for APPC	CRTICFF
Add program device to ICF file	ADDICFDEVE

Advanced Peer-to-Peer Networking (APPN). This is the dynamic networking and routing scheme which enhances SNA node type 2.1. It allows the network to configure itself automatically to changes at remote locations, to route requests automatically to the correct location in the network, and to perform display station pass-through. The nodes in a peer network function as equals without needing the routing services of a mainframe.

Additional configurations

Define network attributes	CHGNETA
Device description can be auto-config	
Create APPN location lists for local and remote	CRTCFGL

Alerts. These notify the network focal point of problems in the network. This enables centralized problem management. You can specify which alerts are forwarded to the APPN focal point.

Additional configurations

Define alert functions	CHGNETA
Create APPN location lists for local and remote	CRTCFGL

Asynchronous communications. These are communications in which the local application program provides the type of data stream required at the remote location. Connection is by X.25 or asynchronous line.

Additional configurations

Create asynch remote location list	CRTCFGL
Create ICF file for Asynch	CRTICFF
Add program device to ICF file	ADDICFDEVE

Binary Synchronous Communications Equivalence Link (BSCEL). This enables remote systems to communicate with each other interactively or in batch. It uses BSC protocols to establish a distributed processing environment.

Additional configurations

Create ICF file for Asynch	CRTICFF
Add program device to ICF file	ADDICFDEVE

5250 display station pass-through. This allows a remote or local 5250 terminal attached to the AS/400 to pass through it to a remote AS/400, System/36, or System/38. The remote session functions just like a local session in terms of data and program access and system control.

Additional configurations

Define network attributes	CHGNETA
Create APPN location lists for local and remote	CRTCFGL
Specify system values for autoconfig and remote sign-on	CHGSYSVAL
Create virtual controllers (or autoconfig)	CRTCTLVWS
Create virtual devices (or autoconfig)	CRTDEVDSP
Create user profiles for remote users	CRTUSRPRF
Start display station pass-through	STRPASTHR

Distributed Data Management (DDM). This allows the applications programmer or interactive user on the source system transparent access to a database on a remote or target system. The AS/400 also supports DDM for documents and folders. PCs can access folders and documents on the AS/400 through Folder Management Services (FMS) in PC Support. DDM implementation requires Source DDM (SDDM) on the source computer to initiate a DDM request to the target computer, Target DDM (TDDM) on the remote system to satisfy the source request, and a DDM file on the source computer to access the remote file. The local and remote Database Manager functions of OS/400 handle the request through the use of APPN and APPC.

Additional configurations

Create APPN location lists for local and remote	CRTCFGL
Create DDM file on source system	CRTDDMF
Set DDM and network parameters	CHGNETA

File Transfer Support (FTS). This enables users on one system to send and receive databases to and from a remote system on the peer network.

Additional configurations

Define network attributes	CHGNETA
Create APPN location lists for local and remote	CRTCFGL

Intrasystem communications. These enable communications between two programs running on the same system.

Additional configurations

Create device description	CRTDEVINTR
Create ICF file for IC	CRTICFF
Add program device to ICF file	ADDICFDEVE

System Network Architecture/Distribution Services (SNADS). This implements the Office Network. Different systems can pass mail, messages, and documents back and forth. OS/400 SNADS uses APPC and APPN to set up the asynchronous distribution network. Distribution lists of remote systems, users, and libraries must be maintained manually for SNADS.

Additional configurations

Define network attributes	CHGNETA
Create APPN location lists for local and remote	CRTCFGL
Start QSNADS subsystem	STRSBS
Configure distribution services	CFGDSTSRV

Transmission Control Protocol/Internet Protocol (TCP/IP). This is a non-IBM industry standard set of communications protocols which can be accessed by the AS/400 as a peer with other non-IBM platforms. It has its own file transfer, mail transfer, programming interface, and remote logon.

Additional configurations

Define TCP/IP configuration	CFGTCP
Start TCP FTP	STRTCPFTP
Start TCP TELNET	STRTCPTELN

23.7 WORKSTATION NETWORK

The AS/400 can serve as host to PC networks, retail devices, finance devices, and nonprogrammable workstations using Ethernet, Token-Ring, and various protocol converters and controllers. Programmable workstations like PCs or PS/2's are capable of performing their own procedures, independently or in cooperative processing with the AS/400. In addition, TCP/IP can be used to connect non-IBM programmable workstations and the IBM PC/RT.

Workstations can be added to the network by defining the usual group of non-APPN configuration objects: line, controller, and device descriptions. Mode descriptions and class-of-service descriptions are APPN routing objects and do not apply here.

From the following list, choose the appropriate entry in each category.

Create line description	CRTLINETH
	CRTLINSDLC
	CRTLINTRN
	CRTLINX25
Create controller description	CRTCTLFNC
	CRTCTLRWS
Create device description	CRTDEVFNC
	CRTDEVDSP
	CRTDEVPRT

In addition to these standard configurations, each communications feature for workstations might require additional configurations as follows.

Finance communications. These are supported by finance processors and controllers operating on SDLC, Token-Ring, or X.25 protocols. Applications programs can be written for finance either using ICF or not using ICF features, depending on the controller used.

Additional configurations for ICF

Create ICF file for IC	CRTICFF
Add program device to ICF file	ADDICFDEVE

Retail communications. These let retail controllers attach to the AS/400 over SDLC lines. This scenario uses ICF to communicate between the remote store and the AS/400 host or pass-through to the System/370.

Additional configurations for ICF

Create device description if pass-through to 370	CRTDEVSNUF
Create ICF file for IC	CRTICFF
Add program device to ICF file	ADDICFDEVE

PC support. This is one of the hottest areas of communications because it enables true distributed processing between the AS/400 and the PC. The AS/400 with its function-rich OS/400, communications capabilities, and powerful SQL-based Database Manager can be coordinated with the PC with its intuitive Graphical User Interface (GUI) and independent or concurrent processing. PC Support runs out of Shared Folders on the AS/400 and on the PC as well. Client-server relations can be set up to share files, folders, printers, and even CPUs. An AS/400 menu which can be reached through GO PCSTSK enables configuration. (See Chap. 24.)

Remote workstation communications. These allow remote sign-on to the AS/400 through communications controllers operating over SDLC or X.25 lines. The AS/400 regards these, once correctly configured, as local sessions. No special configurations are necessary beyond setting up the remote controller and the usual line, controller, and device descriptions.

23.8 OPEN CONNECTIVITY

Open systems and interoperability are topics which are getting increasing attention in the industry. Several standards are being developed to implement open systems (TCP/IP, OSI, DCE, POSIX, etc.), but none has been universally adopted. IBM has maintained its SNA approach to communications, but has committed to supporting developing standards as well. In addition to the SNA techniques and tools we are discussing, IBM offers connectivity on the AS/400 to TCP/IP and OSI, and has released a statement of intention to support POSIX and DCE.

Transmission Control Protocol/Internet Protocol (TCP/IP) allows dissimilar platforms to communicate, and is prevalent in the Unix world. This standardized communications protocol, developed by the Department of Defense, enables the AS/400 to communicate with other architectures which may not fall under the SNA scheme. Connections can be made from non-IBM machines to:

System/370 Multiple Virtual Storage (MVS)

System/370 Virtual Machine (VM)

System/370 Advanced Interactive Executive (AIX)

PC DOS

PC OS/2

PC AIX

AS/400 OS/400

RISC/6000

Token-Ring or Ethernet can be used to create a LAN using TCP/IP, while X.25 supports remote communications. Many of the more powerful native OS/400 communications features are not available through TCP/IP. However, TCP/IP does offer its own communications features:

Simple Mail Transfer Protocol (SMTP)
File Transfer Protocol (FTP)
Remote Sign-on (TELNET)

IBM packages which facilitate communications between Unix-type environments and the AS/400 include:

AIX AS/400 Connection Program/6000: RISC System/6000 can access AS/400 data and applications via Token-Ring, Ethernet, or SDLC.

AIX Viaduct for AS/400: RISC System/6000 or IBM RT can access AS/400 databases through APPC SQL calls.

TCP/IP Connectivity Utilities/400: This package exchange data, applications, and E-mail with non-IBM networks.

The Internation Standards Organization (ISO) designed Open System Interconnection (OSI) is a communications standard which has been gaining international acceptance. To support this protocol, IBM offers:

OSI File Services/400 V2: FTAM protocols support exchange of data with other platforms, including COBOL and C interfaces and an interactive user interface to file transfer.

OSI Message Services/400 V2: This package provides E-mail and messages through OfficeVision to X.400 OSI networks.

OSI Communications Subsystem/400: AS/400 applications communicate with X.25 OSI protocols.

23.9 NETWORK PERFORMANCE

The physical devices and data link protocols which constitute the communications link largely determine performance characteristics. The actual line used to connect remote systems is the biggest factor in speed. Obviously, higher line speed carries a higher price tag, so transaction volume has to be analyzed and weighed against cost. Interactive jobs should not exceed 50 percent of line capacity, while batch jobs can run at close to 100 percent. Avoid mixing batch and interactive line usage if possible. Users don't like to sit and wait for a screen refresh while some batch download is going on. Also, it is important to consider the speed of the applications as opposed to line speed. A faster line won't improve the performance if the program is not sending data fast enough. APPN allows you to set a transmission priority in the class-of-service description which is recognized throughout the network. Remember that SNA and various line protocols add baggage to the data for communications purposes, and that this increases the size of transmitted data.

Different types of lines should be evaluated for performance before a commitment is made. Point-to-point lines offer direct connection between only two devices on a line, while multipoint lines share a line between multiple devices. Nonswitched lines provide a constant connection between devices, but with switched lines the connection is only in effect when needed.

Modems and communications controllers need to be evaluated for aggregate line speed, or the total combined maximum speed of the attached lines. In other words, if all attached lines are operating at maximum, can the modem or controller handle it? Nonswitched lines tend to reduce modem response because the modem does not have to wait for switching to make the line available—the connection is always there. Duplex transmission is also supported best by nonswitched lines (not SDLC).

Distributed database usage requires the evaluation of where the various pieces of a relational database should be kept and maintained. A database should generally reside on the system where it is most frequently accessed. This cuts down on communications time. File maintenance should also be considered in terms of coordination of updates by users and file integrity. It is usually a good idea to make one system responsible for table maintenance where possible.

AS/400 Performance Tools can help you estimate the performance of your network based on line and application considerations. The batch job trace can be used to show how a batch job is doing as compared to other system transactions. The IBM communications manuals contain formulas to help in the evaluation of transmission speed.

23.10 SUMMARY

Connections can be established with remote devices and systems for a large variety of services. The standard configurations necessary to accomplish remote communications are the line description, the controller description, and the device description. In addition to these basic communications object descriptions, some services require additional configurations, such as ICF functions and DDM files. The System/370, AS/400, and IBM PC are designed to implement SAA communications between themselves. Correctly configured, they can provide distributed processing, client-server relations, and remote database access. APPN autoconfiguration can handle much of the connection description processing as devices are attached.

Chapter

24

PC Support

PC Support is an important addition to IBM communications which makes extensive use of APPN/APPC technology. It allows users to access the AS/400 from a PC front end, using all the Graphical User Interface (GUI) features of that platform. This means that you can use the AS/400 through a Windows-like environment, with pull-down menus and push buttons and the mouse and all of that. The AS/400 is thus made much more intuitive and accessible to users who are either familiar with PCs or not that familiar with computers at all. Productivity can also be enhanced by using the PC as a development platform. CODE/400 enables the programmer, for example, to point and click fields onto displays instead of counting spaces and calculating screen positions. Shared folders provide AS/400 disk space as PC local drives. 5250 terminal emulation is included, as well as file transfers using SQL/400 Database Manager functions and virtual printers. Cooperative processing is implemented in a client-server relationship. PC Support can work with either DOS or OS/2. PC Support works with existing networks consisting of SDLC, Token-Ring, asynchronous, or twinaxial topologies.

24.1 INSTALLING PC SUPPORT

PC Support is installed fairly easily through the use of shared folders on the AS/400 and diskettes on the PC. PC Support comes on a tape in a folder called QIWSFLR. Use the PC Support Tasks menu on the AS/400 to install the software to the AS/400 (Fig. 24.1). Most of the software required to start and run PC Support is contained in this shared folder, ensuring software version control and saving PC disk space. The PC Support Tasks menu also allows you to enroll PC Support users on the AS/400.

The PC side comes on installation diskettes which will tailor the PC environment to the use of PC Support, including creating a subdirectory with the PC Support software, rewriting the AUTOEXEC.BAT and CONFIG.SYS files, and creating STARTPCS.BAT to start PC Support. Basically, the PC has enough software to establish the connection to the AS/400 shared folder where the PC Support functions reside. The local PC I: drive is assigned to the AS/400 QIWSFLR to access PC Support functions as though they were local. CONFIG.PCS is the PC file which configures the way PC Support works when started. You can change the parameters of CONFIG.PCS by using an interactive interface invoked by CFGPCS (Fig. 24.2). This menu interface uses lists, panels, and action bars to select the various parameters you want for your PCS session. Once installed and configured, PC Support can be started from the PC command line by using the STARTPCS.BAT file or by issuing the appropriate commands (like STARTRTR) yourself. PC Support can use a lot of PC memory, so it is important not to start elements of it you don't really need or to remove them when finished with them (RMVPCS).

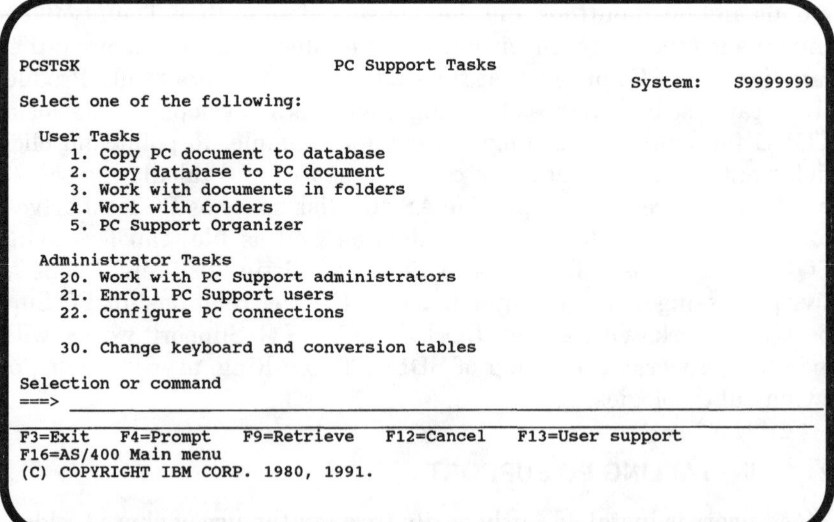
```
PCSTSK                        PC Support Tasks
                                                      System:    S9999999
Select one of the following:

  User Tasks
     1. Copy PC document to database
     2. Copy database to PC document
     3. Work with documents in folders
     4. Work with folders
     5. PC Support Organizer

  Administrator Tasks
    20. Work with PC Support administrators
    21. Enroll PC Support users
    22. Configure PC connections

    30. Change keyboard and conversion tables

Selection or command
===> ________________________________________________________________

F3=Exit   F4=Prompt   F9=Retrieve   F12=Cancel   F13=User support
F16=AS/400 Main menu
(C) COPYRIGHT IBM CORP. 1980, 1991.
```

Figure 24.1 PC Support Tasks menu.

```
2
                    PC Support Configuration

Your configuration is stored in the files specified in your current working
set.  To change to a different set of files, press F7.

Select one of the following to configure.

       General options
        Startup options
        Folders
        Printers
        Messages
        Connection to AS/400
        Work station function
        Organizer
        Application program support

 Enter  Esc=Cancel  F1=Help  F3=Exit  F7=Change working set
 F9=Additional options
```

Figure 24.2 PC Support Configuration.

24.2 MEMORY

PC Support can use up a lot of PC memory. The Router and the device driver for Shared Folders and other TSRs can eat up most of your available RAM, not leaving enough to run PC applications. Expanded and extended memory cards help ease memory constraints. PC Support will automatically use expanded memory if it is available. A PC with an 80386 processor and 2 Mb of extended memory is sufficient for PC Support to coexist with other applications.

The PC Support folder QIWSFLR can be copied to the local PC drive so Shared Folders doesn't have to be started in order to access PC Support functions which reside there. This uses up some PC disk space in return for freeing up memory if Shared Folders is not needed. Watch out for version updates in QIWSFLR on the AS/400. In general, analyze your PC Support needs and start only those functions which are necessary. The Router is necessary (see following). Functions can be removed when no longer needed (RMVPCS) to create room for new ones. Each emulation session takes memory, and the printer emulation on-line help also uses memory. By trimming the extras you should be able to arrive at a functional and operational environment. Any TSR or device driver which is loaded outside PC Support should also be carefully considered.

24.3 ADAPTER HANDLER

At the lowest level of PC Support, the Adapter Handler takes care of the actual physical link and protocol transmission to and from the

AS/400. The actual decoding and functions invokation is done at the next level up by the Router.

24.4 ROUTER

The Router is the core of PC Support because it is APPN/APPC's window to PC functions. It directs data between the Adapter Handler and the various applications on the PC. It must be started (STARTRTR) in order to invoke any of the other PC Support functions. An APPC session is established when the Router is started. All communications requests which involve the AS/400 and the PC are directed through the Router. The STARTPCS.BAT file which was created on the C: drive at installation contains this command, so you don't have to type it if you use the batch file.

CONFIG.PCS can contain several identifiers which influence the way the Router works. Use CFGPCS to modify this file. Among these identifiers are:

ADRS	Add remote system to table
EMLI	5250 emulation link identifier (TDLC)
INTL	Interrupt number (watch out for conflicts)
RMRS	Remove remote system
RTCU	Default common user name
RTDN	Default system name
RTLN	Unique PC network location name
RTYP	Physical link identifier
SDLI	ASYNC or SDLC identifier
TRLI	Token-Ring link identifier with host adapter card address

The local PC CONFIG.SYS file has an entry for the Token-Ring device driver (DXMC0MOD.SYS), which contains the PC adapter address.

24.5 SHARED FOLDERS (SF)

AS/400 DASD can be made to look like a local disk drive to the PC through the use of shared folders. This is one of the main client/server features of PC Support. The AS/400 functions as a network file server for multiple users. Its advanced security features can be used to control access to the shared folders. Some files can even be accessed by applications on both sides, such as documents edited in both DisplayWrite4 (PC) and OfficeVision/400. You can set up a folder drive to access a single folder or a system drive which will make all of the AS/400 folders look like the subdirectory tree of a PC drive. Folders are selected on the PC side with the SLFR command and configured with CFGFLR.

Since most of the main functions of PC Support reside in Shared Folders on the AS/400, it is necessary to start Shared Folders on the PC before you can access the rest of PC Support. You must consider PC RAM limitations when using Shared Folders, as with any PC Support Function. Shared Folders can be customized to your PC environment by changing such parameters as memory usage, buffers, and cache.

Once Shared Folders are set up, you can access them from the PC in much the same way as you would local PC drives. DOS commands like COPY, MD, RD, and DIR work on Shared Folders just like they do on the PC. File sharing is supported so that multiple users can access a file in a folder at the same time. Some computer sites even use Shared Folders for PC network backup.

24.6 WORK STATION FUNCTION (WSF)

PC Support provides up to five simultaneous workstation or printer emulation sessions for each PC. WSF lets you toggle between any of these sessions and to DOS. 5250 terminal emulation sessions from the PC to the AS/400 are supported. In addition, WSF provides 3270 terminal emulation to be used in APPN pass-through to the System/370. Master, session, and keyboard configuration files control how the WSF behaves. Session profiles define each individual session; the keyboard profile remaps the keyboard. Master profiles can invoke several (up to five) session profiles and one keyboard profile. Use CFGWSF to perform these configurations using the PC Support configuration menus (Fig. 24.3). Session parameters can be set, including memory usage, keyboard click, printer help on-line, autodim of display screen, etc.

Display emulation lets you have both the AS/400 and the PC in one terminal on your desk. Actually, you could have the System/370, the AS/400, and the PC network all available in one PC on your desk. This is a very convenient way to work back and forth between systems without having to change between terminals to access each system. Also, it provides many of the user-friendly GUI features of the PC, such as action menus and mouse point-and-click as a front end to the larger systems. You can customize your screen colors (WSFCOLOR) to distinguish sessions and record key sequences for playback of OS/400 commands and parameters at the touch of a key. If you are going to use a GUI interface, you must be sure that the appropriate device drivers are invoked by your CONFIG.SYS file when the PC is booted. WFGSHOW starts the graphics session from the DOS command line and disables the DOS session. Sessions can be started as needed with STARTWSF and stopped when not needed with STOPWSF (but memory is not released).

```
Create  Change  Exit  Help
------------------------------------------------------------------------------
                    Work Station Function Configuration
To select an action shown above, first press F10.

This program allows you to build the following profiles for use with the work
station function program:

--Session profiles, which define the type of workstation or printer a session
  will imitate.

--Keyboard profiles, which define the type and style of keyboard you will use
  in a session.

--Master profiles, which contain a keyboard profile and information to be used
  by up to five session profiles.

You should complete the work station function checklist found in the
PC Support/400 DOS Installation and Administration Guide before continuing.

------------------------------------------------------------------------------
 Enter  Esc=Cancel  F1=Help  F3=Exit  F10=Actions
```

Figure 24.3 Support configurations.

Another feature of the Work Station Functions is Printer Emulation, which lets you use the PC printer as an AS/400 printer. These print servers automatically translate printer data streams from the AS/400 EBCDIC to PC ASCII formats. The Print Operator Panel of PC Support provides such options as Start, Stop, Suspend, and Cancel (Fig. 24.4). You can also change fonts, setups, and forms from this screen. Printer status is displayed.

Virtual Printer sets up an AS/400 printer as a PC printer. Anything sent to the PC printer will be routed to the AS/400 printer through the services of WSF Virtual Printer function. You need to configure a system name and printer ID for Virtual Printer to use in determining where to send print requests. Printers can be assigned and released by using SETVPRT to bring up the interactive VP interface. CFGVPRT configures Virtual Printers in terms of many variable parameters such as printer port, system name, printer device, data type, lines per inch, characters per inch, etc.

24.7 5250 SESSION MANAGER (SM)

Session Manager controls the way 5250 terminal emulation sessions operate. Mouse and windowing functions between sessions, as well as cut and paste between sessions, are supported by SM. Start the Session Manager with SM5250. Session Manager is a TSR which rides on top of Work Station function, so beware of memory constraints. The underlying DOS session is suspended until you toggle

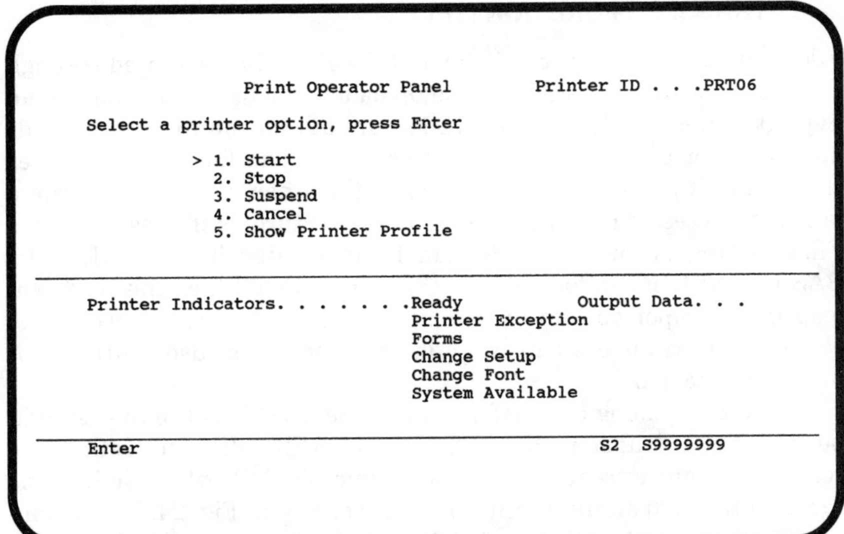

Figure 24.4 Print Operator Panel.

back into it. You can see all five of your sessions overlapping on the same screen at the same time and copy data from one to another, including DOS applications. You simply select the session you want to copy from, mark the text, select the target session, and copy in the marked text at the cursor location—all with pop-up menus. Only text mode sessions can be windowed; graphics sessions take the whole screen.

You can alter the size and position of session windows on the screen. One window is in "focus" or active at a time; all windows are live in the sense that any updates to their data are displayed at once. The Session Manager interface works with either a mouse or with the keyboard, although the mouse may be more effective in certain situations—such as working with pop-up menus or selecting sessions by pointing and clicking.

Printer sessions can be monitored in Session Manager. You can see the status of a given printer or work with it in pop-up Printer Panels. Options include Start, Stop/Reset, Suspend, Cancel, Forms, Change Setup, Change Fonts, etc. Printer sessions automatically switch from background to foreground when their status changes in order to ensure user attention.

Start the Session Manager with SM5250. SM can be customized to personal requirements with CFGPCS. There are options to choose number of lines on the display, fixed foreground window parameters, automatic display of session after starting; always use EMS if available and 8514/A adapter.

24.8 TRANSFER FUNCTION (TF)

File transfer between the AS/400 and the PC is implemented through the Transfer function. Files can be uploaded and downloaded using an SQL-like query facility. This SQL feature allows you to select records and fields for transfer, as well as to sort and join files. TF translates the data as it passes from one system to the other, so that each system is able to access data on the foreign architecture as if it were native. Files coming down to the PC can be translated into ASCII, DOS, BASIC, and DIF file formats. In this way, AS/400 files can be downloaded and imported into PC spreadsheets, databases, and word processors. File transfers can be interactive or batch, user-initiated or program-invoked.

TF works by using a transfer request file, so this is the first step in performing a transfer. Use RTOPC or RFROMPC to define the request. A transfer request is a special type of PC file which defines the function through an interactive interface or menu (Fig. 24.5). You simply answer prompts as to which AS/400 file(s) you want, which records, which fields, grouped how, etc. When you save this, it creates an object which defines for APPN/APPC how to perform this particular data request across the platforms. Once created, this file can be accessed for interactive or batch data transfer by issuing the interactive commands RTOPC or RFROMPC, or the batch transfer commands RTOPCB or RFROMPCB, with the name of the transfer request file as a command line parameter.

```
                 Modify an AS/400 System-to-PC Transfer Request
                                                               More:
Select options and then press Enter

 System name. . . . . . . . [NEWYORK ]

 FROM . . . . . . . . . . . [USERLIB/file1                                ]

 SELECT . . . . . . . . . . [*                                            ]

 WHERE. . . . . . . . . . . [state = 'NY'                                 ]

 ORDER BY . . . . . . . . . [                                             ]

 Output device. . . . . . .  1. Display
                             2. Printer
                            3. Disk

 To . . . . . . . . . . . . [c:\nyfile.txt                                >

 Replace
 old file . . . . . . . . .  1. Yes
------------------------------------------------------------------------------
  Enter  Esc=Cancel  F1=Help  F3=Exit  Shift+F4=Group functions  Spacebar
```

Figure 24.5 Transfer Request.

24.9 SUBMIT REMOTE COMMAND (SRC)

This function allows you to submit an AS/400 CL command from the PC side without using an AS/400 interactive session. In this way, you can implement cooperative processing from the PC to the AS/400. Use PCSMENU to get the AS/400 PC Support Menu and choose number 9 for Submit Remote Command. A pop-up window appears in which you can enter the CL command you wish to execute on the AS/400. Alternatively, you can enter the name of a PC file which contains all of the CL commands you want to run. You get a message saying whether the remote submission was successful.

24.10 MESSAGE FUNCTION (MF)

Message function handles messages between workstations on the AS/400. MF can send a message to a message queue, a workstation, a user, or group of users, using an OfficeVision/400 distribution list. Type STARTMSG to start the message receiver and then MSG at the PC command line to start the Message function interactive interface. This function can be configured in various ways to specify system name, receive options, receive interval, and display timeout. Using MF's interactive interface, you can send or display messages, deleting those you don't need to keep or placing your messages in an ASCII file for PC access. The MSG command located on the I: drive (shared folder) can use command line parameters to send the message directly, without using the menu. This feature can be used in PC applications to send messages to users. RCVMSG receives messages. The Message function may conflict with the Work Station function's message handling, so use the two separately.

24.11 PC SUPPORT ORGANIZER (PCO)

PCO ties all the PC Support functions together into one menu which looks like an AS/400 menu for the familiarity of AS/400 users (Fig. 24.6). You can access all DOS and AS/400 functions from here without toggling between sessions. You can choose PC Support functions from the menu without having to enter the .EXE names at the DOS command line with parameters. Working with AS/400-type menus and screens, you can access the PC. This is really the converse of the Session Manager approach. Instead of using the GUI windowing functions of the PC as a front end for the AS/400, you use the AS/400 menu interface to access the PC and the functions of PC support. AS/400 users will be much more comfortable with this approach. AS/400 applications as well as users can call PCO functions to invoke PC applications.

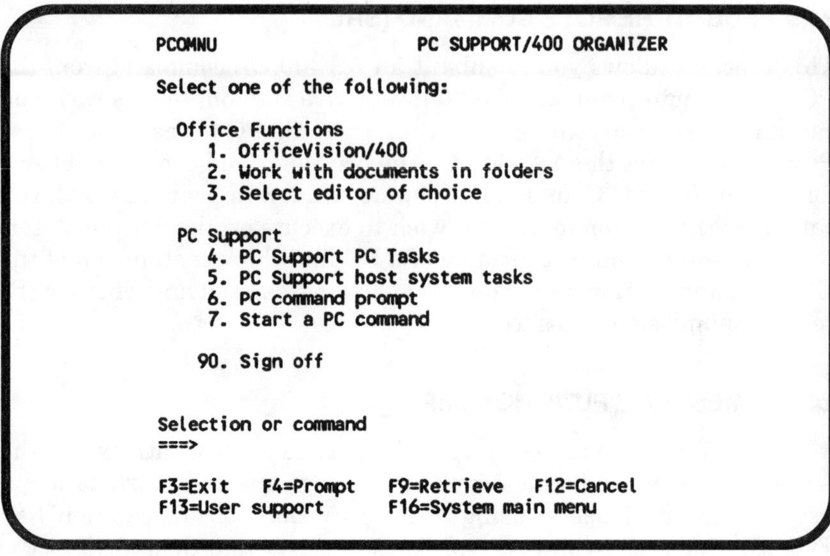

Figure 24.6 AS/400 menu.

One of the PCO functions, Editor of Choice, lets you specify an editor for documents. Choices include DisplayWrite4 (DW4), DisplayWrite5 (DW5), and OfficeVision/400. The editor can then be used to work on documents in shared folders. Documents created with one editor can be accessed in shared folders using another editor by converting them to Revisable Form Text (RFT). PCO automatically handles print format conversion to Final Form Text (FFT) when using Virtual Printer.

Type PCO to start PC Support Organizer on the PC and the OS/400 command STRPCO will automatically be run to start it on the AS/400. When you go into a DOS session through option 6 you can type EXIT to get back to PCO, or you can toggle back if you specified /HOTKEY as a parameter to the PCO command. Other command line parameters for PCO are LOADTA to load Text Assist and TA1 to load enhanced Text Assist. GO PCOMNU gets you to the PCO menu from the AS/400 command line (once it is started with STRPCO). The PCO menu can be customized through Screen Design Aid (see Chap. 12) to include virtually any AS/400 or PC task. Default PCO menu functions are: OfficeVision/400, Work with Documents in Folders, Select Editor of Choice, PC Support PC Tasks, PC Support host system tasks, PC command prompt, and Start a PC command. PCO can be invoked in any or all of your WSF 5250 emulation sessions. The PC Support configuration file CONFIG.PCS or your own PCS file can be used to customize the way PCO behaves, whether it uses Text Assist, which menu comes up on the AS/400, etc., by using the PCOP 1 parameter. For example, to start

PCO automatically and check your spool files, you would include these entries in the .CFG file:

```
PCOP 1,STRPCO
PCOP 1,WRKSPLF
```

Any AS/400 commands can be entered in this way to determine how PCO comes up and what it does.

PC commands can be run from the AS/400 when PCO is active. STR-PCCMD is the CL command used to run PC programs, whether they be DOS commands or user applications. In this way, it is possible to write a CLP program which would start PCO, run a PC application, return to the AS/400, and continue processing. This ability to control the PC from the AS/400 is important for distributed processing capability.

24.12 APIs

Application Program Interfaces are used by PC Support to communicate directly to the Router and the Adapter Handler. These APIs are also available for programmers to use in developing in-house communications functions to supplement PC Support. APIs enable remote disk access and cooperative processing. The Router API implements the SNA communications functions needed to connect to the AS/400. It can be used by applications programs to access the AS/400 databases directly by record and key. Once the Router is started, application programs can take advantage of its APPN/APPC communications features directly, without using the other functions of PC Support. The PC program needs to access the interrupt vector table and find the APPC entry that the Router is using. This can then be used by the application program to invoke Router functions. An in-depth knowledge of C or Assembler is required to accomplish these in-house Router API programs which establish conversations with remote devices.

The Work Station function API enables the programmer to develop functions which enhance PC Support sessions. Information from the sessions can be routed to virtually any desired device; for instance, you could point at a screen position to execute a program or place a phone call. Use WSFAPI to load this API into memory (TSR). It is then accessed much like the Router API by finding its vector in memory and then sending an interrupt to the WSF API interrupt handler which implements the requested service.

The Transfer function API can be used directly to connect local PC programs to the AS/400 databases. In this case, you must handle the functions of the transfer request and the actual data transfer yourself by invoking the API's features explicitly in the program. SQL-like statements can be used to give you access to the powerful data handling features of the AS/400 Database Manager.

The Submit Remote command API allows you to link EHNSRAPI.LIB objects contained in the shared folder QIWSFLR to PC programs to provide remote submission capability to PC applications.

DDM/PC is not really a PC Support function, but it works through the PC Support Router using APIs. With DDM/PC, you can write applications which access data on the AS/400. Record-level access as well as key searches are supported. An application program running on the PC issues a request for AS/400 data and DDM takes over to pass the request to the target system's Database Manager. This satisifies the request with a data excerpt from the AS/400's database and passes the result back down to the PC application through APPC/APPN. You can do just about anything to the data that you can do as a native AS/400 user, including key searches, updates, and deletes.

PC Control files are used by DDM/PC to define the communications requests, as with the Transfer function. They are the configuration file CONFIG.DDM and the format description file. The configuration file sets up drive and file mapping between the source system (PC) and the target system (AS/400). The format description file contains data and field descriptions in the source and target databases to be used in data translation between the systems.

The DDM/PC API allows you to access AS/400 files from a PC application through the PC Support Router. It is available in the form of DDMPCAPI.OBJ for linking to the PC application program. This technique provides transparent access for PC users through applications to the AS/400 databases.

24.13 SUMMARY

PC Support is a powerful implementation of AS/400's APPN/APPC network capability. It provides communications and distributed functions between the AS/400 and the PC. In the Work Station function, 5250 sessions, virtual and emulated printers, and 3270 pass-through sessions are implemented. The 5250 Session Manager makes AS/400 sessions available from a GUI windowing environment with mouse support and cut and paste between sessions. The Message function allows a PC Support to send and receive messages with any other user on the AS/400. Shared folders allow file access from the PC to the AS/400 and the Transfer function enables downloads and uploads of files using special transfer request files and SQL-like calls to the AS/400 databases. Submit Remote Command can execute a CL command on the AS/400 from the PC side. PC Support Organizer accesses all of these tasks from an AS/400-type menu for the user who is used to that environment. APIs can be used to create PC applications which interface directly to the APPN/APPC functions which enable PC Support. Other third-party applications for the PC which implement client server relations with the AS/400 also require the services of at least the Router portion of PC Support to be running. PC Support is the key to effective distributed processing between the AS/400 and the PC.

Part

5

Environment

Chapter

25

Migration

Moving applications and data from one system to another is the process of *migration.* IBM provides easy-to-follow migration paths for the two systems from which the AS/400 was born. Significant support is provided directly from IBM for migrations, and for a successful migration this should be used.

Migration is an easy, viable decision which is often the best path for your system, enabling your business to grow with systems that can support your needs. IBM has developed the AS/400 with a commitment to technical support never before seen on any single product. Numerous migrations have occurred, and relevant knowledge has accumulated.

25.1 THREE SYSTEMS IN ONE

The System/36 and System/38 are the forerunners of the AS/400. The IBM AS/400 can be best described as the optimum mix of the programming and data manipulation world of the System/38 and the ease-of-use and friendly approach of the System/36. If you have used either of these systems, or both, you will immediately notice similarities and differences.

One of the advantages of moving to the AS/400 platform from the System/38 (S/38) or the System/36 (S/36) is that every detail of your current environment will exist on the AS/400 when your migration is complete. With a minimal amount of effort, each and every application program can be "migrated" (converted) to the AS/400. There are several ways that this migration can occur (discussed later in this chapter).

Planning is absolutely the key to your migration. Perform a complete inventory of your current system. Consider all of the information in the IBM migration manuals and planning guides. Consider the consequences of migrating specific applications in a phased approach or the entire system in a single step. Answers to these questions, outlines of basic hardware and software expenditures, and impact analysis to your business will help you form a qualified "cost-benefit" analysis of all of your options. Consider the media format being used and consider your business risk of a "down system" (how long you can really afford to be down and how quickly your system needs to return to operation).

AS/400 environment

Migration software consists of two pieces. First, one piece of software operates on your current system (S/36 or S/38). This software provides a structured method of identifying and saving libraries, files and folders, and other data on your system. The software will also help identify where differences may exist between your existing S/36 or S/38 system and the AS/400. This information may lead you to additional research or directly into the migration. Either way, you will have a clear understanding of what exists, so that this information can be mapped to your new system.

Second, a piece of software needed to complete the migration executes on the AS/400. This is commonly referred to as the Migration Support Programming in the IBM Operating System (OS/400). In essence, this software will assist in restoring the items from the S/36 or S/38 systems as they are transferred to your new environment. Most important, this software will begin to recompile your programs (RPG, COBOL, etc.), messages, screen formats, and menus. In the AS/400, each internal object needs to have a special "AS/400 header." This header is processed during this piece of the migration. Finally, the software provides an audit report of migrated items which can be mapped back to the work you did with the first piece of software on your "old" system.

The reports from the migration aids assist you in tracking your progress as you migrate to the AS/400. If you migrate in stages, a status report will identify the items that have been migrated, as well as those that have not yet been migrated.

System/36 and System/38 environments overview

This environment on the AS/400 is much like an emulation function. You can think of the System/36 environment on the AS/400 as emulating the device called "the System/36."

Because the AS/400 "emulates" the S/36 or S/38, it can be said that the System 3X environment on the AS/400 is much more strict in its interpretation of program code than the S/36 or S/38 itself. The set of rules for emulation do not have the flexibility for modification that they did on your previous system. For this reason, you may want to explore going beyond migration, into a process in which your code is transferred into native AS/400 code. Also, there is overhead involved with S/36 and S/38 environments running on the AS/400, and you cannot take advantage of significant advances characteristic of the native AS/400 environment.

25.2 MIGRATION AIDS

Migration, conversion, and *upgrade* are some of the words commonly used when referring to a platform change involving System/36, System/38, and the AS/400.

Migration planning is a decision-making process whereby you select a strategy, prepare schedules for people and resources, and especially plan to install both hardware and software.

AS/400, System/36, and System/38 migration aids are licensed programs that will transfer data of all types (programs, files, etc.) on your S/36 or S/38 to diskette, tape, through data lines or user-written communication programs to the AS/400. The flexibility in the programs is designed to make the migration as easy as possible for you—they are best utilized if options are planned in advance of the migration. These aids reduce the time it will take to become productive on the AS/400. Like other application program software for the AS/400, the menu paths and prompting help facilitate the use of migration aids. Some System/36 code may need to be rewritten, depending on specific System/36 functions used.

Planning for migration aids

Migration aids to help you move your current environments to the AS/400 are provided by IBM. When planning, it is important to step back from specific systems and think of computers in general for a few minutes.

Every computer system is based on input and output (I/O). I/O is accomplished through the use of attached devices. Devices are attached to your S/36 or S/38 and have a specific way of dealing with data, based on instruction sets specific to the hardware platform and the device itself. In moving to any new hardware platform, it is important to think through the changes related to these I/O devices.

The first step in analyzing your S/36 or S/38 is to look for two details:

1. Devices that will not be supported in the new environment
2. Devices that will be supported differently

Remember that devices can also be lines and control units which are used for I/O in your applications.

Determine the feasibility of migrating your system as it currently exists. Make sure that you have a complete listing of all information (data) on the system currently. Make an inventory of all libraries and application programs with as much documentation as possible. Verify that the compiled programs match the source code. Get rid of all deadwood (data, files, and libraries never used or long-since forgotten), making sure that it is backed up in case it turns out you do need it.

Next, study IBM-supplied migration manuals. These manuals help you identify all the features in your systems that are not supported on your new system. This includes everything from programs to devices such as tape and diskettes.

As you will soon discover on the AS/400, security causes a variety of problems if it is not used wisely. Most System/36 users are accustomed to using menu security (which in any system can leave your system open for security violations), whereas on the AS/400, menu security will only be the beginning of your security planning. By using the top AS/400 security level, every object in the system can be secured by rights, thereby planning for even the most implausible types of security breaches.

Library organization is another key to a peaceful migration. By organizing your applications into environments such as production and test, libraries can be organized through the use of library lists for applications paths on the AS/400. You should note that your program libraries will require more space (DASD) on the AS/400 than on the S/36 or S/38. Many of the IBM sources on this topic recommend reduction of additional overhead by checking that your source code and procedures are no more than 80 characters per line. By using this rule, shorter record lengths in the source files will be created on the AS/400. The software migration aids will assist you in identifying source members and procedures that infract this guideline.

Migration aids will allow you to:

Subtype source libraries (required for the AS/400).

Create a System Summary of all items on your S/36 or S/38.

Create an analysis report for unsupported features.

Choose items to migrate to the AS/400.

Save selected items to your migration media.

Some of the items the migration aid will transfer are:

Program Source Members

Screen Formats

Messages

Menus

Procedures

Data File and alternate indexes

Libraries

Folders

Data Dictionaries

Security and master configuration information

Migration aids will also transfer data necessary to operate the following:

Advanced Printer functions

Business Graphics Utilities

Data File Utility programs

Distributed Data Management

Multiple Session Remote Job Entry

PC Support

Query

The following are not supported by the migration aids:

Communications definitions

User-defined configuration records

These items can be moved to the AS/400 from your S/36 or S/38, but they will not be supported on the AS/400. In this case, the only value in moving these items would be as samples in "duplicating" them on the AS/400:

User-written assembler programs and subroutines

Fortran programs

Any Workstation Utility (WSU) programs

Basic Programs (require a lot of special attention)

Expect delay

In any project which deals with migration or conversion, the primary factor is good planning. Diagramming the correct steps for a migration and all of the related items will ease your transition from system to system. As with all projects, there will be unanticipated hurdles and obstacles.

These obstacles can range from data storage space (lack of DASD), to unsupported third-party input devices at your remote locations (requiring a large investment in devices in order to proceed with the migration), to unplanned operational support for your new system. Plan on a 10 to 15 percent delay in your framework to resolve these unexpected puzzles.

Typical delays. Delay can come in many forms, but here are some typical delays you may encounter:

- Ordering and delivery of your new system
- Determining what to do with the "old" system
- Determining a phased approach, or a single cutover point
- Planning for unsupported functions
- Setting up, configuring, and testing your new system
- Finding a location for your new and old systems
- Determining the need for outside assistance
- Obtaining budget approval for all of these changes
- Explaining all of the changes to management

We are not saying that you will have all, none, or some of these problems. The preceding are typical problems associated with a migration. You will undoubtedly encounter some problems. The key is to be prepared and take the time to deal with them. Otherwise, your migration will snowball into an unmanageable task. Migration is a big step—embarking on a new way of thinking related to your system. Your new system will change many things; give yourself a break and plan for the unexpected.

25.3 SYSTEM/36 ENVIRONMENT

To run your System/36 applications effectively on the AS/400, you have to have an accurately configured System/36 environment. Nearly all of the information you will be required to specify concerns the mapping between new AS/400 device names and the S/36 environment device IDs (as they existed on your "old" system).

A word about devices: AS/400 device names can be up to ten characters but S/36 device IDs can only be two characters. In your systems, you might have a Systems/36 Operation Control Language (OCL) and programs that depend on a two-character ID to run. As you can see, this can be a problem. This is the reason for the tables contained in the S/36 environment; the tables provide the map between device name and S/36 IDs for displays, printers, tapes, and diskettes from system to system.

On the AS/400, both the S/36 and S/38 environments must be started in order to use the environments. After the S/36 environment is started, the AS/400 will automatically create the tables and load the current device configuration for the AS/400 into the tables. When you add or delete devices to the AS/400, the system will automatically update the device-mapping tables in the environments. To view or change the tables, use DSPS36 or CHGS36.

Common use

Both environments on the AS/400 (the S/36 and S/38) require special use of specific CL commands designed exclusively for their use. Each of the special environments must be started and stopped when used.

STRS36	starts the System/36 environment
CALL QCL	starts the System/38 environment

For the System/36 and System/38 user, the AS/400 offers a number of recovery functions previously unavailable to help in recovering data in case of failures. Careful investigation of these functions will assist you in managing the critical issue of backup and recovery.

AS/400 commands and parameters for System/36 environment

There are some special system values that affect your S/36 environment:

QCONSOLE. This is a value telling the system where the controlling console of the system is located. To display or change the current value, use the DSPSYSVAL or CHGSYSVAL for QCONSOLE command. For a valid change to occur, the device description has to exist before the change can be recorded. The console device description must be located on port 0.

QPRTDEV. This system value defines the printer name used as default or system printer for all of the programs on the system. This is an important value, in that all output will be directed to the device indicated. Many people discover in a migration that AS/400 printers do not handle output in the same manner as the S/36 or S/38.

QSPCENV. This system value outlines the special environment. The valid values include *S36 or *NONE. This system value works together with the SPCENV parameters in the user profile. SPCENV in the user profile can be *NONE, *S36, or *SYSVAL. By specifying this parameter in the user profile, users can work in the S/36 environment without any special commands, such as STRS36 for the S/36 environment explicitly. This makes the separate environment more “transparent” to users.

There are a set of System/36 Control Language commands to be used exclusively with that environment. Please see Fig. 25.1 for the System/36 command screen.

Likewise, there are a special group of CL commands for the S/38 environment, as shown in Fig. 25.2.

Special considerations

The special considerations are far too numerous to outline here; however, some of the major points include the following:

1. The AS/400 employs output queues as the System/36 uses a spool file. On the System/36 you may have one spool file, but on the AS/400 you have an output queue for each printer on the system. When a printer description is deleted, the corresponding output queue is also deleted if it contains no entries, so you will not have to worry about unused output queues.
2. If you want printer spooling to mirror the System/36, use System/36 device names for your printers (i.e., P1, P2, P3). Then, both the printer and the output queues will have the same name of P1, P2, P3 and there should be less confusion in managing your printing on the AS/400.
3. Security on the System/36 is less stringent than the AS/400. The AS/400 emulates many of the same functions found on the System/36.

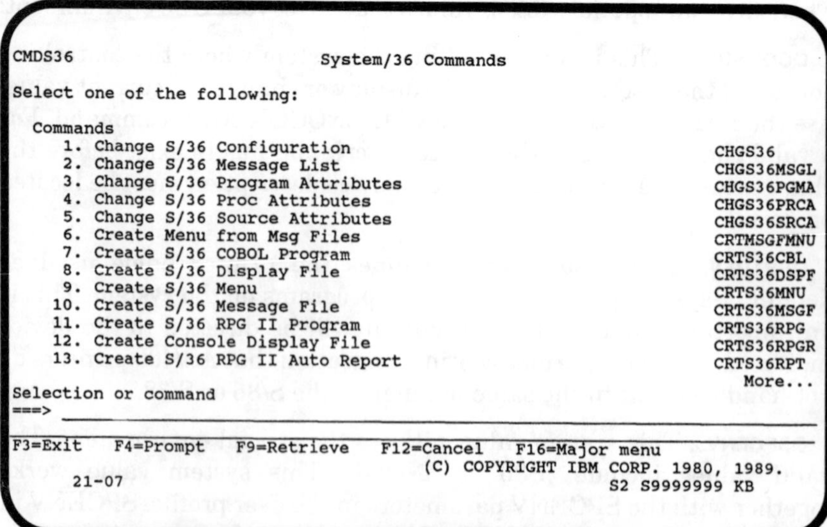

Figure 25.1 GO CMD S/36.

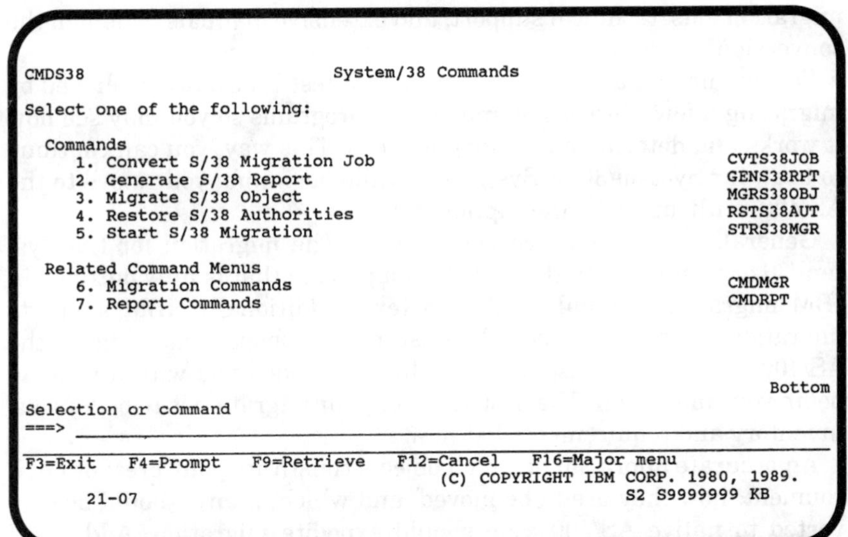

```
CMDS38                          System/38 Commands

Select one of the following:

  Commands
     1. Convert S/38 Migration Job                                   CVTS38JOB
     2. Generate S/38 Report                                         GENS38RPT
     3. Migrate S/38 Object                                          MGRS38OBJ
     4. Restore S/38 Authorities                                     RSTS38AUT
     5. Start S/38 Migration                                         STRS38MGR

  Related Command Menus
     6. Migration Commands                                           CMDMGR
     7. Report Commands                                              CMDRPT

                                                                        Bottom
Selection or command
===> ____________________________________________________________________

F3=Exit   F4=Prompt   F9=Retrieve   F12=Cancel   F16=Major menu
                                        (C) COPYRIGHT IBM CORP. 1980, 1989.
      21-07                                            S2 S9999999 KB
```

Figure 25.2 GO CMD S/38.

Again, the migration aids available from IBM will walk you through all of the conversions and comparisons that your migration requires.

There are many details to consider when migrating your system. The following are additional factors to be considered:

Current system size

Your storage capacity (DASD and MEMORY)

Number of users

Number of applications

Number of products

Time allocated for your migration

Expertise of users and operations staff

Modifications of your application programs

Production schedule

The new configuration

Test time

25.4 SUMMARY

Migration of S/36 or S/38 systems to the AS/400 may be accomplished with relative ease, considering the magnitude of the project. IBM offers migration aids, technical support, and extensive manuals to help in the conversion.

We recommend a test migration. A pilot test is best accomplished by migrating a few libraries of application programs so you may see how it works and determine how long it takes. This way, you can continue to use your System/36 or System/38 while beginning your move to the AS/400, without user interruption.

Generally, there is no reason to wait. The migration for the System/36 or System/38 to the AS/400 is a process that is fully outlined in IBM migration manuals and help text. Additionally, IBM supports migrations and offers special assistance to shops migrating to the AS/400. The topics presented here have provided you with a basis to begin your migration. The best start for your migration is to begin your inventory and requirements list now.

An accurate appraisal of which objects constitute your present environment, how they are to be moved, and which, if any, should be converted to native AS/400 code should expedite migration. Additional questions or issues can be resolved through IBM technical support, migration manuals, and migration aids.

Chapter 26

Performance Tuning

26.1 PERFORMANCE FACTORS

When the AS/400 is shipped, it is configured to perform work in a simple, standard way. It is possible to leave it alone and it will adjust itself to the work being done as best it can. However, it is often better to tailor the system to your needs. Performance tuning or work management is a way to optimize the capacities of the AS/400. Three elements of the computer are involved in performance: memory or main storage, DASD, and the processor. Three types of work make demands on these components. They are systems tasks, batch processes, and interactive sessions. System tuning is a matter of balancing these different types of work with a carefully adjusted set of existing system resources. A careful appraisal of the needs of the system should be carried out in order to determine priorities of work flow.

26.1.1 Memory

Memory is one of the most critical factors in work management. AS/400 performance is directly affected by how much memory it has. One of the best and least expensive ways to increase performance is to add main storage. AS/400's should be configured with as much memory as is reasonably possible in order to maximize response. For instance, although the 9406 model E35 is configured with base memory of 8 Mb, it will not yield satisfactory performance with much less then 40 Mb. And its maximum memory capacity is 72 Mb. Once adequate main storage is installed, it then must be divided into pools and allocated to subsystems appropriate to the work being done.

26.1.2 DASD

It is important to monitor and control disk usage on the AS/400. It is generally not desirable to operate at a percentage higher than about 65 percent of total disk capacity. Performance degrades seriously above 80 percent. Configure your machine with enough DASD to handle your growth needs as indicated by capacity planning. Then monitor disk usage and institute a regular system of cleanup to avoid clogging up the system with unnecessary message, spool, or work files. Refer to Chap. 7 to see how automatic cleanup jobs can be run by the system on a regular prescheduled basis (or GO CLEANUP for the Cleanup Menu). Just performing an IPL regularly helps to clean up DASD as it erases some temporary work and spool files used by the system. Every so often you can use RGZPFM to reorganize physical file members and reclaim memory from deleted records. This requires a lot of resources and should be performed when the system is not busy. Also, you should change journal receivers (CHGJRN) and clear out message queues regularly, as these can really accumulate. It is a good idea to create a batch program for submission at night to clean up some of these DASD problems.

26.1.3 Processor

The processor (CPU) is the heart of a computer system. Processor speed is the factor which mostly determines performance (along with memory management). The type of processor is what gives the computer model its name. For example, an AS/400 model E45 defines a particular processor. There is nothing you can do with it. DASD and memory can be added and managed. Subsystems and job queues can be created and controlled to optimize the work. But the processor is the processor and, if it is not powerful enough for the workload, the only solution is to upgrade.

26.2 JOB TYPES AND PRIORITY

Different types of jobs constitute the workload. At any one time, many different kinds of jobs can be running in the system, making demands on and sharing system resources. Jobs can be managed by assigning run priorities to them and by routing them to the different subsystems with their different resource levels. System jobs, interactive jobs, batch jobs, and spooled output are typical of jobs on the system.

26.2.1 System jobs

System jobs are transparent to the typical user, but are essential to the successful operation of the machine. An example of a system job is access path maintenance, updating indexes when a user adds a record to a database. Save and restore are two more examples of system jobs.

26.2.2 Interactive jobs

Interactive jobs are those which handle display stations when users sign on to the system. They interact with the user in the sense that the user types something at the keyboard and the system responds to it. The data input function is a typical interactive job, as is programming. Interactive jobs can be a tremendous drain on system resources, so care should be taken not to overdo it. The AS/400 has some notorious interactive resource users, like OfficeVision, Query, and SQL. If all of these are running at the same time, especially against the same files, the system can slow down to a crawl.

A user's profile contains information about how that user's work is to be accomplished. Output queues, object authority, and job descriptions are assigned to users by their user profiles. An initial program may be called for a particular user or a menu may be displayed. It is possible to set up a user profile with an initial program which provides a display at sign-on, allowing only certain programmed functions, no interactive command line, and automatic sign-off when the user leaves the screen. In this way, the interactive user session may be controlled completely.

26.2.3 Batch jobs

Batch jobs do not involve this kind of give-and-take between the user and the system. Typically, they are submitted to a batch queue and wait their turn to run in a subsystem, sharing system resources with the other active jobs. An interactive job can submit a batch job to wait on a queue, and then continue with its interactive work. One of the most important ways to relieve overburdened resources is to submit jobs to batch rather than running them interactively. Compiling programs and running queries, for example, should never be done interactively. When jobs run in batch they are controlled by the fact of being queued. They have to wait their turn to become active, whereas interactive jobs all vie for the system's resources simultaneously. Use SBMJOB to submit jobs to batch. The system uses the job description associated with the job (from the SBMJOB command, the user profile, or the session) to determine how the job will run. Job descriptions determine which job queue is used, as well as output queues and priority level. Batch jobs may share system memory with other types of jobs if they are set up to run out of *BASE, or they may have their own subsystems set up with private memory pools (recommended).

26.3 SUBSYSTEMS

A subsystem is a subdivision of system resources (main storage) where work is performed. Some subsystems come with the AS/400, while others are created by the user to manage specific categories of work. Two typical subsystems are the interactive subsysem (QINTER) for display sessions and batch subsystem (QBATCH) for batch processing. Since all subsystems make demands on the same system resources, it is necessary to divide resources between them in an efficient manner. When a subsystem starts (STRSBS), memory storage pools are allocated to it according to the subsystem description. In addition, any display sessions, communications devices, and job queues are set up. Autostart or prestart jobs associated with the subsystem are started.

IBM ships the system with two default subsystem schemes set up. One runs all jobs out of shared resources in QBASE. It is easy to use but does not provide much control over resource allocation in the sytem. There are only QBASE and QSPL to worry about, and QBASE is the controlling subsystem:

QBASE	controlling susbsystem running interactive, batch, communications, etc.
QSPL	printer spooling jobs

The more useful and typical configuration is the other subsystem configuration supplied by IBM with the AS/400. It consists of several susbsystem descriptions and allows very precise management of system resources.

QCTL	controlling subsystem accessed from the system console which starts the other subsystems through an autostart job entry
QINTER	interactive user display sessions
QBATCH	batch jobs
QCMN	communications jobs
QSPL	printer spooling
QSNADS	system document interchange and interchange services

This configuration is obviously more adaptable to managing work on the system in that jobs are isolated in their own appropriate subsystems and memory pools. Other user-defined subsystems may be added to the preceding list of IBM-supplied subsystems. For instance, it may be desirable to create another subsystem for batch jobs to run in, to separate different types of work. In this way, end users could have their own batch queue for their needs, while programmers submit their programs to compile in their own separate batch subsystem. Thus, both types of jobs would run concurrently, sharing system resources. A long list of programs to compile need not hold up the running of reports for the accounting department. Sufficient traffic validates this type of subsystem; otherwise, the separate resources are wasted if they are remaining inactive most of the time.

A subsystem may be created with the CRTSBSD command, but an easier method is to copy an existing subsystem description and modify it. Use the CRTDUPOBJ command to copy the subsystem description, and then use CHGSBSD to alter the subsystem for your needs. Parameters which can be changed include storage pools accessed, maximum active jobs, work and routing entries, and system library list (see Fig. 26.1). Changing the size of the subsystem's storage pool in memory is one of the main techniques in performance tuning. When the system is powered down and then restarted, these additional subsystems do not automatically start. Use STRSBS interactively or in a CLP to bring up the necessary subsystems at IPL.

The controlling subsystem is the interactive subsystem which starts automatically at IPL. QBASE can be the controlling subsystem, or QCTL. The system is shipped with QBASE as the controlling subsystem but this may be changed through the QCTLSBSD system value. QCTL has an autostart job called QSTRUP which may be modified to

```
                      Change Subsystem Description (CHGSBSD)

Type choices, press Enter.

Subsystem description . . . . .   __________    Name
  Library . . . . . . . . . . .     *LIBL____    Name, *LIBL, *CURLIB
Storage pools:
  Pool identifier . . . . . . .   *SAME_        1-10, *SAME
  Storage size . . . . . . . . .   ___________   Number, *BASE, *NOSTG...
  Activity level . . . . . . . .   ______        Number
              + for more values
Maximum jobs . . . . . . . . . .   *SAME_        0-1000, *SAME, *NOMAX
Text 'description' . . . . . . .   *SAME________________________________

                          Additional Parameters

Sign-on display file . . . . . .   *SAME_____    Name, *SAME, *QDSIGNON
  Library . . . . . . . . . . .     __________   Name, *LIBL, *CURLIB
Subsystem library . . . . . . .   *SAME_____    Name, *SAME, *NONE
                                                                  Bottom
F3=Exit   F4=Prompt   F5=Refresh   F12=Cancel   F13=How to use this display
F24=More keys
```

Figure 26.1 Parameters which can be changed.

bring up the system in various ways, including starting subsystems. Use RTVCLSRC to retrieve the CL source for this program, modify it for your purposes, recompile, and the system will automatically come up at IPL with the new parameters.

26.4 MEMORY POOLS

Main storage is divided up into memory pools of various sizes and functions. One pool is for machine functions, while another is base memory for batch jobs and other functions. It is important to allocate adequate pool size for the tasks at hand. The machine pool must first receive enough memory if anything at all is going to perform well. Then the base pool and other shared and private pools should be allocated. If the system has enough memory, it is possible to arrive at an efficient subdivision of pools assigned to subsystems.

26.4.1 Private and shared pools

The AS/400 supports private and shared memory pools. Subsystems created for exclusive use by one type of job, for instance, batch processing (QBATCH), may use private pools or shared pools. Other subsystems share resources to support system functions maintained by the operating system. The machine pool (QMCHPOOL) is an example of this, as is the base pool (*BASE). AS/400 installations generally keep the shared pools provided with the machine and may add a few pools of their own to accommodate the work that they do.

Subsystems run in memory pools as follows.

26.4.2 *MACHINE

The *MACHINE pool is where many system functions transparent to the user take place. Tasks such as maintaining access paths, save and restore, and device emulation make demands on the machine pool. If it is too small, it will affect most jobs running on the systems. No user jobs run in the machine pool, but they may draw on resources in the machine pool. View *MACHINE pool allocation with WRKSYSSTS (pool 1).

26.4.3 *BASE

Memory not specifically allocated elsewhere resides in *BASE. Subsystems can draw their resources from their own private pools, or they can draw from what is in *BASE. That is why *BASE is called a *shared pool.* If it is necessary to assign exactly how much memory a subsystem will always have, you can create its own memory pool which will not be drawn from *BASE. This, however, diminishes *BASE by that amount. You can set the minimum level beneath which *BASE will not fall with the system value QBASPOOL. Batch jobs not explicitly assigned elsewhere run in *BASE and share *BASE memory, reducing it to the QBASPOOL limit. Check *BASE pool allocation with WRKSYSSTS (pool 2).

26.4.4 *INTERACTIVE

This is the memory pool where the QINTER subsystem controls all interactive display sessions. Adequate allocation here will speed up the response of user terminals. It may be desirable to set up a private memory pool for QINTER to run out of so that display sessions do not degrade as a result of competing with heavy batch traffic. In this case, QINTER would not use *BASE any more.

See *IBM Work Management Guide* (performance tuning chapter) for formulae and suggestions as to pool size allocation.

26.5 MONITORING THE SYSTEM

Several CL commands and displays make it possible to monitor the system as it is running. By keeping an eye on these performance factors at regular intervals, it is possible to be aware of the current state of the system and to adjust it where necessary. Remember to use the <F5> key every few minutes to update the statistics which are shown. <F10> restarts the statistics.

WRKSYSSTS	Shows percentage of disk usage, size of storage pools, percent of CPU usage, number of page faults in memory. (See Fig. 26.2.)
WRKACTJOB	A list of jobs active in the system. You can display low-level messages, list open files, work with job locks. Job status is displayed and, if a job has blown up, you can answer the message to free up the remaining jobs waiting in the batch queue. (See Fig. 26.3.)
WRKJOBQ	A list of jobs waiting in job queues. You can work with them and change them. For instance, you can move a job up the queue by changing its priority level, or you can hold a job or change its queue. (See Fig. 26.4.)
WRKDSKSTS	Displays list of disk units and statistics concerning each. The "% Busy" column on the right should not exceed 45 percent. (See Fig. 26.5.)
WRKWTR	Shows a list of system printers. You can display the spool queue for each printer to see what is waiting to print. Answer messages, change number of copies and priorities, etc. (See Fig. 26.6.)

```
                        Work with System Status                        S9999999
                                                            11/04/92   09:32:14
% CPU used . . . . . . . :        80.5   Auxiliary storage:
Elapsed time . . . . . . :    00:00:00     System . . . . . . . . . :    3682 M
Jobs in system . . . . . :         421     % used . . . . . . . . . :   76.9526
% addresses used:                          Total  . . . . . . . . . :    3682 M
  Permanent  . . . . . . :       4.116     Current unprotect used :     348 M
  Temporary  . . . . . . :        .112     Maximum unprotect  . . :     353 M

Type changes (if allowed), press Enter.

System     Pool    Reserved    Max    -----DB-----  ---Non-DB---
 Pool    Size (K)  Size (K)  Active  Fault   Pages  Fault  Pages
  1      __5000       3664     +++     .0      .0    1.8   18.5
  2      __1651          0     __6     .0      .0     .0     .0
  3      ____80          0     __4     .0      .0     .0     .0
  4      _22737          0     _15     .0      .0   18.5   29.6
  5      __1500          0     __1     .0    59.2     .0     .0
                                                                        More...
Command
===>
F3=Exit   F4=Prompt              F5=Refresh   F9=Retrieve    F10=Restart
F11=Display transition data      F12=Cancel   F24=More keys
```

Figure 26.2 System status.

```
                         Work with Active Jobs                         S9999999
                                                            11/04/92   09:32:45
CPU %:   68.6     Elapsed time:   00:05:24      Active jobs:   36
Opt  Subsystem/Job  User        Type  CPU %  Function           Status
__   QBATCH         QSYS        SBS      .0                      DEQW
__     JOBACCT      TACCT       BCH    52.6  PGM-XXXX999         RUN
__   QBATCH2        QSYS        SBS      .0                      DEQW
__   QCMN           QSYS        SBS      .0                      DEQW
__   QCTL           QSYS        SBS      .0                      DEQW
__   QINTER         QSYS        SBS      .1                      DEQW
__     DSP02        CCCC        INT      .2  PGM-XXXXPGM         DSPW
__     DSP03        AAAA        INT      .2  PGM-XXXXPGM         DSPW
__     DSP07        BBBB        INT      .0  CMD-DSPMSG          DSPW
__     DSP12        FRED        INT     2.2  CMD-WAJ             RUN
__     DSP19        DDDD        INT      .3  PGM-XXXXPGM         DSPW
__     DSP20        DDDD        INT      .7  PGM-XXXXPGM         DSPW
__     DSP24        DDDD        INT      .2  PGM-XXXXPGM         DSPW
__     DSP25        EEEE        INT      .8  PGM-XXXXPGM         DSPW
__     DSP28        FFFF        INT      .0  PGM-XXXXPGM         DSPW
__     DSP30        FFFF        INT     1.2  PGM-XXXXPGM         DSPW
                                                                        More...
===> ____________________________________________________________________________
F21=Display instructions/keys
```

Figure 26.3 Status of active jobs.

```
                          Work with Job Queue

Queue:   QBATCH          Library:   QGPL            Status:   RLS/SBS

Type options, press Enter.
  2=Change   3=Hold   4=End   5=Work with   6=Release

Opt   Job            User          Number     Priority    Status
 _    PROGRAM1       USR1          109980        5          RLS
 _    ABC            FRED          109998        5          RLS
 _    ABC            FRED          109999        5          RLS
 _    ABC            FRED          110000        5          RLS
 _    ABC            FRED          110001        5          RLS
 _    ABC            FRED          110002        5          RLS
 _    ABC            FRED          110003        5          RLS
 _    ABC            FRED          110004        5          RLS
 _    ABC            FRED          110005        5          RLS
 _    ABC            FRED          110006        5          RLS
 _                                                                   Bottom
Parameters for options 2, 3 or command
===>
F3=Exit   F4=Prompt   F6=Submit job   F12=Cancel   F21=Subsystem
F24=More keys
```

Figure 26.4 Status of job queues.

```
                         Work with Disk Status                      S9999999
                                                          11/04/92  09:34:26
Elapsed time:    00:00:00

             Size    %      I/O   Request    Read  Write    Read  Write    %
Unit  Type    (M)  Used     Rqs   Size (K)    Rqs    Rqs     (K)    (K)  Busy
  1   2800    320  82.1      .0        .0      .0     .0      .0     .0     0
  2   9332    200  75.8      .0        .0      .0     .0      .0     .0     0
  3   9332    200  76.2      .0        .0      .0     .0      .0     .0     0
  4   9332    200  75.7      .0        .0      .0     .0      .0     .0     0
  5   9332    200  76.0      .0        .0      .0     .0      .0     .0     0
  6   9332    200  75.7      .0        .0      .0     .0      .0     .0     0
  7   9332    300  75.7      .0        .0      .0     .0      .0     .0     0
  8   9332    300  75.7      .0        .0      .0     .0      .0     .0     0
  9   9332    300  75.6      .0        .0      .0     .0      .0     .0     0
 10   9332    300  76.0      .0        .0      .0     .0      .0     .0     0
 11   9332    200  86.3      .0        .0      .0     .0      .0     .0     0
 12   2800    320  75.7      .0        .0      .0     .0      .0     .0     0
 13   2800    320  75.7      .0        .0      .0     .0      .0     .0     0
                                                                     More...
Command
===>
F3=Exit   F5=Refresh   F12=Cancel   F24=More keys
```

Figure 26.5 Disk status.

```
                         Work with All Printers

Type options, press Enter.
  1=Start    2=Change    3=Hold   4=End    5=Work with    6=Release
  7=Display messages     8=Work with output queue

Opt  Device      Sts    Sep     Form Type   File          User        User Data
 _   PRT01       STR    *FILE   *ALL        QPQUPRFIL     USR1
 _   PRT02       STR    *FILE   *ALL
 _   PRT03       STR    *FILE   *ALL        QPRINT        USR2        PGMXX99
 _   PRT04       STR    *FILE   *ALL
 _   PRT05       STR    *FILE   *ALL
 _   PRT06       STR    *FILE   *ALL

                                                                          Bottom
Parameters for options 1, 2, 3, 4, 6 or command
===>
F3=Exit   F11=View 2   F12=Cancel   F17=Top   F18=Bottom   F24=More keys
```

Figure 26.6 Status of system printers.

26.6 PERFORMANCE ADJUSTMENT

Performance adjustment is primarily a matter of adjusting pool size and activity level for the various system pools. You have to balance pool size with activity level (how many jobs are allowed in the pool at one time) in order to achieve the desired page-fault rate. See *IBM Work Management Guide* (performance tuning chapter) for formulae and suggestions as to acceptable fault rates and wait-to-ineligible transitions.

Type WRKSYSSTS to get to the Work with System Status screen. System pools and pool size are shown, as well as disk percent used, CPU percent used, and database and nondatabase page-fault rates (how often the subsystem has to go to disk for programs or data). Nondatabase fault rate should be lower than 1 for the machine pool (pool 1). Give the machine pool enough memory to bring this fault rate down, but you need not bring it much below 1. Other pools should have a combined database and nondatabase fault rate of less than 15 to 25 depending on your machine. Use <F11> to show the wait-to-ineligible transitions to see how the activity level is set.

Use WRKDSKSTS to see the Work with Disk Status display. It shows each disk unit and relevant statistics. The most important statistic here is the "% Busy" on the far right. It tells you what percentage of the time the disk actuator is busy. It should be below 40 percent when observed over a period of time. Remember to use the <F5> key to refresh the statistics, averaging them out over the time you are watching. If you see "% Busy" consistently higher than 40 percent across the disks over time, you are overworking your DASD and probably need more.

WRKACTJOB produces the Work with Active Jobs screen. This display shows each job currently running in the system, together with which user initiated it and CPU percent allocated to it. Again, use the <F5> key to average out the statistics over a representative viewing period. <F11> shows elapsed data for Auxiliary I/O and CPU percent. This screen shows you the results of any performance adjustments you have made.

Methods for performance tuning include PURGE(*NO) for interactive jobs, separating subsystems from *BASE, and multiple pools for different types of user jobs. You must determine whether your system warrants these adjustments. For example, it makes no sense to set up a separate batch subsystem with its own private memory pool for two batch jobs a day. However, a constant stream of batch jobs will run more efficiently in its own subsystem. See the *IBM Work Management Guide* for details of these more advanced techniques.

26.7 SYSTEM VALUES

Various system values determine the resources allocated to the subsystems and pools. By managing these, you can manage the performance of the machine. Use the CHGSYSVAL command to change system values to desired parameters. These are a few of the more useful system values in tuning the system:

QACTJOB	Number of active jobs allowed by the system.
QBASACTLVL	Number of jobs which can compete for *BASE resources at one time.
QBASPOOL	Minimum size of the base pool (*BASE). Subsystems can share resources from *BASE, drawing what they need up to a specified limit. This value is the lowest that *BASE is allowed to drop.
QMAXACTLVL	Number of jobs which can compete for resources at one time.
QMCHPOOL	Size of the machine pool in memory—a critical adjustment because many system functions are accomplished here. If this is too low, the machine will surely drag.
QPFRADJ	Determines whether the system will self-tune at IPL. Set this value to 1 to allow the machine to adjust pool size and activity level at IPL. Set it to 0 if you have set your own pool sizes and activity levels.
QTOTJOB	Total number of jobs allowed by the system.

26.8 SUMMARY

The AS/400 provides a default work environment when it is installed. This may be sufficient for your needs, but does not provide much opportunity for adjustment. Different levels of customization are possible, depending on the degree of flexibility you need and complexity you can manage.

Many tools exist on the system to aid in work management. You can monitor the status of various system elements such as CPU usage, disk usage, active jobs, print queues, and the like. Most of the displays which show statistics and information on these topics allow changes to be made. Subsystems may be set up and certain type of jobs allocated to them. System values which control many of the operating system's parameters can be adjusted.

The AS/400 operates best with plenty of memory, and the surest way to increase performance without an upgrade of the processor is by adding memory. Adjustment of existing resources can only go so far. The well-tuned machine consists of a balanced combination of processor power, memory capacity, and DASD. Performance deficiencies which result from inadequate resources must obviously be addressed with hardware, then by tuning.

Refer to the *IBM Work Management Guide* to determine specific algorithms and suggestions for setting up your subsystems and system values.

AS/400 Performance Tools can also be installed to evaluate system performance.

Chapter

27

Hardware Specifics

This chapter contains a representative sample of available products for the AS/400, and brief notes on each. Many different configurations are possible to meet individual needs. Products are listed, as well as technical configuration charts and performance charts of systems. This machine can be set up to run stand-alone, as a file server, as part of an SNA-based communications network with PCs and 370's (local and remote), and to communicate with non-IBM platforms using TCP/IP protocols. The rack-mounted modular design of the 9406's makes upgrade fairly easy.

27.1 THE MODELS

Since its introduction in 1988 the AS/400 has gone through rapid new hardware releases. The progression from the original B models through C, D, and E models has taken relatively little time, with more new models on the horizon. Each generation has brought dramatic increases in power. The E models are 25 to 30 percent more powerful than the comparable D models. They range in price from around $10,000 for the E02 to over $1 million for the E90 and E95.

The AS/400 comes in three different families of processors:

9402. On the low end, the 9402 is appropriate for small businesses or applications. It consists of a small rack (24 × 14 × 30 in) which fits in easily next to a desk. It requires no special environment. 9402's can be ordered with Plug'N'Go, a system completely configured with system unit, terminals, printers, operating system, and even application software.

9404. A step up from the 9402 is the 9404 processor group. These models are roughly twice as powerful as the 9402 group, and offer much more in the way of configuration options (up to 15.8 Gb DASD, 80 Mb memory, and 240 terminals). With dimensions of 26 × 14 × 30 in, about the size of a two-drawer filing cabinet, these units are hardly larger than the 9402's. They fit easily into the office environment, requiring no special wiring or air conditioning.

9406. The high end of the AS/400 family. The E95 with its powerful N-Way processor rivals mainframe power. These machines are considerably larger than the 9402's or 9404's. They come in rack units about the size of a refrigerator (62 × 26 × 37 in) and require a computer room with dedicated wiring and air conditioning. The rack-mounted structure allows easy expansion and upgrading.

All B's and D's are field-upgradable to E's, and all E's are upgradable within the processor group.

27.2 TECHNOLOGY

Offering state-of-the-art technology, the 9406 series uses Very Large Scale Integration (VLSI) and 32-bit data path and 48-bit addressing up to 281 terabytes of storage. In addition, high-density CMOS logic, high-speed SRAM cache memory for faster I/O, and IBM's new 16 Mb DRAM memory chip enhance the power of the 9406's. N-Way multiprocessing in the E90 paves the way toward true mainframe processing capabilities in a midrange machine and price level.

27.3 CONFIGURATIONS

The 13 E models are available in the following configurations:

	Memory (megabytes)		DASD		CRTs	RAMP-C
	min	max	min	max	max	TPS
9402:						
E02	8	24	988 Mb	1.98 Gb	14	2.8
E04	8	24	988 Mb	3.95 Gb	42	3.6
E06	8	40	988 Mb	3.95 Gb	68	4.9
9404:						
E10	8	40	988 Mb	11.9 Gb	160	4.9
E20	8	72	988 Mb	11.8 Gb	160	6.6
E25	16	80	988 Mb	15.8 Gb	240	7.9

9406:						
E35	8	72	1.28 Gb	28.7 Gb	360	6.4
E45	16	80	1.28 Gb	28.7 Gb	480	9.0
E50	32	128	1.28 Gb	49.2 Gb	720	12.0
E60	64	192	1.28 Gb	76.7 Gb	1000	19.1
E70	64	256	1.28 Gb	76.7 Gb	1400	27.6
E80	64	384	1.28 Gb	124.7 Gb	2400	47.3
E90	64	512	1.28 Gb	124.7 Gb	2400	64.5

IBM offers a Total System Package (TSP) in order to provide a fully configured, ready-to-go system. TSP includes the following:

- Easy-to-order, easy-to-install system package(s)
- Optional hardware, software, I/O, and cables
- Price advantage over non-TSP systems
- Standard volume discount agreements
- All TSP software preloaded
- System delivery in one shipment
- Standard manuals and a supplies kit

27.4 PERFORMANCE COMPARISON

The AS/400 is now much more powerful than when it was first introduced in 1988. The E model represents approximately a 15 to 45 percent performance improvement over the previous D model and an 80 to 100 percent improvement over the B model.

Compared to the original B10, the performance of the AS/400 models is greatly increased as shown in this chart:

9402		9404		9406	
Model	Performance	Model	Performance	Model	Performance
C04	1.1	B10	1.0	B30	1.4
C06	1.3	C10	1.3	B35	1.6
D02	1.3	B20	1.7	B40	1.0
D04	1.5	C20	1.8	B45	2.3
E02	1.5	D10	1.9	D35	2.6
D06	1.9	C25	2.2	B50	3.2
E04	1.9	D20	2.4	E35	3.4
E06	2.6	E10	2.6	D45	3.7
		D25	3.4	E45	4.8
		E20	3.5	D50	4.8
		E25	4.2	B60	5.2
				E50	6.4
				B70	7.0
				D60	8.3

(Continued)

9402		9404		9406	
Model	Performance	Model	Performance	Model	Performance
				E60	10.2
				D70	11.2
				E70	14.2
				D80	19.8
				E80	25.2
				E90	34.4

27.5 TAPE

The Multi Function Input/Output Processor comes standard on all E models. It supports attachment of a ¼-inch cartridge tape unit which can use data compression. Also, it supports two communications adapters, for the IBM 5838 or 7855 modem, enabling Electronic Customer Support access as well as remote access. OS/400 V2R2 allows Save While Active, a feature which allows files to be saved to tape while they are in use.

7208 8mm tape drive. Helical scan technology provides up to 2.3 Gb of backup at 245 Kb per second transfer rate. Data Compression (HDC) function provides two-to-one data compression.

3490E enhanced capability magnetic tape subsystem. This is the high end of IBM's ½-inch cartridge tape drives. Cartridge System Tapes provide 400 Mb capacity and Enhanced Cartridge System Tapes hold 800 Mb. Improved Data Recording Capability (IDRC) can compress the data three-to-one. The Auto Cartridge Loader (ACL) can feed six cartridges for unattended backup.

9348 magnetic tape unit. ½-inch reel-to-reel records at 1600/6250 bpi. Rack-mounted for the 9406 or tabletop for the 9402 and 9404. Hardware Data Compression (HDC) function provides two-to-one data compression.

525 Mb ¼-inch cartridge tape unit. For the 9402 and 9404, reliable 200 Kb per second transfer rate. Standard on these two processor groups, it provides 525 Mb of storage. Hardware Data Compression (HDC) function provides two-to-one data compression.

27.6 DASD

Some recent developments in AS/400 DASD enhance disk operations. The 9406 models come with 1.28 Gb of internal DASD in the rack. Save While Active allows the system to back up files which are currently in use by making copies of them in storage for use in a synchronized backup. DASD Mirroring consists of a duplicate image of the date on disk wherein I/O performance is enhanced. Auxiliary Storage Pools (ASPs) enable database management to protect data in the event of power failure. New input/output processors (IOPs) significantly enhance DASD performance.

9332 disk unit. This drive has been around for several years and is the old standby of the original Model B AS/400's. The model 400 has 400 Mb of storage, while the model 600 has 600 Mb. If your data volume is not heavy, these could satisfy the requirement.

9336 disk unit. A 5.25-inch disk with up to 20 Gb of storage in a single rack. This unit is more reliable, efficient, and affordable than the preceding 9335. The model 10 holds up to 2.656 Gb, while the model 20 goes up to 3.428 Gb. They can be configured with two to four drives in each unit.

3995 compact optical library dataserver. This unit provides 20 Gb of memory, and several can be installed (up to eight for E35 and E45, up to fourteen for E50 through E90). High-volume applications such as imaging can be served by this device.

27.7 MEMORY

AS/400's are offered with a minimum memory configuration. This is almost always insufficient to the ultimate needs of the system. This machine needs to have plenty of memory, so it is necessary to configure it accordingly. The system will consequently support more sessions and run faster. Also, memory upgrade may be necessary at some point to improve performance. By increasing pool sizes, you can sometimes get dramatic gains in performance without the trouble and expense of a processor upgrade. Alternatives to new IBM memory include used IBM memory and IBM-compatible memory from third-party vendors such as EMC. IBM memory prices have been dropping, so it is significantly more affordable to improve performance.

Main storage cards are available for the various models in 8, 16, 32, and 64 Mb. Each machine has its own particular memory scheme, so it is important to check with your vendor before planning upgrades. IBM will swap out any cards which do not work from one model to another, charging only for an increment in memory. The E90 can use the Dynamic Random Access Memory (DRAM) chip for faster processing speeds.

27.8 COMMUNICATIONS

From local communications to remote, the AS/400 family provides extensive connectivity through protocol converters, bridges, routers, MAUs, and other devices. Communications are possible to PCs and PS/2's, other AS/400's, System/36 and System/38, RISC System/6000, System 370, and System/390. One of the strongest points of the AS/400 is that this machine can connect with many platforms. The AS/400 can function as part of a LAN through Token-Ring, Ethernet, or TCP/IP.

The Six-Line Communications Controller, Integrated Services Digital Network (ISDN) Adapter, and the Token-Ring or Ethernet interface give the AS/400 its open communications capability. These features allow the machine to connect to other IBM and non-IBM computers in various network configurations.

16/4-Mbps Token-Ring network adapter. 16- or 4-Mbps configurations provide high-speed network functionality. Connections are made to PC, PS/2, other AS/400's, or 370's on the Token-Ring network to provide resource sharing and file transfer.

8228 Multistation Access Unit (MAU). A concentrator which attaches up to eight devices to the Token-Ring LAN.

Ethernet/IEEE 802.3 CSMA/CD LAN adapter. This unit allows connections to non-IBM platforms through Ethernet or IEEE 802.3 networks using TCP/IP and SNA protocols.

5494 remote control unit. Increases the number of remote twinaxial connections to the AS/400 to 28. Model 002 can support two Token-Rings or it can function as a Token-Ring gateway to connect up to 40 devices (including 28 twinaxial) using SDLC, X.21, or X.25 connection. Supports multiple interfaces.

5394 remote control unit. Connects up to sixteen 5250 displays, printers, PCs, and PS/2's via modem to the AS/400. Three twinaxial ports can each handle seven devices.

5159 programmable I/O controller. Four asynchronous communications lines connect real-time devices. Designed to withstand a wide range of temperature and humidity.

5209 link protocol converter. Attaches up to seven 3270 terminals and printers to the AS/400. It can also connect to a System/370 through the 3174/3274 Control Unit.

5853 modem. Stand-alone unit which communicates on the Public Switched Telephone Network. 300 bps in asynchronous mode and up to 1200 and 2400 bps in synchronous and asynchronous mode. Autodial.

7855 modem. Synchronous data rates of up to 12,000 bps over leased lines and 9600 bps on Public Switched Telephone Networks. Compatible with the 5853 modem.

786X modems. High-speed, microprocessor-based modems which operate on nonswitched voice-grade lines to provide synchronous rates of 4800 to 19,200 bps. These modems provide advanced communications functions such as point-to-point or multipoint facilities, full- or half-duplex, and data multiplexing.

27.9 PRINTERS

There are many printers which work with the AS/400, from high-speed line printers to tabletop laser jets. Because of the connectivity options between the AS/400 and PCs, many PC printers can be used as printers for the AS/400 at a very reasonable price.

Floor-standing printers

3820 LaserPrinter. 20 pages per minute. IPDS, cut sheet, duplex.

3825 LaserPrinter. 58 pages per minute. IPDS, cut sheet, duplex.

3835 LaserPrinter. 88 pages per minute. Continuous forms.

3827 LaserPrinter. 92 pages per minute. IPDS, cut sheet, duplex.

4234 Printer. Dot band printer. Wide range of print styles. APA graphics, IPDS functions. 800 lines per minute.

6252 Impactwriter. Heavy-duty printer which stands on the floor. Can connect to AS/400, PCs, System/36 and System/38. Up to 2200 lines per minute.

Tabletop printers

4224 Printer. Dot matrix. APA graphics, and data/text/graphics merge. 100 to 600 cps.

4230 Printer. Dot matrix. 375 to 480 cps for heavy printing. Small and quiet.

3816 Tabletop Page Printer. 24 pages per minute, APA graphics, IPDS, AFPDS, text and graphics merge. Up to 62 resident fonts.

4028 LaserPrinter. RISC processor, 3 Mb memory. Forms, graphics, IPDS, at 10 pages per minute. Large-drawer capacity.

Convenience printers

2380 2381 Personal Printer II. Impact printers, 320 cpi.

2390 2391 Printer. Operator panel facilitates typestyle changes. 240 cps.

4226 Printer. Serial dot matrix printer for heavy-duty jobs. 533 cps.

4072 ExecJet Printer. 64-nozzle ink-jet, 360 dpi. Small footprint and affordable.

4019 LaserPrinter. 5 to 10 pages per minute. Reasonable price.

4029 LaserPrinter. 5 to 10 pages per minute. 300 dpi.

PC printers

Many personal computer printers can connect with the AS/400 through PCs with a parallel port or directly attach to the AS/400.

4208 Proprinter. Dot matrix printer.

5202 Quietwriter. PC printer.

Advanced Function Printing (AFP) allows the design and integration of data with forms, eliminating the need for preprinted forms. Advanced Function Print Data Streams (AFPDS) merges user-designed forms and data on the printed page.

27.10 WORKSTATIONS AND INPUT DEVICES

Workstations come in many models, from NPW (nonprogrammable workstations or "dumb" terminals) to PWS (programmable workstations: PS/2's and PCs), scanners, and point-of-sale devices.

3151 ASCII Display. 14-inch monitor in green or amber with 102-key keyboard. Horizontal windows and printer port.

3476 InfoWindow Display. Entry-level display in green or amber. 122-key keyboard with special data entry or IBM enhanced option. OCR support.

3477 InfoWindow Display. Nonglare 14-inch screen in green, amber, or color. Can split screen between two sessions. Coax or twinax attached.

IBM PC. Attached through PC Support (Token-Ring) or terminal emulation (twinax), offers the versatility of intelligent workstation and cooperative processing.

In addition, the IBM displays made for the System/36 and System/38 are nearly all supported. 3270 terminal emulation allows attachment to the AS/400 as well. Check with your marketing representative for specific details.

27.11 FINANCING

In addition to outright purchase and third-party financing, IBM offers financing for your new system as well. IBM Credit Corporation financing programs are offered for most IBM machines.

Term leases and rentals

- 3-, 4-, or 5-year term for most machines
- Fixed monthly payments
- Flexible upgrade choices
- Renewal and purchase options
- Tailored financing for large transactions

Installment payments

- 10 percent minimum down payment
- Maximum financing term of 60 months for most machines
- $5000 minimum financed amount
- Separate plan for state and local government

27.12 SUMMARY

The AS/400 is a very flexible environment. Many different configurations are possible for each model in order to meet your processing needs. Memory, DASD, controllers, printers, terminals, and tape drives are available in a variety of options for your machine. Extensive connectivity to other platforms is one of the main design principles of the AS/400, enabling cooperative processing as well as file serving.

Configure your system with your marketing representative and try to project your system needs for at least three years. Upgrade, when necessary, is easily accomplished within and between models. The AS/400, when configured properly, can provide a flexible and efficient solution.

Appendix

A

Additional IBM References

TECHNICAL REFERENCES

There are many IBM publications which will accompany your system. A partial listing of the most important IBM publications is included here.

All of these publications are available from IBM or your system source (business partners or reseller). In addition to these publications, be sure to talk to your marketing representative about Red Books on selected topics. The Red Books often describe the same processes in implementation terms rather than the theoretical terms presented in many IBM publications. In the Red Books you will find many more specific code examples than in the manuals.

Planning and installation information units

The following set of references are for planning, configuring, migrating and/or installing your new or existing AS/400 systems.

IBM AS / 400 ASCII Work Station Reference, SA21-9922-1.
IBM AS / 400 Attaching Work Station and Communications Cables, SA21-9957-2.
IBM AS / 400 Data Communications Planning Guide, GA21-9902-1.
IBM AS / 400 Device Configuration Guide, SC21-8106-2.
IBM AS / 400 Installation Directory, GA21-9981-1.
IBM AS / 400 Installation Guide—9404, SY31-9066-3.
IBM AS / 400 Installation Guide—Customized, 9406.
IBM AS / 400 Licensed Programs and New Release Installation Guide, SC21-9878-0.

IBM AS/400 Migrating from System/36 Planning Guide, GC21-9623-1.
IBM AS/400 Migrating from System/38 Planning Guide, GC21-9624-1.
IBM AS/400 Network Planning Guide, SC21-9861-0.
IBM AS/400 New Products Planning Information, GA21-9984-0.
IBM AS/400 Planning Guide—9404, GA21-9914-1.
IBM AS/400 Planning Guide—9406, GA21-9913-1.
IBM AS/400 Preloaded System Guide, GA21-9574.
IBM AS/400 System Upgrade Guide—9404, SA21-9919-2.
IBM AS/400 System Upgrade Guide—9406, volume 1, SA21-9906-1.
IBM AS/400 System Upgrade Guide—9406, volume 2, SA21-9979-1.
IBM AS/400 System Upgrade Planning Guide—9406, GA21-9897-1.

Customer and system operation information units

This group of reference books will help you operate the day-to-day activities at a detailed level. In addition, this section will list all of the references that your programming staff will need most often.

IBM AS/400 Information Directory, GC21-9678-2.
IBM AS/400 Application Programming: Application Development by Example, SC21-9852-0.
IBM AS/400 Programming: System Concepts, GC21-9802-0.
IBM AS/400 Programming: Backup and Recovery Guide, SC21-8079-1.
IBM AS/400 Programming: Command Reference Summary, SC21-8076-2.
IBM AS/400 Programming: Concepts and Programmer's Guide for the System/36 Environment, SC21-9663-1.
IBM AS/400 Programming: Control Language Programmer's Guide, SC21-8077-1.
IBM AS/400 Programming: Control Language Reference, volume 1, SC21-9775-1, volume 2, SC21-9776-2, volume 3, SC21-9777-2, volume 4, SC21-9778-1, volume 5, SC21-9779-2.
IBM AS/400 Programming: Database Guide, SC21-9659-1.
IBM AS/400 Programming: Data Description Specifications Reference, SC21-9620-1.
IBM AS/400 Programming: Data Management Guide, SC21-9658-1.
IBM AS/400 Programming: Office Services Concepts and Programmer's Guide, SC21-9758-0.
IBM AS/400 Programming: Performance Tools Guide, SC21-8084-2.
IBM AS/400 Programming: Structured Query Language/400 Programmer's Guide, SC21-9609-1.
IBM AS/400 Programming: Structured Query Language/400 Reference, SC21-9608-1.
IBM AS/400 Programming: Security Concepts and Planning, SC21-8083-1.
IBM AS/400 Programming: System Reference for the System/36 Environment, SC21-9662-1.
IBM AS/400 Programming: System Reference Summary, SC21-8104-1.
IBM AS/400 Programming: System/38 Environment Programmer's Guide and Reference, SC21-9755-1.
IBM AS/400 Programming: Work Management Guide, SC21-8078-1.
IBM AS/400 Query: User's Guide, SC21-9614-1.
IBM AS/400 System Introduction, GC21-9766-2.
IBM AS/400 System Operations: Common Tasks, GA21-9573-0.
IBM AS/400 System Operations: Online Education Administering Guide, SC21-9770-2.
IBM AS/400 System Operations: Operator's Guide, SC21-8082-1.
IBM AS/400 Utilities: Interactive Data Definition Utility User's Guide, SC21-9657-1.

Communications information units

These reference books will guide you through the complex world of communications. We have listed only subjects mentioned in this book.

IBM AS/400 Communications: Advanced Program-to-Program Communications and Advanced Peer-to-Peer Networking User's Guide, SC21-9598-1.
IBM AS/400 Communications: Asynchronous Communications Programmer's Guide, SC21-9592-1.
IBM AS/400 Communications: Communications and Systems Management User's Guide, SC21-9661-1.
IBM AS/400 Communications: Distributed Data Management User's Guide, SC21-9600-1.
IBM AS/400 Communications: Distributed Services Network Administrator's Guide, SC21-9588-1.
IBM AS/400 Communications: Intrasystem Communications Programmer's Guide, SC21-9864-0.
IBM AS/400 Communications: Programmer's Guide, SC21-9590-1.
IBM AS/400 Communications: Remote Job Entry Facility Installation Guide, SC09-1201-1.
IBM AS/400 Communications: Remote Job Entry Facility User's Guide and Reference, SC09-1168-1.
IBM AS/400 Communications: Telephony Support Reference, SC21-9867-0.
IBM AS/400 Communications: User's Guide, SC21-9601-1.
IBM AS/400 Communications: 3270 Device Emulation User's Guide, SC21-9602-1.

Customer support information units

In operating your system, you will often need research and specific references—these references will assist you in these tasks.

IBM AS/400 System Operations: Question-and-Answer Database Coordinator's Guide, SC21-8086-1.
IBM AS/400 System Support: Analyzing Problems Guide—9404, SY31-9064-2.
IBM AS/400 System Support: Analyzing Problems Guide—9406, SY31-9063-1.
IBM AS/400 System Support: Service Guide—9404, SY31-9051-2.
IBM AS/400 System Support: Service Guide—9406, SY31-0683-2.
IBM AS/400 System Support: System Upgrade Guide—9406, vol. 1 SA21-9906-1.
IBM AS/400 System Support: System Upgrade Guide—9404, vol. 2 SA21-9979-1.
IBM AS/400 System Support: Unit Reference Code Guide—9404, SY31-9062-2.
IBM AS/400 System Support: Unit Reference Code Guide—9406, SY31-9061-2.
IBM AS/400 System Support: Diagnostic Aids, LY21-0597-1.

Office information units

Regarding office automation, Office/400 and OfficeVision 400 are integrated application products available with your AS/400. These applications have extensive reference material:

IBM AS/400 Office: OfficeVision/400 Adapted Word Processing Function User's Guide, SC21-9879-0.
IBM AS/400 Office: OfficeVision/400 Common Tasks, SX21-9868-1.
IBM AS/400 Office: OfficeVision/400 Learning Guide, SC21-9615-1.
IBM AS/400 Office: OfficeVision/400 Planning Guide, SC21-9626-1.
IBM AS/400 Office: OfficeVision/400 Setting Up and Administering Guide, SC21-9627-1.
IBM AS/400 Office: OfficeVision/400 User's Guide, SC21-9616-1.
IBM AS/400 Office: OfficeVision/400 Word Processing Learning Guide, SC21-9617-1.
IBM AS/400 Office: OfficeVision/400 Word Processing User's Guide, SC21-9618-1.
IBM AS/400 Office: OfficeVision/400 122 Typewriter Keyboard Template, SX21-9937-1.

PC Support information units

IBM AS/400 PC Support: Planning and Installation Guide, SC21-8089-2.
IBM AS/400 PC Support: Messages and Problem Analysis Guide, SC21-8093-1.

IBM AS/400 PC Support: Operations Reference, SC21-8090-2.
IBM AS/400 PC Support: Technical Reference, SC21-8091-1.
IBM AS/400 PC Support: User's Guide, SC21-8092-1.

System/38 compatibility information units

IBM System/38 Compatibility: Data File Utility/38 User's Guide and Reference, SC09-1217-0.
IBM System/38 Compatibility: Query/38 User's Guide and Reference, SC09-1218-0.
IBM System/38 Compatibility: Text Management/38 User's Guide and Reference, SC21-9759-1.

Languages information units

The languages supported on the AS/400: RPG, COBOL, BASIC, C, PASCAL, PL/1, SQL, and REXX (and soon FORTRAN) have detailed documentation available for implementation on the AS/400 as listed in this section.

IBM AS/400 Languages: C/400 Reference Summary.
IBM AS/400 Languages: C/400 User's Guide.
IBM AS/400 Languages: COBOL/400 Reference, SC09-1240-1.
IBM AS/400 Languages: COBOL/400 Reference Summary, SX09-1049-1.
IBM AS/400 Languages: COBOL/400 User's Guide, SC09-1158-1.
IBM AS/400 Languages: BASIC Reference Summary, SX09-1050-0.
IBM AS/400 Languages: BASIC User's Guide and Reference, SC09-1157-0.
IBM AS/400 Languages: Pascal Reference, SC09-1210-0.
IBM AS/400 Languages: Pascal User's Guide, SC09-1209-0.
IBM AS/400 Languages: AS/400 PL/I Reference Summary, SX09-1051-0.
IBM AS/400 Languages: AS/400 PL/I User's Guide and Reference, SC09-1156-0.
IBM AS/400 Languages: RPG Reference Summary, SX09-1164-0.
IBM AS/400 Languages: RPG/400 Reference, SC09-1089-1.
IBM AS/400 Languages: RPG/400 User's Guide, SC09-1161-1.
IBM AS/400 Languages: System/36-Compatible COBOL Reference Summary, SX09-1047-1.
IBM AS/400 Languages: System/36-Compatible COBOL User's Guide and Reference, SC09-1160-1, TNL SN09-1562-0.
IBM AS/400 Languages: System/36-Compatible RPG II User's Guide/Reference, SC09-1162-1.
IBM AS/400 Languages: System/38-Compatible COBOL Reference Summary, SX09-1048-0.
IBM AS/400 Languages: System/38-Compatible COBOL User's Guide and Reference, SC09-1159-0.

Utilities, application development, and migration information units

Programming on the AS/400 most often involves using applications such as PDM and ADT to form a programmers workbench. The reference materials for the workbench are listed in this section.

IBM AS/400 Application Development Tools: Data File Utility List User's Guide and Reference, SC09-1169-1.
IBM AS/400 Application Development Tools: Programming Development Manager User's Guide and Reference, SC09-1173-1.
IBM AS/400 Application Development Tools: Screen Design Aid User's Guide and Reference, SC09-1171-1.
IBM AS/400 Application Development Tools: Source Entry Utility User's Guide and Reference, SC09-1172-0, TNL SN09-1566.

IBM AS/400 System/36 to AS/400 Conversion Guide for Work Station Utility Applications, SC09-1221-0.
IBM AS/400 System/36 to AS/400 Migration Aid User's Guide and Reference, SC09-1166-2.
IBM AS/400 System/38 to AS/400 Migration Aid User's Guide and Reference, SC09-1165-2.
IBM AS/400 Utilities: Business Graphics Utility User's Guide and Reference, SC09-1167-1.
IBM AS/400 Utilities: Data File Utility List User's Guide and Reference, SC09-1222-0.

Electronic customer support information units

Electronic Customer Support has recently begun to have its own documentation. You will find many references in operation sections and following.

Key to Service—Software, GA21-9992-0.

EDUCATIONAL REFERENCES

The following describes a set of educational offerings for the IBM AS/400 system. The education is provided for a variety of audiences to help ensure effective installation planning, implementation programming, and efficient day-to-day operations.

AS/400 education is provided in multiple formats:

- Online education

  Tutorial system support

  Discover education

  Personalized learning series
- IBM learning centers
- Classrooms
- Interactive satellite education network

Curriculums are described for:

- D.P. professional
- Communication specialists
- Office users

Appendix

B

Selected CL Commands

The Control Language of the AS/400 is the key to the system. The following commands provide a reference to the most common, most helpful control language commands.

In the *Control Language Reference Guides* (vols. 1–5), each of the commands are detailed and diagrammed showing all of the possible syntax associated with the command.

You should find this list to be comprehensive for your initial needs.

Selected work commands

Command description	Command
Work with Active Jobs	WRKACTJOB
Work with Commands	WRKCMD
Work with DB Files using IDDU	WRKDBFIDD
Work with DDM Files	WRKDDMF
Work with Documents	WRKDOC
Work with Remote Document Lib	WRKDOCLIB
Work with Document Print Queue	WRKDOCPRTQ
Work with Data Dictionaries	WRKDTADCT
Work with Data Definitions	WRKDTADFN
Work with Files	WRKF
Work with Folders	WRKFLR

Work with Job	WRKJOB
Work with Job Descriptions	WRKJOBD
Work with Job Queue	WRKJOBQ
Work with Libraries	WRKLIB
Work with Libraries using PDM	WRKLIBPDM
Work with Members using PDM	WRKMBRPDM
Work with Menus	WRKMNU
Work with Message Descriptions	WRKMSGD
Work with Objects	WRKOBJ
Work with Object Locks	WRKOBJLCK
Work with Objects by Owner	WRKOBJOWN
Work with Objects using PDM	WRKOBJPDM
Work with Output Queue	WRKOUTQ
Work with OUTQ Description	WRKOUTQD
Work with Problem	WRKPRB
Work with Product Information	WRKPRDINF
Work with Queries	WRKQRY
Work with Questions	WRKQST
Work with RJE Session	WRKRJESSN
Work with Reply List Entries	WRKRPYLE
Work with Submitted Jobs	WRKSBMJOB
Work with Subsystems	WRKSBS
Work with Subsystem Desc	WRKSBSD
Work with Subsystem Jobs	WRKSBSJOB
Work with Spooled Files	WRKSPLF
Work with Spooled File Attr	WRKSPLFA
Work with TIE	WRKTIE
Work with User Jobs	WRKUSRJOB
Work with User Profiles	WRKUSRPRF
Work with Writers	WRKWTR

Selected file commands

Close File	CLOF
Copy File	CPYF
Declare File	DCLF
Delete File	DLTF
Display File Description	DSPFD
Display File Field Description	DSPFFD

Receive File	RCVF
Send File	SNDF
Send/Receive File	SNDRCVF
Work with Files	WRKF
Communications File Commands	CMDCMNF
Create File Commands	CMDCRTF
Data Base File Commands	CMDDBF
Display File Commands	CMDDSPF
Logical File Commands	CMDLF
Member Commands	CMDMBR
Message File Commands	CMDMSGF
Spooled File Commands	CMDSPLF

Selected display commands

Display APPN Information	DSPAPPNINF
Display Breakpoints	DSPBKP
Display Command	DSPCMD
Display Debug	DSPDBG
Display Database Relations	DSPDBR
Display DDM File	DSPDDMF
Display Device Description	DSPDEVD
Display Directory	DSPDIR
Display Document	DSPDOC
Display Data	DSPDTA
Display Data Area	DSPDTAARA
Display Data Dictionary	DSPDTADCT
Display Edit Description	DSPEDTD
Display File Description	DSPFD
Display File Field Description	DSPFFD
Display Folder	DSPFLR
Display Help Document	DSPHLPDOC
Display Job	DSPJOB
Display Job Description	DSPJOBD
Display Keyboard Map	DSPKBDMAP
Display Library	DSPLIB
Display Library List	DSPLIBL
Display Menu Attributes	DSPMNUA
Display Messages	DSPMSG

Display Message Description	DSPMSGD
Display Object Authority	DSPOBJAUT
Display Object Description	DSPOBJD
Display Physical File Member	DSPPFM
Display Program	DSPPGM
Display Program Adopt	DSPPGMADP
Display Program References	DSPPGMREF
Display Program Variable	DSPPGMVAR
Display Program Temporary Fix	DSPPTF
Display Record Locks	DSPRCDLCK
Display Save File	DSPSAVF
Display Spooled File	DSPSPLF
Display S/36 Configuration	DSPS36
Display Tape	DSPTAP
Display User Profile	DSPUSRPRF
Override with Display File	OVRDSPF
Display File Commands	CMDDSPF

Selected print commands

Emulate Printer Keys	EMLPRTKEY
Print Command Usage	PRTCMDUSG
Print Document	PRTDOC
Print Error Log	PRTERRLOG
Start Printer Writer	STRPRTWTR
Verify Printer	VFYPRT
Advanced Printer Func Commands	CMDAPF
Device Management Commands	CMDDEVMGT
File Commands	CMDFILE
Printer File Commands	CMDPRTF
Print Queue Commands	CMDPRTQ
Spooling Commands	CMDSPL
Writer Commands	CMDWTR

Selected create commands

Create BASIC Program	CRTBASPGM
Create COBOL Program	CRTCBLPGM
Create CL Program	CRTCLPGM
Create Class	CRTCLS
Create Command	CRTCMD

Create Ctl Desc (APPC)	CRTCTLAPPC
Create Ctl Desc (Async)	CRTCTLASC
Create Ctl Desc (BSC)	CRTCTLBSC
Create Ctl Desc (SNA Host)	CRTCTLHOST
Create Ctl Desc (Local WS)	CRTCTLLWS
Create Ctl Desc (Remote WS)	CRTCTLRWS
Create Ctl Desc (Virtual WS)	CRTCTLVWS
Create DDM File	CRTDDMF
Create Device Desc (APPC)	CRTDEVAPPC
Create Device Desc (Async)	CRTDEVASC
Create Device Desc (BSC)	CRTDEVBSC
Create Device Desc (SNA Host)	CRTDEVHOST
Create Diskette File	CRTDKTF
Create Document	CRTDOC
Create Display File	CRTDSPF
Create Data Area	CRTDTAARA
Create Data Dictionary	CRTDTADCT
Create Data Queue	CRTDTAQ
Create Duplicate Object	CRTDUPOBJ
Create Edit Description	CRTEDTD
Create Folder	CRTFLR
Create Job Description	CRTJOBD
Create Job Queue	CRTJOBQ
Create Logical File	CRTLF
Create Library	CRTLIB
Create Line Desc (Async)	CRTLINASC
Create Line Desc (BSC)	CRTLINBSC
Create Line Desc (SDLC)	CRTLINSDLC
Create Line Desc (TDLC)	CRTLINTDLC
Create Line Desc (Token-Ring)	CRTLINTRN
Create Menu	CRTMNU
Create Menu from Msg Files	CRTMSGFMNU
Create Message Queue	CRTMSGQ
Create Output Queue	CRTOUTQ
Create Physical File	CRTPF
Create Printer File	CRTPRTF
Create Q/A Database	CRTQSTDB
Create Q/A Database Load	CRTQSTLOD

Create RPG Program	CRTRPGPGM
Create Save File	CRTSAVF
Create SQL COBOL Program	CRTSQLCBL
Create SQL PL/I Program	CRTSQLPLI
Create SQL RPG Program	CRTSQLRPG
Create Source Physical File	CRTSRCPF
Create Console Display File	CRTS36RPGR
Create User Profile	CRTUSRPRF

Selected delete commands

Delete Command	DLTCMD
Delete Device Description	DLTDEVD
Delete DFU Program	DLTDFUPGM
Delete Document Library Object	DLTDLO
Delete Document List	DLTDOCL
Delete Data Area	DLTDTAARA
Delete Data Dictionary	DLTDTADCT
Delete Data Queue	DLTDTAQ
Delete Edit Description	DLTEDTD
Delete File	DLTF
Delete Job Description	DLTJOBD
Delete Job Queue	DLTJOBQ
Delete Library	DLTLIB
Delete Menu	DLTMNU
Delete Message File	DLTMSGF
Delete Message Queue	DLTMSGQ
Delete Output Queue	DLTOUTQ
Delete Program	DLTPGM
Delete Problem	DLTPRB
Delete Query	DLTQRY
Delete Questions and Answers	DLTQST
Delete Q/A Database	DLTQSTDB
Delete Search Index	DLTSCHIDX
Delete Spooled File	DLTSPLF
Delete User Profile	DLTUSRPRF

Selected start commands

Start Advanced Print Function	STRAPF
Start COBOL Debug	STRCBLDBG

Start Copy Screen	STRCPYSCN
Start Debug	STRDBG
Start Data Base Reader	STRDBRDR
Start Data File Utility	STRDFU
Start Diskette Reader	STRDKTRDR
Start Diskette Writer	STRDKTWTR
Start Education	STREDU
Start 3270 Display Emulation	STREML3270
Start IDDU	STRIDD
Start Index Search	STRIDXSCH
Start AS/400 Office	STROFC
Start PC Command	STRPCCMD
Start PC Organizer	STRPCO
Start PDM	STRPDM
Start Programmer Menu	STRPGMMNU
Start Printer Writer	STRPRTWTR
Start Query	STRQRY
Start Question and Answer	STRQST
Start Screen Design Aid	STRSDA
Start Source Entry Utility	STRSEU
Start SQL Interactive Session	STRSQL
Start Word Processing	STRWP

Selected other commands

Go to Menu	GO menuname
Call a Program	CALL programname
Run a Query	RUNQRY queryname

Appendix

C

System Values

System values store configuration information for the AS/400. By changing system values, you can manage the way the AS/400 works. The CL command WRKSYSVAL displays system value names with descriptions and contents. The CHGSYSVAL command requires QSECOFR authority to alter system values. For example, you can set the system time with CHGSYSVAL QTIME (prompt for parameters with <F4>). System tuning is accomplished partly through such system values as QMAXACTLVL for maximum system activity level and QMCHPOOL for size of the all-important machine memory pool. Following is a listing of AS/400 system values with types and descriptions.

System value	Type	Description
QABNORMSW	*SYSCTL	Previous end of system indicator
QACGLVL	*MSG	Accounting level
QACTJOB	*ALC	Initial number of active jobs
QADLACTJ	*ALC	Additional number of active jobs
QADLSPLA	*ALC	Spooling control block additional storage
QADLTOTJ	*ALC	Additional number of total jobs
QASTLVL	*SYSCTL	User assistance level
QATNPGM	*SYSCTL	Attention program
QAUDLVL	*SEC	Security auditing level

QAUTOCFG	*SYSCTL	Autoconfigure devices
QAUTOVRT	*SYSCTL	Autoconfigure virtual devices
QBASACTLVL	*STG	Base storage pool activity level
QBASPOOL	*STG	Base storage pool minimum size
QCCSID	*SYSCTL	Coded character set identifier
QCHRID	*SYSCTL	Graphic character set and code page
QCMNRCYLMT	*SYSCTL	Communications recovery limits
QCNTRYID	*SYSCTL	Country identifier
QCONSOLE	*SYSCTL	Console name
QCRTAUT	*SEC	Create default public authority
QCTLSBSD	*SYSCTL	Controlling subsystem
QCURSYM	*EDT	Currency symbol
QDATE	*DATTIM	System date
QDATFMT	*EDT	Date format
QDATSEP	*EDT	Date separator
QDAY	*DATTIM	Day
QDBRCVYWT	*SYSCTL	Database recovery wait indicator
QDECFMT	*EDT	Decimal format
QDEVNAMING	*SYSCTL	Device naming conventions
QDEVRCYACN	*SYSCTL	Device I/O error action
QDSCJOBITV	*SYSCTL	Time interval before disconnected jobs end
QDSPSGNINF	*SEC	Sign-on display information control
QHOUR	*DATTIM	Hour of the day
QHSTLOGSIZ	*MSG	Maximum history log records
QIGC	*SYSCTL	DBCS version installed indicator
QINACTITV	*SEC	Inactive job time-out
QINACTMSGQ	*SEC	Inactive job message queue
QIPLDATTIM	*SYSCTL	Date and time to automatically IPL
QIPLSTS	*SYSCTL	IPL status indicator
QIPLTYPE	*SYSCTL	Type of IPL to perform
QJOBMSGQSZ	*ALC	Job message queue initial size
QJOBMSGQTL	*ALC	Job message queue maximum initial size
QJOBSPLA	*ALC	Spooling control block initial size
QKBDBUF	*SYSCTL	Type ahead and/or attention key option
QKBDTYPE	*SYSCTL	Keyboard language character set
QLANGID	*SYSCTL	Language identifier
QLEAPADJ	*DATTIM	Leap-year adjustment

QLMTDEVSSN	*SEC	Limit device sessions
QLMTSECOFR	*SEC	Limit security officer device access
QMAXACTLVL	*STG	Maximum activity level of system
QMAXSGNACN	*SEC	Action to take for failed sign-on attempts
QMAXSIGN	*SEC	Maximum sign-on attempts allowed
QMCHPOOL	*STG	Machine storage pool size
QMINUTE	*DATTIM	Minute of the hour
QMODEL	*SYSCTL	System model number
QMONTH	*DATTIM	Month of the year
QPFRADJ	*SYSCTL	Performance adjustment
QPRBHLDITV	*MSG	Problem log hold interval
QPRTDEV	*SYSCTL	Printer device description
QPRTKEYFMT	*SYSCTL	Print header and/or border information
QPRTTXT	*MSG	Print text
QPWDEXPITV	*SEC	Password expiration interval
QPWDLMTAJC	*SEC	Limit adjacent digits in password
QPWDLMTCHR	*SEC	Limit characters in password
QPWDLMTREP	*SEC	Limit repeating characters in password
QPWDMAXLEN	*SEC	Maximum password length
QPWDMINLEN	*SEC	Minimum password length
QPWDPOSDIF	*SEC	Limit password character positions
QPWDRQDDGT	*SEC	Require digit in password
QPWDRQDDIF	*SEC	Duplicate password control
QPWDVLDPGM	*SEC	Password validation program
QPWRDWNLMT	*SYSCTL	Maximum time for PWRDWNSYS *IMMED
QPWRRSTIPL	*SYSCTL	Automatic IPL after power restored
QRCLSPLSTG	*ALC	Reclaim spool storage
QRMTIPL	*SYSCTL	Remote power on and IPL
QRMTSIGN	*SEC	Remote sign-on control
QSCPFCONS	*SYSCTL	IPL action with console problem
QSECOND	*DATTIM	Second of the minute
QSECURITY	*SEC	System security level
QSFWERRLOG	*MSG	Software error logging
QSPCENV	*SYSCTL	Special environment
QSRLNBR	*SYSCTL	System serial number
QSRVDMP	*MSG	Service dump control
QSTRPRTWTR	*SYSCTL	Start print writers at IPL

QSTRUPPGM	*SYSCTL	Startup program
QSTSMSG	*MSG	Display status messages
QSYSLIBL	*LIBL	System part of the library list
QTIME	*DATTIM	Time of day
QTIMSEP	*EDT	Time separator
QTOTJOB	*ALC	Initial total number of jobs
QTSEPOOL	*STG	Time slice end pool
QUPSDLYTIM	*SYSCTL	Uninterruptible power supply delay time
QUPSMSGQ	*SYSCTL	Uninterruptible power supply message queue
QUSRLIBL	*LIBL	User part of the library list
QUTCOFFSET	*DATTIM	Coordinated universal time offset
QYEAR	*DATTIM	Year

Index

ABOUT THE AUTHORS

TONY BARITZ has extensive experience in the computing field, including three years as MIS director at a large New Jersey insurance company and eight years as a systems analyst and computer consultant, designing and coding systems for major New York banks and insurance companies. He is currently an adjunct lecturer at New York University.

DAVID DUNNE has nine years' experience as a systems and business analyst on IBM Systems 36, 38, and AS/400 for major New York financial institutions, museums, and other nonprofit organizations. He also has extensive experience in technical documentation and training.

ABOUT THE SERIES

The J. Ranade IBM and DEC Series, with more than 90 published titles, are McGraw-Hill's primary vehicles for providing mini- and mainframe computing professionals with practical and timely concepts, solutions, and applications. Jay Ranade is also Editor in Chief of the J. Ranade Workstation Series and Series Advisor to the McGraw-Hill Series on Computer Communications.

Jay Ranade, Series Editor in Chief and best-selling computer author, is a Senior Systems Architect and Assistant V.P. at Merrill Lynch.